THE MISTREATMENT OF ELDERLY PEOPLE

Second edition

edited by
Peter Decalmer and Frank Glendenning

SAGE Publications
London · Thousand Oaks · New Delhi

First edition published 1993
Second edition published 1997

 SAGE Publications Ltd
6 Bonhill Street
London EC2A 4PU

SAGE Publications Inc
2455 Teller Road
Thousand Oaks, California 91320

SAGE Publications India Pvt Ltd
32, M-Block Market
Greater Kailash - I
New Delhi 110 048

British Library Cataloguing in Publication data

A catalogue record for this book is available
from the British Library

ISBN 0 7619 5262 4
ISBN 0 7619 5263 2 (pbk)

Library of Congress catalog card number 97-066778

Typeset by Typestudy, Scarborough
Printed in Great Britain by The Cromwell Press Ltd,
Broughton Gifford, Melksham, Wiltshire

Contents

List of Contributors

Jeremy Ambache is Director of Social Services, Knowsley Metropolitan Borough Council and is currently leading the response to elder abuse of the Association of Directors of Social Services.

Simon Biggs is Reader, Department of Applied Social Studies, University of Keele.

Michael Davies is Principal Lecturer (Gerontology courses), Division of Post-Registration Nursing, University of Hertfordshire.

Peter Decalmer is Consultant in Old Age Psychiatry, Halton General Hospital Acute Healthcare Trust, Cheshire.

Frank Glendenning is Honorary Senior Research Fellow in Social Gerontology, University of Keele, and was formerly Visiting Professor in Gerontology, University of Waterloo, Ontario.

Aled Griffiths holds degrees in law and social science and is Head of Business and Social Administration, School of Community, Regional and Communication Studies, University of Wales, Bangor.

Jill Manthorpe is Lecturer in Community Care, University of Hull.

Alison Marriott is Consultant Clinical Psychologist, Central Manchester Healthcare National Health Service Trust.

Michael Nolan is Professor of Gerontological Nursing, University of Sheffield.

John F. Noone is a General Practitioner and Clinical Tutor in General Practice, Post-Graduate Medical Centre, North Manchester General Hospital.

Maggie Pearson, formerly Professor and Director of the Health and Community Care Research Unit, University of Liverpool, is Visiting Professor of Health Service Research, University of Liverpool.

Chris Phillipson is Professor of Applied Social Studies and Social Gerontology, University of Keele.

Sarah Richardson, formerly Research Associate, Health and Community Care Research Unit, University of Liverpool, is currently Research Assistant, Department of Social Work, University of Central Lancashire.

Gwyneth Roberts holds a degree in law and is Honorary Research Fellow in the School of Sociology and Social Policy, University of Wales, Bangor.

Teri Whittaker lectures on ageing and community care at the University of Liverpool.

John Williams is Senior Lecturer in Law, University of Wales, Aberystwyth.

Preface

We are immensely grateful to all the contributors to this edition for their commitment to and encouragement of the project. It was one thing for contributors to the first edition to agree to participate in a second edition, but quite another to discover that four years further on, major rewriting had to be undertaken as the 1993 chapters came to be updated and revised. It has also been an exciting experience for us to have been joined by five new contributors who have brought with them their own special flair and knowledge which they have placed at our disposal in order to enable this project to be completed.

We are especially grateful to Michael Davies for his continuing contribution to the checklist on indicators of physical abuse in Chapter 4. We are grateful to a number of people who assisted us to obtain elusive published material: especially Karl Pillemer of Cornell University, Ithaca, New York; Gillian Crosby and her colleagues in the library at the Centre for Policy on Ageing in London; Sonia Coffrey and Deborah Dunton of the North Manchester Post-Graduate Medical Centre Library; Roger Clough of Lancaster University; Simon Biggs, Paul Kingston and Chris Phillipson of the Keele University Centre for Social Gerontology.

We are grateful also to Dr Tanya F. Johnson of the University of Hawaii at Hilo for permission to reproduce once again her grid of indicators of possible elder mistreatment in Appendix A; to Dr Karl A. Pillemer of Cornell University for permission to reproduce Figure 11.1; to Paul Davies for the graphics in Appendix D; to Bury and Rochdale Partnership Group for Older People for permission to reproduce their guidelines to staff in Appendix F; and to Maxine Offredy for her invaluable help with the pilot studies of the nursing assessment protocols.

We are grateful to Sue Allingham, Helen Bland and Wendy Heap for word processing skills. Wendy Heap and Sue Allingham both gave us great support. Sue was responsible for typing the final manuscript and we were very appreciative of her considerable technical expertise.

Beth Humphries, Rosemary Campbell, Karen Phillips and Kiren Shoman of Sage Publications have given us every assistance and watched over us with patience and care.

Peter Decalmer and Frank Glendenning

1
Introduction

Peter Decalmer and Frank Glendenning

When the first edition of this book was published in 1993, it became the first theoretical text in Britain on the mistreatment of elderly people, apart from the training manual by Phillipson and Biggs which was published in 1992. Since then there have been a number of other books: McCreadie (1993, 1994, 1996a, 1996b), Department of Health Social Services Inspectorate (SSI) (1993, 1994), Bennett and Kingston (1993), Eastman (1994), Kingston (1994), Kingston and Penhale (1995), Biggs et al. (1995), Bright (1995), Pritchard (1992, 1995), Clough (1995, 1996), Stevenson (1996) and sundry papers in journals and chapters in books. Recent publications from North America have included Pillemer and Hudson (1993), Pillemer (1994), Wolf (1994), T.F. Johnson (1995), Kosberg and Garcia (1995) which contains papers from a dozen countries, Lachs and Pillemer (1995), Baumhover and Beall (1996) and in Europe, Saveman (1994) and Wetzels et al. (1995).

Thus the problem of elder mistreatment is gaining an international profile and the first edition of this book has already been translated into Japanese. However, there is a consensus that apart from the categories of abuse developed by Wolf and Pillemer, which we affirmed in 1993 and continue to do so, the ability to define precisely what we mean by elder abuse remains elusive. See further, Chapter 3 of this volume.

The Social Services Inspectorate of the Department of Health (SSI) has offered these definitions of abuse to older people in domestic settings:

> Abuse may be described as physical, sexual, psychological or financial. It may be intentional or unintentional or the result of neglect. It causes harm to the older person, either temporarily or over a period of time. (SSI, 1993)

> The physical, emotional or psychological abuse of an older person by a formal or informal carer. The abuse is repeated and is the violation of a person's human and civil rights by a person or persons who have power over the life of a dependant. (Eastman, 1984, cited ibid.: 3)

In 1995, the pressure group Action on Elder Abuse defined elder abuse as:

> A single or repeated act or lack of appropriate action occurring within any relationship where there is an expectation of trust, which causes harm or distress to an older person.

In Britain we still have insufficient training materials and curricula to support care professionals in the recognition of the signs and symptoms of elder abuse through screening and assessment (Kingston et al., 1995). We also still lack prevalence studies apart from the findings of Ogg and Bennett

(1992b) and, as will be broached several times in the ensuing pages, while the social problem of elder abuse has been recognized publicly by the SSI and to some extent by the media (especially television and radio: see British Broadcasting Corporation, 1995), public and press awareness is limited and the responses of the statutory caring agencies have by no means been uniform. One reason for this must be that, as Ambache suggests in a later chapter, the government's recognition of the problem in 1993 through the SSI Guidelines coincided with the implementation of the 1990 National Health Service (NHS) and Community Care Act. This implementation brought with it the necessity to understand the implications of the concept of case or care management throughout health and social welfare provision.

Little has yet been written about the application of care management skills, although Hughes (1995) has gone some way towards developing the concept, and more recently Sonntag (1996) has addressed ethical issues in relation to case management. In Chapter 4 an attempt is made to review existing case studies specifically involving the mistreatment and neglect of older people in multidisciplinary care management terms. Biggs analytically questions in Chapter 5 if care workers can fulfil their responsibilities satisfactorily if they are untrained in psychosocial skills. We concur with this latter view and regret that this emphasis has been virtually absent from social work, nursing and health and social welfare management training for a quarter of a century. Legal skills are now an essential part of the training too.

All the contributors to the 1993 edition of this book have substantially rewritten their chapters for this volume which endeavours both to rework and to bring up to date the 1993 material as well as to take account of recent developments in the debate. This edition is therefore longer than its predecessor, with eight completely new chapters and, we believe, complements it so that, where necessary, students of elder mistreatment may use both volumes alongside one another, while regarding this volume as being representative (we believe) of the current state of the art in Britain. We have attempted to balance theory and good practice and Chapters 4, 9, 12, 13 and 14, particularly, have been written with practice very much in mind, dealing with clinical cases, clinical psychology, social work, nursing and primary health care.

As in the first edition, we are still unable to present coherent data which reflects the experiences of elderly people in the minority ethnic communities of Britain. We have been continually frustrated in our inability to find reliable research studies which are relevant and we have continued to be reticent about including personal material of this nature lest it be misinterpreted and used as a stereotype. This matter continues to require special attention, in relation to specific cultural backgrounds (see also SSI, 1992: 20). One specific piece of good news is that during 1995 Action on Elder Abuse were able to introduce an Asian language service for their telephone Response Line.

Sixteen chapters follow this introduction.

Chapter 2 attempts to set out briefly the socio-economic context within which elder mistreatment has to be studied.

Chapter 3 asks 'What is elder abuse and neglect?' and is a shortened version of Chapter 1 of the original book.

Chapter 4 explores clinical examples in care management terms and considers the role of each profession in the multidisciplinary team, based on the categories of Wolf and Pillemer (which will be outlined in Chapter 3), in relation to detection and assessment tools. This provides a more detailed overview of case studies than was possible in the first edition.

Chapter 5 considers policy responses to the existence of elder abuse within the context of the 1990 NHS and Community Care Act.

Chapter 6 brings the original chapter on law up to date and discusses criminal prosecution, acts and omissions, civil action, false imprisonment, medical treatment, negligence, wrongful interference and the recent Law Commission report on incapacity.

Chapter 7 enlarges our sociological understanding with new material which discusses the history of the debate about elder abuse and also develops the discussion of recent research findings on family and kinship networks.

Chapter 8 recognizes that because the majority of elderly people are female, the socially constructed feminization of poverty is a key feature within the context of any study of elder abuse. Very little attention, the author affirms, has been paid to establishing an age- and gender-integrated theory of elder abuse which can take into account the power relationships that exist within the family.

Chapter 9 stresses the need to address the psychological issues involved in elder mistreatment and neglect, the nature of the relationships that are formed and the psychological factors involved in these relationships, as well as in team-working.

Chapter 10 discusses recent qualitative research data which throw light on social and family networks and societal response in the face of the breakdown of care in domestic situations as a result of lack of resources.

Chapter 11 discusses abuse and neglect in residential centres and considers American and British research findings from the last decade.

Chapter 12 looks at key issues in social work practice in the light of the changes that have resulted from the 1990 NHS and Community Care Act. The chapter also reflects on the role of care management systems in relation to abuse and neglect and on child protection procedures and what we can learn from them. It ends with a discussion of the values espoused by social work practitioners.

Chapter 13 considers central issues in nursing training and practice, including detection, identification and assessment. The assessment protocols proposed in the 1993 edition subsequently underwent pilot studies and in the light of the responses received have been included in a revised form.

Chapter 14 reflects on the role of the general practitioner in relation to the treatment of elderly patients suffering from abuse and neglect and pays particular attention to the question of screening in primary care.

Chapter 15 examines the nature of caregiving and its satisfactions, based on recent qualitative research findings.

Chapter 16 assesses the responses both in America and Britain in relation to adult and elder protection and asks: what can be learnt from existing procedures?

Chapter 17 provides a summary and looks towards the future.

The contributors to this book share a common conviction that they wish to raise public awareness about elder mistreatment and neglect, which is now recognized as an established social phenomenon in Britain, a recognition that is shared by others at work in the caring professions, in North America, Australia, Europe and many other areas in the world. For this reason, we believe it is essential that a close working relationship is developed between social services departments, the health authorities, the health care trusts, the voluntary agencies and the police.

It is our hope that this volume will provide the reader with an up-to-date presentation of the issues.

2
Attitudes to Older People

Frank Glendenning

There are many derogatory stereotypes of older people: 'senile', 'crumbly', 'wrinkly', 'gaga', 'old git', 'geriatric'. But as Norman pointed out in her paper on ageism in 1987, 'we don't call a sick child a paediatric, or a woman having a hysterectomy, an obstetric'. She went on further to declare that the words used about old age were invariably infantilizing: 'old folk', 'old girls', 'second childhood' (Norman, 1987: 4).

Jones wrote twenty years ago:

> We learn to be old. . . . We acquire the stereotype from literature, film and from the stage. Above all there comes a time when we are treated differently by the young. We learn the myths and we are taught what it is to be old. So effective is the learning and the role performance that we actually feel more comfortable in fitting the niche created for us: The stereotype of the old is pernicious but very effective, because it permeates the self-image of the older person. (Jones, 1976: 9)

Georges Minois, in his *History of Old Age* quotes a Greek philosopher from the seventh century BC: 'Happy are they who die at the age of 60, since once painful old age has arrived, which renders man ugly and useless, his heart is no longer free of evil cares' (Minois, 1989: 47). It is not surprising that elsewhere he records that the men of Chios committed suicide at the age of 60 (p. 63) and a contemporary Greek commentator reflecting on the existence of elder abuse in modern times has reminded us that Greek history reveals clear cases of selfish carelessness and coarse insolence towards the old. Athenian history, for example, offers several instances of children taking over their parents' property without proof of incapacity in the elders, 'even though Athenian law required that sons must support their infirm or aged parents' (Pitsiou-Darrough and Spinellis, 1995: 45).

Minois also reflects, as others have done before him, on Shakespeare's seven ages of man, where the final age is 'second childishness and mere oblivion, sans teeth, sans eyes, sans taste, sans everything'. This was Shakespeare's sixteenth-century evocation of the ageing process, describing the experience of later life as one of inevitable dysfunction and disintegration. Montaigne also wrote in about 1580 of 'this calamity of age' which returns us to childhood, and went on to say in his essay, *On Age*, that it was hypocrisy to claim that old age was a good thing because it brought wisdom. 'There is no merit in not being able to indulge in debauchery. If one must make a virtue of one's decrepitude, it is still preferable to lead an enjoyable life' (cited by Minois, 1989: 265).

But the recurrent negative theme about old age is still with us in the twentieth century. It has a long pedigree.

One of the popular myths about old age in the past was that elderly people who were without private means ended their days in the workhouse (Thomson, 1983: 44). But this fear was a simplification of history. While 'the workhouse' was synonymous with poverty and is painfully ingrained in the British collective memory, poverty itself is not a myth.

In the middle decades of the nineteenth century, between half and three-quarters of all English women over 70 received a weekly Poor Law allowance, a kind of pension, of 2s. 3d. to 3s. Elderly women were not expected to have their own financial resources. Elderly men were treated less kindly. All men under 67 were expected to be in work and capable of making their own living, but over 70, relief was available and between a quarter and a half of all men over 70 in England received it. When Charles Booth published his survey of the aged poor in 1894, people were shocked to learn that a third of all those over 70 were compelled to seek Poor Law relief (Norton, 1990: 15). Nearly a hundred years later, the government's Family Expenditure Survey published in 1992 showed that retired households (however that is defined) depended on social security benefits for 41 per cent of household income in contrast to 11 per cent for all households (Oppenheim, 1993: 68). One may ask, what has changed? Smeaton and Hancock demonstrated recently the difficulty of establishing the meaning of 'poverty'. They affirm that 'poverty is most often defined by means of some threshold which corresponds to a minimum acceptable standard of living', and by 'poor' they mean those whose incomes fall below the supplementary benefit levels. They also show that in 1987, 31 per cent of the poor were elderly (Smeaton and Hancock, 1995: 2–3). And we may go further than this by affirming that the majority of those living on 'the margins of poverty are lone elderly women' (Groves, 1993: 54; Arber and Ginn, 1991a; see also Whittaker, Chapter 8, this volume).

The facts about poverty in old age throughout the centuries have contributed massively to the stereotyping of older people, because for the majority, old age has always been equated with poverty and feared because of the massive shame and resentment it will bring. An important aspect of the development of this stereotype has been the correlation between work and productivity and the consequent notion that older people are unproductive. Until the middle of this century most men worked until they dropped. Phillipson has estimated that at the time of the Old Age Pensions Bill in 1908, 606 out of every 1,000 men over 65 were still working (Phillipson, 1977: 15). In the parliamentary debate on pensions Lloyd George argued in favour of the pension being given at 65, saying that between 65 and 70 the test for continued employment was to be 'infirmity' and the question of 'the broken down old man of 67 and 68 who is left to charity' (Phillipson, 1977: 15). Phillipson comments that the very term 'broken down old man' reflects a historical tradition of identifying the retired working class male as useless, worn out and unemployable, to be grouped with the infirm and feeble-minded as a category in social policy. The establishment of the stereotype of old age as enfeeblement had by now been established. This was further compounded when the Pensions Act became law on 1 January 1909. Pensions would be withheld from those 'who had failed to work habitually according to their ability and need, and those who had failed to save money regularly' (cited in Roberts, 1978: 84). 'Here,' wrote Roberts,

> was a means test with a vengeance. Paupers were not entitled to any pension. . . . [Indeed] 'elderly paupers still went to the workhouse – a word that rang like a knell among us – or died to be borne away in a black glassless hearse to a common grave. There lay the final indignity. For old folk who lived in the district, now dead and under-insured, would have the usual whip-round to prevent the deceased being 'put away on the parish'. My mother would often give away a sheet to make a shroud. Two women went from house to house to collect enough for a wreath. (Roberts, 1978: 85)

By the mid-1950s, it was being argued in social medicine that retirement was detrimental to health and this pessimism came together with the notion of enfeeblement and the constant fear of poverty in old age, which by now was deeply ingrained in the collective memory. Indeed, the state retirement pension has been steadily reduced as a proportion of average male earnings since 1979, when it became related to price increases rather than to earnings, as had previously been the case. By 1992, the pension for a single person was equivalent to 17.8 per cent of average male earnings.

Together with this background, we have become accustomed to the language used in contemporary studies on the ageing population: words and phrases like 'burden', 'danger', the 'demographic time bomb' and 'the rising tide'. If we add to this the dominant biomedical model that older age is a process of inevitable decline then it is not difficult to understand how what we now call 'ageism' has come about.

The word 'ageism' was first used by Robert Butler, the internationally respected American psychiatrist, in 1969, in an article for the *Washington Post*: as Director of the National Council of Aging he rebuked the residents of a fashionable part of Maryland for 'ageism' because they were opposing the use of a high-rise block for the public housing of elderly people. The debate centred on the provision of a swimming pool, air conditioning and parking facilities which, the residents argued, were inappropriate for elderly tenants.

In 1973, he and Lewis defined 'ageism' as 'a process of systematic stereotyping of and discrimination against people because they are old, just as racism and sexism accomplish this for skin colour and gender'. They went on to say:

> Prejudice begins already in childhood and is an attempt by younger generations to shield themselves from the fact of their own ageing and death and to have to avoid having to deal with the social and economic problems of increasing numbers of older people. (Butler and Lewis, 1982: 176)

And over twenty years later, Butler wrote:

Ageism, the prejudice of one group against another, has been applied mostly to the prejudice of younger people toward older people. Underlying ageism is the awesome dread and fear of growing older and, therefore, the desire to distance ourselves from older persons who are a proxy portrait of our future selves. We see the young dreading ageing and the old envying youth. Ageism not only reduces the status of older people but of all people. (Butler, 1996: 12)

In his famous book *Why Survive? Being Old in America*, which won the 1975 Pulitzer Prize, Butler wrote of the myths and stereotypes about the old. As in all stereotypes, clichés and myths, there are bits of truth. But many current views of older people represent confusions, misunderstandings and lack of knowledge about old age. The concept of chronological ageing (measuring age by the number of years one has lived) is a kind of myth, because, as Butler claims, physiological indicators show a greater range in old age than in any other age group and this he says is true of personality as well. In his book he charts a number of myths about old age (Butler, 1975: 6–16).

The first is what he calls *the myth of unproductivity*. It is a myth because substantial numbers of people become unusually creative for the first time when they are older. The second myth is the *myth of disengagement,* which gained great currency in the 1960s as a result of the book by Cummings and Henry, *Growing Old* (1966): the myth that after retirement older people prefer to disengage from activities in society and that this is a natural part of the ageing experience. As Phillipson has said: 'The most powerful image of the elderly which emerged was of large numbers of people dying a slow death in their armchairs, utterly disorientated by an embarrassing surfeit of leisure time' (Phillipson, 1977: 28). But there is no evidence at all to support the disengagement theory, and disengagement is only one reaction to growing old. What is more, 'retirement' itself is becoming a myth in the industrialized world of the late twentieth century. There are increasingly fewer jobs to retire from if you are over 45 or 50. We used to define the Third Age as that part of the life course which came after the cessation of full-time work at 60 or 65. The recent Carnegie Inquiry into the Third Age (1992), defined the Third Age as beginning at 50, so that many people these days may not even be what we used to call young-old when they stop work. They have at least a third of their lives ahead of them. This puts into per-spective the stereotypes and myths about retired people and further ques-tions the validity of the disengagement theory, which was in effect functional for society because it encouraged younger people to take over older people's practical roles.

Third, *the myth of inflexibility*. This has little to do with age and more to do with character formation. Fourth is *the myth of senility*. The notion that older people are forgetful, with confusional episodes and reduced attention, is a popular view held both inside and outside the medical profession in an attempt to categorize the behaviour of older people. But there is often a confusion between brain damage and other mental and emotional problems in later life. Depression and anxiety for example are treatable and often reversible. Irreversible brain damage such as senile dementia of the

Alzheimer type is of course not a myth. The use of the word 'senile' is usually an inaccurate diagnostic label and should be avoided in the same way that we should avoid regarding older people as a homogeneous mass. Each person is different and each is unique.

The fifth myth is that of *serenity* which portrays old age as an adult fairy-land. With retirement comes peace, relaxation and serenity. This Butler denies, observing that older people experience more stresses than any other age group, with depression, anxiety, anger, chronic discomfort, grief, isolation and lowered self-esteem.

These attitudes and myths are very old and lodged in the folk memory of Western society. Moreover, they have also been influenced by the observations of famous men.

One of the most noted of these was Professor William Osler (1849–1919), a distinguished Canadian physician. On 22 February 1905 (only three years before Lloyd George's infirmity speech in the House of Commons), Osler gave his valedictory address as physician-in-chief at the Johns Hopkins University hospital in Baltimore, where he had worked for 16 years. He had just been appointed Regius Professor of Medicine in Oxford at the age of 56, and was later to be knighted. He spoke of 'the comparative uselessness of men above 40 years of age', claiming that men over 40 produced little creative work. Warming to his theme, he went on to speak of 'the uselessness of men above 60 years' and to claim that the best work was done between the ages of 25 and 40. 'It would be of incalculable benefit if men stopped work' at 60 and 'retired for a year of contemplation before a peaceful departure by chloroform'. This idea he had gleaned from Anthony Trollope's novel *The Fixed Period* (Graebner, 1980: 4; Bytheway, 1995: 26) and his views led to a protracted debate in America, which included many now familiar arguments. Graebner (1980) has pointed out that as early as 1892 Osler 'had publicly proclaimed the insidious nature of the ageing process' (p. 7) and its consequences for medical science and future employment policies. 'As a spokesman for efficiency and progress, he threatened those in every class and every line of work whose continued employment was, or seemed to be, a source of inefficiency' (p. 9). Indeed, his interpretation of demographic projections at the beginning of the twentieth century led him to warn about the implications of what he saw as the 'spectre of an ageing population' (p. 10). But, as Laslett has pointed out, when Osler's address was published, he apologized to people of 61 and over in the Preface and protested at being taken seriously about killing them off (Laslett, 1989a: 98).

And there was the surprising statement made by Sir Peter Medawar, one of the most gifted and humane of British biologists in 1946, which he republished in 1981: 'In 40 years' time, we are to be the victims of at least a numerical tyranny of greybeards. The problem of doing something about old age becomes . . . progressively more urgent. Something must be done, if it is not to be said that killing people painlessly at the age of seventy is, after all a real kindness' (cited in Laslett, 1989a: 98). Donald Gould, a medical journalist, writing in the *New Scientist* in 1987, commended killing off all over the age of 75, though as Peter Laslett, the social historian has commented, Gould thought this a bit too strong to be adopted (Laslett, 1989a: 99).

Turning to another point of great importance: the popular misconception that cognitive decline is inevitable as we grow older. H.C Lehman wrote the classic book *Age and Achievement* between 1928 and 1953, when it was published during the booming modernizing years to inform education and training policies about how the development of knowledge and skills is affected by age. He assembled information about the ages, between 30 and 40, at which people had made significant contributions and deduced that the highest output was between 30 and 34. He showed that the peak years of established leadership were between 50 and 70, whereas in sport the peak years were between 20 and 40. Lehman maintained that after 34 output fell steadily until 49, when it was less than half of the output 15 years earlier and was nearly at zero by 70 (Bromley, 1988; Glendenning, 1995). Weschler the developmental psychologist also noted that 'most human abilities decline progressively after 18 and 25' (Weschler, 1958: 135).

Bytheway in his recent monograph on ageism asks the question 'How important have these kinds of claims been in setting the basis for age prejudice?' (Bytheway, 1995: 24).

From the 1960s, however, much more research has been done, in America particularly. In 1969, Green wrote: 'Weschler's work on decline will have to be directly attacked' (1969: 618). The Americans were fortunate that several lifespan developmental psychologists were able to obtain funding for longitudinal surveys and evaluations on ageing, the most famous of which was established in Seattle in 1956. There are also important studies in Baltimore and North Carolina and in Europe, in Gothenburg, Berlin and Bonn. (We have never had a longitudinal study on ageing in Britain. This is a matter for regret, but such studies are very costly.)

The evidence that is now emerging in published papers is that only a small proportion of physical decrements in old age can be adduced to inevitable physiological deterioration and that it is the duration and intensity of training and physical activity which to a large degree determines the performance of many people as they grow older. The Seattle study is showing after 40 years of measurement that cognitive decline is not inevitable either and that where intellectual decline has been shown to exist, it is possible, through carefully planned instruction strategies at the ability level, to reverse the process and although it is not universally true, Warner Schaie and his team have found that 40 per cent of those who cognitively declined significantly over 14 years were returned to their pre-decline level (Schaie, 1990: 302).

Without going into this in detail, it is interesting to recognize that 30 years ago the evidence relating to psychological development in early and middle adult life was virtually non-existent. There was however a considerable body of evidence relating to the later years. Until the 1960s, these studies had been dominated by research designs where equal numbers of cohorts from different ages had their performances on psychological or other measures compared at a single point in time. The performance of older adults was then compared with the 'norms' (the average levels of performance) of younger people and researchers were expected to group and compare the different cohorts on the basis of socio-economic class, gender distribution and past levels of formal education, ignoring in effect the presence of socio-historical change during the development of the life course. So a 70-year-old would be compared with a 20-year-old and any variations were attributed to developmental change.

This disguised the fact that some older people performed as well or better than some younger people in the study. In order to have established the norms in the first place large statistical samples were required and these were provided by existing aggregations of people – young people in schools and older people in institutions, rather than those who lived at home or independently. It is a complicated story, but Schaie and his associates over the years refined their research designs so that it became possible to distinguish between age differences and age change, and they describe the pattern that emerged. What they found was, as has been mentioned, that intellectual decline can be reversed. The implication is that there is human potential for cognitive and intellectual development throughout the whole of life; some researchers say that such development can continue into the 90s and whether people's abilities develop or decline as they grow older is not caused by chronological ageing. It is therefore unacceptable on the basis of scientifically obtained psychological evidence to maintain that older people enter into intellectual decline as a matter of course. Thus another stereotype about ageing can be rebutted.

Any serious discussion about the mistreatment of older people must be seen against this complex background which has led in part to the development of elderly care as a poor quality service and to the marginalization of elderly people within their structured dependence, a process which has been described so eloquently over recent years by Townsend (1981, 1986), Phillipson (1977, 1982) and Walker (1980, 1981, 1983a, 1983b, 1986) (see also Chapter 7, this volume).

One thing that we need to learn is, as Kertzer and Laslett have said: 'We cannot expect to understand ourselves as we are now in the industrialized countries – and what we shall become – unless we also understand what we have been' (Kertzer and Laslett, 1995: ix). Hence the requirement to understand the origins of our attitudes to ageing. Very recently, social historians have been urging sociologists who are concerned with the history of old age to place more emphasis on biographical accounts of the past, so that the personal role of the ageing individual can be recognized, thus compensating for the anonymity of ageing populations (Troyansky, 1996). The editors of *The Oxford History of Aging* exclaimed in their introduction: 'Many people have trouble reading their own experience outside culturally dominant expectations of youthfulness, health or success. Conventional wisdom fails to convince. Stereotypes blunt the imagination' (Cole and Winkler, 1994: 7). That imagination needs to be informed and quickened.

In conclusion, the demographic reality: the size of the very elderly population is escalating. Death is more often occurring within a narrow age range in later life. We can all increasingly expect a lifespan of 80 years, with all that that implies. Nearly a million people in the UK suffer from some form of dementia. One in ten of us will suffer from it and the older we are, the more likely we are to be sufferers (Marshall, 1993: 4; see Kitwood, 1997). There will be a rise of 16 per cent in the number of demented people in Britain by the year 2005 (Decalmer, 1993: 36). Recent American figures suggest that one in four of the over-85s and by 2040, 12.5 million will suffer from some form of dementia. By 2040 also, the over-85s will account for 18 per cent of the elderly American population, with all that that implies for caring and the expenditure of resources (Binstock et al., 1992: 2). The implications for social policy, ethical decisions and attitudes towards older people are immense.

Given the centuries-old background of stereotypes and attitudes to old people, and given that so many older people are trapped within their own models of ageing – models which are ultimately unacceptable to those with a positive view of ageing (see further, Bernard, 1988, passim; Poxton, 1996: 2, 9) – it is perhaps not surprising that in spite of clear evidence of the abuse and neglect of old people, which has been in the public domain in Britain for over 10 years and in North America for much longer, and although the Social Services Inspectorate of the Department of Health has been advising policy-makers, managers and practitioners on this issue since the late 1980s, according to a recent survey in Britain by Action on Elder Abuse (1995), the majority of the local social services departments have policies or practice guidelines in place, but only a minority of health authorities and National Health Service trusts do. This is a matter to which we will return (see especially Chapter 17).

3

What is Elder Abuse and Neglect?

Frank Glendenning

The neglect and abuse of old people is not new. What is new is the attempt, since the end of the 1970s, to find out why it happens. It is established that miscare, mistreatment, abuse and neglect takes place. It is what Bennett (1992) has called 'another iceberg phenomenon'. The focus of this chapter will be to examine what has been written about the mistreatment, abuse and neglect of older people. It is from the United States of America, Canada and Britain that the main thrust and exchange of ideas about abuse and neglect has come. In Europe, the acknowledgement that elder mistreatment exists has been slow to mature (Fisk, 1991: 901; Ogg, 1993b:15), although recently there have been studies in Sweden (Saveman, 1994) and Germany (Wetzels et al., 1995). Ogg has suggested that Australia's response has also been slow to mature (Ogg, 1993a: 23; see also Biggs et al., 1995: 53). But in fact the work of McCallum et al. (1990), Kurrle and Sadler (1993), Kurrle (1995) and Dunn (1995) suggests otherwise. In addition, there is now evidence of elder abuse from Greece, Hong Kong, India, Israel, Japan, Nepal and South Africa (Kosberg and Garcia, 1995). Clearly, there is an increasing international awareness that the mistreatment of elderly people is a social problem assuming world-wide proportions.

In the USA and Britain, about 5 per cent of older people live in institutional settings (Hudson and Johnson, 1986; Fennell et al., 1989). In Canada, the figure is approaching 9 per cent (Forbes et al., 1987). There is chilling evidence that these elderly people are more likely to be at risk than the 95 per cent in Britain or the 91 per cent in Canada who live in the community.

However, although the vast majority of elderly people are cared for and tended with affection at home, a considerable amount of violence takes place within the family. Whitehead, for instance, has written in a British nursing journal: 'Interest and concern about non-accidental injury grew out of a general awareness that individuals sometimes assaulted people close to them and then either forced or conspired with them to make out that the resulting injuries were sustained accidentally' (Whitehead, 1983: 32–3).

It is unclear whether there is a connection between child abuse and elder abuse, but it is singular that several times in the literature there appears, with minor syntactical changes, the anonymous verse which from folk memory presents such a view:

When I was a laddie,
I lived with my granny,
And many a hiding me granny gi'ed me.
Now I am a man,
And I live with my granny.
And I do to my granny,
What she did to me.

The connection, however, remains to be substantiated. What is clear is that in Britain research into the causes and reasons for family violence has been an undeveloped field of inquiry. This matter has now begun to be addressed, however (Penhale, 1993a; Kingston and Penhale, 1995; Biggs et al., 1995). What can be said is that commentators such as Pillemer and Wolf (1986; Wolf, 1988; Wolf and Pillemer, 1989) have been urging an increased study of family dynamics. Brubaker (1990) has pointed out that we must be sensitive to later life family relationships, recognizing that there can be both a positive and a negative side. Steinmetz (1990: 194) has considered family relationships in previous centuries and concluded that 'The romantic view of close-knit, multi-generational families of yesteryear is a mythical representation rather than an accurate account of family life in the past.' Steinmetz suggests that evidence from family papers and civic records indicates that the traditional belief that care was always provided for elderly people by their family requires examination. Similarly, Laslett's study of English social structure has led him to the conclusion that 'there never was a time when all elderly English people lived in large, extended households' (Laslett, 1989a: 112), while Kosberg and Garcia have suggested that elder abuse has probably always existed (Kosberg and Garcia, 1995: 186).

During the past ten years, in particular, society has become more overtly aware of the existence of elder abuse and neglect. Observers agree that the quantity (not the proportion) of abuse and neglect will inevitably rise, as will the actual numbers of those suffering from senile dementia of the Alzheimer type, because of the demographic changes taking place. In Britain in 1901, there were half a million people over 75 and 57,000 over 85 (Glendenning, 1993: 3). By 1981, these numbers had increased to over three million and half a million. In Canada, nearly 900,000 people were over 75 in 1981 and nearly half a million over 80 (Denton et al., 1987). In the USA, in 1901, less than one million were aged over 75 and only 100,000 were over 85. By 1988, nearly 12.5 million were over 75 and nearly 2 million over 85 (United States Department of Commerce, 1990).

Hudson and Johnson, writing in 1986, believed that between 4 and 10 per cent of the elderly population in the USA were abused, primarily within a family context and they suggested that certain questions needed to be addressed:

(1) How do families who abuse or neglect their elders differ from those who do not? (2) How can families at risk for elder neglect or abuse be identified? (3) What are the circumstances in family settings that generate elder neglect and abuse? (4) How can families be helped to effectively prevent or control neglectful and abusive situations? (Hudson and Johnson, 1986 : 113)

Even in the 1960s in Scotland, an examination of the hypothesis that old people are less well cared for by the 'younger generation' led to the conclusion that between 1959 and 1966 out of 1,500 patients discharged from a geriatric unit, in only 12 cases was home care by relatives unreasonably refused. The hypothesis could not be sustained (Lowther and Williamson, 1966). A subsequent study, however, showed that the generalized actuality was not as they had thought. Isaacs studied 612 patients in another department of geriatric medicine in Scotland between 1966 and 1967 and concluded that 'the prolonged survival of many severely disabled and ill people into advanced old age . . . has created unprecedented strain on our family and social system' (Isaacs, 1971: 286). Four years later, Baker reported the ill-treatment of elderly people and this was perhaps the first time that the term 'granny battering' was used (Baker, 1975; Burston, 1975). Later, Burston wrote:

> Hitting elderly people is not a new phenomenon; there can be little doubt that old people have been subjected to physical violence since time began . . . It is in the community that the trouble starts. The majority of elderly patients are not known to the primary health care team as a whole . . . In the past, the medical profession has disregarded the problems of old age and must accept a share of responsibility for those who are subsequently physically assaulted . . . The catalyst seems to be the continued and continual presence of the older person. (Burston, 1977: 54–5)

The main thrust for the next ten years in Britain came from Eastman, then a practising social worker in London, who enabled a growing number of professional social workers to admit the existence of elder abuse. The terms 'granny battering' and 'granny bashing' in Britain (Baker, 1975; Burston, 1975; Eastman and Sutton, 1982; Eastman, 1983) changed in the mid-1980s to 'old age abuse': *Old Age Abuse* became the title of a book by Eastman in 1984.

While the interpretation of the case material lacked the sophistication of the American and Canadian studies, this volume stands as a landmark in the British literature. With the support of Age Concern England, Eastman helped to bring the British Geriatrics Society firmly into the debate in 1988 with their conference on elder abuse which was attended by some 400 people. General practitioners in Britain are nevertheless still slow to respond to the problem.

Eastman's approach was challenged by Cloke (1983) who regarded his work in relation to problem-solving as being underdeveloped. Stevenson (1989: 28) reflected that Eastman's

> concern about the issue does not seem to be adequately conceptualized nor related to more general issues concerning the strains on family life. To separate consideration of old age abuse from the range of powerful emotions, positive and negative, which are present in those who depend and those who care, and which affect all interactions, is both limiting and stigmatizing.

The same may be said about Pritchard (1989, 1990a, 1990b, 1992). 'Old age abuse' is still in use as a term, as is the term 'elder abuse' and the 'abuse or mistreatment of elderly (or older) people'.

In America, in 1975, Robert Butler wrote in *Why Survive? Growing Old in America* of the 'battered old person syndrome'. One of the first American academic studies was never published, although it is referred to frequently in the American and Canadian literature: 'The battered elderly syndrome: an exploratory study' by Block and Sinnott (1979). Conducted in Maryland, with 24 agencies, 427 professionals (randomly selected) and 443 elders (randomly selected), the response rate was very low (17 per cent overall, including 4 per cent from the agencies, i.e. one agency), and typifies the climate of opinion a decade and a half ago. They found 26 cases of elder abuse, the majority of which had been reported to the relevant agency. Little action was taken and, not surprisingly, the study went no further.

The Canadians during the past 15 years, like the British, have been highly dependent on the American material. According to Hudson (1988), serious interest in elder abuse has only existed since the 1980s. The first study was that of Shell in Manitoba in 1982. Gnaedinger published a detailed discussion paper in 1989 for the National Clearing House on Family Violence. Podnieks and Pillemer carried out the second major study, a national study of prevalence (the Ryerson Study) which reported in 1989. In 1991, the Canadian National Advisory Council on Aging, which advises the Minister of National Health and Welfare, published a report on elder abuse (Wigdor, 1991).

Just as child abuse entered the general public's consciousness in the 1960s, followed by spouse abuse in the 1970s, the 1980s brought us face to face with the abuse of older people. Several myths about the family have therefore been shattered (Wolf and Pillemer, 1989: 1–8; Gnaedinger, 1989). The Schlesingers (1988) identified over 200 North American research papers relevant to elder abuse and neglect and some of these will be referred to in order to outline the argument.

Definitions

During the 1980s, there were many definitions of elder abuse and elder neglect, and there is wide recognition that they lacked clarity and precision (Johnson, 1986; Hudson, 1988; Finkelhor and Pillemer, 1988; Wolf, 1988; Filinson, 1989; Stevenson, 1989; Wolf and Pillemer, 1989; Bennett, 1990a; McCreadie, 1991; Glendenning, 1993; Bennett and Kingston, 1993; Biggs et al., 1995; Kosberg and Garcia, 1995). Johnson wrote in 1986, 'It is impossible to evaluate or build knowledge in a field in the absence of a common definitional frame of reference . . . until we can adopt a standard definition of elder abuse, causal theory cannot be explored' (Johnson, 1986: 168). The issue is critical and we will not solve it on this occasion. A clear difficulty has been that investigators have approached elder abuse from different perspectives – that of the victim, the carer, the physician, the nurse, the agency, the social worker, social policy – and, as a result, there has been a lack of clarity. In addition, by 1988 some 32 investigations had been completed and every state in the USA had legislation dealing with the maltreatment of adults. Yet the basic critical questions were still unanswered. 'What is, and is not elder abuse? Elder neglect? Exploitation? Self-abuse? Who should define these terms?' (Hudson, 1986: 160).

Typologies of domestic abuse

From the beginning there was a distinction between those who sought to establish a typology of various kinds of elder abuse and neglect and those who attempted to conceptualize elder abuse and neglect (see Tables 3.1 and 3.2). From 1979 onwards, there was some understanding of what the discussion was about. Physical abuse involved being hit, sexually assaulted, burned or physically restrained, while psychological abuse involved the abused person being insulted, frightened, humiliated, intimidated or treated as a child (Hickey and Douglass, 1981b). Medical abuse involved the withholding of, or careless administration of, drugs (Block and Sinnott, 1979). Social and environmental abuse included the deprivation of human services, involuntary isolation and financial abuse (Chen et al., 1981). Material abuse included misuse of property or money, theft, forced entry into a nursing home, financial dependence and exploitation (Rathbone-McCuan and Voyles, 1982). Passive neglect referred to the elderly person being left alone, isolated or forgotten (Hickey and Douglass, 1981b). Active neglect involved the withholding of items that were necessary for daily living (food, medicine, companionship, bathing), the withholding of life resources and not providing care for the physically dependent person (Rathbone-McCuan and Voyles, 1982). Eastman (1984: 23) defined old age abuse as 'the systematic

Table 3.1 *Definitions of elder abuse and neglect*

Investigators	Typologies
Lau and Kosberg, 1979	Physical, psychological, material abuse and violation of rights
Block and Sinnott, 1979	Physical, psychological, material and medical abuse
Kimsey et al., 1981	Physical, psychological, material and fiscal abuse
Hickey and Douglass, 1981b	Passive neglect, active neglect, verbal and emotional abuse, physical abuse
Chen et al., 1981	Physical, psychological, sexual, social/environmental abuse
Sengstock and Liang, 1982	Physical, psychological, financial abuse; physical and psychological neglect
Rathbone-McCuan and Voyles, 1982	Physical assault, verbal and psychological assault, misuse of money or property, theft, misuse or abuse of drugs, not providing care
Eastman, 1984	Systematic maltreatment, physical assault, emotional or financial abuse, threatening behaviour, neglect, abandonment, sexual assault
Hirst and Miller, 1986	Maltreatment divided into types of abuse and neglect
Finkelhor and Pillemer, 1988	Physical violence, psychological, emotional mental abuse; neglect
Wolf and Pillemer, 1989	Physical, psychological, material abuse; active and passive neglect

Table 3.2   *Definitions of elder abuse and neglect*

Investigators	Concepts
O'Malley et al., 1979	The wilful infliction of physical pain, injury or debilitating mental anguish, unreasonable confinement or deprivation by a caretaker of services which are necessary to the maintenance of mental and physical health.
Rathbone-McCuan, 1980	A heretofore unrecognized form of intra-family violence.
O'Malley et al., 1983	Active intervention by a caretaker such that unmet needs are created or sustained with resultant physical, psychological or financial injury . . . Failure of a caretaker to intervene to resolve a significant need despite awareness of available resources.
Johnson, 1986	A state of self-inflicted or other-inflicted suffering unnecessary to the maintenance of the quality of life of the older person.
Fulmer and O'Malley, 1987	The actions of a caretaker that create unmet needs . . .The failure of an individual responsible for caretaking to respond adequately.
Wolf, 1988	Not only is it impossible to compare the findings from the early studies, because of variations in the meaning of elder abuse, but it is also not possible to compare or aggregate data obtained from state reporting systems.
Wolf and Pillemer, 1989	We believe it is necessary to include . . .the more general literature on relations between spouses and between elderly parents and adult children . . .The determinants of the quality of family relationships of the elderly can provide important insights into elder abuse, especially in concert with family violence research.
Filinson, 1989	Because the lack of empirical work is an intrinsically significant feature of the transformation of elder abuse into a social issue, the implications for practice and policy in the light of the paucity of sound data are considerable . . .The complexity of the elder abuse phenomenon and the various motivations and circumstances for abuse suggests that a multi-faceted approach to dealing with the problem is needed.

maltreatment . . . of an elderly person by a care-giving relative. This may take the form of physical assault, threatening behaviour, neglect and abandonment (when the relative is either thrown onto the street with their belongings, or is put in a room with no furniture), or sexual assault.'

Hudson and Johnson (1986: 114) commented on the nature of these developing typologies: 'Physical and psychological mistreatment are consistently included, whereas inclusion of separate classifications of neglect (active and passive), financial or material abuse, self-neglect, violation of rights, sexual abuse and medical abuse, vary from study to study.' Investigators were using different words and different descriptions of categories of abuse. Hudson and Johnson noted that Lau and Kosberg (1979) referred to 'physical abuse' as 'withholding personal care', while Sengstock and Liang (1982) applied 'withholding personal care' to 'psychological neglect'.

These discrepancies might be explained by variations in sampling techniques and differences in research design, but there is a certain incongruity when investigators do not work with definitions that have an accepted meaning. The situation caused Cloke (1983: 2), writing from a British perspective, to say: 'There has been a tendency to include such a wide range of abuses within the overall term "old age abuse" that the concept becomes almost meaningless as a heuristic tool.' Nevertheless, the issue was now unmistakably in the public domain even if it could not claim public legitimation. In the years to come, not only was the medical profession to become in principle more involved, but more honesty was to be asserted both in relation to domestic abuse and neglect, and also in relation to abuse taking place, sometimes in horrific circumstances, in institutions.

Conceptualization

Some investigators attempted to conceptualize the issues. Some of these attempts are listed in Table 3.2. O'Malley et al. (1979) sought to place abuse and neglect within the wider context of inadequate care. They defined elder abuse as 'the wilful infliction of physical pain...mental anguish...or deprivation by a caretaker of services which are necessary to the maintenance of mental and physical health' (1979: 2). Hudson and Johnson (1986) criticized this definition because the label of abuse could only be applied if it was clear that the carer or caregiver intended to do the harm. The assumption is also that the patient is dependent, thus excluding independent older people who may also become victims of abuse.

In a paper written in 1983, O'Malley et al. simplified the conditions of abuse to 'physical, psychological or financial injury' and developed a new definition of neglect: 'the failure of a caretaker to intervene to resolve a significant need despite awareness of available resources' (1983: 1000). In 1984, they wrote:

> The terms 'elder abuse and neglect' are being applied to situations in which an elderly person is subject to battering, rough handling, verbal abuse, denial of rights, neglect of care needs, infantilization, abandonment or misuse of resources . . . The terms used to describe cases of family mediated abuse and neglect emphasize the behavior of the individual alleged to be responsible for the abuse and neglect. (O'Malley et al., 1984 : 362)

Hudson and Johnson (1986) suggested that here abuse was an act of commission and neglect an act of omission. Rathbone-McCuan (1980: 296) broached the hypothesis that elder abuse is a formerly unrecognized form of intra-family violence: 'Conceptual confusion...is reinforced by rapidly changing norms and values, social policies and definitions that are applied to describe the social problems faced by the elderly.' Her conclusion was that 'the brief history of clinical intervention in intra-family violence in the United States is very discouraging' (Rathbone-McCuan and Voyles, 1982: 192).

Lack of consensus

Investigators continued to publish their findings in the 1980s without a consensus emerging. Hirst and Miller (1986) argued that to include too many broad types of abuse would result in an overstatement of the problem, making it impossible to determine the aetiology of abuse. They suggested a general heading of maltreatment, subdivided into various types of abuse and neglect. This, however, proved to be merely cosmetic.

Finkelhor and Pillemer (1988) noted the failure of an expert conference in the USA in 1986 to reach agreement on a definition of elder abuse. They spoke of 'definitional disarray' and found 'no generally accepted definitions of elder abuse and neglect'. They believed, however, that a consensus had been established about types of mistreatment. These they stated to be: physical violence; psychological, emotional or mental abuse; and neglect (the failure of a clearly constituted caregiver to meet the needs of an elder). Tomlin (1989: 5) follows a similar path and quoted a working party of Bexley Social Services Department (1988): assault (including force-feeding); deprivation of nutrition; administration of inappropriate drugs and deprivation of prescribed drugs; emotional and verbal abuse; sexual abuse; deprivation of help in performing activities of daily living (glasses, hearing aid, etc.); involuntary isolation and confinement; and financial abuse. (However, Hildrew, 1991, noted that this working party which at that time had been a pioneer in the UK was in abeyance in 1991.)

Since 1982, Callahan has consistently suggested that the definitional problem is so great that it would be prudent to abandon the concept (Callahan, 1982, 1986, 1988). He admitted in 1988 that elder abuse 'may have reached a new plateau of legitimacy' by appearing on the front page of the *Wall Street Journal* (4 February 1988), but he continued to question the need to elevate elder abuse as a central concern of social policy. While it is an urgent concern for the victim, it affects a relatively small number of people, he maintained, although he recognized that this might be the result of under-reporting.

Pointers to future developments

Wolf (1988: 758) refers favourably to Johnson's (1986) study of definitions and her definition of elder mistreatment as: 'a state of self-inflicted or other-inflicted suffering unnecessary to the maintenance of the quality of life of the older person' (Johnson, 1986: 180). Later, Johnson was to add to this definition: '[older person] by means of abuse and neglect caused by being overwhelmed' (Johnson, 1991: 4). The discussion had now shifted to what is important, namely, avoiding labels and seeking a consensus about care. Wolf also added her weight to those criticizing the continuing search for definitions: 'Not only is it impossible to compare the findings from the early studies because of the variations in the meaning of "elder abuse", but it is also not possible to compare or aggregate data obtained from the state reporting systems' (Wolf, 1988: 758). And Filinson (1989: 17) wrote that 'the implications for practice and policy in the light of the paucity of sound data are considerable'.

Wolf and Pillemer (1989) and Godkin et al. (1986, 1989) used the following classification of abuse and neglect in their review of the Three Models Project (Massachusetts, Syracuse and Rhode Island, set up in 1981): *physical abuse* (the infliction of physical pain or injury, physical coercion, sexual molestation, physical restraint); *psychological abuse* (the infliction of mental anguish), and *material abuse* (the illegal or improper exploitation and/or use of funds or resources); *active neglect*: refusal or failure to undertake a caretaking obligation (including a conscious and intentional attempt to inflict physical or emotional distress on the elder); *passive neglect*: refusal or failure to fulfil a caretaking obligation (excluding a conscious and intentional attempt to inflict physical or emotional distress on the elder). Gnaedinger (1989) follows the same classification in Canada.

It was not surprising then that Bennett (1990a: 53) said: 'The difficulty in defining elder abuse is a major thread throughout the published literature.' It is mainly the Americans who have sought to clarify our understanding of the abuse and neglect of older people. But the case material is perfectly recognizable elsewhere (Kosberg and Garcia, 1995: 184). American investigators have been largely concerned with domestic abuse. Very little work was done on abuse and neglect in institutional settings in the USA and Canada until Pillemer and Moore's survey of nursing homes in 1987, which will be discussed in Chapter 11, but in Britain as a result of official boards of inquiry, episodes involving the ill-treatment of patients and poor standards of care in hospitals and residential homes are well documented. There was a succession of reports in Britain on the abuse of old people in institutions in the 1970s and 1980s: Ely Hospital, Cardiff (National Health Service, 1969); Besford House, Shropshire (Medd, 1976); Moorfield, Salford (Hytner, 1977); Stonelow Court (Derbyshire County Council, 1979); Nye Bevan Lodge, Southwark (Gibbs et al., 1987) – and there have continued to be others since. They are, however, not analysed, apart from Clough's unpublished evidence to the Wagner Committee on residential care in 1988 (1988a; see also Chapter 11, this volume).

There has been uncertainty as to the relation between domestic and institutional abuse, and an unresolved question is whether elder abuse has characteristics which distinguish it from the abuse of other adults. We also have too little information about the relation between neglect and other forms of abuse. Definitions of abuse so far vary according to the purpose for which they are needed, although Pillemer and Wolf have probably reached an important stage in reaching a workable classification.

How much abuse and neglect is there?

There has been no major study of the prevalence or incidence of elder abuse in Britain. By 'prevalence' is meant 'the number of cases...in a given population at a specific point of time'. By 'incidence' is meant 'the number of new cases occurring in a given population within a defined period of time' (Victor, 1991: 4–5). Tomlin (1989), writing the report of the British Geriatrics Society conference in 1988, quotes the figure of 500,000. Eastman and Sutton (1982) arrived at this figure in their paper 'Granny battering', saying that in the USA, 42 per cent of the over-65s were being supported by caregiving relatives and that 'evidence from the United States indicates that 10 per cent of such people supported by family members are at risk' (1982: 12). They concluded, on that assumption, that nearly 500,000 were at risk in Britain. Hocking (1988), who pioneered a study of non-accidental injury (NAI) found in old people in the 1970s, claimed that one in ten was at risk then and one in 1,000 suffered physical abuse, but she provided no source for this figure. Writing in 1994, she revised these figures to 'up to 10 per cent may be at risk' and 'abuse actually occurs in only 2 to 4 per cent of cases' (Hocking, 1994 : 52). Ogg and Bennett (1992a : 63) have ventured an estimate (translated from American figures) of 'eight elderly people who are [subjected to] abuse or inadequate care within a patient register of 200'. These estimates seem to be misleading, and to apply American statistics elsewhere is an unsafe procedure. Very recent figures given by Ogg and Bennett at the end of 1992 (based on an Omnibus survey by the Office of Populations, Censuses and Surveys in May of that year, with 2,130 interviews) suggested that in the experience of the over-60s in the sample, verbal abuse was much more significant than physical or financial abuse. But they cautioned against taking their findings 'in isolation from other attempts to systematically identify elder abuse' (Ogg and Bennett, 1992b: 998; see also Bennett and Kingston, 1993: 144–52; McCreadie, 1994).

McPherson, one of Canada's leading sociologists, has suggested that 'it is difficult to identify either the incidence per 1,000 elders, or the absolute number of cases that may be present in a given community or society...[because] most elder abuse and neglect is hidden or unreported' (1990: 360). However, he refers to Shell's Manitoba study (1988) and suggests that, transposed on to a national basis, this represents about 22 cases per 1,000 elders; and in the Ryerson national study, Podnieks (1990) found that about 40 persons per 1,000 experienced some form of mistreatment: that is to say, 98,000 people. Regional variations were discovered also. British Columbia, at 53 per 1,000 was much higher than the Prairies with 30 per 1,000. Health and Welfare Canada (the government ministry) has estimated that 100,000 elderly Canadians were being abused (Brillon, 1987).

The methods for obtaining estimates of prevalence rates in the USA have not been satisfactory. Among the early attempts to estimate the prevalence of elder abuse and neglect, Block and Sinnott (1979) found 40 per 1,000 in Maryland, and Gioglio and Blakemore (1983) 15 per 1,000 in New Jersey. As in the case of the Ryerson survey, these regional variations require further study. The Block and Sinnott (1979) survey gave rise to the widely cited figure of 4 per cent of elderly people suffering abuse, but it has to be said that there are no reliable statistics because of the lack of uniformity in state reporting laws and in the keeping of records. Definitions of elder abuse are unclear because of the use of professional and agency reports rather than interviews with victims, and the failure to use rigorous research designs (for example random sample surveys and case-comparison studies) (Finkelhor and Pillemer, 1988). With the exception of the work of Wolf and Pillemer and their associates, it is now recognized that much of the early American work has inbuilt weaknesses.

The first large-scale random sample survey of elder abuse and neglect was by Finkelhor and Pillemer (1988) in Boston involving over 2,000 older people. Their prevalence findings showed that the sample translated into a rate of 32 per 1,000. 'If a survey of the entire United States were to find a rate similar to the one in Boston, it would indicate between 701,000 and 1,093,560 abused elders in the nation' (Pillemer and Finkelhor, 1988: 54). The rates for types of mistreatment were: physical violence, 20 per 1,000; verbal aggression, 11 per 1,000; and neglect, 4 per 1,000. Wolf and Pillemer (1989) remark that these rates are lower than other forms of family abuse. The rate for child abuse in the USA is 110 children per 1,000. Nevertheless, there are potentially over a million abused elders in the United States.

It is worth noting Stevenson's remarks in her *Age and Vulnerability* (1989: 22) 'There seems little point in wasting research time on the incidence of old age abuse; as with child abuse, it can lead to a kind of spurious precision, in which figures are cited which will not bear scrutiny.' She gives three reasons. First, without agreement on definitions, we may be attempting to compare different phenomena. Secondly, estimates are likely to be based on reported abuse, which is dependent on the highly variable practices of agencies and practitioners. Thirdly, much abuse is likely to be hidden and difficult to discover. However, as Biggs et al. (1995: 40) point out, the North American and British prevalence studies confirm the reality of abuse in the lives of a significant number of people.

Who are the victims and who are the perpetrators?

Tomlin (1989), in the British Geriatrics Society report on elder abuse, suggested that the most vulnerable elderly people are those with whom it is difficult to communicate and who show fluctuating disabilities. Those with dementia or Parkinson's disease, she remarked, are more likely to be abused than others. (No source was given for this statement.) She quoted Hocking (1988) as saying that those who are particularly vulnerable are women over 80 with dementia, Parkinson's disease or cerebrovascular disease, who may have communication difficulties, hearing impairment, immobility and/or incontinence. She also reported that 'American studies have shown the classic victim to be an elderly person over the age of 75, female, roleless, functionally impaired, lonely, fearful and living at home with an adult child' (cited in Tomlin, 1989: 5). Eastman (1984 : 41) writes that 'the majority are female over 80 and are dependent as a result of physical or mental incapacity . . .They are not confined to any particular social group, but are to be found in all social classes.' (Steuer and Austin, 1980, had also made this latter point in America.) Horrocks (1988: 1085) spoke of the abused victim being 'over 75, female, physically heavy, often immobile, incontinent, aphasic and demcnting'. Bennett (1990b: 46) wrote that victims were more likely to be 'female, average age 76, living in houses with spouse or family'. The age differs from case study to case study, but the contexts are similar. There is a generality in all these claims, and the lack of specificity as to how these conclusions were arrived at is noticeable.

Perpetrators are frequently seen as being the victims of stress and isolation and Tomlin gives a useful summary of the caring process (Tomlin, 1989), as does Eastman (1984). But there are no studies in Britain that illuminate this problem apart from Homer and Gilleard (1990), who reported from their sample that all carers who committed some form of abuse lived with their victim. Abuse was significantly associated with alcohol consumption. Abusers who admitted physical and verbal abuse scored significantly higher on the depression subscale of the questionnaire than did the non-abusive carers. There was poor communication between victim and perpetrator. Abusive caregivers were likely to have stopped work in order to care for their relative. Non-abusers by and large had not.

The Manitoba and Ryerson studies

In Canada, certainly until 1988, when the Schlesingers published *Abuse of the Elderly*, practitioners were almost entirely dependent on American sources. Shell (1988), however, in the Manitoba study had found that two-thirds of victims were women aged 80–84 who had lived with a family for 10 years or more. Vadasz (1988) believed from the literature up to 1983 that victims were most likely to be female, over 75, confused and physically dependent. The caregiver was seen as being driven to a sense of helplessness, rage and frustration. Podnieks (1990) in the Ryerson study found little to distinguish between the abused and the non-abused as far as gender, marital status and living arrangements were concerned; and, according to McCreadie (1991), she found that victims of material abuse were more likely to live at home, while 40 per cent of the perpetrators of material abuse were known to the victim. Those who were abused physically or verbally were likely to be married, or married and living with an adult child.

Early observations in the USA

Responses to the question 'Who are the victims?' in the American literature are frequently scarce and, as in Britain, based on the observation of case material. The majority of the early investigators did not use a case-comparison or control group method but simply looked at what material was available in aggregate. Thus, 'based on an analysis of case materials', Rathbone-McCuan (1980: 300) listed (without explanation) the victim's characteristics: female, over 65, functionally dependent, a history of alcoholism, retardation or psychiatric illness for either the victim or the caregiver, a history of intra- and inter-generational conflict, a previous history of related illnesses. She did not build up a profile of the perpetrator, but regarded him/her as a member of the family. She believed there to be a background of intra-family violence, with all that that implies. Abusive behaviour might be associated with alcohol. There was an intolerance of dependency and members of the family might reinforce the violent behaviour of others. Rathbone-McCuan's conclusion was that the position of abused elders was similar to that of wives and children who were abused and neglected, which seems a simplistic view from our perception 15 years later. The tendency merely to extend the concepts relating to other forms of family violence will not go far enough in a study of elder abuse (Wolf and Pillemer, 1989). We need to extend the study of family relationships and older people alongside research into family violence which certainly in Britain has been under- researched, as was mentioned earlier (see, for example, Kingston and Penhale, 1995).

The early debate about elder abuse and neglect was still in its infancy 15 years ago and many of the early investigators found themselves in a cloud of uncertainty and ignorance. Hence Hickey and Douglass (1981b) were not specific beyond 'family members' and made a plea for 'in-depth studies of victims and their families', believing that abusive behaviour was probably triggered by parental dependency which recalled parent–child hostilities of earlier life. They also reported that in 63 per cent of cases of physical abuse, the abuser was suffering from alcohol and/or drug abuse and severe stress. Douglass (1983), cited in Schlesinger and Schlesinger (1988: 6), described victims as 'the older elderly persons, frail, mentally or physically disabled, female and living with the person responsible for the abuse'. Gesino et al.(1982) were interested in spouse abuse which existed throughout married life and spoke of the dearth of knowledge about spouse abuse in later life.

O'Malley et al. (1983) were responsible for one of the earliest surveys (of the reports of professionals and para-professionals) in Massachusetts. Their analysis of existing reports from professionals concluded that the victims were chiefly over 75 and female and that 75 per cent had significant mental or physical impairment. Sengstock and Liang (1982: 198) reported from their survey that the age-span was from 60 to over 90 and predominantly female. More whites were involved than blacks and 80 per cent were in receipt of an income of less than $10,000 a year. Taler and Ansello (1985) agreed on the basis of their records that the majority of victims were female, over 75, widowed and unable to be financially independent, with at least one physical or mental impairment. Similar responses came from Hirst and Miller (1986) and Mildenberger and Wessman (1986), but over 65; Soule and Bennett (1987), over 70; and Powell and Berg (1987), over 75.

O'Malley et al. (1983), turning to the perpetrators found them to be caregivers, suffering from stress, and/or the products of domestic violence which had become learned behaviour and normative for them. The abusers, in

O'Malley's study, frequently suffered from drug and alcohol abuse or were pathologically violent people. Taler and Ansello (1985) noticed that 40 per cent of perpetrators in their sample were spouses of victims and 50 per cent were children or grandchildren. Hirst and Miller (1986) identified daughters as abusers, with marital conflict, alcohol or drug abuse and ineffective coping patterns. Mildenberger and Wessman (1986) describe the daughters as white, middle-aged and middle-class.

The Boston study

Alongside these studies, Pillemer and Wolf were involved in their major study the Three Models Project (see p. 21 above). Among their findings were the results of the first large-scale rigorous random survey, involving 2,020 elderly people in Boston who were interviewed by telephone: these included interviews with abused persons, which I have already mentioned in another context. Here the profile was quite different from previous studies. Finkelhor and Pillemer (1988) noted that no longer were the results showing that elderly women were being mistreated by an adult child. Instead, in older people living in the community, abused men outnumbered abused women by 52 per cent to 48 per cent. Of the perpetrators, 58 per cent were spouses and 24 per cent were children. Because more elders live with spouses than with adult children, the chances of being mistreated by a spouse rather than an adult child are greater. If that is so, they suggest, it may account for the greater visibility of abused older women in previous surveys and trawls, because they suffer more severe injury and are more likely to report or be reported to a service agency.

Some of the other findings confirmed the picture painted by previous investigators. Abused elderly people were likely to be living with someone else. They were more likely to be in poor health. Neglected elders tended to have no one to turn to for support. In previous studies (Johnson et al., 1985; Hudson, 1986) as Finkelhor and Pillemer point out, victims appeared to come more from the older and disadvantaged sections of the community. They draw attention also to two more 'striking differences' between their study and earlier reports of elder abuse. There were high rates of spouse abuse and of men as victims. This study established that elder abuse in future could be the subject of general population surveys. Until Wolf, Pillemer, Finkelhor, Kosberg and others, most of the results of surveys, with the possible exception of O'Malley et al., had been obtained through unsound methodology. The findings were, for this reason, unreliable.

Later observations

Throughout the 1980s, some commentators emphasized the dependency of the victim on the perpetrator (Steinmetz, 1983; Quinn and Tomita, 1986), together with the stress to the carer that results. Wolf and Pillemer disputed this in 1989, maintaining that few research findings supported this view. They pointed out that while a large number of elderly people are dependent on relatives, only a small minority of these are abused. Therefore, they claimed, no direct correlation between the dependence of an elderly person and abuse could be established. Similarly, they continued, many elderly people are physically impaired, but without case comparison and control groups, it is inadequate to claim that abuse victims have some physical dependency. There had in the past been a tendency to generalize and Wolf and Pillemer exercised caution, concluding that 'a better way to conceptualize the issue is to view a serious imbalance of dependency in either direction as a potential risk factor' (Wolf and Pillemer, 1989: 27). There has been a tendency for some investigators to claim that abuse is the result of carer stress (Eastman, 1984; Traynor and Hasnip, 1984). However, some American researchers have criticized the methodology that has led to this conclusion and Bennett and Kingston in Britain have judged carer stress to be 'a victim-mentality' (Bennett and Kingston, 1993: 30). In the United States, Lachs and Pillemer and also Kosberg and Garcia have suggested that abusers are frequently carers with a history of mental ill-health, substance abuse problems or dependency on the elderly person for financial assistance (Lachs and Pillemer, 1995 : 438; Kosberg and Garcia, 1995: 190; see also from Britain, Homer and Gilleard, 1990).

Indicators of abuse

Burston's letter to the *British Medical Journal* in 1975 drew attention to the physical abuse of old people (who, he said, often had mental impairment). We had entered the world of 'granny battering', as he called it. Eastman, from the early 1980s, listed 'signs of facial bruising, grip marks on limbs, burns (caused perhaps by cigarettes), cuts or fractures' (1984: 58). In addition, as examples of abuse, he listed sexual abuse, the misuse of medication, recurring or unexplained injuries, physical constraints (tying people to beds or chairs), malnutrition and/or dehydration, lack of personal care. There may be responses from both the abused person and the abuser. Both men and women who have been abused may cower when approached (Hocking, 1988).

The early literature from America had moved quite quickly to describe the manifestations of abuse and neglect of older people (Block and Sinnott, 1979; Lau and Kosberg, 1979; O'Malley et al., 1979; Steuer and Austin, 1980; Hickey and Douglass, 1981a, 1981b; Rathbone-McCuan and Voyles, 1982). Their descriptions are strikingly similar to those from Britain. In the USA, Hall (1989) studied a sample of 284 cases of abuse and mistreatment with, by this time, a considerably more sophisticated analysis of what was happening. Hall found 43 separate acts or situations which related to the 284 cases. Two elements appeared in 15 per cent of the cases and 63 per cent contained two or more elements of mistreatment. Furthermore, the most frequently recurring items were (a) care of the person and the immediate living area, and (b) not seeking medical care. The items concerning self-care and health status accounted for 38 per cent of the recorded elements in this study: what Hall defined as personal maintenance (hygiene, clothing, food), care of the immediate living area, medication problems and food.

He went on to suggest that there may be a core of deterioration in the victim which makes the more extreme forms of mistreatment easier to commit. Abuse of elders' resources (theft, misuse of resources and/or coercion) constituted 14 per cent of the whole. Hall identified the most common indicators of abuse as 'not caring for health or seeking medical care'; the theft of material resources; physical abuse (including beating up, pushing, shoving, grabbing and slapping, kicking, hitting, sexual molestation), emotional and psychological abuse (calling names, insulting, swearing at, abandonment for long periods of time, threats, non-specific verbal aggression, restraint, locking up); and violation of elders' rights (forms of restraint, imposition and abandonment). Such a list exemplifies the great variety of acts of mistreatment that may be present and which were being increasingly recognized during the 1980s.

O'Malley et al., whose work in Massachusetts has been discussed approvingly by Wolf (1988), developed an identification chart in 1983 which provides a good summary:

Conditions that may be manifestations of abuse or neglect
Recurring or unexplained injuries
Non-treatment of medical problems
Poor hygiene
Malnutrition
Dehydration
Depression, withdrawal or fearfulness
Imposed social or physical isolation
Over-sedation or misuse of medication.

Conditions associated with high risk of abuse or suggesting potential for abuse
Severe cognitive impairment
Severe physical impairment requiring heavy care
Depression
Mention of punishment by elder or caretaker
Family norm of violence
Isolation of caretaker
Refusal of outside services
Control of elder's financial affairs or assets by another
Inconsistency of information by family or caretaker.

They also included a useful flow chart to assist decision-making, which asked the following questions:

Does the elder want to remain at home?
Are the reasons sound and justifiable?
Can the needs be met by the family and others?
Are the family and the patient willing to accept inadequate care to remain at home?

In the light of the answers to these questions, they continue:

Either provide support services which involve one or more of home health aide, homemaker/chore services, transportation, medical, nursing care, counselling, respite care.

Or, explore the choices, and counsel the family and the patient.

Or, explore alternative living arrangements for the patient, with another member of the family: foster care, residential home, nursing home. (O'Malley et al., 1983: 1000–2)

O'Malley et al. emphasized that in domestic cases of abuse and neglect it was useful to divide them into two categories: those in which the elderly person had physical or mental impairments and was dependent on the family for daily care needs and those in which care needs were minimal and were overshadowed by the pathological behaviour of the caregiver. They emphasized that access and intervention must be negotiated with both the abuser and the abused, neither of whom might desire help. The aim must be to benefit the elderly person, and in the negotiation it should be emphasized that services would resolve unmet needs for the patient while providing support to the caregiver.

American commentators continued to write about how to recognize the indicators of abuse (Hudson, 1986; American Medical Association, 1987; Soule and Bennett, 1987; Kosberg, 1988). The papers were numerous. Extended studies were virtually non-existent apart from the longitudinal studies of Pillemer and Wolf, who were cautious to report, until the end of the 1980s.

Breckman and Adelman (1988) included in their list of physical indicators: unexplained genital infections; soiled bed linen or clothing; unexplained or unexpected deterioration in health; absence of glasses, hearing aid and/or dentures. They suggested some indicators for psychological abuse: insomnia, sleep deprivation, need for excessive sleep, change in appetite, unexplained weight gain or loss, tearfulness, unexplained paranoia, low self-acceptance, excessive fears, ambivalence, confusion, resignation and agitation. Indicators of financial mistreatment might be the elderly person's inability to pay bills; an unexplained or sudden withdrawal of money from the elderly person's account; a disparity between assets and satisfactory living conditions; an unusual interest by family members in the older person's assets.

They also set out a detailed protocol (devised by Quinn and Tomita, 1986) for identification and assessment. This takes the reader (the worker) step by step, question by question, through the procedure and also lists a thorough raft of options, as did Podnieks (1988).

Unlike the USA, where there has been universal support for adult protection procedures and screening instruments, Britain has been very slow to set in place policies and guidelines for the protection of older people who are being mistreated. Bennett and Kingston have analysed the reasons for this (Bennett and Kingston, 1993: 1–22). It needs to be said, however, that the Social Services Inspectorate, which is part of the Department of Health and responsible for monitoring service delivery in social services departments, commissioned a review of the literature on elder abuse (McCreadie,

1991). It also reviewed cases of elder abuse in domestic settings in two London boroughs, in order to suggest ways in which practice in social services departments might be improved (SSI, 1992). It published its own guidelines (SSI, 1993), and a report on two seminars which were organized as a means of consciousness-raising (SSI, 1994). The Association of Directors of Social Services (ADSS) issued guidelines on adults at risk in 1991 and on elder mistreatment in 1995.

Kingston (1990), Hildrew (1991) and Penhale (1993a) have all carried out surveys of elder abuse procedures, but found a very incomplete picture. Action on Elder Abuse (AEA), which came into existence in 1993, carried out a survey of social services departments, health authorities and National Health Service (NHS) trusts in 1994. Five hundred and fifteen questionnaires were sent. There were 351 replies and a report was published (AEA, 1995). This revealed that 124 policies were in place. Half of the policies of social services departments and health authorities had been written jointly with the police, but only one-third of the policies of healthcare trusts had been so written. Most policies were said to be reviewed and updated regularly. A small number of areas were found to have 'elders at risk' registers. None of this is mandatory and advice from the SSI does not cover mistreatment in residential settings. There is little compatibility between existing policies and procedures and there are no national criteria. So nearly 20 years after Burston's letter to the *British Medical Journal*, there is still a long way to go.

A promising development in the USA in relation to the treatment of elder abuse and neglect has been the work of the neighbourhood justice centres (also referred to as mediation centres). They attempt to solve personal disputes between people who have a continuing relationship. Their techniques include counselling, mediation and arbitration (Nathanson, 1983). Mediation developed quite quickly in America in the 1980s and is now beginning to be discussed in Britain (Craig, 1992, 1994).

Establishing a theory

Most of the reasons given for abuse are reminiscent of ·the typologies in relation to definitions. In cases of domestic abuse, there were those who stressed psychological and psychosocial causes, concerned with family relationships, violence and family history. Others suggested a variety of other possibilities.

Reasons advanced for elder abuse by selected investigators:

Psychological and psychosocial causes
Rathbone-McCuan, 1980; Steuer and Austin, 1980; Hickey and Douglass, 1981b; Cloke, 1983; O'Malley et al., 1983; American Medical Association, 1987; Hudson, 1988; Godkin et al., 1989; Homer and Gilleard, 1990.

Other possibilities
Drugs and/or alcohol (Mildenberger and Wessman, 1986; Homer and Gilleard, 1990).

Chronic medical problems (O'Malley et al., 1983).

Financial problems (Hickey and Douglass, 1981b).

Dependency of victim (Hickey and Douglass, 1981b; American Medical Association, 1987; Soule and Bennett, 1987; Hudson, 1988).

Provocation by the victim (Mildenberger and Wessman, 1986).

Internal stress of the caregiver (Block and Sinnott, 1979; Rathbone-McCuan, 1980; Soule and Bennett, 1987; Hudson, 1988).

External stress of the caregiver: age, financial, work or unemployment (Soule and Bennett, 1987; Hudson, 1988; Godkin et al., 1989).

Social isolation (Godkin et al., 1989).

Hudson (1988) and Stevenson (1989) have suggested that the abusing caregiver may also be dealing with unresolved conflict. Pillemer and Moore (1989) have pointed to frustration engendered by long hours of work, low pay and low prestige; Kimsey et al. (1981) to discouragement, understaffing, underfunding and inadequate facilities, a point echoed by the American Medical Association (1987) and by Pillemer and Moore (1989), who also pressed for a study of conflictual staff–patient relationships. Block and Sinnott (1979) pointed to internal stress; Hudson (1988) to external stress and negative attitudes towards older people. The AMA (1987) also suggested that formal caregivers often had pessimistic attitudes to life and death, which frequently resulted in callousness.

None of these suggestions alone, however, provides a theoretical base which has been empirically tested. As early as 1981, Hickey and Douglass wrote of the need for a model that was free of professional bias, from which could be developed appropriate crisis intervention and prevention techniques.

The situational model

Phillips (1986) explored three theories of elder abuse and the way in which they reflected the empirical data. The earliest theory was the 'situational model'. The premiss fits easily within an intervention framework and is derived from a theoretical base associated with child abuse and less strongly with other forms of family violence:

> As the stress associated with certain situational and/or structural factors increases for the abuser, the likelihood increases of abusive acts directed at a vulnerable individual who is seen as being associated with stress. The situational variables that have been linked with abuse of the elderly have included (1) elder-related factors such as physical and emotional dependency, poor health, impaired mental status, and a 'difficult' personality; (2) structural factors such as economic strains, social isolation and environmental problems; and (3) caregiver-related factors such as life crisis, 'burn-out' or exhaustion with caregiving, substance abuse problems, and previous socialization experiences with violence. (Phillips, 1989: 198)

However, Phillips had difficulties in relating this model to the empirical data, mainly because of the lack of clarity in definitions of elder abuse and the confusion between physical or emotional neglect and other forms of abuse. Existing samples have differed from agency to professional to victim. Few studies used comparison groups. Usually, studies have described a sample of abused elders and then generated a theory to explain the observed data. The assumption that different forms of abuse within the family can all be explained by the same theory has not been tested. Phillips concludes that for these and other reasons the situational model may be inappropriate.

Social exchange theory

Social exchange theory is 'based on the idea that social interaction involves the exchange of rewards and punishments between at least two people and that all people seek to maximize rewards and minimize punishments in their interaction with others' (Phillips, 1989: 202). Phillips suggests that, conceptually, social exchange theory can easily be used to explain elder abuse, assuming that abused older people 'are more powerless, dependent and vulnerable than their caregivers and have fewer alternatives to continued interaction' (1989: 204). Deriving empirical support for this stance, however, has been far less simple. For instance, researchers have failed to produce unequivocal evidence that abused elders are more dependent than non-abused elders, thus 'violating the essential assumption that abused elders are more powerless, and as a result, caregivers have little to lose by their actions' (1989: 205). Phillips concludes that social exchange theory does not afford a complete explanation of elder abuse. It does not enable us to predict who will use violence and who will not. However, further testing of social exchange theory is likely to be productive (see Wolf, 1992; Jack, 1994; Biggs et al., 1995).

Symbolic interactionism

A third theoretical perspective which has been advanced for elder abuse is 'symbolic interactionism'. 'Social interaction is a process between at least two individuals that (1) occurs over time; (2) consists of identifiable phases that are recurring, interrelated, and loosely sequenced; and (3) requires constant negotiation and renegotiation to establish a "working consensus" ... about the symbolic meaning of the encounter' (Phillips, 1989: 207). This is about cognitive processes, the adoption and improvization of roles, the imputation of roles, role support, reciprocity and compatibility. When there is a mismatch, then there is the probability of conflict and termination of the interaction. In such a context, elder abuse can be conceptualized as an inadequate or inappropriate role enactment. Phillips (1989) obtained data from abusive and non-abusive caregivers and found that 'an important part of formulating personal images of the other person concerns reconciling the image of who this person was conceived to be in the past and the image of who this person is now conceived to be' (1989: 209). An obvious example is the case of someone suffering from dementia. Conflict can be particularly acute for 'adult children and elders who had not had a continuous live-in relationship throughout the years and among spouses where one spouse had sustained a personality-altering illness' (Phillips, 1989: 210). After using this model in rigorous test conditions, Phillips believes that there are some advantages, as well as disadvantages, in using symbolic interactionism as an explanatory base for elder abuse. These three perspectives are not mutually exclusive, 'nor do they include all the explanations that have been advanced in the literature for elder abuse' (Phillips, 1989: 214).

Abusers and victims

There are numbers of studies which have focused on the abuse of children by their parents and the abuse of women by men. In recent years, Pillemer has been developing a theoretical approach towards elder abuse which is based on the literature about child abuse and spouse abuse. He matched abused older people against non-abused older people and identified five areas:

1   Intra-individual dynamics (the psychopathology of the abuser).
2   Inter-generational transmission (the cycle of violence).
3   Dependency and exchange relations between abuser and abused.
4   External stress.
5   Social isolation. (Pillemer, 1986; see also Godkin et al., 1989; Wolf and Pillemer, 1989)

The study showed that abusers of elderly people were more likely to have mental and emotional problems, to abuse alcohol/drugs and to have been in hospital for psychiatric reasons (see also Kosberg and Garcia, 1995: 189). The study did not indicate that the perpetrator had been a victim of child abuse. Abused elders were not found to be more ill or functionally disabled than the control group. However, the abusers were likely to be dependent on their elderly victims. External events did not significantly differ between the two groups. The perpetrators had fewer overall contacts. This tended to isolate the victim.

There was general support for theories of elder abuse that related abuse to the problems of the abuser and the relationship between the abuser and the victim. The early family lives of the perpetrators were not unusually violent. Chronic economic stress and stressful life events played only a small part. Wolf and Pillemer (1989: 146) have reflected that 'the characteristics of the abuser, rather than those of the old person, may be strongly associated with violence against the elderly'. As a result of this model, the authors believed that they were nearing a consensus model. More research was required to see if their findings could be replicated. They are singular in that they run counter to the usually accepted view which depicts the victim as very dependent and the perpetrator as an overburdened caregiver.

The role of the physician

The progress that has occurred over the past ten years in bringing the problem of elder abuse and neglect to the attention of the public, professionals and politicians has taken place, by and large, without the involvement of the medical profession. (Wolf, 1988: 761)

The role of the GP . . . is of the utmost importance. (Eastman, 1984: 75)

In Britain, remarkably little has been written about the physician and elder abuse; McCreadie (1991) does not mention the physician. Nor is it clear why this is the case. Is it simply that the average physician is not interested in the ageing patient? A more likely reason is that the differential existence of guidelines across the country inhibits both recognition and intervention. There is plenty of anecdotal evidence for that. A handful of essays from America has attempted to draw the attention of physicians to the increasing visibility of the abuse and neglect of elderly people.

Solomon (1983a: 151–2), in describing the way in which physical complaints frequently mask underlying psychological or psychiatric problems, stressed that 'physicians are frequently unable to identify the results of victimization and abuse of the elderly'. Hooyman (1983: 382) went further and maintained that physicians encounter abused elderly people, 'but do not take any action'. O'Brien (1986: 620) reported that 'most physicians felt abuse was difficult or very difficult to detect' and in a survey he conducted in 1984, he found that 70 per cent of physicians in Michigan and North Carolina were unaware of mandatory reporting and in consequence underreported.

Taler and Ansello (1985), like Solomon, suggested that victims of elder abuse usually present to their physicians with complaints of a medical nature. They listed physical indicators as:

bruises or welts on the shoulder, back, chest or arms in various stages of healing; rope burns around the wrists or ankles; hemorrhaging beneath the scalp and multiple fractures of the long bones or ribs [These] are all signs of purposeful injury. On the other hand, pallor, dehydration and weight loss may not be evidence of willful neglect . . . These findings are common in confused and immobile patients. Bedsores should also be evaluated in context and may not represent neglect. (Taler and Ansello, 1985: 111)

They wrote also of behavioural indicators such as generalized fear on the part of the victim. Hostility, excessive concern, improbable explanations of symptoms or a harping on the burdens of caregiving may be behavioural clues to an abusing caregiver. Locks and barriers, the position of the elderly person's bedroom, lack of assistive devices for moving about, absence of a bedside commode, when the need for one seems appropriate, and the existence of unreported drugs for sedation might all be relevant as environmental indicators.

Taler and Ansello (1985) also comment on counselling the patient and caregiver. The caregiver should not be present with the victim during a discussion about potential abuse or neglect. If allegations or suspicions are aroused about the behaviour of the caregiver, unless immediate counselling and follow-up can be offered, it is wise not to discuss the matter with the caregiver at all at this stage. If the matter needs immediate attention then 'pejorative or accusatory language should be avoided' and follow-up and counselling arranged immediately (1985: 111).

The Council on Scientific Affairs of the American Medical Association (AMA) published a report on abuse and neglect in 1987. In recognizing the complexity of the problem, it strongly recommended that intervention and management of abuse cases should be multidisciplinary. A typical team would consist of primary care physician, a nurse, a social worker, a psychiatrist, a psychologist, a lawyer, a police officer and a case data coordinator. The need for harmonious relations between the agencies was emphasized by Wolf and Pillemer in 1989.

Writing in the *Illinois Medical Journal*, Cochran and Petrone (1987) provided an introduction to the identification and treatment of abuse cases. They included a classification table of types of abuse, quoted from the 1987 AMA report and provided a list of some 30 indicators. They suggested that if a physician suspects abuse, there are three points to be borne in mind. First, identification and treatment are complicated because of embarrassment or reluctance to admit the abuse. Secondly, victims have probably been traumatized over a long period of time and may, therefore, exhibit passivity, low self-esteem and indecision. Thirdly, the abused elder must make his or her own decisions. Cochran and Petrone (1987: 246) stress the need for:

- privacy when interviewing;
- the need to listen before beginning the physical assessment;
- documenting the history of the injury;
- observation of the emotional status of the patient;
- discussion of the relevant services which would be required for an adequate package of care;
- making arrangements for follow-up.

Wolf (1988) has maintained that physicians must be able to recognize the potential risk factors and symptoms of abuse. They should become familiar with elder abuse laws and procedures and, as members of a multidisciplinary team, they can both educate other professional groups about the physical problems of old age and act as a link with the health service or medical care system. Wolf (1988: 761) believes also that:

> Physicians have an obligation to make known their opinions about the laws, especially regarding some of the controversial aspects that affect medical practice, such as mandatory reporting, competency, professional judgement, patient self-determination, immunity and liability.

Bloom et al. published a paper for physicians which also stressed the importance of documentation. This, they emphasized, was an essential first step towards necessary involvement. 'Physicians . . . have a special responsibility to promote [a] greater awareness [of elder abuse] and effective interventions' (1989: 44).

In Britain, Hocking (1988) pointed out that, in cases of non-accidental injury, everyone in the household is at risk. The physician as coordinator of the primary care team has a central role in preventing the occurrence of NAI. The case notes of people in stressed households should be marked to facilitate a regular (monthly) review. Chapter 14 of this book refers specifically to the role of the physician.

Legislative developments in America

It may be helpful to conclude this overview with a brief consideration of the principal legislative developments in the USA, bearing in mind that in Britain there is still no legal requirement to report cases of abuse. In the USA every state, by 1988, had some form of adult abuse and protection laws in place as a result of the federal elder abuse legislation of 1981 (Biggs et al., 1995). Much of this legislation was based on child abuse legislation and most of it was applicable to all adults, although it has been designed for and primarily used in relation to elder abuse. Much of the early legislation was drafted quickly and without recourse to expert advice. Because of this there is a lack of standardization in terminology; 'abuse' and 'neglect' may be used interchangeably.

Definitions of 'elderly' are not always helpful, particularly where, as in Florida, ageing is regarded as a form of disability. Their statute defines an aged person as one 'suffering from the infirmities of aging as manifested by organic brain damage, advanced age, or other physical, mental or emotional dysfunctioning' (Crystal, 1986: 339).

Definitions of elder abuse are not clear in the legislation either. (Salend et al., 1984 and Fulmer and O'Malley, 1987 among others have drawn attention to this.) Distinctions between different types of abuse are frequently not included. The majority of states failed to make provision for a central database of reports. Some required only physicians to report. Some required some professionals and not other professionals to report. Some required both professionals and lay persons to report. Some provided immunity. Some included provisions about confidentiality. All required names and addresses of victims and perpetrators. Not all laws included penalties for mistreatment or failure to report. Some specified penalties for one and not for the other. The work of identification and prevention has been under-resourced.

Some practice issues

Nevertheless, in some states teams of workers were appointed as adult protective agencies. Assessment tools were developed. In most cases, if there is suspicion of abuse, the law requires investigation as soon as possible (within, say, 24 to 72 hours), with a service plan elaborated immediately if the case is proved (Bennett, 1990c).

Kosberg (1988) drew attention to the result of most of the legislation as it stands, namely that it focuses on abuse after it has occurred and necessitates both detection and reporting. This caused him to urge the development of assessment protocols for carers in order to prevent elder abuse.

Salend et al. (1984) urged the importance of immunity for those reporting cases and the necessity for assessment guidelines which could be used in a sensitive and informed way. They also raised the question of the rights and well-being of the alleged victim (as do Taler and Ansello, 1985; Mildenberger and Wessman, 1986) and the fundamental question of a thorough conceptualization of what should be reported and why.

Daniels et al. (1989) regarded the mandatory reporting laws as merely symbolic. In their study of the operation of elder abuse laws in Alabama, they found considerable scepticism among physicians about the reporting procedures. In fact, they confirmed O'Malley et al. (1979) and O'Brien (1986) in finding that physicians as a group tended to under-report cases of abuse. Crystal (1986) reported that a Syracuse study in 1983 found that only 2 per cent of reports came from physicians. Three-quarters were uncertain how to report cases. Most were uncertain about their own immunity in reporting cases. Eighty per cent felt that prompt action would not be taken by service agencies. Daniels et al. (1989) pointed out that most politicians in enacting this legislation assumed that service delivery would be accomplished with available resources. This they regarded as a serious flaw in the elder abuse legislation, as did Crystal (1986) and Wolf and Pillemer (1989).

It is therefore not surprising that in 1990 the US House of Representatives issued a Select Committee on Aging report entitled *Elder Abuse: A Decade of Shame and Inaction* (United States House of Representatives Select Committee on Aging, Sub-Committee on Health and Long-Term Care, 1990). The Committee found that in terms of funding their adult protection services, the states spent an average of $3.10 on each elderly resident compared with $45.03 for each child resident (McCreadie, 1991).

There is, however, evidence to show that amendments can be made to existing legislation. Foelker et al. (1990) describe how in Texas an amendment was passed in 1987 to sharpen the legislation at the point of caregiver responsibility and caregiver neglect. They also achieved an expansion in both staffing and financial resources.

Canada and Britain

The situation in Canada and Britain is very different. Sharpe (1988) and Gnaedinger (1989) list a variety of charges in relation to abuse and neglect that could be laid under the Canadian Criminal Code and the Power of Attorney Act (1979). Under Canadian law in 1988, there was still no legal protection for an endangered and mentally incapable adult (Sharpe, 1988: 64). There was the possibility of protective intervention under the Mental Health Act, and the Mental Incompetency Act provided for guardianship of the person and the estate of a mentally incompetent adult.

Gnaedinger (1989: 11) suggested that 'the primary hindrance to reporting cases of elder abuse is the reluctance of the victims to admit to their own abuse'. She also described the basic difficulties of mandatory reporting: the violation of family privacy, the minimization of complaints because of lack of interest by elderly people, disbelief, fear of accusing the perpetrator, being sued and lack of awareness. She also noted that, since 1988, the federal government funded at least six federal departments to prepare a national approach to family violence. By 1989, special legislation concerned with adult abuse, including elder abuse, existed in Ontario, Nova Scotia, Prince Edward Island, New Brunswick and Alberta.

In Britain, when an elderly person is considered to be at risk or mentally incapacitated, the law in relation to decision-making on his or her behalf is fragmented and complex. Remarkably little has been written on the subject. The first texts available in Britain on English law and elderly people were by Griffiths et al. (1990), Griffiths and Roberts (1995) and Ashton (1995). It is necessary to move towards positive legislative developments in this area of human vulnerability and this theme will be returned to in Chapter 6.

Conclusion

This brief overview has attempted to introduce the reader to some of the complexities of elder mistreatment. What is the way forward to good practice? Kosberg (1988: 49) provides us with a summary:

> Elder abuse will continue as long as ageism and violence exist ... Elder abuse results from the dynamic interaction between personal, family, social and cultural values, priorities and goals. Therefore, attention must be given to those factors which, although not causing abuse, contribute to its likelihood: poverty and unemployment, lack of community resources, intra-family cycles of abuse, and personal hedonism.

It is in the area of 'intra-family cycles of abuse' particularly that more information is required. Elder abuse has often been compared or related to child abuse (Rathbone-McCuan, 1980; Eastman, 1984). This is because the relationship between the carer or caretaker and the elder (according to Finkelhor and Pillemer, 1988: 248) is often thought to have 'a parent–child character in the extreme dependency of the elder'. American commentators have gone on to point out that in some states in the USA the same agencies handle both child and elder abuse cases: the problems were first identified by professionals working with both populations. This kind of abuse differs from spouse abuse, which was first identified by the women's movement through volunteers and private agencies. The point is also made that both child and elder abuse are social problems which have been 'medicalized' by health professionals, who have their own intervention strategies established within health care institutions and this is not the case with spouse abuse.

To press the parallel between child and elder abuse is dangerous. We have already noted that much elder abuse is not committed by a carer against a dependent victim. In many cases, as Wolf and Pillemer have shown, it is the abuser who may be dependent. Furthermore, even if the elder is dependent, the relationship is different. Parents have a legal responsibility for children who are minors, but in most cases adult children do not have a legal responsibility for their parents.

> Older persons are considered to be independent, responsible individuals. More-over, most [of the] elderly do not live with their children (fewer than one in ten do so), and there is only a small and disappearing social expectation that they should do so . . . The elderly are in a very different structural relationship to their abusers than are children. (Finkelhor and Pillemer, 1988: 249)

Finkelhor and Pillemer go on to affirm that elder abuse is often spouse abuse that has been going on for years, and they refer to their Boston study, which has already been mentioned. Even when the perpetrator and the victim are not husband and wife, the situation of elder abuse is more akin to spouse abuse than to child abuse. 'Both parties are independent adults; they are living with each other by choice; the elder is connected to the abuser by ties of emotional allegiance and perhaps economic dependence, but certainly may have more social, psychological and economic indepen-dence than a child' (Finkelhor and Pillemer, 1988: 250). For this reason, Finkelhor and Pillemer (1988) and Breckman and Adelman (1988) are con-vinced that further studies in family violence are required.

Finally, Wolf and Pillemer (1989: 148–50) have recommended in relation to elder abuse victims and their families that:

1 A need exists for specific elder abuse programmes.
2 An elder abuse project should be located in, or affiliated to, a high profile community agency.
3 An elder abuse project should offer direct services.
4 Inter-agency coordination is critical for the success of the project.
5 The existence [in the USA] of a mandatory reporting statute, with insufficient financial appropriations, can hinder elder abuse inter-vention.

They also recommend direct interviews with abused elders and with perpe-trators; and moving away from agency samples to population surveys, based on control group designs. They regard it as necessary to focus research on the consequences of abuse; the context of abusive acts; why abusive children come to live with their parents; the relation between physical abuse and parent–child relationships and child-rearing practices. They press for further definition of what is meant by 'case resolution' and 'neglect', and for further investigations into spouse abuse.

Wolf, Pillemer and their colleagues have arrived at these conclusions after a decade of rigorous fieldwork and research. In so doing, they have provided an agenda for action and research. Ideally, what is required is a series of cross-national projects based on compatible designs, which can begin to create a database of international and meaningfully coherent proportions. In this context, we would undoubtedly further benefit in Britain from a rigorous examination of 'neglect' within the community, and a more extensive study of the prevalence of abuse and neglect. A great deal of the debate until now has centred on physical, psychological and material abuse within the domestic environment, but the delicate question of elder abuse and neglect in residential settings requires detailed study and resolution too. In terms of human vulnerability, it is unacceptable that investigations of this nature should apparently have been discouraged for so long (see further Chapter 11, this volume). There have been so many official inquiries in Britain into alleged mistreatment in residential centres, and so many adverse findings, that we now require a responsible and analytical commentary on the experience of both elderly people and staff in residential centres in the statutory, voluntary and private sectors.

When the first edition of this book was published in 1993, our understanding in Britain of elder mistreatment was still largely dependent on the findings of American and Canadian investigators. While it remains true that much more fieldwork and clinical study is required in Britain, there have been developments in conceptualization as attempts are made to establish a theoretical understanding of elder mistreatment. Readers might be interested to compare the findings of the first edition with those of Bennett and Kingston, published later in 1993, Eastman (1994), Biggs et al. (1995), Kingston and Penhale (1995) and the chapter on 'protection' in Hughes (1995).

Biggs et al. have suggested that

> a perspective is needed that explains the complex nature of abusive situations on at least three levels. This should take account of the personal, interpersonal and socially constructed nature of mistreatment. It is not enough simply to categorize types of abuse and neglect ... It is also important first to unpack the ways that different conceptions of abuse emerge and how behaviour is influenced. Second, we must also examine the systems that perpetuate and reproduce mistreatment at each level and how these levels interact. (Biggs et al., 1995: 123)

Hughes approaches elder abuse in a similar way to Biggs et al., insisting that it can only be understood within the context of its social location. In her view a conceptual understanding of elder abuse must

> begin from an analysis of the concept of ageism and old age inequality;
> connect conceptually different forms of abuse at different levels in society;
> locate domestic and institutional abuse within the wider context of social attitudes;
> offer an explanation for current levels and types of abuse;
> offer an explanation why not all elderly people are abused;
> suggest factors within the overall analysis, which might predict abusive and non-abusive situations. (Hughes, 1995: 134)

Kingston and Penhale suggest that the inbuilt attitudes to older people, which were discussed in Chapter 2 above, may increase the likelihood of abuse due to the marginalization of older people and their carers (Kingston and Penhale, 1995: 230). They point out further (p.233) that for any social problem to develop as an acknowledged problem it requires a reasonable degree of public legitimation, rather than solely professional concern. Although in the last two or three years there have been a number of encouraging signs, as we have just noted, 'a reasonable degree of public legitimation' of elder mistreatment as an acknowledged social problem remains hard to achieve in Britain.

4

Clinical Presentation and Management

Peter Decalmer

> Disease is very old, and nothing about it has changed. It is we who change as we learn to recognize what was formerly imperceptible. (Jean Martin Charcot, French neurologist, 1825–93: *De l'expectation en médecine*).

Elder abuse is a serious and much-neglected subject. However, its profile and recognition has been raised considerably over the last five years with the publication of several English textbooks which have been influenced by work in the United States of America by Wolf, Pillemer and Johnson and in Canada by Podnieks and others. Politically, and in terms of promotion and raising awareness, the organization Action on Elder Abuse has considerably helped the group of people who are subject to abuse. Numbers of social services departments and healthcare trusts have now started to consider seriously their strategies, policies and procedures dealing with either vulnerable adults, or elderly people who are subject to abuse. The recognition of elder abuse in this country has been patchy. In 1975, Burston and Baker first recognized the phenomenon described as 'granny battering' or 'granny bashing'. In the 1980s, Eastman, with the British Geriatrics Society (BGS) helped to raise the profile, together with the reports of researchers from the United States and Canada. However, this did not lead to substantial research in Britain and it has yet to be done in any depth, with particular reference to prevalence and incidence; there are areas that are totally neglected in terms of research, for example the incidence of institutional abuse in Britain, abuse in minority ethnic communities and of most importance perhaps, the fact that although policies and procedures have been set up, outcome measures are a very rare commodity and much work needs to be done in that area.

The clinical presentation of cases that were outlined in the 1993 edition of this book will not be repeated in this chapter. The purpose of this particular presentation is to consider the recognition and management of people who are exposed to the risk of elder abuse. It examines several instruments and how they can be used to identify, collate and manage cases. The chapter will also deal with the recognition of elder abuse and the various roles of the multidisciplinary team. Multidisciplinary teams are now being carefully examined in this country, together with the development of several models, one of which will be described here and in Chapter 14, from Bury and Rochdale. I will describe the role of each member of the team involved and how their expertise can help with the management of people who are suspected of being abused, as well as the role of the care manager in helping the perpetrators of this potential abuse.

Further work has been done on definitions. What I use in this chapter will be the categories proposed by Wolf and Pillemer in 1989. However, it is important to examine one of the newer definitions which was adopted in 1995 by Action on Elder Abuse. This has already been cited in Chapter 1:

> Elder abuse is a single or repeated act, or lack of appropriate action occurring within any relationship where there is an expectation of trust which causes harm or distress to the older person.

There are certain key elements to this definition which seem to set it apart from other definitions, mainly the expectation of trust. This seems to push the definition in particular towards carer abuse where there is a relationship. It also highlights the issue of actions or lack of actions, which addresses many of the difficulties that are encountered by researchers who ask, 'Is active or passive neglect actually part of elder abuse?' The weakness of the definition is that it does not contain any reference to people's legal rights or civil liberties. At the time of preparing this chapter, the Law Commission was attempting to make recommendations to Parliament concerning vulnerable elderly people, with the extension of guardianship, the expansion of the Court of Protection and the possible inclusion of a Protection Order. However, at present these have been rejected by the government. The Wolf and Pillemer categories (which were listed in Chapter 3, this volume) are probably the most useful research tool as they are tight definitions which give us five categories with which to work, and these have also been found to be useful when health and social services have attempted to put together policies and procedures. Many have adapted these categories for day-to-day purposes, especially in relationship to care management.

The categorization of cases has its limitations as there is often considerable overlap between, say, physical abuse and psychological abuse, or psychological and financial abuse. Clinicians have found descriptive formulations in many ways a more useful tool, the assessment tool developed by Johnson having been found to be particularly useful. She uses a holistic approach and defines what she calls 'elder mistreatment' as 'self or other imposed suffering, unnecessary to the maintenance of the quality of life of the older person by means of abuse or neglect caused by being overwhelmed' (Johnson, 1991: 4). She has developed a questionnaire which includes a grid and is concerned with suffering as a consequence of abuse, neglect as the means, and being overwhelmed as the causal antecedent.

This definition and the grid are being used by clinicians when assessing cases individually and by managers who have to construct policy documents. As soon as clinicians start to work with this grid they will begin to understand the broadness of the presentation of the cases, and this will be highlighted later in this chapter. It is a considerable advance on the case studies which were so popular in this country, especially in social work, for example Eastman (1984), and were used particularly for clinical and teaching purposes. When designing the Bury and Rochdale Policies and Procedures (Community Care Act) in 1993 it was decided to build in clinical assessment, which was centred around the principles of care management, and to train professionals to use this as their basic tool and to incorporate four assessment procedures.

The first of these was the assessment instrument devised by Johnson in 1991: Indicators of Possible Elder Mistreatment. The second was the High Risk Placement Worksheet developed by Kosberg (1988). The third was the Caregiver Strain Questionnaire developed by Robinson (1983). The fourth was the Elder Abuse Assessment Protocol for Nurses (Davies, 1993). These will all be found in Appendices A, B, C and D, this volume. The instruments are used in conjunction with care management procedures. Health and social services colleagues using these instruments have found that they did not need to adjust their normal practices in terms of training and additional work. Our experience in Bury and Rochdale has been that many cases have been successfully worked through, using the above methods. We have also found that we have been able to train over 250 people from health and social services, voluntary agencies and from both providers and purchasers, in the recognition and management of elder abuse (Bury and Rochdale Partnership Group for Older People, 1993). I will now describe three of the four instruments that are used. These will be demonstrated in the case examples later in the chapter. The Assessment Protocol for Nurses (Davies, 1993) will be discussed in Chapter 13.

The Indicators of Possible Elder Mistreatment (Johnson, 1991) is a grid accompanied by a questionnaire which asks standardized questions relating to the physical, psychological, sociological and legal aspects of people who are possibly being subjected to abuse. The grid gives the clinician a 'picture of the case', often demonstrating symptoms that are overlooked. The clinician, care manager and line manager often begin to understand the multifaceted nature of each case of elder abuse. We have found that by using this model and giving it to all the professionals and carers involved, it became very apparent that different people were picking up different aspects of the abuse. This also allowed the care manager, when preparing for the case conference, to address very specific questions to the doctors, psychiatrists, social workers and members of the legal profession based on the areas highlighted in the grid devised by Johnson. Our experience of using this grid is that it is an extremely useful tool, both in analysing and managing cases, and often defines resources that the line manager then needs to address, to allow the care manager to manage the particular case.

The High Risk Placement Worksheet (Kosberg, 1988) was originally designed to make decisions about placement. Our experience with this model has been that it brings together all the risk factors and allows the assessment, both in a qualitative and quantitative way, to understand the risk factors of the older person and the major carer, the family systems that are involved, and also the issues that are perceived surrounding placement of the older person, both the reality and the ideal. This instrument, used in conjunction with the previous one described, and with the Caregiver Strain Questionnaire, provides an overall picture which is of great use when examining complex social issues, such as whether separation needs to be examined as an option, placement issues and the risk factors that may lead the clinician to have to consider using such instruments as the Mental Health Act, 1983 or the National Assistance Act, 1947.

The Caregiver Strain Questionnaire (Robinson, 1983) examines independently the stresses on the carer, his/her coping mechanisms and often gives clues as how near to breakdown the carer is, without making any reference to the abuse that is suspected. It focuses very much on the carer's needs and is an extremely useful and non-threatening instrument. It explores with the carer aspects of behaviour exhibited by the elderly person which provoke stress, as well as examining the potential and actual consequences of caring for that older person. It identifies the needs where assistance would often be of benefit to the carer.

The role of the interview

Noone and Decalmer deal with the first presentation of a case for initial screening and assessment in primary care in Chapter 14 of this volume, while the present chapter addresses the issues surrounding assessment and management by a trained multidisciplinary team. When a referral of a case of suspected elder mistreatment is made, the specialist may be faced with a potentially explosive situation. The abuser and victim are often very frightened, defensive and vulnerable. Great sensitivity is needed to obtain a clear picture and work out a care plan that is owned by all the parties. The first step is to try and take a standard psychiatric history. The assessment tool developed by Hwalek and Sengstock (1986) is very useful as a screening instrument to establish the range and type of abuse. There are leading questions which can be incorporated within an interview if the victim becomes unduly distressed :

1 Has anyone tried to hurt or harm you?
2 Have you been forced to do things you did not want to do? Give an example.
3 Have you been threatened with being placed in a nursing facility?
4 Has anyone stolen from you or taken your possessions without permission?
5 Has anyone sworn at you or threatened you?
6 Has anyone confined you at home against your will?
7 Has anyone refused to provide you with food or with your medications?
8 Has anyone beaten or assaulted you?
9 Have you ever signed any documents that you did not understand?
10 Are you afraid of anyone in your home?

The useful guidelines listed below are fairly standard practice developed from child abuse protocols:

1   Ensure privacy.
2   Always interview in pairs.
3   Separate victims from caregivers – interview separately.
4   Ensure confidentiality.
5   Allow adequate time for response.
6   Progress from general (screening) to specific (direct) questions.
7   Keep questions simple and appropriate for educational level.
8   Respect cultural, ethnic differences.
9   Do not blame victims.
10 Do not blame or confront perpetrators.
11 Do not show frustration.
12 Be prepared to terminate the interview if situation goes out of control.
13 Acknowledge that this process may require multiple interviews.
14 Determine whether cognitive impairment is present.
15 Use other people, such as office or emergency room nurses, to conduct the interview if this is less threatening to victims.

These guidelines set the protocol for the use of the various assessment tools in a safe and non-threatening way. To acquire all this information requires tact, sensitivity and professionalism. The clinical procedures for the detection of abuse of an elderly patient have also been summarized by Lachs and Pillemer (1995: 440) and it is a useful checklist to enable the clinician to consider the most important aspects of these cases.

The Elder Abuse Assessment Protocol for Nurses (Davies, 1993) is of course primarily designed for nurses, but it has the great advantage of being simple to use, if added to medical notes. Other professionals as a result of their clinical assessment can provide additional information concerning the patient. Accurate records of injuries sustained by the victim are recorded, as are assessments of the mental state of the abused person, their social functioning, and whether there is acute or chronic neglect. The carer section deals with the attitudes of the carer to the victim. Aspects of caring and deficits of the older person are recorded. Risk factors are assessed. The other advantage of this instrument is that it is signed and dated and is very useful if legal action is being contemplated at some later stage. An accurate record is kept of each incident of the suspected abuse. It is important when filling in the Davies questionnaire to consider the checklist of possible physical indicators for types of physical abuse and neglect, and these are outlined below.

Cases of institutional abuse have to be approached in a different way. The High Risk Placement Worksheet and Caregiver Strain Questionnaire are chiefly for domestic use, although they were found to be particularly useful in case example 7, p. 66ff. The assessment form that is really helpful is the Indicators of Possible Elder Mistreatment. We are also finding the Theoretical Model of Patient Maltreatment (Pillemer, 1988), which is described in Chapter 13, to be invaluable. Pillemer's self-proven model suggests that abuse and neglect may occur, given factors relating to the characteristics of staff members and patients which are influenced by aspects of the nursing home environment and by certain exogenous factors (Pillemer, 1988: 230). These factors are discussed in Chapter 11 of this volume.

All of these assessment tools, including Pillemer's Theoretical Model, require practice and patience. They do not replace the need to undertake a proper interview.

Checklist of possible physical indicators for types of physical abuse and neglect

Physical abuse

1 Unexplained bruises and welts:
   (a) on face, lips, mouth, on torso, back, buttocks, thighs
   (b) human bite marks in various stages of healing (it is advisable to note site of bruising)
   (c) clustered, e.g. forming regular patterns
   (d) reflection of shape of article used to inflict abuse (e.g. electric cord, belt buckle)
   (e) different surface areas noted
   (f) regular appearance after absence: weekend or vacation
2 Unexplained burns:
   (a) cigar, cigarette burns, especially on soles, palms, back or buttocks
   (b) immersion burns (sock-like, glove-like, doughnut-shaped, on buttocks or genitalia)
   (c) patterned like electric burner, iron, etc.
   (d) rope burns on arms, legs, neck or torso
3 Unexplained fractures:
   (a) to skull, nose, ear (cauliflower ear), facial structure
   (b) in various stages of healing
   (c) multiple or spinal fractures
4 Unexplained lacerations or abrasions:
   (a) to mouth, lips, gums, eyes, ears
   (b) to external genitalia
5 Unexplained hair loss:
   (a) haemorrhaging beneath scalp
   (b) possible hair pulling, self or other
   (c) possible evidence of underlying severe head injury (subdural haematoma)
6 Evidence of past injuries:
   (a) Deformities – skull, nose and ears, cauliflower ear, hands (twisting reflex)
   (b) Contractures resulting from restraint and delay in seeking treatment
   (c) Dislocation, pain, tenderness and swelling (NB: dislocation may be due to incorrect lifting)

Bruises can be roughly dated by colour as follows:

0–2 days: swollen, tender
0–5 days: red-blue
5–7 days: green
7–10 days: yellow
10–14 days: brown
2–4 weeks: clear

NB: It is important to look for bruising in minority ethnic groups who tend to be darker. Injuries on their own are often difficult to interpret. An important clue is the appearance of haematomas of differing ages. If possible, any suspicious injuries should be photographed to provide an accurate record.

Physical neglect

1 Consistent hunger, poor hygiene, inappropriate dress, including soiled clothing, unexplained weight loss, dehydration
2 Consistent lack of supervision, especially in dangerous activities or over long periods
3 Constant fatigue or listlessness, unexplained or increasing confusion
4 Unattended physical problems or medical needs, including urine burns or pressure sores
5 Lost or non-functioning aids, e.g. glasses, dentures, hearing aids, walking aids and wheelchairs
6 Over/under-medication
7 Abandonment, immobility, hypothermia/indicating possible isolation

Sexual abuse

1 Difficulty walking or sitting
2 Torn, stained or bloody underclothing
3 Pain or itching in genital area
4 Bruises or bleeding in external genitalia, vaginal or anal areas
5 Unexpected and unreported reluctance to cooperate with toileting and physical examination of genitalia

Emotional mistreatment

1 Habit disorder (sucking, biting, rocking, etc.)
2 Conduct disorders (anti-social, destructive, self and others)
3 Neurotic traits (sleep disorders, speech disorders, inhibition of play)
4 Psychoneurotic reaction (hysteria, obsession, compulsion, phobias, hypochondria)
5 Post-traumatic stress disorder
Note: It is necessary to assess whether symptoms and signs disappear in hospital or residential care over a period of time. Particular attention

should be paid to appearance after a weekend or holiday. (Decalmer and Davies, 1993 adapted from United States Department of Health and Social Services, 1980 and Hocking, 1988)

The multidisciplinary assessment

Before examining the cases described under physical, sexual, psychological and material abuse it is important to describe the ways in which each of the professionals is involved, the use of their professional expertise and the strategies of care and intervention in the setting of a multidisciplinary team.

A team conference is a well-established method of drawing together all information and it leads to a strategy for managing these very complicated cases. In the guidelines of the Bury and Rochdale Partnership Group (see Appendix F) a case conference is held within ten working days. This team conference provides a method of open discussion, reporting of findings and formally formulating cases so that a written record can be drawn up in the care management plan. The record should consist of information obtained from all sources, including an account of the type of abuse of the victim, the characteristics of the perpetrator, the assessment by each professional, an agreed strategy of care and intervention, and an assessment of risk. Clear statements are necessary about whether it is definite or a probable case of abuse. Conclusions should declare methods of intervention, making it clear who is responsible for each of the decisions that have been made and who is the key worker and coordinator responsible for the overall management of the case.

The line manager is responsible for providing the funding implications of that particular case as decided through the care manager and the multi-disciplinary team. Regular reviews need to take place at stated intervals to ensure that strategies of intervention are working and to address new developments or facts of the case which begin to appear as the patient or client is care-managed. Any unmet need that is found must be carefully recorded. There is an urgent need to develop these strategies (Allen et al., 1992). However, the NHS and Community Care Act 1990, since its implementation in 1993, has helped many professionals to be trained in care management and multidisciplinary working and has allowed them, with additional training, to feel comfortable about managing cases of possible elder abuse, addressing openly the issues surrounding the management and care of the possible perpetrator.

The care manager's role is in many ways a much broader one. It allows, through the recent legislation, not only for the client to have rights, but also for the carer to demand interventions to help him/her to cope with the stresses of managing often a very disabled elderly person (Carers (Recognition and Services) Act 1995). Although case management, as defined in the White Paper *Caring for People* (Department of Health, 1989b), should have been in place from 1991, there have been considerable problems in implementing this. It is pleasing to note that case management is now fully operational throughout Britain and although there are many teething problems, it does provide an excellent model for helping people with elder abuse.

Of particular importance are two new pieces of legislation. The Supervision Register allows people who are being abused, after a full assessment, to be clearly identified as being at risk and to be highlighted, both to social and health services, to have key workers appointed, with regular reviews required by law, and to have provision made to look at unmet need with an onus both on health and social services to pay particular attention to this vulnerable group. Additional legislation came in on 1 April 1996. Supervised Discharge is, in many ways, similar to Guardianship Order under the Mental Health Act and provides the responsible medical officer with the duty to place the person in a safe environment, to require that person to attend for treatment and to nominate a key worker who has responsibility for the case and has the responsibility to transport that patient to a treatment area or safe environment, or to see the responsible medical officer in the out-patients department.

This piece of legislation is of particular use in the case of people who are being abused. It is important, therefore, that there is a co-ordinator who can mobilize resources and integrate service allocation with cost information (Worsam, 1991; Goldberg and Huxley, 1992). All of these are provided by the Care Programme Approach and the Care Management, which are intending to amalgamate.

Worsam (1991) studied assessment and broke the process down into:

- purpose
- process
- method
- occasions for assessment
- outcome of assessment

The care management team

When deciding who to invite to a multidisciplinary team for an elder abuse case conference the following should be considered essential: the general practitioner, a consultant psychiatrist or geriatrician, a social worker, a specialist nurse or community psychiatric nurse, a clinical psychologist and either a legal adviser or the police. The other important people to be invited are the line manager, who is kept involved, the elder person and the carer.

The *general practitioner* is the physician with responsibility for primary care medical services. His/her duties include:

1 maintenance of a confidential relationship between doctor and patient;
2 the determination of clinical needs of an individual patient which may include the victim and the perpetrator;

3 provision of the best possible medical treatment within his/her experience for elder and carer;
4 the power to delegate authority (to diagnose or treat) but not responsibility;
5 screening cases using the over-75 assessment procedure, and an abuse assessment scale;
6 screening health and functional status.

The *consultant's* responsibilities include:

1 his/her role as ultimate medical authority within the hospital service for patients within his/her care, and those on the Care Programme, Supervision Register and Supervised Discharge;
2 the same duties as listed in 1–3 above for the general practitioner;
3 describing deficiencies in the service, especially if they impede the satisfactory implementation of clinical and ethical duties to patients;
4 a special role as responsible medical officer, as defined within the Mental Act 1983;
5 supervision and training of junior medical staff and other doctors in training;
6 effective coordinating of the contributions of the variety of disciplines involved in clinical care.

The *psychiatric nurse* possesses general skills in the assessment of nursing needs and in the planning and delivery of nursing care. In addition, he/she often has skills in:

1 the assessment and observation of mental state in a community setting;
2 behavioural modification;
3 group work and leadership;
4 community psychiatric nursing;
5 family therapy and prevention;
6 individual counselling.

He/she should establish a relationship when visiting the client at home (Sladden, 1979):

1 to look at nursing needs (SSI, 1993: 15) particularly in a home setting;
2 to establish social and rehabilitation programmes;
3 to help the elder abused person regain lost skills, and to provide diversion;
4 to be able to monitor medication schedules and drugs safety policies, especially if there are problems with medication abuse;
5 to establish individual care plans;
6 to develop close links between the primary care teams and the psychiatric teams to assist both parties in difficult nursing problems through internal liaison;
7 to develop close links with other agencies, e.g. community-based services (Skidmore and Friend, 1984).

He/she should follow up complex management problems when the patient is discharged from hospital and liaise with the multidisciplinary team, often acting as a key worker.

The *social worker's* duties can be summarized under four headings:

1   Casework: a range of techniques employed by the social worker with the client to enhance the latter's personal functioning. This includes support and counselling (Goldberg and Huxley, 1992).
2   Statutory powers, as defined by the Mental Health Act 1983.
3   Liaison and consultation between social services, other local authority departments and the health service.
4   In elder abuse, serious consideration may need to be given to the social worker carrying a central administrative role.

The social worker does encounter structural and cultural obstacles to the achievement of multidisciplinary work in community psychiatry, because of the fear that he will be treated as a 'medical auxiliary' (Bruce, 1980).

The *clinical psychologist* has responsibility for the following areas:

1   planning and carrying out treatment, particularly on counselling or behavioural modification;
2   psychological and psychometric assessment to include formulation of the patient's problems and mental capacity in objective terms. In elder abuse, capacity and understanding may be a vital issue (BMA, 1995);
3   education of other team members in the principles and findings of scientific psychology;
4   contributing to the (social) psychological perspectives of abuse cases;
5   undertaking research in relevant areas.

The *police and legal advisers* have duties:

1   to assist the group in legal matters, or if a crime has been committed;
2   to help with collecting evidence or to make clear the legal position and subsequent courses of action in often very complex cases;
3   to advise the team on the correct course of action, especially if prosecution is advised, and to suggest the correct procedures with both parties.

Problems of a multidisciplinary team

These can only be summarized here as a full description would be beyond the remit of this chapter:

1   *Outside accountability*. The doctor is probably the only member of the team with clinical autonomy. Other representatives of the team have line managers to whom they are responsible. To overcome this, the other members have to negotiate autonomy within the group. The NHS

and Community Care Act 1990, using case management, should help to formalize this problem and so lead to the provision of probable solutions.

2 *Failure to distinguish between specific and shared skills.* Each discipline is now developing its own professional identity in relation to its respective skills and this has the potential to cause considerable rivalry, which will be divisive unless roles are agreed and the group is accountable. to the team manager (Lomas, 1991).

3 *Clinical versus executive function.* This may lead certain members of the group to have to withdraw from the team (Bebbington and Hill, 1985; Bennett and Freeman, 1991) to ensure that their statutory responsibilities are met, especially if they are overruled by the group. This applies to medical officers and social workers in particular.

Once the multidisciplinary team has decided on a course of action with a case of abuse, a key worker system is best identified (Care Programme/Care Management). This person can act as a facilitator, coordinator and an integrator of the action to be taken (Mechanic, 1989), thus making sure that the case is properly managed and information is disseminated to all members of the group, with each professional's responsibilities and functions put down in writing. The case can then be reviewed at regular intervals with the key worker calling and organizing further case conferences at prescribed intervals. The cases described give some insight into the management of these complicated cases using the key worker system.

When the multidisciplinary team has a case conference dealing with the complex issues that arise, the Model Abuse Prevention Training Programme, described by Keller (1996), which uses the technique called RETHINK, provides a step-by-step approach to dealing with conflict and is of great assistance:

R *Recognize* when you are angry or stressed and learn to help yourself relax.
E *Explain* the situation from the other person's point of view (i.e., empathize).
T *Think* about how you may contribute to the problem.
H *Hear* what the other person is saying; actively listen to the feelings as well as to the words.
I *Include* 'I' statements to explain how you feel, rather than starting a sentence with 'You . . .'
N *Negotiate*; try to work things out to everyone's satisfaction.
K Show *kindness* even when expressing frustration. (Keller, 1996: 236)

The case examples that follow are composites of several elder mistreatment cases referred to the author for clinical consultation. All identifying information has been changed to protect the confidentiality of the victims. In order to assist in the analysis of each case it will be necessary to consult the four assessment procedures already discussed, because they will be used in the commentary on each case example. The procedures are to be found in Appendices A, B, C and D of this volume.

Case examples of abuse in domestic settings

Case example 1

A.B. is a 76-year-old married woman who lived with her husband aged 78. They had been very happily married for 56 years, totally devoting their lives to each other, even to deciding not to have children. A referral was made by the general practitioner because of A.B.'s memory loss, depression and anxiety, and because she had been easily flustered over the last six months. On assessment she showed moderate short-term memory loss, a dressing apraxia, an inability to use or recognize money, and her attention and concentration was very poor (described by her husband as 'feather-brained'). A nominal aphasia was becoming very evident. Incontinence, both urinary and faecal, was frequent. The problem was that she would hide the excreta. This caused enormous friction between the two of them, as she would also hide the pension books and even food. The couple's personal history is very important here. The husband was a research chemist, with marked rigid, perfectionistic traits, making him intolerant of any 'unexpected' behaviour. Verbal abuse was first noticed soon after the referral. A diagnosis of Alzheimer's disease was made and a care package was offered. There were difficulties, as every month they would disappear without warning, on holiday. After a further year, the picture changed. He became unwell with cancer of the bowel, requiring major surgery. A.B. over this period, was placed in residential care to which she reacted violently, attacking staff, becoming very restless and demanding. She could only be quietened by her husband visiting her. This was resolved by admitting her to our care until her husband recovered from his operation. She went home but within two weeks she was coming to the day hospital with facial bruising and ear and finger injuries consistent with twisting injuries. She was very distressed and cowered on approach, indicating that her husband had hit her. She was admitted for assessment. He was counselled, admitted to being under enormous pressure, but never quite to hitting her. Emotionally they remained very close. He failed to understand her unpredictable behaviour and could not cope with her non-goal-directed behaviour, such that her slowness in dressing to go to the day hospital would cause him severe anxiety about the fear of being late, and he admitted to holding her down to dress her. Once the responsibility for physical care was taken up by carers and professionals, they resumed a very close private, emotionally satisfying relationship which continued until they died three years later within six weeks of each other. For these last three years they would spend an average of 18 out of every 24 hours together.

Commentary

At the many case conferences that were held and during all the interviews that had taken place, it became very apparent that although he acknowledged the enormous strain that his wife placed on him, he would not admit to the assault. It became clear that they needed each other to survive, but the carer could not cope with the physical demands placed upon him. If this case was handled insensitively he would take one of three courses of action:

(a) remove her from our care
(b) abandon her, saying no one believed or trusted him
(c) kill her and then himself

Everybody agreed to a programme of shared care, without involvement increasing as they became frailer. He retained his dignity and control and agreed to be educated in a relatives' support group, which he found very useful. She was given a key worker to ventilate her feelings about her husband's obsessional nature. The abuse stopped immediately. The most interesting caveat was that they would attend the elderly severely mentally infirm (ESMI) day hospital, rotational care and long-stay care as a couple, refusing even up to the end to be separated.

Assessment tools used

Indicators of possible elder mistreatment   This highlighted some important additional features as the husband's physical state deteriorated and her dementing illness progressed. She showed evidence of physical abuse. There was increasing concern of a homicide/suicide act which the husband was quite open about, if any attempt was made to separate them. As the assaults continued, she became increasingly agitated and fearful, often cowering when approached.

Caregiver strain questionnaire   This showed the husband's very high levels of stress. The most important stressor to affect him was his wife's inability to go on holiday and his own life-threatening illness. This led him to feel overwhelmed and imprisoned with no sleep and no outlets for his stressors, so that with his obsessional personality he internalized his feelings, which exploded into violent episodes.

Analysis

The analysis of the assessment tools shows, then, some very interesting features. A.B. did reveal lifelong dependency needs, which when challenged by her husband's illness were internalized and reappeared as severe challenging behaviour, of sufficient severity to precipitate assaults in the nursing home. The husband showed a severe obsessionally rigid personality where he appeared to lack understanding of his wife's illness and became severely stressed by his own illness. He would become violent when he was unable to control his wife's wandering. The most important feature of this care was not to separate this couple as they would become very disturbed if we attempted to. It was essential to allow them to deal with their emotional needs, but to remove the physical demands they made on each other.

Case example 2

C.D. is an 81-year-old married woman living with her 82-year-old husband and a 30-year-old unmarried grandson. Both men were carers. She was referred by her general practitioner with a three-year history of depression and increasing forgetfulness. She was found to be suffering from Alzheimer's disease with severe short- and long-term memory loss, dressing apraxia, persistent agitation, intrusive behaviour and wandering, both day and night. On physical examination she was found to be frail, agitated, constipated and tremulous, as well as suffering from pernicious anaemia and myxoedema. All these problems put considerable strain on both carers. She started attending the ESMI day hospital. Bruises became very noticeable on her face, arms and legs as well as cuts on her legs, especially after a weekend. Her agitation steadily increased. She became disorientated and unsteady when put on a major tranquillizer which she had been given previously. Even though these drugs were stopped, she continued to present with bruising and abrasions. Evidence of neglect started to appear. Her personal hygiene deteriorated and she became doubly incontinent. Additional support was offered but refused by the carers. Rough handling from the carers was noticed by the nurses, as well as verbal abuse, such as threatening to slap her, when home visiting. Careful surveillance was set up by the multidisciplinary team as admission seemed imminent. Within a week she was admitted with pneumonia. On the ward she deteriorated rapidly and was found to have two subdural haematomas requiring drainage by the neurosurgeons. The family stated prior to admission that she had fallen downstairs. After the operation, she made a good recovery and was functioning better than before admission. The family demanded her discharge which failed as soon as 24-hour support was withdrawn. She developed pressure sores and lost one stone in a week before being readmitted. We resisted all attempts to discharge her.

Commentary

This is an extremely complex case, highlighting almost all the features of physical, psychological and financial abuse, and active neglect. The indicators of possible elder mistreatment reveal key factors in this case. C.D. is an elderly lady with severe dementia, who was fiercely independent. Her husband was dementing himself, was very rigid, with unrealistic ideas about her recovery. Emotionally, they were totally dependent upon each other. All the family, particularly the grandson, were financially dependent upon her, especially on her attendance allowance. The grandson was a loner, abused drugs and alcohol, had a history of violence and was unsympathetic, hypercritical and refused to engage with any of the agencies concerning his grandparents' care. Further problems were highlighted when assessing the family system. Management and care planning were virtually impossible because of the intra-family conflicts and lack of support despite many promises of help, and tangential comments: 'We would help Mum if our brother was not on the scene.'

Assessment tools used

Indicators of possible elder mistreatment This highlighted many of the problems that led us to such a rigid care plan. It was clear that early on there had been abuse of medication to reduce the challenging behaviour. Unmet medical needs were neglected because of the grandson's indifference. The grandson's probable assaults became more serious until they were life-threatening. The grandfather also had shown signs of a beating on more than one occasion. Psychologically, this elder had been harassed and intimidated by her grandson. She showed fearfulness and agitation, especially when her environment was changed. Sociologically, her environment was unfit. She was found at 6 p.m. on a November evening lying in a urine-soaked bed, unfed since the previous day, with her grandson preparing a meal for himself. No medication or sustenance had been provided all day. She had developed a pressure sore. The financial abuse began to emerge in the legal section, especially when the attendance allowance was reduced, as it was supporting the grandson's alcohol and drug habit: if he could be a recognized carer he would not have to get up to go to work!

Caregiver strain questionnaire This highlighted the difficulties experienced by the husband, who, despite his own disabilities, put himself under enormous stress. The grandson was not even prepared to make anyone a meal, heat the house or give his father a break.

Analysis

The case presented here has many complex issues. It seems fairly clear that if someone is being frequently assaulted the offender should be arrested and prosecuted. C.D. was unable to prefer charges. The family were too frightened and none of us had witnessed any of the assaults. The police were unable to act, so we were forced into a careful recording of injuries, waiting for further evidence, and putting together care plans that offered the patient care and protection. The patient was only allowed home on a full care plan which included a Supervision Register. The family deeply resented anyone going into the family home and the last two full care plans collapsed when there was any relaxation in total care, as none of the family either would or could fill in the gaps, and the patient was immediately subjected to unacceptable risks, as described earlier.

On discharge, the Care Programme Approach (CPA) and Supervision Register obtained agreement:

1   Attend the ESMI day hospital three days per week.
2   Senior nurse to visit and assess daily for six weeks.
3   Regular home visits by the consultant and general practitioner.
4   A trial of a week at home prior to discharge.
5   CPA review after one week.
6   To have a baby gate to stop her falling downstairs.
7   Granddaughter/daughter to do bathing at home.
8   Bathing at other times at ESMI day hospital.
9   Regular or immediate respite on request by family or professionals.

Everyone agreed to and signed the CPA, including the husband and all the professionals.

As the husband was so vulnerable, an advocate was suggested, but this was, until the last few weeks, refused. He has now accepted the Community Health Council as advocate.

The other options we are now exploring after taking extensive legal advice are as follows:

If she remains in hospital because of the severity of her illness and her vulnerability, she will be placed on a Section III (a treatment order). This will require the husband's consent. If he refuses, an application to the Courts will be made to remove him as the next of kin. She will be made a ward of court.

If it was decided to move her to a nursing home, a guardianship order would be applied for, which is very similar to a Section III except that it allows a person to be required to reside at a specified place for the purposes of treatment and to attend an out-patient clinic. You cannot treat under this part of the Act.

The ideal solution, if we could get agreement, is for her to be placed in an ESMI home which has a residential part to the building, so that the couple can be together, as they are devoted to each other.

Case example 3

E.F. presented as an emergency referral from the general practitioner after her daughter, who was the main carer, was admitted to hospital with a stroke. She was placed as an emergency into an aged persons' home by the social worker, where she was noted to be psychotic. Her symptoms were that she had delusional beliefs that her dead husband's ghost was residing in her council house. She was very agitated, constantly searching for her dead husband. There was no evidence of cognitive impairment initially. Her home was very unusual. It was in a very poor state of repair. There were no carpets or usable furniture, no food, and the wallpaper was peeling. When the wallpaper was removed there was found to be no plaster on the walls. There were holes in the walls where the bricks had been chipped away revealing only breeze-blocks. In the living room and the bedroom there was evidence of frequent fire-setting to exorcize a spirit. The history from the grandson was that each morning his mother would enter the house and put all the wallpaper back with Polyfilla to cover the excavation work of her mother from the night before. There was no food in the house because the daughter delivered it on a daily basis. E.F. would use the building tools stored in the fridge. She was trying to find her dead husband's tombstone. She believed that the headstone had been used to build her flat. Each night she would light fires to exorcize his ghost. She refused all medication from the general practitioner and all offers of help from social services. She had no insight into her illness and was admitted under Section II of the Mental Health Act for assessment. On admission she was found to be acutely confused with pneumonia and on further investigation had carcinoma of her uterus requiring surgery. She made a good recovery following a long illness but was beginning to show evidence of senile dementia with poor short-term memory and poor skills to look after herself, in terms of aids to daily living. Her psychotic illness quickly responded to major tranquillizers and she remained symptom-free from her psychotic breakdown. After a six-month admission she was placed in a rest home, where she lived until her death three years later.

Commentary

This case incorporates all the arguments for the Community Care Act. This elderly person should have had a full care management assessment with a full health and social care package. Her mental illness needed assessing, treating and careful follow-up arrangements by the psychiatrist and community psychiatric nurse. The general practitioner should have physically examined her and arranged an early gynaecology appointment to treat and carefully follow up. The patient's social care needs should have been met, including ensuring that her nutritional needs were met. A home help would have built up trust, allowing her to go shopping, attend a day centre and making the home habitable. This programme would have reduced the stress on the daughter, possibly improving the daughter's health.

Assessment tools used

Indicators of possible elder mistreatment   This highlighted the neglect by the statutory agencies; an absence of medication; the absence of community care, care support and social care needs led to the elder's illnesses and her nutritional status deteriorating. There was a great deal of falsification of information, voluntary withdrawal and inadequate supervision, which led to profound neglect.

High risk placement worksheet   When you analyse the high risk placement worksheet, the most important features are that this isolated woman was both physically ill with cancer and had a severe mental illness of paraphrenia with destructive behaviour. The caregiver also was vulnerable with hypertension and a shared psychosis (*folie à deux*). The collusions, both mental and financial dependence, worsened the danger. The neglect only came to light when the daughter had a stroke and the family refused to become involved as the elder wanted to stay at home until she herself underwent surgery.

Caregiver strain questionnaire   This confirmed that the daughter's time was taken up by caring for her mother and that she became physically, socially and psychologically overwhelmed.

Analysis

This was a case of profound neglect incorporating all the worst aspects of a fragmented service. The general practitioner, although he had received occasional reports of her psychiatric state, did not act on them or follow them up. No mechanism existed to identify this woman's health and social care needs, until the daughter's illness. The situation had deteriorated to such an extent that admission under Section II of the Mental Health Act 1983 (which enables a patient to be detained in hospital in the interests of his or her own health and safety) was the only viable management strategy.

When she had made a complete recovery her social circumstances were so poor that admission to residential care was the only option. As this case presented in the 1980s, none of the advantages of health and social services working in unison, as outlined in the National Health Service and Community Care Act 1990 were available.

Case example 4

G.H. is a 68-year-old man who was referred to the old age psychiatry service from another hospital after an admission showed him to have memory loss of seven months' duration, a four-week history of visual hallucinations and severe occipital headaches. He was a married man who had retired from his job as a welder five years previously. He drank moderately. Examination revealed him to be a fit man with early pernicious anaemia. The diagnosis of senile dementia was made. The brain damage was confirmed by his ECG and brain scan. He presented with short-term memory loss, which had worsened since his myocardial infarction. His long-term memory was remarkably well preserved. At home he was experiencing severe nocturnal confusion, a dressing apraxia, episodes of depression, marked confabulation, was developing third person auditory hallucinations, but no visual hallucinations. His eyesight was deteriorating quite markedly. Unfortunately, his wife was becoming physically very ill. He was referred to the ESMI day hospital where lack of motivation was identified as well as the onset of visual hallucinations. Marked deterioration in his mood was noted, and as his wife's physical deterioration continued, his demands on her increased. Further problems with dressing and bathing were noted. Home support and additional day care was requested from social services. Within a month his mental state was deteriorating with the onset of incontinence, sleeplessness and episodes of aggression, terminating in a serious assault on his wife. He was admitted to the assessment unit; it emerged that the family were unable to cope. His physical state deteriorated further; wandering off the ward started to become a major problem, as well as his increasing sensitivity to medication. A further assessment showed him to have markedly deteriorated. Assessment for placement revealed that because of the severity of his challenging behaviour his placement on an ESMI long-stay unit was the only possible solution. He was admitted to a specialized unit where he settled well until the death of his wife; his family made the decision not to take him to the funeral despite advice to the contrary. During his grief period he was found having sexual intercourse with a fellow female patient and was, at the instruction of the senior managers, charged with rape, while the responsible medical officer (RMO) was on annual leave. The charges were dropped on the return of the RMO. However, he had lost all trust in the Unit and blamed the family for not allowing him to grieve. He then started to try to escape from the ward as he felt no one trusted him and after several 'escapes', even though he was placed under continuous supervision, managed to evade all his carers and was found dead five days later after an extensive search, having 'drowned' within half a mile of the hospital.

Commentary

This is a tragic case of a man who developed a dementing illness causing such intra-generational conflict that when his wife became terminally ill he was admitted to residential care. When his wife died he internalized his feelings of grief because the family did not allow him to go to the funeral. In his abnormal grief reaction he felt rejected by the staff and constantly had to leave the residential home, challenging the staff until he lost himself and died.

Assessment tools used

Indicators of possible elder mistreatment   Physically G.H. had been over-sedated, was in a poor state of nutrition, and had sleep disturbance, all of which contributed to his deterioration. The sexual incident was clearly a cry for help from a grieving man. It was apparent that this man had no wish to continue living without his wife.

The psychological assessment compounded the physical problems. His low esteem, loss of role and abandonment were confirmed by his family when his wife died. They felt the rest home had rejected and punished him for the sexual incident. Although the medical staff advocated for him he lost all sense of trust. This was confirmed by the close observation policy he was subjected to and the loss of his civil liberties.

High risk placement worksheet   The caregiver characteristics revealed an unrealistic belief that the patient would recover; when the caregivers realized that he would not, the reaction was rejection, anger and abandonment. They displaced these feelings onto the staff.

The family characteristics revealed a caregiving reluctance, especially when his wife became terminally ill.

The placement section revealed many of the reasons which led to such tragic consequences. The husband and wife only wanted to be together. When she died, he initially went through the phases of grief (Bowlby, 1982) and wandered in search of his wife.

Caregiver strain questionnaire   This showed stresses with all the questions which were attributed by the family to a combination of his personality change, the terminal illness of his wife (who was the main carer), and their inability to adapt to a carer role.

Analysis

This case shows how an institution that has rigid policies and procedures can become punitive and abusive, and the tragic consequences of prolonged and sustained psychological abuse can lead to anomie (Durkheim, 1952).

The case should have included a complete Care Management assessment addressing G.H.'s health and social care needs.

1　He could have stayed at home with 24-hour support to experience his wife's terminal illness, and grieve for her normally, choose her head-stone and gain some control over his life.
2　If it was necessary to place him in residential care, this should have been delayed until after his wife's death to allow him more choice. If he did not settle, he should have had his needs re-evaluated and he should have chosen another home.
3　Family support should have been sought through the voluntary sector, such as the Alzheimer's Society, to educate and support the family to understand the father's dementia.

Unfortunately, events moved so rapidly that these care plans were only partially implemented. It is important that emergency procedures are built into abuse protection procedures and policies, even in institutions.

Case example 5

I.J. is a person with a manic depressive psychosis who was severely financially abused over many years in such a clever way that health and social services had enormous difficulty controlling the abuse. This case shows how the assessment can help to unravel such a complex case and allow strategies to be developed for managing such complicated cases. The role of the law is explored, particularly if concrete evidence is not enough for the police to act upon.

This woman aged 74 was widowed, with two grown-up children who have at different times been her carers. She was referred from another consultant because of severe problems in management. She had a 20-year history of severe manic depressive psychosis, Ativan and alcohol abuse, poor compliance with medication, and a history of moving between Ireland and Britain. She lived with her sister who had a severe schizophrenic illness, in a symbiotic relationship. Her physical health was poor with severe chest problems due to a consumption of 60 cigarettes per day, as well as diabetes and an under-active thyroid gland. Problems became very apparent when her sister died quite suddenly and her son 'allowed' her back into her own flat, which she was paying for. The son then started to destabilize his mother's mental state by stopping or omitting her medication, on which she was very dependent. Her mood started to fluctuate very rapidly and she had to be admitted to hospital in a severely depressed and suicidal state. Whilst she was an in-patient the son announced that he was selling the flat and moving abroad to further his career. Health workers and social services started to investigate this and found that I.J. had signed over the flat 15 times, transferring it back and forth between her son and herself. It was impossible to establish that she had given informed consent. She would not admit publicly to any impropriety and refused to allow any legal proceedings to be taken against her son, even when the family found that another £55,000 was missing. This left this woman in sheltered housing with no money, and only a colour TV courtesy of her son (which she was very grateful for). His only failure, in her view, was that he wanted her in a nursing home. I.J. was left in a very vulnerable and agitated state needing a full package of care including five days a week at a day hospital for the severely mentally ill, two days a week at a day centre, a community psychiatric nurse and a social worker involved in her case on a weekly basis, as well as a carer going in to give her general assist-ance twice a day. She has, over the last two years, been sexually assaulted and abused on a number of occasions, but again will not allow any investigation or interference, because she remains intensely loyal to the people who care for her and will only discuss issues privately with her doctor.

Commentary

This is a case of psychological and financial abuse of a vulnerable, elderly lady with a mental illness which affected her judgement and who showed excessive loyalty to her children by internalizing her feelings. The caregiver used his position of trust to manipulate the elder to his own needs for money, drugs and alcohol. He used his education (a degree in psychology) to attack the professionals by criticizing the services to confuse and deflect them from the main issues.

Assessment tools used

Indicators of possible elder mistreatment   This revealed how by withholding medication the elder's mental state deteriorated until she was admitted to hospital. Psychologically she was repeatedly humiliated. She felt ashamed that she had brought up a son like this and blamed herself. He eventually rejected her. The harassment was frightening, as fear and intimidation were very powerful weapons used against her. Manipulation, particularly of information, were very difficult to counter as the son constantly interfered with any decision-making.

The sociological section naturally expands the information about the totality of the mistreatment, with inadequate supervision, dissolution of the elder's role and eventual abandonment.

The financial abuse, which is part of the legal section, highlighted the stealing of property and contracts, and extortion of property. Unfortunately, she refused to press charges.

High risk placement worksheet   The family networks revealed weaknesses in the other siblings, who were frightened of their brother and would only stand up to him with support from the professionals. When he attempted to institutionalize I.J., the elder wanted sheltered housing with companionship.

Caregiver strain questionnaire   The son was undoubtedly under enormous pressure from his mother's wandering, agitation and mood swings. He felt trapped socially, wanting to get married, and professionally.

Analysis

This case was managed by the elder being protected by admission to hospital. She agreed to an Enduring Power of Attorney with the daughter as the executor, only after most of the assets had been removed. The victim refused to prosecute but she did show her severe displeasure against her son in a case conference, publicly humiliating him sufficiently to ensure he left the country the following day. This action allowed the team to treat and stabilize her manic depressive illness. She was able to choose suitable sheltered housing. A full programme of care was set up. The daughter felt confident enough to become the main carer.

The patient lives in the community, still very vulnerable to exploitation and occasional sexual abuse, but she is happy, independent in her own way and cooperates fully with her care plan. This case highlights the need for more legal protection for vulnerable people to ensure they do not lose everything.

Case example 6

This is a very sad case of betrayed trust that led to severe sexual abuse, intense psychological intimidation and massive financial abuse.

> K.L. is an 84-year-old widow who was born in Germany and came to England after the war after marrying an alcoholic soldier who died from his addiction ten years later. She started to take student lodgers. Over a period of 15 years a particular lodger developed a friendship with her, which became intense. About five years ago she had a stroke, quickly followed by another. This left her with left-sided weakness, unsteadiness, dysarthria, incontinence and episodic confusion with a patchy short-term memory loss. His role changed to that of carer. He would visit her two or three times a week, bringing her food, helping her with the housework and assisting her with her personal hygiene! Social services were asked to put in services after her discharge from hospital but found that the student would be obstructive concerning any interference, especially if it involved entry into the house or any involvement in her finances. It was very evident that the patient–carer relationship was abnormal. She was referred to our service; she had an early multiple-infarct dementia. The cerebral vascular accident (c.v.a.) had left her with incontinence and unsteadiness which made her feel very vulnerable. She also had intense feelings of depression because she felt very betrayed by the student. We found her to be very frightened of her carer because she was being intimidated. She admitted to handing over large sums of money: she had signed for money to be withdrawn from her deposit accounts in building societies, post offices and banks. When the student was asked by social services to account for this money he became very evasive and disappeared, except at the weekend when he would visit her and blackmail her into refusing help from health and social services, even getting her to write out that she did not want anyone to investigate this money; he interrogated her for four hours, pressurizing her to write the note by threatening that she would never see him again and lose his love and support. This left her profoundly disturbed. With this kind of pressure her health began to suffer and she was admitted with a heart attack. Moving carers into the home proved very difficult. She is now in a nursing home but he continues to put severe pressure on her. She felt very depressed and betrayed when she found he had married, but she is still infatuated and even though he visits every three months she would go with him any time. He is now threatening to remove her from the home, and this is a real concern. She still has considerable assets. She is much frailer and is in need of constant attention. She has become quite cognitively impaired as her multi-infarct state progresses.

Commentary

The impact of the severity of this case is not fully appreciated until the extent of the psychological, financial and sexual abuse is explored.

Assessment tools used

Indicators of possible elder mistreatment This showed clearly that medication, especially the antidepressants, were not being given. K.L.'s physical state and personal hygiene were deteriorating. Sexual assault occurred at the weekend and made her sore, vulnerable and scared. The lodger would make her write notes consenting to his actions and taunt social services with these. She would not challenge him for fear of losing him. The psychological abuse was the most powerful weapon. Harassment, intimidation in the form of the threat that he would leave her or expose her publicly, led her to become very agitated. He would threaten to emotionally deprive her if she did not agree to falsify information, so decisions made to help her were very difficult to sustain. Her environment deteriorated and the household became increasingly disorganized. In legal terms, large amounts of money, property and jewellery were removed. He coerced her into signing for everything: none of it was ever retrieved.

High risk placement worksheet The elder shows all the risk factors except for alcohol abuse. The most influential risk is the previous abuse which primed her. She had been raped during the war, physically assaulted by her alcoholic husband and severely sexually abused and coerced by her carer, who was a lodger. She had lent this perpetrator vast sums of money – up to £75,000.

The caregiver showed very strong evidence of a personality disorder. He would threaten and blackmail to obtain money and property. He abused drugs. The victim wanted to go into residential care but was too frightened to ask, as he dominated her totally. The stresses on the carer amounted to disruption of his time and extra demands made upon him by social services to improve the quality of his care. He deeply resented this, along with the financial monitoring which was set up.

Analysis

The enormity of the psychological, financial and sexual abuse was beyond dispute; the police were involved but K.L. denied everything because of her strong emotional ties, which were only loosened when she discovered her lodger had married someone else. One of the problems we all faced was to decide when the sexual intercourse became abusive to the victim; the victim admitted that after her strokes, and the resulting incontinence, she felt assaulted, but she continues to have very strong feelings towards the carer.

Eventually, we persuaded her to be admitted to hospital for rehabilitation and move on to residential care, where she has settled. He continues to threaten to remove her and take her to live with him. After a series of multi-disciplinary case conferences it was agreed to place her on a guardianship order of the Mental Health Act 1983 and the perpetrator is only allowed to visit with an advocate in attendance to ensure that no financial abuse occurs. Her health, both physical and psychological, is steadily deteriorating and she is now too frail to live independently, but still recognizes her beloved carer.

Case examples of abuse in institutional settings

Case example 7

M.N., a 66-year-old man, was referred by the general practitioner to the specialist because of a rapidly progressive memory loss and wandering. He was seen at home and was found to have a two-year history of increasing short-term memory loss with poor recall, a marked nominal aphasia, dressing apraxia, acalculia and agnosia and episodes of agitation, particularly during the day. At times, he would become very depressed and tearful, especially when talking about his occupation. This illness had forced him into early retirement. His wife and daughter were supportive but very anxious about the social stigma of Alzheimer's disease. They had taken him to faith healers and herbalists in search of a 'cure'. After he was assessed, a day hospital place was allocated but his wife did not want anyone in the community to know that her husband was ill. Her denial failed to respond to counselling from all the agencies. Her demands on the day hospital increased, centred on what would happen if her husband wandered off. One incident gave her the opportunity to insist that he should be locked away. He had been found urinating in a public place, in an alleyway next to his normal drop-off place from day hospital for going home; she insisted that he be admitted, which we did for assessment. However, she demanded that he should be placed in a locked facility. He was removed from hospital and subsequently placed by the family in a nursing home out of the district, on a locked ward. He responded to this by continually trying to escape. He was placed in a Buxton chair and tied in. The social services and consultant were refused entry. When we eventually gained entry we found a man who had deteriorated rapidly and was chairbound and heavily medicated. He died six weeks later of a chest infection following a myocardial infarction.

Commentary

This case vividly illustrates both psychological abuse by the spouse, and severe institutional abuse. The damaging effects of denial of this man's illness and the fear of his family's perceived stigmatization led to him being put away out of sight.

Assessment tools used

Indicators of possible elder mistreatment   This revealed how the physical abuse appeared in residential care; and the improper use of medication to ensure passivity. M.N.'s nutritional needs led to a physical deterioration and dehydration. He loved to walk but the family insisted that he was restrained in a Buxton chair. Psychologically, he was abused in all the indicators, but the most damaging was rejection and interference with his decision-making. He was reduced to a problem, no longer a person with problems associated with Alzheimer's disease.

High risk placement worksheet   We see a man who had increasing dependency needs, who was excessively loyal to his wife and never questioned her decisions. The only time that he exhibited provocative behaviour was having to urinate in a public place and this landed him in institutional care. The carer could not accept her husband's illness as irreversible. Once she worked through her denial, rejection and abandonment followed. The family were ashamed of his disability and just wanted him 'out of circulation'. The victim wanted to stay at home. His family wanted him in a secure facility, never to embarrass them again.

Caregiver strain questionnaire   She became stressed almost to breaking point, but the most distressing features were M.N.'s incontinence, unpredictable behaviour and the loss of a stabilizing figure in the family. The carer dealt with this by seeking sympathy for her plight in the community.

Analysis

This case of physical and psychological abuse demonstrates clearly how the problems persist when alternatives are available and it is essential to deal with the underlying problems. The multidisciplinary team which included the general practitioner, consultant, approved social worker (ASW), occupational therapists and nurses from the community and the ESMI day hospital decided to offer him a place in the day unit, which he enjoyed. We instituted family counselling which they all attended but their belief was that 'Dad would get better'. We all concluded that, however much support or education they were given, abandonment was the most likely outcome.

The incident where M.N., who for psychological reasons, had to urinate anywhere, urinated in a public place had a dramatic effect. He was withdrawn from the day hospital. Demands were made for him to be placed in a medium secure facility where he would have been at severe physical risk. Admission to an open ward was refused by the family. He was immediately placed in private care where the family could dictate the care, the general practitioner was changed as well as the geographical sector, so social services had problems gaining access. The ESMI team was also denied this right. Legal advice was taken. Eventually the ASW gained entry, but M.N. had had a heart attack. An internal investigation resulted in the abolition of Buxton chairs and a more open visiting policy being instituted.

Case example 8

An 84-year-old widower O.P. was suffering from a well-established multiple infarct dementia and had been a resident in a nursing home for two years. When he was referred by the general practitioner his presenting problem was aggression, sexual disinhibition and verbal abuse. The history was that he was cohabiting in a double room with another male resident. Seven months previously he had been moved without his consent into a single room. He became very angry about the separation and his reaction to this was to sexually assault female residents, mainly the most vulnerable, and he would verbally abuse the staff when approached. He was isolated using 'time out' but he became more isolated, neglected and angry, feeling victimized. We saw him in the nursing home and found him in a very neglected state, isolated in a side room, doubly incontinent, and his clothes were very dirty, covered with food. He was showing evidence of advanced vascular dementia with a very poor, patchy short-term and long-term memory. He had problems with his speech, with a motor and sensory aphasia. He had had a large number of strokes and suffered from epilepsy. In his personal history, he was an ex-boxer who was described by the family as a very difficult, aggressive man who drank heavily and was violent towards his family. As a result of his personality problems, his history of violence and his deteriorating state he had been placed in a nursing home. There was also a positive family history of psychiatric illness in the siblings, whom he had sexually abused as children. His diagnosis was frontal lobe dementia which was partly vascular in origin and partly due to his boxing.

Commentary

It is important to point out that the high risk placement worksheet and the caregiver strain questionnaire are not particularly useful instruments for cases of abuse which occur within institutional settings because the dynamics of an institution do not fit in with those particular documents. This led us to employ a different approach. The indicators of possible elder mistreatment is a useful instrument because it addresses the problems of the individual. We found also that Pillemer's model allowed us to understand the factors that lead us to abusive situations in an institution.

Assessment tools used

Indicators of possible elder mistreatment   This reveals a lot of information that tends to become lost because of the massive sexual abuse that appears throughout O.P.'s history. He has massive unmet needs which include the sequelae of his stroke, leading to a failure to understand and communicate language; poor mobility, incontinence and sexual disinhibition. Psychologically, he had personality problems, worsened by frontal lobe damage caused by boxing. This caused him to be isolated and emotionally deprived, so I found him alone in a filthy state (food all down his clothes and doubly incontinent). It was obvious that he was inadequately supervised. No one had discussed his problems or tried to help him. 'Time out' (i.e. seclusion), as it was put to me, was basically 'out of sight out of mind'. The family were of no help because of their own mental health problems and they blamed him for his wife's death. He had abused her and the children sexually. The same behaviour pattern was exhibited in the home.

Theoretical model of patient maltreatment This model showed that the home was a good nursing home, but could not cope with patients with severe challenging behaviour who need a specialist/elderly mentally ill (EMI) care home with registered mental health nurses. The abusive situation was the response so often seen when the wrong client is in the wrong home, with the wrong care plan, for the following reasons:

1 inadequate support mechanisms among the staff, with inadequately trained carers;
2 custodial orientation which isolated and disempowered him;
3 levels of care – he was placed in a room, alone and unsupervised;
4 social isolation which was compounded by the family;
5 high stress levels amongst the staff;
6 an additional factor that was very noticeable was that he was very unpopular with the staff and was disliked by his family.

Analysis

The multidisciplinary case conference was held with the specialist (old age psychiatrist), ASW, community psychiatric nurse (CPN), occupational therapist (OT), speech therapist, representatives from the nursing home and EMI home. The family refused to attend. The issues which needed immediate decisions were:

1 Did he need relocation to a specialist home and what could they offer him? The unanimous answer was placement in an EMI home which would give the elder the best quality of life, if we could reduce his challenging behaviour, which was achieved with low doses of medication and a strict behavioural programme.
2 OT and speech therapy would help him communicate and reawaken many of his dormant skills.
3 Physically we found he was hypertensive and diabetic. Both were treated, with a dramatic improvement.
4 He was offered day care, which he accepted. His sexual outbursts have stopped.
5 We are now working with the family. This is much more difficult and is in its early stages.

Case example 9

Q.R., widowed with four children, was admitted to a nursing home four years ago following the death of his wife. He had suffered a stroke a year prior to admission. Since living in the home he had formed a close homosexual relationship with another resident who shared a room with him. This posed no problems and was accepted by the other residents of the nursing home. However, two years ago a new matron was appointed, who separated these two men because of her own personal prejudices, and fear for the reputation of the home. No discussions occurred with the two residents or the staff, who were all opposed to the move. However, the staff started to question their own values. Q.R. felt very hurt and became very depressed and suicidal. He became aggressive towards the staff and started to sexually assault the vulnerable female residents. He did this openly and in front of the staff as a cry for help. He would also masturbate in the lounge as a provocative act but would be moved into a side room as 'time out'. He was referred to me and I visited him at his residence where the deputy matron was a strong advocate for him. She had met a lot of resistance from the matron, who wanted both men removed. It was clear that Q.R. was a very frightened man who was initially very evasive and aggressive. When we were alone, I made it clear that I was not judging him, but trying to help him. He started to tell me about the things which were important to him: for example his army life revolved around being a bandsman in Burma, and he had lost contact with his army friends. He was a professional musician who loved classical music, but hated the military music which everyone assumed he liked. He was very isolated by his family, who kept him short of money so that he was unable to go to concerts, which he loved. He felt there was nothing to live for once the relationship with the other male resident was damaged. He was bisexual and comfortable with that. He also felt isolated, lonely and victimized and very angry. He wanted to enjoy his music on his own, go to concerts with his friends and spend quality time with his family.

Commentary

This is primarily a case of severe psychological abuse with some sexual abuse of vulnerable female residents.

Assessment tool used
Indicators of possible elder mistreatment

When you analyse Johnson's indicators of possible elder mistreatment other factors begin to emerge. Physically, Q.R. had been sedated without his knowledge and no one had followed up his profound weight loss, which revealed an advanced cancer. He had been sexually assaulted by this other male resident. The victim's psychological abuse showed up in all categories. The most potent were the public humiliation by the matron, who made her feelings of disgust very clear; this led to some rejection by the younger staff and a few residents, but by no means a majority. He was severely intimidated about the falsification of information and betrayal of confidence about his supposed sexual deviancy. His role of decision-making was destroyed when he lost his room without prior discussion. Financially his family had withheld his pocket money, which denied him independence.

Pillemer's model helps us further with this case. The exogenous factors led this man to be trapped because no other home had a vacancy. The nursing home was a good one but the staff were not trained to manage this type of case, so the senior nurses felt unsupported and fearful for their jobs. In addition, the new matron started to set up a custodial orientation which proved very damaging.

The nursing environment was excellent, showing none of the worrying predictors. The patient characteristics which led to abuse were that Q.R. was a sensitive man who tended to isolate himself.

Analysis

After the assessment was performed it was clear that there were three main areas of intervention:

1 The patient was a sensitive man who internalized his feelings, but was very angry and lonely; he also enjoyed his own company. We agreed with him that he should manage his own pocket money to re-establish some of his independence. He attended the Hallé Orchestra concerts, bought his own Walkman and tapes of classical music. He decided to have treatment for his tumour, which was limited in its success. We treated his depression with antidepressants and supportive psychotherapy. He asked for treatment for his high sex drive, which was treated chemically.

2 His role as an important member of the nursing home was re-established by setting up weekly residents' groups, of which he was an active member.

3 The training needs of the staff were clearly identified and a model mentioned in Chapters 11 and 13 of this volume (CARIE, Hudson et al., 1991) was set up for all the staff using the pneumonic RETHINK (see p. 53, this chapter). This was made available to all the staff and residents as a cornerstone and had a dramatic effect on all involved. The man died peacefully in his sleep in the nursing home six months ago.

Case example 10

S.T., a 72-year-old single Irish man, was referred by the general practitioner because of his aggressive outbursts. He was found to have a very patchy short-term memory and was aggressive towards the staff in the aged persons home (APH) and also refusing to talk to them. He had been ostracized by the staff. He was admitted to hospital. The APH knew little about him other than his name and his occupation. He had not been bathed for six months and had pressure sores on the front of his lower abdomen and his umbilicus. He had an undiagnosed carcinoma of his penis which was inoperable. He did have a multiple infarct dementia with minimal frontal lobe damage which was the cause of his patchy short-term memory, irritable behaviour and minor verbally aggressive outbursts, but this settled within 48 hours with staff who treated him with respect. He became talkative, particularly with our black nurses, and was able to discuss his problems, especially his cancer, with impressive confidence. Once the pain from the pressure sores was controlled and then treated, his aggression disappeared. He was able to attend the case conferences and chose a home that met his needs. He was highly critical of the original APH, and verbalized his feelings very eloquently. He moved there and lived for a further two years in his eccentric fashion.

Commentary

This case could have been summarized by Hall (1989) who found that in cases of active neglect:

1 There was a failure to care for the person in the immediate living area.
2 No medical attention was sought.

3 There was a failure to provide patients' maintenance, including hygiene, clothing and food.

4 There had been theft of personal possessions.

This case is unfortunately only too familiar. An elder who is moderately eccentric encounters a rigid, abusive institution. The mixture is often explosive.

Assessment tools used

Indicators of possible elder mistreatment When analysing the possible indicators of abuse, medication applied as a chemical restraint, often without the client's knowledge or consent, is often the first form of abuse. Because he is being ignored his medical needs are not being met. In this man's case his cancer and his severe pressure sore had become severely infected. Psychological mistreatment took many forms, the most severe being rejection by staff and residents. He was inadequately supervised as he had no care plan or key worker, which led to active and passive neglect. His role as a respected elder was slowly dissolved until he was abandoned in hospital. He was subjected to financial abuse in terms of his pocket money, which meant that he had no independence, and had to beg for cigarettes, his only pleasure.

Theoretical model of patient maltreatment When this case is analysed using Pillemer's model the factors leading to abuse are obvious. The important exogenous factors were all present: high unemployment, poorly trained staff, low levels of trained to untrained staff, with no patient advocacy. If the nursing home environment (with its custodial traditions and lack of openness, smallness of the home and lack of financial resources to spend on the resident) is added on to the personal factors we can illustrate that proprietary institutions breed a fear to complain, as retaliation by the staff is a very powerful weapon and was one of the main factors in this case. Staff characteristics showed all the features that would lead to abuse: poorly educated, young staff who had little experience of older people and their problems. 'Burnout' was important here; the staff were triumphant when S.T. refused to go back – another problem case disposed of! An examination of patient characteristics revealed a singular lack of humane treatment, which socially isolated him until he was ill enough to be disposed of into hospital.

Analysis

This case of active and passive neglect was partially solved by the elder being admitted to hospital as he came to the notice of the service. Many do not. After the salient features were assimilated there were several clear issues:

1 The patient's health: after a lot of advice from medical staff *he* decided not to have the operation and to rely on conservative treatment, mainly painkillers, which was successful.

2 He agreed to placement in a nursing home where he was very happy, popular and made many friends.

3 The original home was reported to the Inspection Unit of Social Services. Senior staff were replaced, training and monitoring programmes were instituted, advocacy was set up, structural alterations were made to accommodate single and double rooms.

This man lived happily for four years, regularly followed up by our team.

A final word

These ten case examples show the different presentations of abuse and how complex they are. Without proper screening, assessment, interviewing of the victim and the perpetrator/institution, professionals are left with a confused and frightening picture. It is my hope that these case examples and assessment procedures will help multidisciplinary teams to manage their cases with more confidence.

5

Social Policy as Elder Abuse

Simon Biggs

With the publication of Department of Health guidelines on the subject, elder abuse has now achieved official status as a recognized social problem in England (SSI: Social Services Inspectorate, 1993). However, professional understanding of it as a psychosocial phenomenon is underdeveloped (Phillipson and Biggs, 1992) and wider public awareness minimal.

In such circumstances, social policy has two functions. First, it enables responses to be made by nominated agencies, in this case local authority social service departments. In other words, it discriminates between key institutions, such as health, welfare and criminal justice, and gives permission for certain forms of action to take place. These responses will be shaped by the culture and allocations of resources that already exist, what these institutions see as their legitimate domain and expertise. Second, social policy will tend to position the new social problem in the public mind. It will reinforce certain beliefs about an issue and underplay others. This second function is often overlooked by professionals who find themselves faced with having to make the new procedures work, so that the assumptions underlying them quickly become an unquestioned 'common-sense' guide to decision-making (Berger and Luckman, 1972).

In large part, this chapter explores the relationship between these two functions: the policy and the positioning. My chosen structure has been to move from the general to the particular, as a series of focusing lenses to discover more specifically the positioning of elder abuse as a phenomenon of a particular kind. Through the first lens it is possible to recognize a tension between welfare and criminal justice approaches to the problem, possibly reflecting the influence of debates in the United States. A second examines trends within British social policy toward older age in general. A third constitutes the particular nature of community care in contemporary British policy, and the last, the guidelines themselves. This is not a view that sees abuse as self-evident yet in need of further elaboration and classification, something that requires a moral crusade for greater legal powers, but rather one that attempts to discern why elder abuse has come to be seen as a particular sort of phenomenon in particular historical circumstances.

As the preceding paragraphs would suggest, the approach taken draws on the work of Michel Foucault (1977, 1979) in so far as an attempt has been made to trace a theme, or genealogy, through these different levels and time frames of policy formation. In the course of drawing out such themes, an earlier observation that a defining characteristic of the British experience of policy was elder abuse's seeming ability to be simultaneously recognized and ignored (Biggs et al., 1995), came back to me with renewed force. Why was emphasis repeatedly placed on monitoring with so little proposed for the creation of new and appropriate services? Foucault's (1977) concept of panopticism came to hand. The panopticon was a form of institution envisaged by Benthamites in the early nineteenth century. Wherever inmates were, staff could see them and supervise their moral behaviour. Foucault proposed that the symbolic value of this arrangement has been extended as services have moved away from institutions and into what we would now call community settings. A guiding principle behind care, then, continues to be to discipline the conduct of persons who are in effect under surveillance. For surveillance to be justified, though not of course named as such, a moral reason is required. Also, a technology, a particular method of caring, needs to be found that suits any one site for observation.

The view that emerges is that contemporary policy has located elder abuse as a problem of the domestic sphere, in a period when the relationship between formal and informal caring arrangements is in flux. The 'discovery' of abuse specifically aimed at older people must be placed against a policy background in which vulnerable elders are perceived as a burden and the costs of care, both fiscal and emotional, are being transferred from the state to families and friends. The role of professional helpers, such as care managers and to a lesser extent workers in primary care, has developed as a capacity for assessment and monitoring, aimed at maintaining the informal carer in the caring role. Under these circumstances it is not only reasonable to ask whether social policy can only be thought of as contributing to a limited awareness of what constitutes abuse, but to consider a more radical position suggesting that policy is itself a form of abuse.

An emphasis on monitoring, in the absence of any serious policy initiative to discover a carer's suitability or willingness to care, constitutes a form of surveillance and the call for more powers of intervention, a bigger stick with which to beat carers who will not conform. The 'discovery' of abuse therefore empowers the policing of informal care. Further, identifying the abuse of older people in the absence of services that can respond to the complexity of late-life relationships, sends a clear message to elders in receipt of care: 'Be grateful for what little support you get; it could be worse for you.'

This is a strong position to take, but it is one that is absent from the current debate, which desperately needs critical analysis if the rights of both carers and vulnerable older people are to be addressed. If we are not careful elder abuse may become a policy giant that eclipses other needs of older people, at once labelling every carer as a potential abuser, whilst paradoxically enforcing inappropriate informal care. Surveillance in the absence of reparation leaves 'abuse' as a sword hanging over the heads of caring relationships and lends a vicarious reassurance to common prejudices about old age. Blaming the burden is not just done, in other words; it can be seen to be done.

Positioning social problems

Policy in the USA and Britain

Whilst elder abuse had been recognized at approximately the same time in the USA and Britain, until comparatively recently policy had only developed on one side of the Atlantic. In the USA initial concern at state level influenced the re-authorization of the Older Americans Act in 1992 to achieve national legislation. This had built upon the position that all states had instituted some form of adult protection legislation by 1988 (Wolf, 1994: 11), and an increased public awareness of abuse as a social problem. In 1981, for example, a Harris poll indicated that 79 per cent of the American public believed elder mistreatment to be a serious problem. The American system has tended to rely on specialist elder protection services and the mandatory reporting of suspected abuse by professional workers. Recourse to law has led to concern that this policy has contributed to the criminalization of mistreatment in situations where it may not always be easy to discern a clear perpetrator and victim (Faulkner, 1982; Crystal, 1986; Formby, 1992).

In Britain, and for that matter the rest of Europe (Biggs, Phillipson and Kingston, 1995) embryonic policy developments have avoided a criminal justice route, seeing elder abuse as a problem of welfare. It has been argued (Hugman, 1995) that placing elder abuse within a welfarist framework recognizes the ambiguity arising in situations of dependency and family expectation, the stresses associated with the caring role and the need to see abuse within the context of long-term relationships. Concerns that new legislation specifying elder abuse is needed in Britain (*Eagle*, 1994) tends to overlook the fact that existing legislation can be used and has been collated by the Department of Health (SSI, 1993) in their guidelines (see also Chapter 6, this volume). The main policy question is why the specific abuse of older adults was not identified as a practice priority until comparatively recently, from either a welfare or criminal justice perspective.

Formal recognition of elder abuse as a British problem arose in 1993 with the publication of Department of Health guidelines entitled *No Longer Afraid*. This followed a campaign centred around the social work press (*Community Care*, 1993) and the simultaneous launch of the pressure group Action on Elder Abuse. The relative absence of public awareness and grassroots activity around the issue, when compared to similar problems such as child protection or domestic violence, has led a growing number of commentators (Manthorpe, 1993; Biggs, 1994b; Penhale and Kingston, 1995b) to surmise that policy may be developing as part of an 'ageing enterprise'. This term was first coined by Estes (1979) to describe the tendency for practitioners, policy-makers and academics to shape responses to the problems encountered by elders in order to meet their own professional or political interests. A danger lies, then, in the possibility that the voice and requirements of older people themselves become marginalized as policy and procedure develop.

Policy often seems to be based on the tacit assumption of adversity in later life, of which mistreatment would be a part. However, little has been done to ensure that the civil and human rights of older people are sustained. Indeed, if the problem of abuse is as serious as certain commentators would have us believe, the view that generic care management plus a telephone helpline is a sufficient response would lead to the conclusion that whilst policy has an interest in identifying abuse, it evidences little will to act beyond observation.

It is now generally agreed on both sides of the Atlantic (Pillemer and Wolf, 1986; Bennett and Kingston, 1993) that abuse occurs to approximately 3.2 per 1,000 older people in the overall population, with physical abuse occurring to two per 1,000. Figures for child abuse have been estimated to approach between 14 per 1,000 (Straus, 1980) and 10.7 per 1,000 (Gelles and Straus, 1987). Whilst no figures are currently available on the incidence of elder abuse amongst older people in receipt of informal care, it is not unreasonable to assume from the above that we are not dealing with problems of the same magnitude (although this should not be confused with their severity). A recent survey (Action on Elder Abuse, 1995) undertaken a year after publication of *No Longer Afraid* indicated that just under three-quarters of social services departments had fully implemented policies on elder or adult protection, the most prominent feature of which was a propensity toward monitoring (see further, Chapter 17, this volume). Whilst this is encouraging in terms of the promptness of response, it is also reminiscent of Foucault's (1979) panopticon. In other words, as Fox (1995) points out, the nature of care is paradoxical. It is about love, generosity and the celebration of otherness, but it can also become part of the technology of control and surveillance. Monitoring in community settings might easily become an appropriate surveillance once a different moral reason for doing it has been established.

Social policy towards old age

In order to understand the development of a distinctive policy on elder abuse in England (at the time of writing there is no comparable guidance in the rest of the UK) it is necessary to situate it within general policy towards older people.

The defining features of such policy have, since the inception of the welfare state, centred on dependency as a result of physical and mental decline, plus the primacy of child care over the needs of other, adult, groups. Old age is thus conceived of as a burden on other productive, or potentially productive, parts of the population. Evidence for this view can be found in Beveridge's (1942) original document *Social Insurance and Allied Services* on which much of the post-war consensus on health and welfare is based:

It is dangerous to be in any way lavish to old age until adequate provision has been assured for all other vital needs, such as the prevention of disease and the adequate nutrition of the young. (quoted in Wilson, 1991: 39)

As Patel (1990: 4) points out, this view is often unthinkingly reproduced in policy documents. She cites, for example, the 1988 edition of *Social Trends* which states that:

Although the size of the dependent population in 2025 will not be much higher than it was in 1971, its composition will be different in that there will be far less children and many more elderly people, so reducing the demand on education but increasing the burden on health services.

In other words, one generation's need is seen as a demand on resources whilst another's is perceived to be burdensome.

However, a number of influential writers have shown that increased dependency and the subsequent burdensomeness of older people is by no means an inevitable consequence of ageing (Townsend, 1981; Phillipson, 1982; Walker, 1986). In particular Townsend (1981, 1986) has expanded on the view that dependency is socially constructed. He has proposed that this structured dependency occurs as a result of the way that elders are systematically excluded from the working population by retirement policy, the poverty that results for the majority of the aged population, the institutionalization of a minority of older people which then comes to stand for the majority, plus restrictions that are then placed on the expected domestic and community roles made available in later life. One of the consequences of structured dependency would be that disengagement by older people from the rest of society is seen as functional, and that rather than investing in services to support an active later life 'policies of non interference would be a greater kindness', leading to 'minimalist solutions to their problems' (Townsend, 1986: 18–19).

This is in spite of evidence (Wilson, 1991) that rather than being 'downhill all the way', as policy and provision tends to assume, the character of decline in later life is more accurately characterized as a 'terminal drop'. This means that the majority of older people are able to maintain physical and intellectual functioning right up until the final months of life.

Policy assumptions of dependency and decline are reflected in the services that are made available to older people. Thus, Phillipson and Walker (1986: 281) note a 'tendency to ghettoise work with the old, often placing it in the hands of the lowest paid and least trained'. Further, it is often assumed by helping professionals that, whilst their training has largely prepared them for work with children and young adults, it is an equally valid basis on which to make judgements about old age. Although the priorities of later life might be quite different to those of other phases of the life course (Biggs, 1993), it has been observed by Phillipson and Walker (1986: 282), in their review of social policy, that professionals tend to 'interpret and channel these demands (i.e. those of older people) into acceptable and conventional forms'. In this case acceptability is age-structured, with the priorities of youth (as the dominant client group) and mid-adulthood (as the dominant worker group) characterized as central and other perspectives as marginal.

A problem with current policy, then, is that whilst assumptions of dependency may be true for a minority of the most vulnerable of our citizens, and this, in social problem terms, is a valid focus, the minority comes to stand for the dominant experience of ageing and influences future policy-making and public attitudes in an age-structured manner.

An additional characteristic of policy toward old age concerns the site of care. Townsend (1986) alerts us to the fact that the findings of early research, most notably Sheldon's (1948) seminal study, lead to the view that whilst public policy segregated older people from wider society; community, and in particular family life, integrated them into local and inter-generational networks. This view has largely been maintained in social policy and has failed to take the changing nature of family and community into account. Phillipson (1996a) has reviewed research into contemporary social networks in later life and concludes that increased geographical mobility has eroded traditional communities, while changed patterns in relationships, such as increased divorce and cohabitation, have made inter-generational ties more complex (see further Chapter 7, this volume). A consequence of these changing patterns has been that inter-generational relations have become characterized by 'intimacy at a distance' (Rosenmayer and Kockeis, 1963). Further, families are not cemented by 'fixed obligations' as might be expected from a traditionalist model of filial relations, but depend upon a variety of personal 'commitments' that may change depending upon current circumstances and the historical quality of a relationship (Finch, 1995). So, whereas in 1948 elders might have been tied into reciprocal obligations and shared living arrangements with their children, in 1996 they are more likely to be living with a spouse or alone. Commitment is likely to be negotiable, with an expectation that rather than depending on support from younger generations, older family members will offer support down the generational tree (Finch and Mason, 1990). Finch (1995: 62) has outlined the policy implication as follows:

> In future, family responsibilities cannot be relied upon to deliver a consistent pattern of informal care for elderly people. Although present social and demographic trends will not necessarily undermine this aspect of family life . . . the basis of responsibilities is likely to remain highly individual.

Indeed, it is not at all clear that, when asked, older people particularly wish to be looked after by kin. A number of studies, reviewed by Phillipson (1992b) indicate a preference for formal services that preserve independence from other generations of family members. This is supported by social-psychological studies (Pratt and Norris, 1994) indicating a preference for peer relations that are perceived as being both less intrusive and more accepting of age-related priorities. Unfortunately, neither the changing nature of inter-generational relations nor the preferences of older people seems to have found its way into contemporary policy.

The assumptions of social policy – that elders are a dependent burden and that family obligation is alive, well and indeed desirable – are reflected in the historical nature of welfare intervention in the lives of older people as it concerns abuse and neglect. Intervention had been restricted to cases of self-neglect, where the conduct of older people has been judged to be a danger to themselves or to others. Legislation such as section 47 of the 1948 National Assistance Act has provision to.protect elders from self-neglect, and section 45(1) of the 1968 Health Services and Public Health Act allows local authorities to promote the welfare of old people. One of the results of this historical trend is that 'There is no systematic provision, much less a tradition of protecting elders against active abuse by others in community and family settings' (Biggs, 1995: 31).

The problem is not, in other words, conceived in terms of the possibility of active abuse by others; rather, that old age itself may give rise to decrement that might prove harmful to individuals and those around them. Indeed, the possibility of abuse in old age seems not to have been identified, as other forms, such as child abuse and domestic violence, have chipped away at notions of the family as a haven in a harsh world (Phillipson and Biggs, 1995). The great wave of rebellion against familial and welfare paternalism in the 1970s and 1980s seems to have passed old age by.

This constellation of general factors has created three enduring features of policy development with respect to elder abuse. First, there is a tendency to see the older person as in some way responsible for his or her own predicament. A minimalist approach that has historically focused on self-neglect leaves little conceptual space for exterior causes of harm. Secondly, old age is seen as the least valued generation in the caring nexus. In terms of commonsense values and in explicit policy pronouncements, other life phases are positioned as less burdensome and as offering more of a return on societal investments. Thirdly, the family has been identified as the rightful site of care by virtue of its not being an institution and by a presumed embeddedness in community networks.

The stage is thus set for a particular view of elder abuse to take shape, one that is ambivalent about the value of older people, that is biased in favour of younger generations and identifies families as a proper locus of continuing care.

Community care policy and elder abuse

Contemporary community care policy contains a number of complex relations that further specify the site of elder abuse and mirror some of the trends noted above. It also supplies a moral dimension to informal care.

The 1990 NHS and Community Care Act was largely conceived as a piece of social engineering – to consolidate a mixed welfare system that gave greater rein to private forms of care and to inject market mechanisms, such as more explicit purchasing and competition between providers, into traditional caring arrangements. However, the government of the day was faced with a contradiction in so far as it both wished to promote private care which was primarily institutional in nature and to transfer the responsibility for care to the domestic sphere. In the words of the Audit Commission (1986): care *by* the community should take the place of care *in* the community. Motivation for this policy was both ideological to the extent that a 'flourishing private sector' was politically palatable, and fiscal: to transfer the financial responsibility for care to the relatives of vulnerable adults.

These trends in community care policy help to explain why concern about elder abuse occurring in specifically domestic settings should come about at the same time as the promotion of informal care as the key to successful community support and a growth in private residential care.

The first task is to explain why domestic rather than institutional settings were identified as specified sites of abuse. The second task is to identify the nature and consequences of anxiety about domestic settings.

A close association between increased private residential provision and government policy meant that rather than focus on institutions as the primary site of abuse, a strategy of encouragement to increase the quality of residential care was adopted. A series of initiatives such as the Wagner review, *Residential Care: A Positive Choice* (1988) and *Homes are for Living in* (SSI, 1989) were developed rather than the direct confrontation of abuse in such settings. Indeed a much cited report to Wagner on *Scandals in Residential Centres* (Clough, 1988a: see Chapter 11, this volume) remains unpublished at the time of writing. This policy direction has been maintained in spite of a long history of public inquiries and, since 1984, registered homes tribunal decisions which support the conclusion that 'There is chilling evidence that these elderly people are more likely to be at risk than the 95 per cent to 91 per cent who live in the community' (Glendenning, 1993: 1). It has been argued elsewhere (Biggs, 1996) that the ideologically unpalatable nature of the incidence of abuse in this sector eclipsed it as a site for policy development on elder abuse.

Whilst institutional care had effectively been knocked out of the policy picture this was not the case for domiciliary care. The domestic environment had been specifically earmarked by the 1990 Act as the great unrecognized site of care. However, the Act and subsequent guidance (SSI, 1992) failed to recognize the diversity inherent in informal carers, preferring to see them as a homogeneous group selflessly providing cheap support to vulnerable older people. There has thus to date been no serious consideration of the suitability of individuals who find themselves in a caring role, other than a private member's bill (Hansard, 1995) to ensure that carers receive a separate assessment of their own needs, as carers, from the person being cared for. The assumed homogeneity of this group leads one to suspect that other motivations are driving the debate than those that would determine the readiness of nominated carers to care and the acceptability of such arrangements to vulnerable older people. In other words moral, rather than practical, priorities.

It was not necessary to look far to note what this other motivation, or more accurately fear, might be. On both sides of the Atlantic right wing commentators had generated anxiety that the contract between generations was breaking down (see Minkler and Robertson, 1991; Thompson, 1989; and Phillipson, 1991 for a fuller discussion of this policy debate). In Britain this culminated in a 'Back to Basics' campaign in 1993–94 which reinforced the message of familial responsibility, and indeed, culpability. The tone of this debate is deeply rooted in government ideology and is reflected in Prime Minister Thatcher's widely reported view that 'Too many people are given to understand that if they have a problem it's the government's job to cope with it . . . They are casting their problems on society. And, you know, there's no such thing as society. There are individual men and women and there are families. And no government can do anything except through people and people must look to themselves first' (*Woman's Own*, 1987).

Thus, in the face of research evidence cited earlier, social policy was interpreted as a tool to enforce filial obligations to care which seemed to be based on atavistic longings for a family structure that might never have been and certainly failed to fit current trends. The outcome, in terms of the risk of elder abuse, would be that relatives or others who were unsuited or unwilling to care would be obliged to maintain a fantasy of coping.

This conclusion might seem less of a flight of fantasy once one looks at the categories of persons who are likely to abuse. American studies (Pillemer and Wolf, 1986; Pillemer, 1993) have repeatedly shown an association between mental health problems, substance misuse plus dependency *on the part of the perpetrator* and the likelihood of abuse taking place. It would seem, then, that perpetrator characteristics are a more accurate indicator of risk than victim characteristics and that some 'carers' who become perpetrators should never be placed in a position of care in the first place. A moralistic and uniform policy on 'caring' does little to elucidate the actual circumstances that might lead to abuse and discriminate between these and situations of positive care.

Care management, carer support and abusive situations

Once a moral imperative imposes a blanket responsibility on all relatives or other informal carers, regardless of suitability, some form of surveillance technology is needed to ensure that older people are maintained 'in their own homes'.

The preferred model of professional support, that of care management, relies for success on maintaining the carer in a role so as to stop the person being cared for from entering long-term residential or nursing care. As such, carers have been encouraged to see themselves as 'para-professionals' who, whilst unpaid, identify with the professional caring task. In turn, the care manager gauges the success of their overall objective, to maintain the older person in the community, by the ability of the informal carer to cope. Some writers have noted the advantages of such a system. Bond (1992), for example, has valued the increased recognition and self-esteem that is thus given to informal care and suggests that carers should receive training in basic care tasks. Hugman (1995) is again positive, whilst voicing concerns that informal carers cannot be held to the same ethical obligations that regulate the conduct of professional workers. Biggs (1994b), however, has noted that such para-professionalization may increase collusion between care managers and informal carers such that the needs of the original service user can become ignored. Thus, as the carer comes to see him/herself as increasingly para-professional, there is more common ground and thus a closer identification between the worker and the carer. An accompanying danger emerges should the older person become further marginalized and the carer replace the vulnerable adult as the nominated client in the mind of the care manager. This may be the case in instances of unrecognized abuse, such that the victim becomes doubly abused: by the carer through commission and then by the worker through omission. Thus the policy courts failure on two counts: the needs of the older person become eclipsed by those of the carer, and the carer is unable to give voice to their own dependency needs because they are encouraged to see them-selves as coping and not upsetting the care management 'applecart'. When viewed from an age-alert perspective, this policy, often portrayed as a radical break from previous service systems, can be seen as continuing life-course-related trends that prioritize the needs of younger generations and marginalize the requirements of older adults.

The additional factor, from the current perspective, is not so much the often quoted coordination of care packages envisaged by care management technology, but its tendency to distance simultaneously carer and cared for and maintain a surveillance function over the carer–cared-for relationship.

'No longer afraid'

The stage is now set for the official 'discovery' of elder abuse as exempli-fied in *No Longer Afraid* (SSI, 1993). *No Longer Afraid* can be seen as further strengthening the location of elder abuse in the public and pro-fessional mind and a critique of the definitions found therein has been reviewed elsewhere (Brammer and Biggs, in preparation). As its full title suggests – *No Longer Afraid: The Safeguard of Elderly People in Domes-tic Settings* – it reinforces perceptions of abuse as a predominantly family affair. It also implies that dependency on the part of the victim and inter-generational role-reversal are key factors in the development of such abuse within the domestic environment.

These guidelines can be questioned on a number of counts (see Biggs, 1996):

First, they reinforce the use of care management as the appropriate form of intervention and effectively close off the development of alternative approaches to the problem. The particular form of care management chosen is administrative rather than therapeutic and can no longer be assumed to include the direct mediation and counselling skills that could usefully be employed in contexts of suspected abuse. As noted above, these skills have largely been replaced by assessment and monitoring.

In short, care management had been introduced for other policy purposes, and is essentially a means of coordinating routine care. It would be unfair to expect post-holders to address the complex psychosocial problems that occur in many abusive situations. The net effect is to subordinate this 'new' social problem to other agendas in the *realpolitik* of social engineering, avoid providing services designed to address abusive contexts, and, as has been argued above, to observe.

Secondly, carer stress brought on by victim dependency is given prominence as a causative factor in abuse. This view has not been supported by research evidence, as a growing number of reviews indicate (Pillemer and Wolf, 1986; Pillemer, 1993; Bennett and Kingston, 1993; Biggs et al., 1995). Two substantive points have arisen from empirical study that stress does not discriminate between abusive and non-abusive care, and that abuse is most likely when the perpetrator is dependent emotionally or financially on the victim, rather than vice versa. Indeed the degree of dependency also failed to discriminate between abused and non-abused elders. What the stress hypothesis does do, however, is to reinforce the view that 'normal' carers might understandably be prone to abuse, given the burden of care. This view would help to sustain the myth of the independent and coping carer and underplays the vulnerability of those few carers who actually abuse. Situational stress is, after all, a predominantly transient state that would not threaten the integrity of the care management enterprise as outlined above. In one sleight of hand the average carer is seen as prone to abuse and the older person as both dependent and culpable.

Third, an emphasis on inter-generational conflict as a cause of abuse places it firmly in the 'daughter-carer' camp while reducing emphasis on spouse abuse and forms of community harassment. Indeed, by so psychologizing abusive situations, other factors, such as the gendered nature of abuse (Whittaker, 1995; see further, Chapter 8 this volume), its relation to race (Biggs, 1996) and the role of collective scapegoating by certain communities (Pritchard, 1993; Garrod, 1993) have been hidden.

Whether intentionally or not, the net effect of the chosen policy position has been to place responsibility insidiously upon the older person for their own circumstances *and* to lock abuse more securely within domestic care. Case management methods ensure assessment and monitoring but there is no provision for specific service initiatives to tackle abusive situations. In other words it becomes little more than surveillance. The carer stress hypothesis seems plausible not because it is supported by evidence, but because it legitimizes the 'normality' of abuse. The further embedding of abuse in familial and inter-generational settings obscures the role of its relationship to wider social phenomena.

There *is* an alternative

I want to emphasize that to critique the development of abuse awareness in the contemporary British context is not to devalue the efforts of many care managers. Their task is made much harder, however, because the tools and accompanying philosophy at their disposal are simply inadequate to the job at hand. Not only might abuse be obscured in certain settings, but care management can contribute to the continuance of abuse in others.

However, history need not have turned out this way. That progress is being made against the odds should not make us blind to alternative possibilities, a number of which are itemized below.

First, when Phillipson and Walker (1986) edited their book on social policy, much was made of the Elderly Persons Support Unit project in Sheffield. This was later renamed the Neighbourhood Support Unit (NSU). The project attempted to break away from the traditional patterns of service delivery. Community support workers replaced the staff of day centres and domiciliary services, and the workers made a conscious effort to see old age not as a period of decline and burden upon relatives but as subject to rehabilitation within communities. The intention was to involve older service users and their informal carers more directly in decision-making about the kinds of support that they required. It was argued that care should not be pre-packaged in service provider categories, but instead provided along a continuum depending on the needs of the user. The philosophy of the NSUs in the mid-1980s in Sheffield received much attention at the time of the Audit Commission's report, *Making a Reality of Community Care* (1986). Recently there has been an evaluation of this innovatory project (Walker and Warren, 1996).

Secondly, practice in other European countries may offer us a way out of the policy impasse presented by the 1990 Act. In Norway, Johns and Juklestad (1995) describe a system based on specified elder protective services which are not subject to the adversarial nature of the American model. Key to the success of this approach have been specially trained mediators whose job it has been to broker negotiations between parties in abusive situations, including the professionals themselves. Whilst mediation has been promoted in Britain (Craig, 1992, 1994), it has not, as yet, been adopted to any degree. In the Netherlands (Jensen, 1995), specified 'help centres' have been developed that act as a resource for front-line workers. Two help centres were evaluated by Jensen, one based in a home-care organization and another in a victim support agency. The former model was found to be more in tune with the problems faced by older people and responses that might be made. In Italy, a number of public awareness campaigns, which have attempted to draw on inter-generational collaboration in communities, point to another, though less well documented approach, which seems to hold out the prospect of genuine preventive action (Ripamonte, 1995).

Each of these developments indicates that it is possible to escape the dead hand of British community care policy and develop creative responses to elder abuse. Any new approach would need to recognize the counter-intuitive nature of abusive contexts: that, contrary to the 'common sense' of current policy, abuse may not be a predominantly domestic issue, that older victims may not be unduly dependent and that solutions do not consist of repeating a mantra that services designed for other purposes can simply adapt to new and complex challenges. The changes required would be at both the level of the public perception of older age, caring and the positioning of abuse as a social problem and at the level of developing new services to address previously unencountered arenas.

Concluding comments

At the beginning of this chapter, I suggested that the procedures adopted towards a newly recognized social problem and the positioning of that problem through policy decisions ultimately shape how the phenomenon is seen in the professional and public mind. Elder abuse is no different from other problems in this regard, and by viewing it in relation to a number of increasingly specific policy agendas it can be seen how that positioning has taken shape. Thus, it is seen as a welfare, rather than a criminal problem; associated with lowered life course priorities and the family; as a moral imperative to informal care maintained by the technology of care management and by carer stress and dependency.

I have argued that the 'discovery' of elder abuse, in the absence of a concerted policy and practice response, may fulfil a deeper and more primitive need in social consciousness than is generally acknowledged in policy debates. This need can be thought of as voyeuristic in so far as abuse raises the profile of later life in such a way as to emphasize the consequences of nonconformity to established, yet largely tacit, expectations of both carers and elders and, behind this, there is a vicarious confirmation of the dominance of younger generations over older ones. Further, trends in contemporary policy towards old age in general and community care in particular might even be conceived of as abusive in themselves, by virtue of their systematic and negative presentation of later life and, in the particular case of abuse, by their provision of a technology of disclosure and monitoring with no serious attempt to create appropriate services with which to intervene and change such states of affairs.

The function of contemporary social policy would, according to this view, be twofold: to discount abuse as an area in need of specialist resources, preferring instead the use of an established generic practice method designed for other things; and to emphasize the generic, both allowing the surveillance of all informal care and reinforcing the image of older people as the second-class citizens of the welfare world. Specifically, the identification of elder abuse as a social problem at a certain historical juncture may serve to justify the policing of service arrangements that are in flux at a time when processes of care are being reshaped.

It must be remembered, here, that abuse is clearly indefensible as a personal act and I am specifically not saying that it is in some way manufactured. However, any simple moralism that fails to locate it within policy and collective trends will avoid a deeper and ultimately more effective understanding of how to prevent abuse and enhance the lives of marginalized groups such as older people and their carers.

6
Elder Abuse and the Law

Aled Griffiths, Gwyneth Roberts and John Williams

The dearth of law on elder abuse can perhaps be rationalized on the ground that any attempt to categorize elderly people as a group apart from others in society should be resisted. In truth, however, law makers in the United Kingdom, in contrast to those in the USA (Glendenning, 1993), have hardly addressed, as yet, the arguments for and against bespoke law in the area of elder abuse, akin to that which is available in other areas of domestic violence (Williams, 1994; Pollard, 1995). More alarmingly, it seems that little use is made of existing legal and/or quasi-legal processes as a means of protection or redress, despite the considerable body of evidence which indicates that elderly people are vulnerable to various forms of abuse (SSI, 1994).

The current situation gives rise to a number of key questions. Why are legal procedures so little used? Would more use of legal procedures be a positive step forward? If so, how could they be better used, or better shaped, to protect elderly people?

There are several possible explanations for the situation which exists at present. These include the reluctance of many victims to instigate or become involved in legal processes; the attitude of professional workers towards elder abuse (SSI, 1992); and the way in which elder abuse has been interpreted and defined. A contributing factor is that a proportion of the elderly population suffers, to a greater or lesser degree, from mental incapacity. Where such individuals are subject to abuse, particularly complex problems are likely to arise. Unfortunately, the law relating to mental incapacity is, at present, 'complicated, inflexible and piecemeal' (Law Commission, 1995). It consists of a series of separate and discrete procedures which operate in different ways in different circumstances, depending upon whether an issue arises in relation to the property and financial affairs of the incapacitated person, or in relation to personal care and treatment. As a result, an incapacitated elderly person may be deprived of autonomy and self-determination when he/she is capable of exercising both; or may be left without proper protection in situations where he/she is most vulnerable, such as residential care (United Kingdom Central Council for Nursing, 1994). Some residential homes have been described as little better than 'prisons in suburbia' (Counsel and Care, 1991).

Evidence suggests that some elderly victims of abuse refuse to take legal action against an alleged perpetrator because they fear retaliation at some future date, or because they wish to protect the abuser against punishment or liability (Powell and Berg, 1987). These findings may be given too much weight, however. Not so long ago, similar reasons were routinely given by the police, and other law enforcement agencies, to justify non-intervention in cases of domestic violence (Griffiths, 1980). Since then, attitudes have changed and evidence suggests that many victims of domestic abuse are only too willing to cooperate in the criminal process (Pahl, 1985). Indeed, some important lessons might be learnt from the experience of those who have been in the vanguard of the battle against the abuse of women. To quote some American researchers in a publication sponsored by the United Nations Development Fund:

> 'Domestic violence' is now a household word [sic] and the United States has more than 1500 programmes providing services for battered women. In many areas the legal system no longer treats domestic violence as a 'family matter', but prosecutes wife assault as it would assault by a stranger. Through the symbolic force of law, society has declared wife abuse unacceptable and is holding violent men accountable. (Chapman and Chapman, 1993: 257)

To achieve a similar revolution in the context of elder abuse in Britain may be an uphill struggle since the policy response to the needs of older people in post-war British society has been 'welfarization', involving a subtle mixture of diminution and patronage (Fennell et al., 1989; Biggs et al., 1995).

In addition, certain legal procedures, particularly criminal prosecutions, may be inappropriate in many cases of elder abuse, because the perpetrators of the abuse may themselves be seen as victims. There may be factors in the situation which impose considerable stress on the abuser (Costa, 1984), who is often the elderly person's carer and, usually, a son or daughter (Powell and Berg, 1987) for whom there is little by way of support in the community (Millard, 1984). It can equally be argued that many of those professionally employed as carers in the residential sector could be described as victims of the situation, in that their terms of employment have many of the features of other low status occupations, including stressful working conditions, low pay, limited career prospects, few opportunities for training, and minimal support from management (Donovan and Wynne-Harley, 1986; Downey, 1991; Mitchell, 1991).

Persuasive though such explanations may be, they can hardly be regarded as sufficient justification for non-intervention. Indeed, other research, in the context of both community and residential care, points to the significance of 'relationships' as opposed to 'environments' as an explanation for pathology and breakdown in care arrangements (Nolan et al., 1990; Biggs, 1994a). For instance, a study of residential and nursing homes in North Nottinghamshire revealed, contrary to assertions by staff, that there was little correlation between restrictions being imposed on residents and the staff/resident ratio. The clear message was that with good management and determination 'freedoms are possible' (Murphy and Bean, 1992).

It is evident, however, that there may be some reluctance across the relevant professions to make full use of the available legal remedies. This reflects, in part, the education and training of key professionals, such as lawyers and social workers, in the relevant legal provisions. There is evidence, for example, that – in the past, at least – professional social work courses varied considerably in the attention they gave to equipping students properly with a sound knowledge of the law which governs social work practice (Ball et al., 1988). There is evidence of indifference – and even antipathy – by service providers towards the law and lawyers, not only among those who plan and provide residential care, but also among those who supposedly regulate its quality (Carson, 1985).

It is encouraging that these training issues are now being addressed by the relevant academic and professional bodies (Ball et al., 1995). The Law Society, too, has expressed a growing concern about the physical and/or mental abuse of older people, and has suggested that solicitors should take steps to ensure that older people have protection from abuse, whether through legal proceedings, or by alerting the appropriate authorities (Law Society, 1994).

Most social services authorities have developed, or are developing, guidelines on elder abuse for their staff (Penhale, 1993b). The need is pressing, since elder abuse often seems to be given low priority, despite general agreement about its prevalence (SSI, 1992).

Members of the caring professions seldom conceptualize elder abuse in terms of the law. According to Eastman (1984), 'granny bashing' may consist of physical assault, threats of physical assault, neglect, including locking a dependant in a bedroom; abandonment, either to residential or hospital care; exploitation, including appropriation of finance and property; sexual abuse; and psychological abuse. The result is a highly diffuse definition of elder abuse (Cloke, 1983). Eastman (1984) also argues that abuse committed by persons other than relatives who care for an elderly person should not be included within the analytical framework. To differentiate in this way between caregiving relatives and other abusers seems arbitrary and illogical, and makes little sense in terms of the law.

Recent attempts at categorizing abuse appear more satisfactory, in that no regard is paid to whether or not the alleged abuser is also a carer. Categories of abuse developed in America distinguish between the abuse of civil liberties; physical abuse; psychological abuse; financial abuse; and neglect (Decalmer and Glendenning, 1993; see further Chapter 3, this volume). These distinctions are far more easily transposable into legal concepts, such as crimes or torts (that is, actionable civil wrongs).

Physical abuse – criminal prosecution

Instances of physical and/or sexual abuse may give rise to a criminal prosecution. A number of offences exist at common law and under statute law. The most important in this context are assault and battery. It is the Crown Prosecution Service (CPS) which decides whether or not to prosecute in relation to crimes such as assault and battery. In making this decision, the CPS will, in accordance with the Crown Prosecutor's Code, have regard to two factors:

1　that there is enough evidence to provide a realistic prospect of a conviction; and
2　that pursuing the prosecution would be in the public interest.

There is some concern that vulnerable adults may be regarded as unreliable witnesses who will be unmercifully exploited by the defence (Holt, 1993c). A failure to prosecute for these reasons can unfairly deny such people the right to use the criminal law. The Royal Commission on Criminal Justice (1993) suggested that the kind of support currently given to children should be extended to vulnerable adults. Such support includes the use of pre-recorded video interviews, interactive videos and the use of screens in court (Williams, 1994). The Royal Commission recommended that judges should take a more interventionist approach to check unfair and intimidating cross-examination of vulnerable witnesses. For the present, screens to prevent eye contact with adult defendants are used only exceptionally (*R. v. Schaub* [1993] 138 Sol. Jo. LB 11 CA). The competency of a witness is a matter for the judge, who must be satisfied that he/she has the necessary level of understanding.

Even where competency is not in doubt, a witness may face other problems. Many instances of abuse are unwitnessed, and some are of such a sensitive nature that corroborative evidence will be required (*R. v. Spencer* [1987] AC 128). In some circumstances, a part admission by a defendant may be taken as corroboration (*R. v. Simpson* [1994] Crim. LR 436).

Witnesses in criminal cases are usually expected to attend and give oral evidence on oath. The Criminal Justice Act 1988 makes provision for the admissibility of written statements where a person's physical or mental condition prevents them from attending the court (McEwan, 1989). However, such evidence may be excluded. In *R. v. Neshet* [1990] (*The Times*, 14 March 1990) the police took statements from two elderly women in the course of investigating alleged thefts by the matron of a residential home. The Court of Appeal excluded the evidence on the grounds that it was unsafe to rely on it.

If the CPS decides not to prosecute, it is possible for an individual to bring a private prosecution under the Prosecution of Offenders Act 1985. The right is generally acknowledged to be an important safeguard (*Gouriet v. Union of Post Office Workers* [1978] AC 498). Legal aid is not available in such cases, but since common assault and battery are summary offences, the defendant cannot elect for trial by jury so that prosecution is much cheaper. Nearly all the summonses issued by the magistrates' courts, in response to private complaints of violence, are for common assault (Saunders, 1995). It is possible, in such cases, to make a formal complaint to a magistrates' court – a process known as 'laying an information' – and to request the court to issue a summons. Proceedings of this kind are relatively speedy, and provide individuals with the opportunity to present their case in relatively informal surroundings.

Normally, in cases of common assault or battery the victim him/herself is required to initiate proceedings, although elderly and infirm individuals may be treated as exceptions to this rule. In *Pickering v. Willoughby* [1907] 2 KB 296, an elderly woman who had suffered a number of strokes was assaulted by her niece who had moved to live with her. The court held that a great-nephew could institute proceedings on behalf of the victim on the grounds that 'if the person assaulted is so feeble, old and infirm as to be incapable of instituting proceedings, and is not a free agent but under the control of the person committing the assault, the information may be laid by a third person'. This procedure may assist those who are themselves reluctant to use the criminal law (Griffiths and Roberts, 1995).

Those found guilty of common assault can be required to enter into a recognizance to be bound over to be of good behaviour. The police can also, in certain circumstances, arrest a person for a breach of the peace. A common law breach of the peace can take place on private premises (*McConnell v. Chief Constable of Greater Manchester Police* [1990] 1 All ER 43). The police are entitled to enter such premises without a warrant if they have reasonable grounds for believing that a breach of the peace is likely to occur (*McLeod v. Commissioner of the Police of the Metropolis* [1994] 4 All ER 553; Police and Criminal Evidence Act 1984, s.17(1)(e)).

Acts and omissions

A criminal offence is normally the result of a deliberate act and not the result of an omission to act. In England and Wales, no legal duty is placed upon informal or formal carers or other service providers to report criminal acts. This is in sharp contrast to the situation in America where, as of 1988, at least 43 states operated mandatory state-wide reporting systems (Bennett and Kingston, 1993).

However, where a person assumes a duty of care for an infirm person but is indifferent or reckless to an obvious risk of injury, he or she may be guilty of manslaughter should that person die (*R v. Stone* [1977] 2 All ER 341). The defendants had undertaken the care of an infirm relative. They were found guilty of manslaughter when she died as a result of toxaemia caused by infected bedsores and prolonged immobilization. Guilt may be established by showing that there had been reckless disregard for any danger to the health and welfare of the infirm person. Inadvertence is not enough. It must be shown that the defendant was indifferent to an obvious risk of injury to health, or had foreseen the risk, but, nevertheless, did nothing to avoid it.

Civil action

A civil action in tort for damages or an injunction may be brought in addition to a criminal prosecution or as an alternative to it. In general, it does not matter in which order the proceedings are brought, although normally a civil action will be stayed until the criminal proceedings have been completed (Williams and Hepple, 1984), since legislation provides that a conviction in the criminal courts is admissible as evidence in any subsequent civil proceedings (Civil Evidence Act 1968, s.11).

For an assault to be established in a civil action it is sufficient for the threatened person to have reasonable cause to fear that actual harm will be directed towards him/her. Battery, on the other hand, requires actual application of force to the person, that is, an act which directly and, either intentionally or negligently, causes some physical contact with the person without their consent (Brazier, 1988). The essential test is not whether the defendant's action showed ill-will or malevolence, simply that it was hostile (*Wilson v. Pringle* [1987] QB 237). The tort simply requires the defendant to do something to which the plaintiff objects. It would appear from *Forde v. Skinner* [1830] 4 C & P 239 that the least touching of another person, such as an unwarranted kiss, or cutting an individual's hair against his/her will, could be sufficient to satisfy the tort. As a result, the tort of battery protects against intrusion into another person's right to physical privacy and personal autonomy. Thus, pushing an individual in a manner which was undignified and uncalled for, as reported in Registered Homes Tribunal Case No. 9, might well satisfy the essentials of the tort. Although not relevant in determining liability for battery, motive or malice may be relevant in determining damages.

In Tribunal Case No. 95, it was revealed that drugs had been taken by residents for whom they had not been prescribed. It is, however, unclear whether, in English law, this is an example of trespass to the person since the judicial tradition is to insist upon a direct relationship between the wrongful action taken by the defendant and the harm caused to the plaintiff. This requirement has been abandoned in Canada and the USA. Some fairly liberal interpretations of directness have been accepted by the courts (see, for example, *Scott v. Shepherd* [1773] 2 Wm Bl 892). It would appear from the above that the tort of trespass to the person could be developed to provide a check on the indiscriminate prescribing of psychotropic drugs. In any case such conduct might be actionable on the basis of the tort of wrongful interference (Rogers, 1989) which is discussed below.

False imprisonment

False imprisonment arises where a person's movement is restricted by another without lawful authority. It is not false imprisonment if the restrained person consents, although agreement must not be implied simply because he/she did not resist, or because, for example, he/she is living in a residential home. Consent raises the issue of whether the person has the necessary mental capacity and, if so, to what precisely he/she has consented. Contrary to popular belief there is no general legal power to restrict the movements of vulnerable adults even where the person has been assessed as needing, and has consented to, residential care. Any such power to detain a person against his/her will is only to be found within the Mental Health Act 1983. It is far from certain that social workers and other social care professionals have recourse to the *Re F* 'best interests' test available to doctors. Lord Justice Goff in *Re F* stated *obiter dicta*, '. . . the relative, friend or neighbour, who comes in to look after him will commit no wrong when he or she touches his body' (*Re F* [1990] 2 AC).

The Law Commission (1995) correctly considers this *dictum* to be uncertain. There is no clear legal authority which extends to social workers and others the same degree of professional freedom given to doctors to determine clients' best interests (Parkin, 1995).

The cases appear to suggest that a person may be falsely imprisoned even though he/she was unaware of the restraint (see *Murray v. Ministry of Defence* [1988] 1 WLR 692). Restraint itself may take various forms. In some cases it is of a very extreme kind which is deliberate and premeditated. In Tribunal Case No. 87 an elderly resident was tied to a chair by means of a rope and jubilee clip. The records revealed that she was restrained on no less than 18 occasions within one month. On nine occasions within one month, she was restrained all night.

It was alleged in Tribunal Case No. 131 that residents in one residential care home were confined to their bedrooms by the insertion of a nail in the door frame which acted as a bolt to secure the door from the outside. There is no lawful authority for such treatment since the residents were there of their own volition. In other cases, the form of restraint may be less extreme, but may still be restrictive of the person's liberty. A good example of such restraint is the policy of locking doors in residential care homes and denying residents access to the key. A similar result is achieved through the use of numerical key padlocks, the code for which the residents are not told. This method may be used to confine a resident to one part of the home, or to the home itself. One justification put forward for this policy is that it is necessary for security reasons. However, it is also a means of 'protecting' the resident by avoiding the risks inherent in leaving the home or a part of it. Whether such a policy is lawful is debatable. The Law Commission (1995) suggests that it is. When commenting on the results of the consultation process, its report states: 'Some of the consultees confidently asserted that locking a door on a demented resident is illegal, but we doubt the accuracy of this claim' (para. 4.31).

It is submitted that the confident assertions of the consultees more accurately states the law than the view of the Law Commission — there is no general power to detain an adult against his/her will. This is an area in which the dilemma which exists between protection, on the one hand, and autonomy, on the other, is brought into sharp focus.

Current law imposes a duty of care on care staff and this may result in negligence if a resident wanders off and is injured. However, it also raises the possibility of a successful action for false imprisonment where unlawful restraint is used. Although there is no easy legal resolution to this dilemma, two general principles can be identified. First, it is essential that the autonomy of residents is fully recognized. Evidence suggests that the welfare and life expectancy of frail elderly people are enhanced and prolonged if they are allowed to take normal risks (Hibbs, 1991). The duty of care does not require protection from every conceivable risk. Secondly, if the risk is assessed as unacceptable, it will be necessary for the home to provide an appropriate level of support for the resident if he/she goes outside the home. This may require diverting the person in the short term until suitable arrangements can be made. However, restraint effected by the wrongful assertion of authority is enough to establish the tort of false imprisonment (*Harnett v. Bond* [1925] AC 669). Clearly, this has implications for the level and quality of the staffing in the home. Residential care homes should ensure they have a system for identifying which residents have gone out, for example, on a shopping trip, although the idea of electronic tagging of residents is a clear breach of civil liberties (Parkin, 1995).

In an emergency, however, an individual may be lawfully restrained to protect him/herself or others (Hibbs, 1991). According to *Shaper v. Robinson* [1987] (unreported) CLY 87/755, proving the existence of a reasonable cause for restraining a person falls on the defendant, since restraint is *prima facie* a tort and requires justification. Similarly, where detention or restraint is initially lawful, it may, subsequently, become unlawful because circumstances have changed. For example, a crisis may be over (*Middleweek v. Chief Constable of Merseyside* [1990] 3 WLR 481).

Medical treatment

Medical examinations and procedures undertaken without consent could constitute battery. This not only covers surgery but also includes dental treatment, physiotherapy, medication and sedation. As the decision in *Chatterton v. Gerson* [1891] QB 432 indicates, consent may be given expressly or by implication, but it must be 'real' (Hoggett, 1990). An individual who offered no resistance to the infliction of a medical procedure because of the threat of another sanction (such as eviction from a residential care home) might not be giving a 'real consent'. In its most recent guidance to doctors, the General Medical Council (GMC, 1995) states that a doctor must respect the right of patients to refuse treatment, and that they must not refuse or deny treatment because they believe that patients' actions have contributed to their condition.

English law does not, however, require individual patients to be fully informed of *all* the risks associated with a particular treatment. It is enough for individual patients to be informed in broad terms of the likely possible consequences. However, the GMC guidance does require doctors to give patients the information they ask for or need about their condition, its treatment and prognosis (GMC, 1995). Where there is substantial risk of grave adverse consequences disclosure might be so obviously necessary to enable the patient to make a choice that a failure to do so would negate any apparent consent. As has been argued in a different context (Williams, 1983; Hoggett, 1990), the implications of the 'broad terms' explanation as a requirement is that a high proportion of otherwise vulnerable elderly people will have sufficient understanding to exercise the consent which is required in law, and to enable them to refuse treatment as well.

The *Sidaway* test is subject to the principle of therapeutic privilege. This principle recognizes that an 'obligation to give a patient all the information available to the doctor would often be inconsistent with the doctor's contractual obligation to have regard to the patient's best interest' (per Lord Templeman). The legal test on disclosure of information is set out in *Bolam v. Friern HMC* [1957] 2 All ER 118 which states that a doctor must 'exercise such care as accords with the standards of reasonably competent medical men at the time'. It might be tempting for doctors to use therapeutic privilege as an excuse for not giving patients all the necessary information. In the case of older patients medical paternalism may mean that they are not fully informed because 'they only get confused' or they 'cannot understand'. It is worthwhile noting that it is incumbent upon doctors to provide information to patients in a way that they can understand (GMC, 1995).

Where an elderly person lacks the capacity to give real consent what can the doctor do? Failure to examine or treat may result in the patient's condition deteriorating, or in death. This issue was discussed by the House of Lords in *Re F* [1990] 2 AC 1. The case highlighted a gap in the law which results in nobody being able to consent on the part of an incapacitated adult. Lord Brandon in the House of Lords said that 'A doctor could lawfully operate on, or give treatment to, adult patients who are incapable of consenting . . . provided that the operation or treatment is in the best interest of such patients.' Whether or not the 'best interests' test has been met would be based on the *Bolam* test for negligence outlined above. Intermingling the 'best interests' test with the test of medical negligence has, quite rightly, been the subject of criticism (Mason and McCall Smith, 1994; Law Commission, 1995). The House of Lords has also been criticized for the willingness to hand over to doctors an inappropriate degree of unsupervised power over the patient on the basis of 'doctor knows best' (Law Commission, 1995). The Law Commission has proposed that in determining 'best interests', regard should be made to the ascertainable past or present wishes of the patient; the need to permit or encourage the patient's ability to participate in the process; the view of those whom it is appropriate and practicable to consult; and the least restrictive alternative.

Care has to be taken in deciding whether or not a person has the requisite capacity to make a decision on medical treatment. The fact that a patient makes an 'irrational' decision and refuses to heed the advice of professionals, or the fact that he or she may be detained under the Mental Health Act 1983, does not mean that capacity to consent is lacking. The British Medical Association (BMA) stresses that a doctor must assess capacity in relation to the decision in question. For example, is the patient able to understand the nature and effects of the treatment and the consequences of not having it? If so then any refusal must be respected (BMA/Law Society, 1995; *Re C* [1994] 1 All ER 819).

One method of ensuring that an individual's wishes relating to medical treatment are observed could be by means of a living will, that is, a document formally made in advance, in which a person may declare his/her wish that life-prolonging procedures should be withheld should he/she become mentally or physically ill to an extent that recovery cannot be envisaged. In the absence of legislation for living wills, their legal status is unclear although there is some authority for saying they may be legally effective. Given the benefits of living wills, there is a sound argument for putting them on a proper legal footing (Dyer, 1996).

Negligence

A characteristic of the torts discussed above – assault, battery and false imprisonment – is that physical harm must be directly threatened or inflicted upon the plaintiff. The courts have, therefore, recognized that such acts are actionable *per se*, that is, without any need of further proof, that an act caused *actual* harm to the plaintiff. But where actual harm (whether physical or psychological) is caused to the plaintiff, it might also be possible to bring an action in the tort of negligence, which can be founded on either an act or an omission – referred to elsewhere in this volume as active or passive neglect. To succeed, however, it is necessary to establish that the defendant owed a duty of care to the plaintiff. Establishing the necessary duty of care might not be such a problem with respect to a professional carer (Griffiths et al., 1990) but there may be considerable, if not insurmountable, problems in relation to informal carers. In contrast to some other jurisdiction (Steinmetz, 1983), English law imposes no statutory or common law duty upon adult children to care for adult dependants, from which a duty of care in negligence might arise.

No case which concerns the abuse of an elderly person has been reported, although there are numerous examples of circumstances in which elements of the tort of negligence may have existed. The following allegation was made in evidence to the Wagner Committee:

> There must be up to thirty residents and at least four staff. However after their dinner at about midday, the staff are not seen until afternoon tea . . . then the staff aren't seen again until the evening meal at 6pm . . . anyone could have fallen, died, haemorrhaged, wet themselves and the staff wouldn't know. (National Institute of Social Work, 1988: 66)

The concept of vicarious liability can be important in the context of elder abuse. Where it is alleged that a tort has been committed by an employee, it may be possible to bring the action against the employer as well as, or as an alternative to, suing the employee.

Wrongful interference

A more fruitful area of law in relation to establishing the legal liability of informal and formal carers – and which is particularly important in relation to the category of psychological abuse – may be in the tort of wrongful interference, established in the case of *Wilkinson v. Downton* [1872] 2 QB 57. The tort is not well developed, and its scope is a matter of academic debate, with commentators increasingly recognizing its enormous potential (Williams, 1983; Brazier, 1988; Fricker, 1992; Cretney, 1993). The case establishes that liability can arise where physical or psychological harm has been indirectly caused to the plaintiff by an intentional act of the defendant.

It may not, however, be necessary to show a *deliberate* intention to cause the plaintiff the harm which resulted, it if can be shown that the defendant acted recklessly. It might, therefore, apply to a situation in which an individual suffered psychological harm as a result of being tricked into entering residential care by unscrupulous relations or those working in the so-called caring professions (Brearley, 1982).

A legal principle, similar to the tort of wrongful interference, has been developed in America. Liability can arise as the result of extreme and outrageous conduct, which intentionally or recklessly, causes severe emotional distress. It appears that the resulting distress need not amount to a recognizable psychiatric illness. What is 'extreme' and 'outrageous' is to be determined in each individual case. In the leading case of *Nickerson v. Hodge* [1920] 84 50 37, damages were awarded to a mentally infirm elderly woman who had been subjected to unsolicited ridicule. The case illustrates the American concern with the development of 'dignity' law, a development which is long overdue in the British context. At last, the tort of harassment has now been recognized by the English courts. In a recent decision, the Court of Appeal confirmed this as a separate tort and noted the wide powers at common law to make whatever orders the court considers just and necessary (*Burris v. Azadani* [1995], *The Times*, 9 August).

Although verbal abuse leading to psychological suffering may not, in the absence of gesticulation, give rise to an action for trespass to person, an alternative action might be based on the tort of defamation. It would be necessary to show that the effect was to subject the victim to hatred, contempt or ridicule so as to lower the plaintiff's reputation in the estimation of ordinary sensible people (*Parmiter v. Coupland* [1840] 6 M & W 105; *Sim v. Stretch* [1936] 2 All ER 1237).

Financial abuse

Legal intervention is particularly appropriate in cases of financial abuse since it is unlikely that social workers, and those in allied professions, will be competent to deal with these. As with physical and psychological abuse, a range of remedies is available, including possibly rescission of the contract (because undue influence had been exercised by one party in relation to the other party to the contract); an action for damages for trespass to goods or for conversion; or, where a dishonest motive can be established, in the tort of deceit. Prosecution for theft or fraud may also be possible. A discussion of the technical legal rules is, however, beyond the scope of this chapter.

Contracts and wills can be set aside if undue influence can be shown (*Lloyds Bank v. Bundy* [1975] QB 326; *Re Craig deceased* [1971] Ch.95). For trespass to goods to be established, it is probably necessary for the act to have been committed with intent. Conversion is the wrongful interference with a plaintiff's right to possession of his/her goods. It essentially means treating an elderly person's goods as your own, and could include, for instance, destroying or misusing goods, or refusing to return them on demand. If the tort of deceit is established, the plaintiff may be entitled to aggravated, that is, additional damages for injury to his/her feelings (Brazier, 1988). Indeed the legal position has been clarified by the Torts (Interference with Goods) Act 1977.

An action might therefore be initiated simply after a refusal to return the goods on request. Normally, a plaintiff would sue for damages, but the legislation also provides a suitable remedy for those who actually want the goods returned. If the goods, for instance, are predominantly of sentimental value it would be appropriate to apply for an order for the delivery of the goods and for payment for any consequential damage to them (s.3(2)). The law also allows for direct action. A person entitled to the possession of goods of which he/she has been wrongly deprived may re-take them. No more than reasonable force can be used.

Among the examples of financial abuse quoted by American and British studies are instances where family members had removed money from the bank accounts of elderly relatives without permission, and where nursing home proprietors have refused to return possessions and goods (Breckman and Adelman, 1988; Grant and Griffiths, 1993). Considerable sums were often involved. Other victims had their homes or other property put into another person's name, without their permission. Several victims had personal belongings, such as jewellery or furniture, taken from their homes by relatives or by landlords. Research concludes that the threat of legal intervention is often sufficient to rectify the abuse (Sengstock and Barrett, 1986).

One method by which an individual can protect him/herself against the possibility of financial abuse in old age is to create an Enduring Power of Attorney in anticipation of loss of capacity to conduct his/her own affairs. An Enduring Power of Attorney allows the donee to plan for that loss of capacity. He/she can appoint a chosen person to administer his/her affairs upon incapacity, and give general or specific instructions as to the manner in which it is to be done. The Court of Protection exercises a supervisory jurisdiction over Enduring Powers of Attorney. The ability to plan ahead in this way is welcome. It ensures that, so far as practicable, the donor has maximum control over the conduct of his/her affairs following incapacity.

His/her views, expressed during a period of capacity, must be respected and will be binding on the Attorney.

Another means of protecting a person who lacks mental capacity is through the Court of Protection which exists for the 'protection and management of the property and affairs of a person under a disability'. In the words of Ungoed-Thomas, J. in *Re W*. [1970] 2 All ER 502, it 'has exclusive jurisdiction over all the property and affairs of the patient in all their aspects; but not the management of care of the patient's person'. There is no flexibility at present in this 'all or nothing approach'.

Before it can exercise its jurisdiction the Court must be satisfied that the person is, by reason of mental disorder, incapable of managing his/her property and affairs. Mental disorder is defined in section 1 of the Mental Health Act 1983 as 'mental illness, arrested or incomplete development of mind, psychopathic disorder and other disorder or disability of mind'. The nature of the medical evidence needed to satisfy the Court is not specified. This is unfortunate, given the vagueness of the definition of mental disorder. Some confused elderly people may be placed under the Court's jurisdiction without proper consideration of their mental state.

In its recent report on mental incapacity the Law Commission (1995) recognizes that the current arrangements for managing the affairs of individuals without capacity are unsatisfactory and recommends extending the powers of proxy decision-making to include health and personal matters.

Abuse of civil liberties

The United Kingdom lacks a written constitution, but since 1966 British citizens have had the right to make complaints to the European Commission of Human Rights on the basis that their rights under the Convention for the Protection of Human Rights and Fundamental Freedoms (the European Convention) have been transgressed. The Convention addresses a wide range of civil rights including the right to life (Art. 2), the prohibition of torture, inhuman or degrading treatment (Art. 3), the right to privacy, and respect for family life, home and correspondence (Art. 8) and the right not to be discriminated against on the grounds *inter alia* of birth or 'other' status (Art. 14). Discrimination on the grounds of age might fall within the 'other' status category. Family lawyers are increasingly advocating the use of the Convention in respect to parent/child/family relationships (O'Donnell, 1995; Clements, 1994), but its use in relation to the abuse of the rights of elderly people remains untested. However, success with respect to other client groups suggests that much might be achieved by greater use of the procedure. Its purpose is to protect individuals from arbitrary interference by public authorities. According to a Dutch case (*X and Y v. Netherlands* [1986] 8 EHRR 235), however, it seems that a complaint might succeed on the basis of a state's failure to protect an individual's privacy against interference by another private individual. The case concerned the sexual abuse, in a private residential home, of a 16-year-old young woman with learning difficulty. The complaint succeeded because it was held that the Dutch civil and criminal codes provided insufficient legal protection.

Proceedings before the European Court may take up to five years or more. In any case, the primary function of the Court is not to offer a remedy to individual victims, but to expose violations of the Convention by individual states (Bailey et al., 1991).

In the British context, the lack of statutory and common law protection is a cause for concern. There are statutory rules only in relation to matters of race, sex, marital status and, very recently, disability. The common law similarly remains underdeveloped giving, for example, no specific right of action for breaches of privacy (*Kaye v. Robertson* [1991] FSR 62).

Changes in attitude

Some of the worst cases of elder abuse could be dealt with more effectively now, without any change to the existing legislative and constitutional framework. What is mainly needed is a shift in professional attitudes and better cross-disciplinary understanding (Ashton, 1994).

In its recent report on mental incapacity, the Law Commission has set out proposals for general reform of the law in this field. These include a new definition of incapacity; encouraging people to take decisions for themselves which they are able to take; but where intervention is necessary in their own interests, or for the protection of others, that intervention should be as limited as possible and should aim at achieving what the individual would have wanted; and that proper safeguards are provided against exploitation, neglect and physical sexual or psychological abuse. It sets out a number of possible options which include more comprehensive advanced directions, designated decision-making procedures; reform of existing procedures such as guardianship under the Mental Health Act 1983; and a new judicial body with jurisdiction in the field of mental incapacity. Undoubtedly, radical changes in the law are necessary to meet a growing need.

If the hallmark of full citizenship is the exercise of rights, then it appears that many elderly people experience only incomplete citizenship. Nowhere is this more clearly seen than in the context of elder abuse.

Abuse of Older People:
Sociological Perspectives

Chris Phillipson

Maltreatment of older people, within the community and inside residential institutions, has been an enduring feature of our social history. At worst, this has taken the form of outright persecution of those who, lacking resources of any kind, were thrown upon the mercy of their fellow citizens. Thomas (1978), for example, notes that tensions arising from the dependent status of older women played a significant role in the witchcraft craze that swept through many parts of Western society from the sixteenth to the later seventeenth centuries. At another level, maltreatment has been expressed through inter-generational conflicts of various kinds: through the elder's control over property and the blockage of the aspirations of younger kin (Stearns, 1986); through the pressures faced by an unmarried daughter left to care for her parents (Bardwell, 1926); or through the crisis generated by economic recession, as families struggled with the contradictions of meeting the care needs of both older and younger generations (Murphy, 1931).

But the meanings attached to, and the concerns expressed about, mistreatment of the old, have varied greatly from generation to generation. It is in the last two decades (as we saw in Chapter 3) that we have attempted to translate a generalized concern about the suffering of the old into a more precisely defined concept of abuse. But the transition has been a difficult one, raising complex problems about the way in which social relationships in later life are defined, and the reasons given for focusing on some problems to the exclusion of others. The purpose of this chapter is, first, to clarify some of the sociological issues which surround the concept of elder abuse; secondly, to examine some of the questions it raises for understanding the lives of older people; thirdly, to identify some principles for those involved in working in the field of elder abuse.

The issue of domestic violence

The concern with elder abuse reflects a more general focus on the issue of family violence. This is shown in the language of the debate (for example the early description of abuse in terms of 'granny battering', Eastman, 1983), and in the anxiety about the changing pattern of family life and its effects on groups such as older people. In his classic study *The Family Life of Old People*, Peter Townsend had defined the centrality of family relationships in the following way:

> if many of the processes and problems of ageing are to be understood, old people must be studied as members of families (which usually means extended families of three generations); and if this is true, those concerned with health and social administration, must at every stage view old people as an inseparable part of a family group, which is more than just a residential unit. They are not simply individuals, let alone 'cases' occupying beds or chairs. They are members of families and whether or not they are treated as such largely determines their security, their health, and their happiness. (Townsend, 1963: 227)

Yet the anxiety of the 1980s was precisely that the family was in some sense moving away from being concerned with the plight of its elderly members. Despite the extensive literature dealing with the vital role of informal carers, by the end of the decade there was renewed emphasis, expressed in the debate around inter-generational conflict, about the divergent interests as regards financial and social support for the care of the old (Johnson et al., 1989; Callahan, 1987; Walker, 1996). Running alongside this debate was the growing evidence about the way in which families could inflict damage on their most vulnerable and weakest members. Dobash and Dobash, in a major comparative survey of family violence, note that: 'It is . . . known that the family is filled with many different forms of violence and oppression, including physical, sexual and emotional, and that violence is perpetrated on young and old alike' (Dobash and Dobash, 1992: 2; see also Gelles, 1987).

For older people, there are considerable implications (and contradictions) in such observations. On the one side, changes in community care are moving older people back towards support from the informal care system (Phillipson, 1992a). On the other side, there would appear to be evidence that it is precisely this system which can produce damage to the lives of older people, and especially the very old (Department of Health, 1992). At the same time, it might be argued that locating elder abuse within the spectrum of family violence raises more difficulties than it solves. Is family violence the most significant form of oppression experienced by older people? What evidence do we have for maltreatment outside domestic settings? To what extent do theoretical perspectives support a broader view of the problems faced by older people? In dealing with this issue, we shall first look at the question of how family violence is defined before proceeding to examine its attribution to the lives of older people. A major theme of this chapter will be to explore the extent to which elder abuse has become more visible in the 1980s and 1990s. This development will be related to changes in family structure over the past 30 years, and to alternative perspectives on the position of older people in society.

The scope of family violence

Linda George (1989), in a major review of the politics of domestic violence, has challenged the view that the current problems in this area are more significant (or unprecedented in scale) in comparison with the past. She suggests that there has been an ebb-and-flow pattern of concern about violence over the past century, this suggesting that its incidence has changed much less than its visibility (see also Phillips, 1989). George goes on to argue that:

> Concern with family violence has been a weathervane identifying the prevailing winds of anxiety about family life in general. The periods of silence about family life are as significant as the periods of concern. Both reveal the longing for peaceful family life, the strength of the image of home life as a harmonious, loving, and supportive environment. One response to this longing has been a tendency to deny, even suppress, the evidence that families are not always like that. Denying the problem serves to punish the victims of family violence doubly by forcing them to hide their problems and to blame themselves. Even the aggressors in family violence suffer from denial, since isolation and the feeling that they are unique make it difficult to ask for the help they want. (George, 1989: 2)

Following the above argument, George suggests that it is possible to see family violence as historically and politically constructed. This, she argues, can be seen in two senses:

> First, the very definition of what constitutes acceptable domestic violence, and appropriate responses to it, developed and then varied according to political moods and the force of certain political movements. Second, violence among family members arises from family conflicts which are not only historically influenced but political in themselves, in the sense of that word having to do with power relations. Family violence usually arises out of power struggles in which individuals are contesting real resources and benefits. These contests arise not only from personal aspirations but also from changing norms and conditions. (George, 1989: 3)

The framework provided by George offers some important insights into the current debates about elder abuse. First, it is clear that the debate about elder abuse has run parallel with, and has itself been influenced by, the wider debate about the resourcing of an ageing population. Thus, rather than ageing as such (and the growth in the number of very elderly people) being a key factor in the apparent 'increase' in abuse, a more substantive issue has been the support to be provided to older people and the relationships between the different groups providing this help. Following this argument, the key issue with the discourse on elder abuse is the selective way in which the problem has been framed. Over the past ten years, the concern has been with the direct abuse of older people (and especially physical abuse) by their informal carers (Block and Sinnott, 1979; Department of Health, 1992). Yet the actual research from properly conducted surveys (as opposed to studies of the experiences of self-selected professionals) gives no grounds for believing that direct abuse is a significant problem amongst older people. Crystal (1986) argues that the impression given by research is of substantial numbers of older people being beaten up by their children. This, he suggests, is 'palpably wrong'. He comments: 'Carefully read . . . studies typically reflect much lower rates of actual direct abuse; indeed, one of the problems in the research has been the difficulty in identifying sufficient numbers of truly abused victims to study' (Crystal, 1986: 333).

The argument here is not that abuse of older people does not take place (after all, as Sprey and Matthews, 1989, suggest, even *one* case is socially unacceptable) but that recognition should be given to the fact that there are a number of forms of harm or endangerment which affect the lives of older people. Crystal, reviewing the American experience, makes the important point that

> [Elder] abuse . . . while dramatic . . . is not necessarily the most severe [problem facing the old] . . . Experience with a broad range of programs designed to respond to harm and endangerment – adult protection services programs in particular – suggests that abuse is only one of a variety of problems encountered by impaired adults. . . ; that it is not necessarily the most common or most severe form of harm or endangerment requiring protective intervention; and that where abuse does appear to be manifest, it is usually encountered as part of a complex set of problems, often revolving around an unmet or poorly met care need and/or an abuser who is himself or herself functionally compromised. (Crystal, 1986: 333–4)

This argument raises the issue of why abuse, and particularly domestic abuse, has appeared on the agenda of local and central government. Set beside the problems associated with the deprivation of key services from older people, the problems associated with the decline in housing during the 1980s, and the more generalized problem of age discrimination, the focus on abuse would appear somewhat selective. This does not undermine the case for attempting to understand family violence as it affects older people (to repeat, even one case is unacceptable) but it does suggest that issues about the incidence and prevalence of domestic abuse should be placed in a wider context which recognizes important changes in the family and community lives of older people (Allen and Perkins, 1995; Biggs et al., 1995).

Changing family structures

The argument developed by George raises important questions about the construction of abuse within different historical and social settings.[1] Here, and building on the argument outlined by Stearns (1986), it is important to distinguish between the period from the late nineteenth century to the 1950s (the modern age), and the phase from the mid-1950s to the mid-1990s (the contemporary period). These periods represent very different contexts for older people, in terms of their relationships both within the family and with other social and political institutions.

There was a build-up in the size of urban households in the nineteenth century, with the augmentation of the nuclear family coming through children remaining at home for longer periods, a rising incidence of unrelated lodgers, and an increase in the co-residence of non-nuclear kin (Seccombe, 1991). In terms of the last of these, older people were especially important, with a growing tendency for women to return to live with one of their daughters following the death of their husbands. Seccombe (1991) suggests that the taking in of widows appears to have been very common; Anderson's (1974) study of mid-nineteenth century Preston shows that over 80 per cent of women aged 65 and over were living with their children. More generally, it is the density of kinship networks which appears to be an important feature of the way many communities developed.

This last point was clearly illustrated in post-war studies by Sheldon (1948) in Wolverhampton, Townsend (1957) in Bethnal Green, and Willmott and Young (1960) in Woodford. In Wolverhampton, in the late 1940s, one-third of older people had relatives living within a mile (4 per cent with children living next door). In Bethnal Green, in the early 1950s, each older person had an average of 13 relatives living within a mile; 53 per cent of older people had their nearest married child either in the same dwelling or within five minutes' walk away; in Woodford, the figure was 40 per cent, in Wolverhampton, approaching 50 per cent.

The 1960s, however, introduced a significant break with the pattern identified above. Richard Wall (1992) in fact stresses the basic continuities in household structure over several centuries, with a marked change in living patterns only coming in the last 30 years, with the increase in those living alone, and the corresponding decline in those living with people other than their spouse. By the late 1990s, 14 per cent of older people in Great Britain lived with a child, in comparison with 40 per cent at the start of the 1950s. Similar trends have been cited in the case of the United States. In 1900, more than 60 per cent of all persons aged 65 and over resided with their children. Haber and Gratton observe: 'Whether as household head or as a dependant of their offspring, the elderly shared residences with the young, uniting their assets and abilities as well as their conflicts' (Haber and Gratton, 1994: 44). As in the case of Britain, improved personal resources (especially with the growth of pensions) encouraged the development of separate residences. Haber and Gratton note that the allocation of pensions brought two important trends: steep declines in complex living arrangements and striking increases in independent, autonomous households. By 1962, the proportion of the old who lived with their children had dropped to 25 per cent and by 1975 to only 14 per cent.

At first glance, these figures are difficult to reconcile with concern about abuse, given that it developed at a time when older people were becoming more dispersed and separate from immediate kin. On deeper investigation, however, it is possible to identify factors which brought to the surface awareness of the nature of abuse which had not been present in the period up to the mid-1960s. What were the key factors for each period which either limited or enhanced awareness of abuse? In the first period, up until the mid-1960s, three points should be noted: the lack of conceptualization of the problem; the mediating role of the kinship network; and the characteristics of the older population. The first of these is probably crucial in terms of the lack of definition of abuse as a distinctive social problem. This itself is bound up with the very modest expectations about the standard of living which older people had a right to expect. In an important sense, a concept of abuse and neglect can only emerge when society sees the achievement of a particular standard of care for the old as important. This was certainly not in evidence in the pre-war period, and it took some time to develop even after the war (Phillipson, 1982). In the context of scares about the effects of population ageing, the possibility of the maltreatment of the old (if it was taking place) was simply not an area which had to be tackled with any degree of urgency.

Another factor is the extent to which the social relations of the old were mediated by relatively dense kinship structures. One possibility is that these may have provided an informal check on certain types of abuse (though further research is needed to test this possibility). Equally, the external checks on family behaviour were less strong, given the absence of any professional or legislative focus on the needs of older people (a factor which undoubtedly marks this period out from the later one). A further point to consider is that the importance of kinship ran alongside a higher level of tolerance, by society at least, of domestic violence (a point developed in the work of George, 1989, and other feminist researchers working in the area of abuse).

Finally, numbers alone may be an important part of the explanation. In terms of the group cited as the most vulnerable to abuse (those aged 75 and over), this was a relatively small group up until the 1940s. The significant shift comes from the 1950s onwards, with the number of people aged 75 plus in Great Britain increasing from 1.7 million to nearly 4 million by the early 1990s. The changing relationship of this numerically (and proportionately) more important group within the family became a crucial area of concern from the 1970s onwards.

Elder abuse and kinship obligations

As the above would suggest, changing norms and conditions surrounding family care are likely to be crucial in influencing debates on family violence. This point may be especially relevant for understanding the emergence in the 1970s and 1980s of abuse as a social problem. In this context, it is important to relate the debate about strain within family relationships to changes in attitudes to the giving and receiving of family care. The evidence from a number of research studies is that older people are moving away from wanting any dependence on children, especially that which implies a long-term commitment arising out of a chronic illness (Lee, 1985), or the need to provide personal care (Ungerson, 1987). Such arguments about changes in preferences for care are highlighted by research on changing patterns of kinship obligations. Finch (1989), in a major review of work in this area, has highlighted the complex set of rules determining the provision of family care. She notes that kin relationships do not operate on the basis of a ready-made set of moral rules, clearly laid out for older people and their carers to follow. In particular, the 'sense of obligation' which marks the distinctive character of kin relations, does not follow a reliable and consistent path in terms of social practice:

> It is actually much less reliable than that. It is nurtured and grows over time between some individuals more strongly than others, and its practical conse- quences are highly variable. It does have a binding quality, but that derives from commitments built up between real people over many years, not from an abstract set of moral values. (Finch, 1989: 242)

This argument is important because it cuts across a central thrust of current policy on community care, namely, that families act as though there are cul- tural and moral scripts which they follow in supporting older people in times of crisis or dependency. Moreover, the argument is taken a stage further by some researchers with the assertion that older people themselves follow this path, with an almost instinctive tendency to move towards the family rather than bureaucratic agencies. According to Wenger:

> Research from a wider section of developed countries demonstrates that not only does most care come from the family . . . but that most people think that this is where the responsibility should lie. (Wenger, 1984: 14)

But this argument relies upon a historical perspective which may no longer be acceptable as an accurate portrayal of the kind of care that people want. Families are variable in their response to requests for help and, in any event, as Finch points out, the care given is always negotiated within a social and biographical context. In this regard, it is possible to see the debate about abuse as reflecting a wider discussion about the nature of family care: who should provide it? And under what conditions? Abuse, in fact, though a lived experience for some older people, may also be a metaphor for the way in which families and older people are changing in terms of care preferences (Phillipson, 1992a). Care for older people is *not* defined by any clear social norms (in contrast to care for children). It thus follows that our definition of abuse is equally uncertain. The reasons are not just that older people are adults and hence supposedly in control of their lives, but also that issues of who should provide care and on what terms are in a state of flux. The idea of abuse may be as much an expression of this uncertainty as much as a rep- resentation of the real experiences of older people. To repeat: this does not minimize the importance of abuse at an individual level; it does, however, indicate the complexity of abuse as a social issue.

Power and the family

A final set of issues arising from George's work is where older people stand in relation to different forms of family violence. Here, it seems important to distinguish carefully elder abuse from other forms of domestic abuse. It is misleading to argue that: 'Elder abuse is clearly only part of a spectrum of domestic violence which affects all ages' (SSI, 1992). Elder abuse is similar but also very different. Unlike in other types of domestic violence there may not be a clear victim or perpetrator. Because most elderly adults are legally (and actually) autonomous human beings, it may be difficult to determine who is doing the abusing. This leads, as Phillips has pointed out, to difficult questions for professionals working in the field:

> Is it the responsibility of an adult child to enforce rules of cleanliness on a legally competent elder when the elder does not want to be clean? What is the effect of geographic distance or filial distance on legal and moral responsibilities? Who is the victim and who is the perpetrator in situations where a legally competent elder refuses to act in his or her own best interests? And perhaps even more basic than any of these is the question of how can responsibility be assigned in a society that has yet to establish clear criteria regarding the minimum material and emotional rights to which every individual in society is entitled? (Phillips, 1986: 89)

Phillips's argument highlights the complex issues facing professionals working in the field of elder abuse. Contrary to the impression given in much of the elder abuse literature, direct cases of abuse will be the exception. The rule will be a far murkier area, where acts of omission and commission intermingle, and where elders may themselves be partly involved in the construction of abusive situations. In contrast, the problem with the debate on elder abuse is that it too often degenerates into a battle between 'innocent' elders and 'bad' families. On the one side, we have a stereotyped view of the old as relatively powerless, undemanding and invariably blameless in terms of the outcomes of family dynamics. On the other side, there are families for whom various 'risk factors' can be identified, ranging from psychopathology on the part of the abuser to various forms of stress (Breckman and Adelman, 1988). This division has of course been challenged in more sophisticated studies, with researchers such as Pillemer (1986) showing the extent to which the *abuser* may be the dependent one in terms of their relations with an older person. But the tendency (especially in the British literature) has been to ignore such findings and to focus on the older person as a victim within a disturbed or highly stressed network of family relations (Eastman, 1984). This presentation is, however, misleading in how it presents the power relations running through families involved in the abuse of older people. Moreover, it is also important to acknowledge the extent to which abusive situations are themselves socially created, through low incomes, inadequate community care, and ageism within society. Care, and family care in particular, is deeply influenced by this wider context of oppression affecting older people. The tendency has been to focus on the influence of 'family pathology' in creating certain types of abuse. But highlighting the role of individual families ignores wider issues about the labels attached to older people and the resources available to them to resist maltreatment. Attention to these broader issues will be vital if progress is to be made in the elder abuse debate.

Institutionalized abuse

The identification of elder abuse as a form of family violence has led to an additional problem: the failure, especially in the British context, to give proper weight to abuse in institutional settings. This must be considered surprising given the long history of maltreatment of the old within Poor Law institutions, elderly people's homes, and long-stay hospitals (Townsend, 1962; Robb, 1967). Contemporary evidence of abuse is not hard to find. The first 96 cases of the Registered Homes Tribunal provide examples of abuse and neglect. *Verbal* aggression was characteristic of a number of the cases. For example, in *Mattarooa v. East Sussex County Council*:

> Concern from various sources had been expressed over a number of years focusing on the cold and regimented manner in which the residents were treated. It was clear that a number of persons involved in the placing of residents approached Mrs Mattarooa to try to improve the situation, but the regime of strict control, concentration on the minutiae of table manners, humiliation of residents and lack of development of their emotional needs continued. Neighbours who gave evidence reported hearing shouting and abuse and use of such terms as *'idiot'*, *'stupid'* and even *'animal'* to the residents. One resident was observed at a day centre with a bruised face and bleeding nose. The police became involved but no charges were brought and the tribunal accepted Mrs Mattarooa's story that she had not struck the woman and that her face had become bruised when she accidentally bumped it. (Harman and Harman, 1989: 21)

A combination of *physical abuse* and *verbal aggression* is contained in the following case of *Scorer and Akhtar v. Cambridgeshire County Council*:

> There was mental cruelty in that some residents had their hair rinsed with cold water, and that some residents were sent up to their rooms by way of punishment, and that some were abused and insulted by being called names to their faces and humiliated by being shamed in front of other residents. They were physically abused in that some residents were roughly handled, pushed and pulled unnecessarily, frog-marched, slapped; that some had their clothes yanked off; that two residents were roughly treated when certain medical processes were taking place . . . There was verbal abuse in that Mrs Scorer shouted at residents; insulted and humiliated them by calling them names (fat old pig, stupid, dirty, smelly, filthy), so that residents were frightened. All these matters constituted a serious risk to the residents' well-being. (Harman and Harman, 1989: 66)

Abuse may also occur where homes deny basic standards of privacy to residents. This was an area explored in the report *Not Such Private Places* (Counsel and Care, 1991), a survey of private and voluntary residential and nursing homes in Greater London. The study found that 70 per cent of all types of homes expect older people to use commodes within hearing of their room mate. A large proportion of homes (24 per cent) expected residents to use commodes in shared rooms where no privacy curtains were available. The report also found a high proportion of nursing homes failing to ensure that residents could lock their rooms both on the inside and the outside (73 per cent). Finally, a high proportion (one-third) of homes did not provide any specific lockable storage space for residents. The report commented:

The observations of our visiting caseworkers produced some sad anecdotes of individual homes' lack of respect for privacy of their residents, particularly when caseworkers were shown round the homes . . . All too often residents' doors are not knocked on and the officer-in-charge simply entered a room without explaining the reason for the intrusion. This can result in embarrassing situations for the visitor but much more importantly for the residents themselves. Bursting in on a resident on a commode is an all too common occurrence. (Counsel and Care, 1991: 18–19)

Negative attitudes to older people may be more visible in long-term care facilities because of the greater concentration of older people in a single location. Kayser-Jones has grouped the most frequently reported complaints of staff abuse into four categories:

1   *Infantilization* – treating the patient as an irresponsible, undependable child;
2   *Depersonalization* – providing services in an assembly line fashion, disregarding the patient's individual needs;
3   *Dehumanization* – not only ignoring elderly persons but stripping them of privacy and of their capacity to assume responsibility for their own lives;
4   *Victimization* – attacking the older person's physical and moral integrity through verbal abuse, threats, intimidation, theft, blackmail, or corporal punishments. (cited in Monk, 1990: 7)

The categories identified by Kayser-Jones directly correspond to those developed in the area of domestic abuse. It now seems important to accept the view that there is a broad spectrum of maltreatment of the old in both private and public settings. It is invidious to select any one for particular emphasis (unless this is part of a clearly defined research strategy) and we should look for an approach which sees abuse as an issue which is not tied to any one context or relationship. (For further discussion of abuse in residential settings, see Chapter 11, this volume.)

Theoretical perspectives

One way of widening the debate on elder abuse is by clearer integration of social theory and observation about abuse of older people. To illustrate this point three theoretical perspectives will be reviewed: interactionist theory, political economy theory, and critical gerontological perspectives as developed from the humanities. These approaches will be used to identify the complex issues underpinning the debate about elder abuse.

Interactionist theory, following Blumer (1969) and McCall and Simmons (1966), suggests that the way social life is organized arises from within society itself and out of the processes of interaction between its members. In this approach abuse and neglect would be viewed as a consequence of the interaction within either families or institutions. More specifically, the theory would predict that processes arising from social and biological ageing might change role definitions within the social groups with which the older person was interacting. Such alterations might challenge hitherto stable identities, causing stress in social relationships. This could be resolved by the negotiation of new self-validating identities. Alternatively, forms of psychological abuse (such as infantilization) could emerge, possibly leading to other forms of abuse and neglect.

The implication of an interactionist perspective is that our understanding of abuse should acknowledge the way in which ageing processes affect workers and carers at a personal level. Contact with older people may be difficult (or may be avoided) because it is seen as unrewarding or reminds carers of their own ageing. This is partly because they have no direct experience of old age and therefore have to rely on social stereotypes. As these are predominantly negative they create perceptions of our own future old age as a time of dependency, poor health, poverty and vulnerability, even though this may bear little relationship to the lived experience of many older people or the old age we may expect.

The likelihood is, however, that those most vulnerable to abuse may well experience some of the chronic conditions associated with old age. Age is particularly associated with changes to the physical appearance and functioning of the human body. This is both the most obvious visible way of identifying old age as well as being a disconcerting link that workers and carers can see with themselves. Physical decline is often seen to the exclusion of more positive attributes. Ageist attitudes and abusive behaviour may arise from the way in which older people come to be seen as failures as a result of the effects of chronic illness. The prevalence of disability increases from 12 per cent at age 65–69 to over 80 per cent above the age of 85. Arthritis and rheumatism affect 59 per cent of those 75 and over; poor eyesight 42 per cent; swelling of feet and legs 33 per cent, and giddiness 31 per cent (Victor, 1991).

These physical changes raise important issues in terms of how older people view themselves and how they are viewed by society. People are given full accreditation as human beings only when they have reached a relatively high level of cognitive, emotional and biological development. This aspect of how human development is perceived has major implications for older people. Featherstone and Hepworth (1991: 376–7) suggest that:

> If the process of becoming an acceptable human being is dependent upon those developments, the loss of cognitive and other skills produces the danger of social unacceptability, unemployability and being labelled as less than fully human. Loss of bodily controls carries similar penalties of stigmatization and ultimately exclusion. Deep [or late] old age is personally and socially disturbing because it holds out the prospect of the loss of some or all of these controls. Degrees of loss impair the capacity to be counted as a competent adult. Indeed, the failure of bodily controls can point to a more general loss of self-image . . . The loss of bodily controls also impairs other interactional skills, and the loss of real power through decline in these competencies may induce others to feel confident in treating the individual as a less than full adult. Carers may, for example, feel secure in the belief that the person 'inside' will not be able to return to wreak any vengeance on them whatever their former social status or class background.

Changes to the human body may, therefore, be a crucial agent in creating the conditions for abuse and neglect and for disturbing social interaction between older people and other family members. This has important implications for the prevention of abuse which we will turn to in the final section of this chapter.

Interactionist perspectives focus on the question of how individuals adapt and respond to old age. Political economy perspectives, in contrast, examine the impact of society on the lives of older people, both within and beyond domestic settings.[2] This approach adopts the view that old age is a *socially* as well as a *biologically* constructed status. In this context, many of the experiences affecting older people can be seen as the product of a particular division of labour and structure of inequality rather than as a natural product of the ageing process. Walker (1980) encapsulated this perspective in the notion of the *social creation of dependency in old age* and Townsend (1981) used a similar term when he described the *structured dependency* of older people. This dependency is seen to be the consequence of the forced exclusion of older people from work; and of the experience of poverty, institutionalization and restricted domestic and community roles. Finally, Estes (1979) has used the term *the ageing enterprise*: 'to call particular attention to how the aged are often processed and treated as a commodity and to the fact that the age-segregated policies that fuel the ageing enterprise are socially-divisive "solutions" that single-out, stigmatize, and isolate the aged from the rest of society.'

The value of the political economy approach is that it places the struggles of carers and older people within a framework of social and political resources and ideologies. The implication of this approach is that abuse may arise from the way in which older people come to be marginalized by society (and by the services which they are targeted to receive). If people are predisposed to abuse the old because of their biological dependency, the likelihood is increased by social forces which discriminate both against the old as well as against those involved in their care (Bornat et al., 1985; McEwan, 1989; Estes, 1993). Such a perspective would suggest that the challenge to abuse must be seen as an issue of social policy as well as a problem to do with dysfunctional families (Department of Health, 1992).

Finally, the 1980s saw important work emerging from scholars working in a number of disciplines within the humanities.[3] In particular, the work of Cole (1992), Moody (1992), and Kastenbaum (1992) introduced a new set of reflections about the nature of ageing, rooted in a discourse focused on the doubts and anxieties pervading a post-modern age. These writers identified the absence of meaning in the lives of older people, and the sense of doubt and uncertainty which seemed to infuse their daily routines and relationships. Cole in his landmark study *The Journey of Life* (1992), highlighted the complex existential questions faced by all older people. Elderly people, he noted, may live 10, 20 or more years beyond gainful employment. But what sort of life should they have in this period? Is there something special they are supposed to do? Is old age really the culmination of life? Or is it simply an anticlimax to be endured until medical science can abolish it? Cole goes on to comment:

> We must acknowledge that our great progress in the material and physical con-
> ditions of life has been achieved at a high spiritual and ethical price. Social security
> has not enhanced ontological security or dignity in old age. The elderly continue
> to occupy an inferior status in the moral community marginalized by an economy
> and culture committed to the scientific management of growth without limit.
> (Cole, 1992: 237)

This argument is related to a broader theme concerning the anxieties characteristic of a post-modern age. A feature of post-modernity is the way that it reconstructs the life course, with greater flexibility between hitherto stable and predictable transitions (Moody, 1992). This development brings opportunities for positive redefinitions of ageing, linked, for example with some of the ideas associated with the 'third age' (Laslett, 1989a). On the other hand, it increases the ambivalence people may feel about late old age, affected as it is by an increase in major issues associated with poverty and poor health.

The argument from the humanities is that these problems are not addressed within the context of a society which diminishes rather than enriches the store of cultural meanings associated with ageing. From this theoretical perspective, elder abuse may be seen as exemplifying in crucial ways the ambivalent feelings society has towards older people. On the one side, the extension of the lifespan is a triumph of modernity, reflected in the activity of the state in areas such as public health and the development of the welfare state. On the other side, the argument from a post-modern per-spective is that the basis of individual identity and security remains uncertain, and never more so than in the period leading up to death (Giddens, 1991). The idea, experience and metaphor of abuse remains, in this context, part of a world which has manufactured old age but which has left unanswered the question about its purpose and meaning. The impli-cation of this argument is that the ultimate challenge to abuse will come from a clarification of the basis of ageing in what is now a post-industrial and post-modern world.

Conclusion: principles for tackling abuse

None of the above is to suggest that abuse and neglect should not be 'con-fronted' (and hopefully understood) in day-to-day health and social work. But some basic principles need to be observed as a guide for action. In con-clusion the following are offered for discussion:

1   Workers should be encouraged to be both vigilant about the possibility of abuse/neglect while being aware of the fact that there are no clear criteria for identifying abused elders and no good interventions that are totally acceptable to all the parties involved.

2 Shared decision-making is essential. Sharing should be conducted both by involving a range of professional workers in developing a strategy for tackling abuse and by ensuring that workers are supported in the decisions they make about protecting vulnerable elders.

3 Agencies will need to develop policies which empower older people in situations where they are leading marginal lives. Policies for tackling abuse must therefore be concerned with advocacy and strengthening self-care abilities in old age.

4 The emphasis in work with all older people in private households and residential settings, should be on how to develop lives free of mistreatment. This means focusing on a variety of areas, of which activities with informal carers, the primary focus of the Department of Health report, may be a relatively small part.

It seems clear that we are set for a major debate about the extent and nature of abuse of older people. The range of publications devoted to this topic is expanding, especially in areas such as training and research (McCreadie, 1991, 1996a; Pritchard, 1992, 1995; Phillipson and Biggs, 1992; Biggs and Phillipson, 1994; Biggs et al., 1995). However, it is important to place this discussion within a critical perspective which acknowledges the social construction of abuse and the influence of this on dynamics within individual families and communities. So far the debate has tended to focus on the risk factors which may be attributed to individual families. We must, however, pay attention to risks arising from ideologies about older people and the resources at their disposal. This dimension would seem to be an important next step for the debate on tackling the existence of elder abuse in society.

Notes

1 The historical background to abuse is developed more fully in Biggs et al. (1995), Chapter 2.

2 Minkler and Estes (1991) provide an excellent book of readings reviewing the political economy perspective.

3 Some recent work from researchers working in the humanities tradition is reviewed in Phillipson (1996b).

8

Rethinking Elder Abuse: Towards an Age and Gender Integrated Theory of Elder Abuse

Teri Whittaker

The way in which we think about a social problem will determine the methods of investigation and intervention used to explain and resolve it. This chapter starts from a position of dissatisfaction with current thinking and theorizing about elder abuse and from a belief in the importance of treating gender like age as an equally significant dimension of social life in general and of elder abuse in particular. As a researcher and practitioner in the area of elder abuse it has become increasingly clear to me that dominant models of elder abuse relating to carer stress and individual or inter-personal pathology are inadequate as explanatory frameworks and do little to help at the practice level which, as the Social Service Inspectorate report notes, is characterized by uncertainty, confusion, delay and inappropriate procedural guidelines (SSI, 1992).

The chapter does not however represent a bid for the supremacy of any one academic theory over another. All those involved in this area of study and practice are constantly thinking or theorizing about the meaning of elder abuse and grappling with the inadequacy of existing explanatory models. There is an urgent need for theorists and practitioners from various schools of thought to pool their conceptual and experiential resources in order to develop a more adequate theoretical base for future research, policy and practice formulations.

The overall concern, here, therefore, is to encourage theorists and prac-titioners alike to recognize and address the importance of age and gender dimensions of elder abuse at both personal and structural levels. Whether or not, and how, women and men experience and respond to abuse throughout the life course is a product of the interplay between their own unique indi-vidual circumstances and personalities and a wider social structure within which their experiences are mediated not just by age but also by gender and the connections between these and other forms of social disadvantage.

A critique of existing theory relating to elder abuse is followed by some suggestions as to how such theory could be reformulated and expanded to incorporate an understanding of both age and gender dimensions of elder abuse and the connections between personal or interpersonal experiences and wider economic, social and cultural processes. A synthesis of fully age and gender integrated formulations of political economy with life course approaches is proposed as a starting point from which those interested in research, policy and practice could begin to connect the personal or subjective meaning of elder abuse at the practice level to an analysis of the power inequality of older women and men embedded in wider social structures and attitudes.

The gendered nature of ageing

Ageing is a gendered process which men and women experience differently relative to other race and class dimensions and which fundamentally affects their life expectations and opportunities. Although both old men and women share some 'commonalities' in that they are more likely to experience poverty, poor housing and poor health as a result of their location within a social structure with particularly negative attitudes, images, provision and policies towards retirement and old age, there is also real diversity within and between them. Socially, age and gender based attitudes contribute to a double standard of ageing whereby old men are perceived as mature, distinguished and desirable whilst old women are seen more negatively as 'past it' (Sontag, 1978).

Social and cultural rules about women's reproductive and caring roles in the 'family' influence their location within the workforce, and the vast majority of women are employed in caring services. These roles also affect women's work opportunities and material standards of living. The consequences of women's involvement in the family and in caregiving together with institutionalized discrimination in the labour market and shorter and more intermittent employment records limit women's career opportunities, resulting in a lower average income than men throughout the life course (Bernard et al., 1995). This is especially so in later life when the gap between male and female earnings widens and the feminization of poverty becomes a key feature of many older women's lives.The structural disadvantage associated with social ageing is experienced differently at the individual level, according to class, gender and race locations within society, as well as by chronological and physiological ageing, which means that very old, very frail working-class and black women are more likely to lack the material or physical and mental assets they need to enjoy an autonomous old age and avoid abusive situations (Arber and Ginn, 1995).

Interest in chronological ageing has focused predominantly on increased longevity and on 'apocalyptic demography' (Clark, 1993) to fuel fears about rising welfare costs and the dependency associated with old age. These approaches have been used to depict dependency in old age and an intergenerational conflict whereby older people, the majority of whom are women, are perceived as a drain on the public purse and held responsible for poverty and recession (Johnson et al., 1989). This is especially so in relation to what has been called the 'fourth age' (Laslett, 1989a) a term used to refer to 'deep old age' (Featherstone and Hepworth, 1989) and/or to physiological decline. This has become increasingly separated from the 'third age' (Laslett, 1989b) which is seen as the apogee of life and as a period of creative fulfilment associated with younger elderly people and a view of old age as a time of personal growth, consumption and autonomy.

Women are more likely than men to enter and live through the third age into the fourth age and it is here that the gendered nature of physiological ageing is most apparent. Although Laslett's work is not strictly related to chronological age, the fourth age category is commonly used to refer to those over 85 and is associated with more negative views of ageing which have inadvertently been displaced from the young-old to the old-old. Here there is a marked gender imbalance, with women outnumbering men by three to one due to gender differences in mortality and prevalence, type and onset of disabilities. Consequently a significantly higher number of old women depend upon formal and informal care, which itself is a gendered process with women providing both higher levels and different types of more personal and labour intensive care in both formal and informal settings (Martin Matthews and Campbell, 1995). Who provides such care and how, when and where it is provided, and with what attitudes and support, will affect the nature and extent of an older person's sense of freedom, control and power.

Power, like age and gender dimensions of social life varies according to what it is in relation to or with, and how it operates in different contexts and settings is of crucial importance to the problem of elder abuse. In advanced old age, the social networks of old women are more likely to change in response to increasing disability and need for care. Old women are twice as likely as men to enter residential care and to be 'cared' for by other women. Where they do remain in their own homes they are more likely than older men to depend on the support of female adult children, rather than spouses. In either setting, there is significant scope for conflict and tension and for age and gender based power relationships which may be directly connected to violence and abuse.

Theorizing elder abuse

Given the gendered nature of ageing in Western societies and the fact that the world of the very old is predominantly a woman's world (Peace, 1986) with old women experiencing more and different types of abuse than old men, any adequate theory, research, or policy/practice developments should be informed by an understanding of both age and gender dimensions and the links between them and other forms of discrimination and disadvantage.

Such an approach would seek to connect the personal or subjective meaning of elder abuse to an analysis of the power inequality of older women and men embedded in the wider social structures and attitudes of society and to show how this affects their experiences of and responses to abuse. Abuse between two people can occur only if a power imbalance exists between them; one person perceives himself and is perceived by the other as being more powerful whilst the other perceives herself and is perceived as being relatively powerless. These beliefs and perceptions are not necessarily conscious but are derived from the detailed routines of daily life and the establishment of patterns of interaction which confirm and reinforce the relative positions of one as more powerful and the other as less powerful. Such patterns are not solely derived from the personalities, personal histories or interpersonal dynamics of those involved, but also from characteristics endowed by membership of particular groups in society which give some people the inherent advantage of more power while relatively disadvantaging others because they are members of groups whose structural position in society is weaker. In other words, the factors which trigger abuse are important but secondary: the context of a perception of power inequality in the home or institution buttressed by the age and gender-based power inequality in society is the primary context within which abuse occurs (Hughes, 1995).

This is a complex argument which may be difficult to grasp as it is concerned with the interface between society and the individual or between the personal and the political. The way in which the power structures of society infiltrate to a greater or lesser extent our personal lives and intimate relationships is crucial. How these are played out both within and between various groups of both younger and older men and women involved in abusive situations across a wide range of formal and informal care settings requires a theoretical framework which will locate both age and gender as central categories of analysis and treat them and the links between them and other forms of social disadvantage as equally important. However, a careful review of existing theory, research and policy analysis relating to elder abuse reveals a marked absence of such an approach and a failure to integrate fully age and gender dimensions of elder abuse and their connections with other forms of social disadvantage.

Until now, thinking and research relating to elder abuse has been predominantly policy driven and limited by a range of professionally defined, practice-based definitions or by theoretical approaches which have adopted an 'add on' approach to existing theory and attempted to fit elder abuse into it. There has been no attempt to develop a theory specific to elder abuse and the relevance of the 'add on' approach which assumes that elder abuse can be explained by extending mainstream social theory has not been considered critically.

Two approaches to current theorizing about elder abuse will be examined here. The first approach draws on Dollard's (1939) 'frustration–aggression' theory and on research relating to a situational stress model of elder abuse which has been enormously influential at research, policy and practice levels. This approach will be used to illustrate how theorists have sought to add age onto mainstream sociological theory and extend it to the problem of elder abuse. The second approach relates to political economy theories of ageing which have sought to add gender onto existing models and explain abuse in later life by reference to structural inequalities. It is argued that neither approach provides an adequate framework for understanding the interconnectedness of age and gender dimensions of elder abuse at either the personal or the political level.

Age, gender and the situational stress model of elder abuse

Of particular importance here is the use of the situational stress model of elder abuse which has been enormously influential in informing policy and practice interventions relating to elder abuse and in drawing attention to the needs of carers, arguably at the expense of the needs of those experiencing abuse. The situational model extends frustration–aggression theory (Dollard, 1939) which was originally developed to explain aggression and abuse among younger males and draws on research relating to child abuse to explain elder abuse in terms of the dependency of the victim and how this causes stress for the carer.

The situational stress model locates the problem of elder abuse within individual men, women and children and within the relationships between them rather than within an analysis of interpersonal relationships and their connection to the wider social structures that support and reinforce them. Although studies underpinned by this model generally agree that the overwhelming majority of victims are older women, the gender dimensions of elder abuse are rarely identified or discussed in any real depth. Within this model, age is 'added on' as a variable, as something which is interchangeable with other variables rather than being a central category of analysis.

This kind of approach has been criticized by McMullin (1995) who argues that mainstream social theory is inadequate because frameworks relating to the nature of work and family life for younger men, women or children cannot be extended to the lives of older people in general or to older women in particular. In other words, the lives and experiences of older men and women and how these are connected to wider social and political structures are unique, not simply by virtue of their age, but also because of their gender and the connections between these and their personal histories, life opportunities and expectations. Rather than reformulating frustration–aggression theory and treating social and family life and elder abuse as organized and structured around a particular set of age and gender-based power relationships which are in turn linked to and buttressed by wider social divisions, policies and practices, the situational stress model treats old age and associated decline and dependency as the basis for deviation from some ideal notion of caregiving. Within this model, elder abuse is located within a stereotypical and uncritical version of the family and underpinned by notions of burden, stress, inadequate care or personal pathology of either victim or abuser. The age and gender-based power and dependency relationships within the family and other settings and their connections to wider social structures which support and reinforce abusive relationships are not explored beyond the physiological decline and stress assumed to be associated with 'caring' for older people.

Age and gender-based forms of power and dependency are not fixed structures but facets of relationships which are fluid and which change over time and in relation to other dimensions of social life. The nature and extent of power/dependency inherent in abusive situations will therefore vary according to who or what it is in relation to. For example the nature and extent of power/dependency held by a woman at any point in time may vary according to her position *vis-à-vis* her husband, children, older women, younger women, health, race, economic status and so forth. In respect of elder abuse this leads to a concern with how age and gender-based forms of power operate in different contexts and at different levels within and between different groups of men and women.

This kind of approach would allow for consideration of the dynamics of interpersonal relationships and their connection to wider social structures which support and legitimize abusive behaviours, and of the widespread existence of elder abuse in institutional settings where the reality is abuse by women against women. The absence of any kind of public discourse to encompass women's abuse by women other than through the notion of individual or interpersonal pathology is a testimony to the strength of the situational stress model which has functioned to locate elder abuse firmly within the 'family'.

Moving beyond 'add on' approaches to locate age and gender as central categories of analysis and to connect the personal with the political would reveal differences in the meaning and importance attached to caring and to what is perceived as frustration and aggression by men and women. Linking the personal or subjective experiences of men and women involved in abusive situations to the wider social structures which support and legitimize them would allow for a more critical exploration of caring, a term which (as with elder abuse) masks the gender specificity surrounding care and abuse in both formal and informal 'care' contexts.

So far, we have virtually no sense of the views/experiences of those who are abused in old age. Kappeler (1992) argues that this reflects the fact that we live in a society which encourages identification with the subject rather than the object of violence. The situational stress model has functioned to reinforce this position by locating elder abuse within a frustration–aggression paradigm and by trying to establish causes for abusive behaviour in the hope that understanding what motivates abuse may enable its identification and prevention, or intervention and treatment. The focus has been predominantly on the carers and the assumption is that the cared-for will derive secondary benefits from this process.

Although there is virtually no empirical support for this assumption the recent Carers Act 1995 provides a good example of the connection between the personal and the political and the focus on carers rather than those who have been abused. The Act, which was informed by the powerful perceptions and experiences of various carers' lobbies and by theory locating care and abuse firmly within the family or interpersonal relationships, is focused on carers and requires social service departments to take account of their needs and rights when assessing actual or potential cases of abuse. At no time was the voice of elderly recipients of care heard in the debate leading up to the introduction of the Act. This reflects the fact that within the current economic and political climate carers are perceived as a resource and a positive asset, whilst those who need care are perceived and may perceive themselves as a burden and as less powerful. The Act has effectively institutionalized support for informal carers and functions alongside situational stress theory and other forms of ideological buttressing to support and legitimize conceptions of elder abuse as a problem of carer stress or problematic interpersonal relationships.

This is not an argument against support for carers, especially where it is clear that such support will be effective in reducing both carer stress and abuse. However it is important to question the notion of causation implicit in situational stress theory as predominantly a problem of carer or family stress and inadequacy. The assumption that supporting carers will automatically result in less abuse needs to be contextualized and examined critically. Currently the problem of elder abuse is being located ever more firmly within the family rather than within the social structure and the relationship between the two. As a result the marginalized status of those receiving care, the majority of whom are women, is reinforced. Attention is diverted from their experiences, needs and rights as citizens and the potential for abuse is increased by placing greater responsibility for welfare on carers, the majority of whom are also women. In ways such as this, hierarchies of age and gender-based relationships are created and sustained with younger female, and to a lesser extent, male carers perceiving themselves and being perceived by less powerful more dependent groups as having more power and control, thus fuelling conflict and masking the processes which socially construct power, dependency and abuse.

The situational stress model then is not adequate as a conceptual or theoretical framework attempting to explain elder abuse as it locates elder abuse firmly within the family and fails to connect either the personal or the interpersonal dynamics of abuse to the wider political or structural processes which reinforce and support abusive situations leaving them to be played out at the micro level amongst carers and 'victims'.

Age, gender and the political economy model of elder abuse

During the 1960s and 1970s the dominance of a functionalist model of ageing as a form of social disengagement and in terms of role theory (Havighurst, 1954; Cummings and Henry, 1966) was challenged by sociologists adopting a political economy approach which sought to relocate the problems of dependency care and ageing away from individuals and/or families towards a social structure in which old people were marginalized and rendered dependent and powerless relative to other groups. The functionalist approach to ageing had been primarily concerned with the loss of male roles through retirement and with advocating various forms of individually based adjustment, adaptation and 'activism' in old age. The term 'structured dependency' (Townsend, 1981) was coined to shift attention away from the individual characteristics of older men in particular, towards the wider social system and to focus on the resources available to older men and women to enjoy a peaceful and independent old age.

This perspective has informed recent conceptualizations of elder abuse (Hughes, 1995) and is potentially very useful in drawing attention to some very important issues and bringing a much needed structural dimension to the issue of elder abuse which functions as a corrective to the tendency of existing literature to focus on individual characteristics of abuser or abused or on the dynamics of their relationships. However it also has significant limitations.

First, the emphasis on structural or economic factors which create and sustain dependency and abuse in old age is at the expense of the links between personal and political processes. Subsequently the voices of old people and/or their views about the problem of elder abuse or their strategies for coping with it are not heard or used as a check on academic or professional definitions and/or perspectives. This is crucial to the issue of elder abuse, where the marked absence of the voice of those experiencing abuse has hampered the process of problem construction and legitimation and hindered policy and practice developments aimed at victims rather than carers.

Although the emphasis within political economy perspectives on the labour market position of older people highlights important common features of retirement, income, pensions and other structural inequalities in old age, the institutionalized connections are presented in a very generalized way and applied primarily to 'age', with 'gender' being subject to the 'add on' approach and treated as a variable. Whilst the model is useful in drawing attention to the economic dependency which is socially constructed under capitalism through employment and retirement policies that affect all elderly people, there are other forms of culturally created dependency which are equally important but are not considered. Insufficient attention is also given to gender differences in terms of the effects of political and economic forms of age-related dependency or to how these are manifested within and between different groups of men and women in abusive relationships. For example, the connections between the feminization of poverty, disability and dependency in old age and the fact that older women experience higher levels of physical and sexual abuse than older men have not been explored satisfactorily.

The tendency of political economy approaches to emphasize structural or economic issues at the expense of personal or interpersonal facets of abuse or the relationship between them tends to portray older people very negatively and passively as victims of a capitalist social system in which they are marginalized; and elder abuse as primarily a function of their low economic and social status within what has been termed an 'abusive society' (Biggs et al., 1995). The dynamics associated with the context and meaning of abusive situations and how older men and women experience, resist and respond to those situations remains uncharted territory because political or structural analyses tend to neglect cultural change and the diversity of cultural meanings within and between groups of older men and women and to render their voice inaudible within a theoretical framework which is inadequate to the task.

Towards an integrated approach to theorizing elder abuse

The problems associated with each of these 'add on' approaches to theorizing elder abuse can be resolved by recognizing that gender and age are organizing dimensions of the social world, each affecting and being affected by the other and each being influenced or shaped by both personal histories and characteristics as well as by membership of more or less powerful groups within society. Age and gender then cannot be separated from other social systems or divisions. Older people experiencing abuse are not just old: they are either men or women, black or white, middle class or working class. The social and economic world is organized around these dimensions and it makes no sense to try and treat them as separate or unequal systems, or as variables in theoretical frameworks.

A great deal of complex work is needed to adequately explain the situations of older women and men involved in abusive situations and how this is related to both the wider social structure and to the dynamics of their personal and interpersonal relationships. Existing theories relating to elder abuse should not be thrown out with the bathwater. However, it is unlikely that existing theoretical frameworks relating to interpersonal, family violence, or to the structural position of older people within capitalist societies will be able to adequately explain elder abuse without some significant reformulation and expansion.

Connecting age, gender and elder abuse: synthesizing political economy and life course approaches

The study of ageing has been largely policy driven as various governments have sought to address the problems of an ageing population. Consequently, ageing as a field of study has remained underdeveloped theoretically. However, new and more coherent approaches have been developed in recent years which, although paying insufficient attention to the links between ageing and gender, could, with some reformulation and expansion, contribute to the development of a theory specific to elder abuse, thus overcoming some of the problems associated with 'add on' approaches (Bury, 1995).

Life course perspectives on gender and elder abuse

Life course approaches are increasingly being used to explore the experiences of different age and social groups or as a means of uncovering the cultural construction and meaning of ageing. Such frameworks provide the opportunity to contextualize abusive situations at the interpersonal level and to explore their meaning and the individual and collective strategies devised for dealing with them.

There are two broad interrelated strands to theorizing based on life course approaches. The first is concerned with ageing throughout the life course as a social process and the second with age as a structural feature of rapidly changing societies. The latter pays particular attention to how contemporary patterns of ageing reflect a pluralist culture and focuses on different lifestyles and consumerism amongst older people, arguably at the expense of very old, very frail elders who are mostly women and often cannot exercise the financial or political clout enjoyed by younger, middle-class men or women. The former on the other hand is more concerned with the interface between personal or interpersonal experiences of ageing and with the political or structural processes which shape life histories and experiences. It is this approach which shows promise in relation to theorizing about elder abuse.

Political economy and life course approaches to gender and elder abuse: problems and possibilities

Some life course theorists are attempting to link political economy and life course approaches and to make the connection between social and economic policies and the meaning and effect they have for and on individuals and groups (Arber and Evandrou, 1993). Arber and Evandrou's focus on the cultural dimensions of ageing allows for an exploration of the dynamics of elder abuse which moves beyond typologies of abused and abuser towards an understanding of the meaning attached to abusive situations for the men and women involved. The experiences of different cohorts are emphasized in an attempt to bring historical as well as current elements into the picture. This is particularly important as the basis for developing an understanding of how rapid social and cultural change is perceived and acted upon by older men and women and how such change affects the nature and extent of 'caring' relationships and the potential for abusive situations.

Arber and Evandrou note the neglect of life course issues in official policy and the impact that state policies and practices have on interpersonal relationships and matters such as gendered patterns of care and disability across the life course. This kind of approach is directly relevant to the study of elder abuse and has been used to explore the relationship between the introduction and implementation of the NHS and Community Care Act 1990 specifically 'care management' processes and the quality of assessment and intervention practices relating to cases of elder abuse (Whittaker, 1996b).

The recent introduction and implementation of 'care management' processes as the 'cornerstone' of the NHS and Community Care Act is an example of a social policy which claims to empower older people and their carers and to maximize choice and independence while targeting those in greatest need and ensuring that assessments are needs based and user led. In practice relating to elder abuse however, the focus on carers' needs combined with resource constraints and the extra administrative demands inherent in 'care management' have led to the dilution and minimization of elder abuse procedures. Some practitioners acknowledged confusion and uncertainty about how to reconcile the often conflicting aims and objectives of care management and elder abuse procedures and found it difficult to reconcile the needs of caregivers and care receivers within the available time, skill and service resources. A consequent increase in service provision for carers which was itself gender and age specific, with more males being likely to receive services than females in similar circumstances, was evidenced. This corresponds with a decrease in access to professional social work among old people, especially very frail elders, the majority of whom were women and arguably more vulnerable to abuse and less likely to be able to 'talk and tell' or reframe their experiences in ways which would enable them to make informed choices without skilled social work intervention. There was no evidence of a cessation of abuse in this study though some evidence of a decrease in certain types of more overt abuse was identified (Whittaker, 1996b).

This kind of integrated approach to theorizing elder abuse illustrates the importance of connecting the political and the personal or interpersonal and draws attention to the need to focus on the interface between them, thus demonstrating that the rhetoric and the assumptions or intentions which underpin state policies are not necessarily translated into desired outcomes at the practice level and may be more dependent on the character and the priorities and resources of institutional settings or professional groups than on the needs or experiences of those involved in abusive situations.

Synthesizing certain life course approaches with political economy perspectives on elder abuse shows considerable promise as an explanatory framework and as a platform for future research, policy and practice formulations. However, there are also problems with existing attempts to reconcile political and personal levels of analysis, as exemplified by Arber and Evandrou. Bury (1995) notes that the problems associated with trying to focus on the interface between the personal and the political and linking structures with individual experience/history in a detailed way are not really explored in any depth and need to be addressed in future theoretical and methodological formulations. This would necessitate a theoretical approach which conceptualizes elder abuse as a social problem played out at the interpersonal level within a wide range of formal and informal care settings including the family. Such contexts need to be seen as both a reflection of and a response to wider forms of social inequality and disadvantage based not just upon age but also upon gender and the connections between them and other dimensions of discrimination and disadvantage. This type of approach would allow for the exploration of differences in power/dependency within and between different groups of men and women which affect their ability to resist abusive situations and/or to engage successfully in social action aimed at obtaining the resources needed to prevent abuse.

Social inequality and dependency is not related solely to the distribution of money. McMullin (1995) notes that it may be fruitful theoretically to consider other physical, psychological and emotional sources of power imbalance in old age. Cultural dimensions of inequality, including the way in which males and females are socialized and how this influences the kind of age and gender-based social hierarchies which we have illustrated in relation to the emphasis on carers as opposed to victims, are also important areas to consider. How such 'victims' exercise power and autonomy within relationships where they are deemed to be the problem or are perceived and perceive themselves as less powerful but at the same time as a stressful source of burden constrained by limited economic, social and cultural choices are key areas of study.

These aspects of interpersonal relationships cannot be dealt with in a theoretical or methodological framework which prohibits exploration of the interplay between the larger socio-political context of age, gender and power inequality and the substance of personal or interpersonal relationships within both formal and informal care settings. Instead of problematizing the biology of later life, a recognition of the socially constructed aspects of dependency which both younger and older women and men experience, albeit differently, could be used to develop a better understanding of elder abuse and to challenge dominant stereotypes of older women and men as a burden or as passive recipients of care.

This type of approach could do much to shift current thinking about elder abuse as a symptom of individual or interpersonal malfunctioning which, it is implied is remediable through health and welfare interventions, towards a better understanding of the links between the political and the personal or interpersonal and between policy rhetoric or intention and practice-based outcomes. The differential impact of various social and economic structures on different groups of older men and women as they seek to make sense of and respond to their experiences both as caregivers and as care receivers needs to be explored more fully if we are to begin to map, understand and respond effectively to the problem of elder abuse.

Summary

In summary, 'add on' approaches to theorizing about elder abuse tend to focus on the difference that age or gender makes in relation to a particular area of study such as the family, rather than recognizing that social life is organized around age and gender as well as around other forms of social division. Thus, locating elder abuse within paradigms developed to study frustration and aggression patterns amongst younger males, or some idealized version of the family, is unlikely to be very productive.

Similarly trying to compare elder abuse with child abuse or spouse abuse is like comparing grapes with prunes. Ageing is a gendered process and gender and age divisions like social class and race are fundamental to the organization of social life and have to be treated as unique dimensions of the social and economic world in which we live. Future theoretical developments relating to elder abuse must be underpinned by such an understanding and must attempt to link gender and age-based systems of inequality at the social and political level to the way in which elder abuse is perpetrated or experienced and responded to at personal and interpersonal levels by a diverse group of older men and women.

Until now, theoretical developments relating to elder abuse have been limited to 'add on' approaches, which we have shown are inadequate as explanatory frameworks. McMullin (1995) notes that theoretical developments or the lack of them reflects power imbalances in society, with those who are least powerful in economic and social terms, such as old women, attracting the least attention. The study of elder abuse has been policy – rather than theory – driven and there is now an urgent need for a conceptual framework to support more fruitful research which will enable older women's and men's voice to be heard alongside professional definitions and which will enable more effective policy and practice.

The proposed synthesis of political economy and life course perspectives may be one way forward and would provide the basis for the different approach to research, policy and practice formulations that is desperately needed. This relatively simple proposal represents only one approach to existing problems with elder abuse research and associated policy/practice formulations. It is not intended to minimize the complexity of the task. It is however intended to draw on wider developments within sociological theory to provide a starting point from which those interested in this area of study could begin to consider new ideas and new approaches, which would improve our understanding of the social lives of older men and women involved in abusive situations.

9
The Psychology of Elder Abuse and Neglect

Alison Marriott

Just as it has often been difficult to arrive at a clear definition of elder abuse and neglect, it is also difficult to define what the psychological aspects of elder abuse and neglect are. Psychological issues have relevance to almost all aspects of elder abuse, as even the most concrete and situational aspects of abuse may be mediated by psychological factors. A factual account of an incident involving physical violence, for example, is likely to be mediated by a large number of psychological factors, such as how the perpetrator and victim perceive their situation, their attitude to their role in the situation, and their relationship with others involved in the incident. The various theoretical models for elder abuse and mistreatment which have been proposed (Phillips, 1986; see also Chapter 3, this volume), all include a consideration of psychological factors, such as a response to stress in a caregiving situation (situational model), the nature of relationships and interactions between individuals (symbolic interaction model) and issues relating to dependency (social exchange theory). In addition, broader and more general ideas from psychological research – for example from behavioural, cognitive and social psychology – may help towards our understanding of some of the issues involved in elder abuse and neglect.

It is beyond the scope of this chapter to consider all of the ways in which psychological factors may enhance our understanding of elder abuse and neglect. It attempts instead to review some of the psychological issues and will do this through a consideration of one of the most vital and basic currencies with respect to all abusing incidents: *the nature of relationships*.

All victims and perpetrators of elder abuse live within either family relationships or other relational systems, such as institutions which have failed to provide continuing suitable relationships for those living within them. Relationships involve a number of psychological facets, including perceptions and attitudes to others, interactions and rules governing social and other behaviour, and emotional responses (such as anger control) in relation to other people. Psychological factors pertinent to the victim and to the perpetrator individually deserve some consideration, but they are likely to be subsumed within the context of the victim and perpetrator's relationship and how they interact. Relationships are another important issue with regard to how professional staff interact with the victim and/or perpetrator when managing cases of elder abuse. They also determine how different professional staff relate to one another in determining action and procedures when dealing with cases of abuse.

Relationships between victim and perpetrator

There are many different ways in which a relationship between an elderly person and someone else can become neglectful or abusive. Cassell (1989) describes how 'the elderly are abused when others in relationship to them use them to their disadvantage'. However, elderly people may also be involved in relationships which are not unequally abusive, and where instead they are being abused and disadvantaged, while at the same time abusing and disadvantaging someone else. Sometimes this may be in the context of an illness such as dementia, where the elderly dementia sufferer may be more likely to abuse their, often elderly, carer than the converse. Various studies have suggested that dementia sufferers are aggressive towards their carers three to five times more frequently than the carers are aggressive towards the dementia sufferer (Paveza et al., 1992). Relationships may have recently become abusive as a result of changes or may have been abusive on either side for a long period of time. Relationships may or may not involve a caregiving role and may or may not involve an elderly person who is dependent upon someone else.

Within all abusing relationships there exist victims and perpetrators, who each have their own unique, individual characteristics, which may be relevant to the abusing or neglectful relationship. However, a consistent finding from elder abuse research is that characteristics associated with the perpetrator may be more predictive of abuse than characteristics associated with the elder; and these characteristics are often related to the psychological state of the perpetrator. Elder abuse, and in particular physical abuse, has been linked to psychological distress in the perpetrator by studies in Britain, the USA and Australia: the psychological distress is either directly evident in the form of mental health problems in carers, or indirectly evident in the context of the abuser's excessive use of alcohol (Homer and Gilleard, 1990; Pillemer and Finkelhor, 1989; Sadler et al., 1995). In some situations the perpetrator's psychological distress appears to predate the abusive action, and there may be a history of perpetrator psychopathology (Pillemer and Wolf, 1986); or longstanding patterns of inter-generational family violence (Steinmetz, 1977). In other situations, elder abuse has been represented as arising more directly out of an elder/caregiver relationship, and is seen in the situational model of elder abuse (Phillips, 1986) to be the potential response of a distressed and overburdened caregiver faced with an intolerable caregiving environment. Studies which consider elder characteristics in relation to abuse have produced inconsistent findings and this may be partly because there are relatively few elder characteristics which are intrinsic determinants of abuse in themselves. It is psychological factors, such as the way in which the perpetrator perceives and responds to these elder characteristics, or to a caregiving situation, which are more important. The relationship and interaction between the individual characteristics of victim and perpetrator would seem to be vital, and the complexity and uniqueness of different relationships helps to explain why there are few clear-cut findings in elder abuse research which can be easily replicated.

Attempting to understand and support the psychological aspects of elder/carer relationships, may be at least as necessary in maintaining the caring relationship as directing services towards providing practical support. Although many of the physical tasks associated with caring for a frail elderly person are demanding, and carers will require practical assistance, Steinmetz (1988) has suggested that the carer's perception of stress and the problems involved in providing the elder with social and emotional support may be more difficult for the carer than coping with caregiving roles which are more task orientated and practical in nature. This also accords with the findings of Pillemer and Wolf (1986), who reported that elderly victims commonly felt that their relationship with the abuser was the source of more stress than life events such as retirement, unemployment, death or illness of family members and financial worries. Hence it may not be the volume of potentially stressful events and the physical demands of caring which are most significant to the perpetrator/elder relationship, but the psychological factors which mediate the interactions between the carer and the elderly person when facing these tasks of caring. These interactions are likely to be subject to the influence of numerous other factors such as individual differences, differing pre-morbid relationships, and different expectations of the outcome of caregiving.

Although psychological factors seem to be vital in helping to determine whether carers of older people cope with their role or fail to cope and possibly abuse or neglect the elder, few interventive services offer psychological interventions of the same value as practical forms of support. Providing appropriate psychological interventions and support may face professional carers with the same dilemmas as unpaid carers; practical, task-oriented care provision may be more readily identifiable and easier for professional staff to supply than less clearly definable forms of psychological support. Interventive methods of support are addressed in Wolf and Pillemer's (1994) review of four 'best practice models' introduced to address elder abuse in the USA. These models are (1) a multidisciplinary case conference team in San Francisco; (2) a volunteer advocacy programme in Wisconsin; (3) a victim support group in New York; and (4) a training scheme for workers in adult protection services in Hawaii. However, few services for older adults and their families have available the range of psychological interventions that are accepted as good practice for families at an earlier stage of the life cycle. Some services do offer family therapy for older adults, which aims to provide psychological assessment and interventions for older adults and their families, including those who have been victims of abuse (Benbow et al., 1990); but many services are organized in ways which emphasize the importance of providing practical support.

Before one can consider assessment and intervention in cases of elder abuse, the abuse must, of course, be identified and reported. Psychological factors associated with the nature of the relationship between the victim and perpetrator may have important implications. Penhale (1993a) has outlined some of the reasons why elder abuse occurring in a family context may fail to be reported, and many of these explanations are to do with the psychological state of the victim, and how the victim perceives their relationship with the perpetrator. As she points out, the victim may fear the consequences of reporting the abuse, for both themselves and the perpetrator. The victim may be dependent on the perpetrator, or the desire to report the abuse may conflict with the feelings of affection for or loyalty to the perpetrator, if they are a family member. The elderly victim may also fail to report the abuse because they feel that they are to blame for the perpetrator's behaviour, either because they may take responsibility for 'provoking' the perpetrator, or, if they are a parent of the perpetrator, take responsibility for an upbringing which has resulted in abusive behaviour (Steinmetz, 1978). The elderly person's perception of their role and relationship with respect to the perpetrator may be an important psychological determinant of whether they report abuse and seek assistance from others. Staff may have a significant role to play in establishing relationships with elderly people who they feel may be being abused but who seem reluctant to report the abuse, because of fear of the perpetrator or because they are dependent upon the perpetrator for other reasons.

Staff working with victims and perpetrators

Many of the dilemmas facing staff working with elderly people arise from situations where the evidence concerning abuse is not definitive or unambiguous, and where it has not been clearly reported by the elderly person. This may occur when the abuse has been reported or identified by someone other than the elderly person, and the elderly person appears to be reluctant to talk about it, or may be unable to do so because of cognitive or other disabilities. Staff may be faced with the difficult prospect of trying to determine the most appropriate way to gather information about risk to the elderly person, while trying also to maintain a successful working relationship with the client, and possibly with family members too. Difficulties may also arise because the professional worker's perceptions of the situation may not accord with the perceptions of the elderly person or perpetrator. Attempts to develop clearer definitions of elder abuse and neglect, and the development of guidelines for good practice when assessing and intervening in cases of elder abuse, may be seen as attempts to introduce and impose some objectivity upon thought and decision-making, when working in this area. In many ways, this may be important and the definitions which we encounter with regard to elder abuse and neglect are likely to help to shape our perceptions and attitudes to the problem. Baker's (1975) early description of 'granny battering' evokes different images of abuse (an older woman being physically assaulted?), from the images evoked by Fulmer and O'Malley's (1987) discussion of elder mistreatment in terms of 'inadequate care' provision by a caretaker of an older person. Many investigators have commented upon the difficulties in agreeing adequate definitions of elder abuse and neglect, and whilst this may be partly attributable to the multi-dimensional nature of the area, some of the difficulty is due to psychological factors.

Even when workplace guidelines defining abuse and appropriate action exist, and may impose some uniformity upon practice, professional staff working in the area will continue to carry with them different attitudes and perceptions of what significant abuse entails, and their personal and psychological responses to work in this area will differ. Our attitudes and beliefs concerning elder abuse and neglect are likely to be determined and influenced by many factors, such as our previous experience of working with elderly abused people; other experiences from our professional background and training; our own experiences from our family of origin about the place and role of elderly people in the family and in society; and by our own gender and cultural context. An awareness of the effects of these influences is important as they may determine how effectively we utilize definitions and guidelines concerning elder abuse. We must acknowledge our own personal understanding and perception of the abuse of elderly people, as it may help to determine the forms and types of abuse which we ourselves perceive and detect, and the form of intervention and assistance we may offer. Staff attitudes to elder abuse and neglect may also affect and determine the nature of the working relationship which is established with the victim and perpetrator. The staff member's psychological position in relation to the victim and perpetrator could produce a variety of types of working relationships – protective? condemnatory? risk taking? over- or under-concerned? – any of which could influence the outcome of the case and action that is taken. In some cases this may not be in the best interests of the elderly client. Solomon (1983a) has addressed the risks of our own perceptions producing stereotypes of the elderly person, for example as 'dependent' or 'incapable', which in turn may increase the possibility that we will respond to and address only this stereotype when intervening. We may fail to continue to try to work with the older person and their complex situation, but instead 'go beyond caring' for the elderly person, by addressing only their 'dependency' or 'lack of capability'. At the other end of the spectrum, attempts to attend to the rights of elderly people may sometimes include the risk that positive intervention will not be taken by staff when it might help the situation, and as McDonald and Wigdor (1995: 5) point out, empowerment of elderly people should not 'become a euphemism for no service or no protection'.

The various theoretical positions which have been proposed to help to account for elder abuse may also have different implications for the ways in which professional staff perceive and interpret acts of abuse and neglect, and for the relationships they establish with the victim and, in some cases, with the perpetrator. The situational model proposes that abuse can occur in a caregiving situation in which the carer feels unsupported and the stresses and strains of caring result in a loss of control and abusive behaviour. This may contrast with a situation in which, rather than perceiving the carer/elder relationship as an otherwise caring and positive one, which breaks down under the weight of pressures of caring, the professional worker perceives the relationship as a reflection of more widespread and longstanding inter-generational abusive behaviour within a family setting. The psychological issues for the professional worker in relation to this situation of trans-generational violence are likely to be different from those where the situational model could be more readily applied. The worker may feel that the abuse is more easily detectable and easier to acknowledge in a family setting where the family culture of violence is more overt. But he/she may be afraid of discussing abuse with a family, who otherwise appear to have positive relationships which he/she may hope to share with them, in case such discussion gets in the way. This may also have personal relevance for the worker in terms of the relationships which they would view as desirable to achieve and maintain with the members of their own family of origin. There are hence likely to be taboos surrounding the worker's acknowledgement of abuse with a family whom they otherwise view positively.

On the other hand, the professional worker may be hesitant to acknowledge abuse in families for whom they perceive violence to be normative, as they may fear the response of family members and may possibly fear for their own safety. But they may have difficulty in acknowledging this to professional colleagues. There may also be a risk that the worker fails to act upon the evidence precisely because the abuse is viewed as normative by the family or in some way acceptable in the family context, and this may place the elderly person at risk. The risks to the elderly person in these two situations may be similar, but the worker's perception of the situations and the action that they subsequently take may be considerably different. Penhale (1993b) has discussed how attempts to differentiate between different contexts of violence, for example whether the violence seems to be socially acceptable within its context or whether it goes against the prevailing social norms in which it occurs, may prove to be an obstacle to effectively addressing the problem of elder abuse. But it does seem likely that professional staff encountering the abuse of older people will be influenced by the rules governing the system in which the abuse occurs and will not always view the facts surrounding abuse in isolation from its context. One of the strengths of team-working may be to help individual team members to discuss these issues with other staff, who are less closely involved with the case, and this may help to disentangle some of the psychological effects, and may enable discussion of how they may influence assessment and intervention.

The professional worker may also deal with abusive situations differently as a result of factors mediated by the worker's own psychological response to the situation. An example of this is to do with the length of time which the worker may have known and established a professional relationship with the client(s) prior to the possibility of abuse or neglect of the elderly person becoming apparent. Many staff working with elderly people with longer-term mental health problems and dementing illnesses, and also with longer-term physical health problems, may have well-established relationships with the elder and other members of their family *before* the possibility of an abusive relationship becomes apparent. The professional worker may then perceive the carer/elder relationship as an otherwise positive and caring one, which has broken down as a result of the burden of care, as with the situational model of abuse.

Psychological theories concerning the effects of *cognitive dissonance* may help in an understanding of this situation. Cognitive dissonance has been the subject of much research in the area of social psychology and the term was first introduced by Festinger (1957) to describe the, usually unwelcome, feeling experienced when we perceive inconsistencies or incongruities between our perceptions, attitudes or behaviour. In this situation the individual usually attempts to re-establish some 'consonance' by trying to change some aspect of the perception or experience. If the beliefs which the professional worker had developed about the family no longer accord with reality, a state of cognitive dissonance may ensue. The worker may have difficulty in making the cognitive shift necessary to incorporate a new perspective of the elder/perpetrator relationship and there may be a risk that he/she will try to recreate a sense of cognitive consonance and comfort by assuming a position of disbelief. In this case it is likely that the abusive behaviour will be underplayed because of the feelings of personal and professional inadequacy which it may engender in a situation where the worker previously perceived the relationship with the client as being an effective and helpful one. Ideas about cognitive dissonance may have other applications with respect to elder abuse. The very fact that an elderly person has been abused may create a sense of disbelief and dissonance in others, because it may not accord with our ideas about the vulnerability of some older people, and social norms about the unacceptability of violence directed at elderly people. This means that it can be more difficult to acknowledge the abuse openly, because it increases and acknowledges the sense of dissonance we are experiencing.

It is important to remain aware that in the definition of many aspects of abuse there remains a distinctly subjective element, which is subject to many factors other than the actual description by a professional member of staff of the abusive or neglectful incident itself. Whilst it is likely that there will be some agreement in cases of more extreme physical violence towards an older person, many examples of behaviour or acts of apparent neglect are less clear-cut, and are likely to be perceived differently by those involved. In cases of abuse involving family members and an older person, the victim and perpetrator are often likely to define and perceive the abuse differently from professional workers involved in the case, because, in addition to their previous experiences of a relationship with those involved, their very experience of the abuse, either as victim or perpetrator, adds a psychological dimension which the professional onlooker has not shared. Moon and Williams's (1993) work with elderly women from different cultural groups who were presented with the same scenarios of elder abuse to consider, demonstrates how many issues surrounding the cultural and psychological context of the elder may determine their perceptions of an abusive situation and the help that they would subsequently seek, rather than the actual facts surrounding the abusive act itself. This emphasizes the difficulties for the professional worker in addressing cases of elder abuse and neglect, and implementing universally accepted solutions. The cultural and psychological context they are likely to find, and in which they are required to gather information and interact, is likely to be very different for different families, and the action which the elder is likely to view as appropriate is also likely to differ considerably.

Within this context it can often be helpful to try to obtain a clear account of an incident of elder abuse or neglectful behaviour, from the point of view of the victim and perpetrator, either by following clear guidelines or by imposing a clear structure upon the interview process. The member of staff encountering a case of elder abuse may have formal guidelines to follow which are determined by the work setting in which they are employed, or they may have a formal interview schedule to follow. However in some situations it can be difficult to gather the information which needs to be collected and one possible way to help to structure this process is to draw upon psychological behavioural approaches using *behavioural analysis*. This does not necessitate adopting the tenets of behavioural learning theory but can be a useful model to draw upon as a way of structuring an interview where cognitive and emotional issues might be in danger of overtaking and overwhelming the process of gathering information. Behavioural analysis involves trying to find explanations for simple and complex patterns of behaviour, and may be a useful way of considering and structuring the difficult issues surrounding incidents of elder abuse. Behavioural analysis may be utilized by the professional worker required to gather information about a specific instance of elder abuse and can complement any existing guidelines the worker is required to follow.

The simplest form of behavioural analysis involves an ABC approach, which generates questions about the incident, and structures the incident into possible contributory causes and effects (A = antecedents; B = behaviour; C = consequences). It requires a clear description of what the actual problem is, which is a helpful starting point in cases of elder abuse. Behavioural approaches usually try to produce an objective account of the phenomena and therefore typically avoid reference to the cognitions, thoughts and feelings of those involved in the incident. In some circumstances and at the initial stage of information-gathering this can be a helpful position for the worker to take with respect to the client and leads the worker towards establishing a dialogue and hence the beginnings of a working relationship with the client(s). (The ABC approach was used in the first edition of this book to analyse the case of Mr and Mrs Z: Decalmer and Marriott, 1993: 128–32.)

Whilst behavioural analysis may help us to understand some of the features of an abusive incident, and help to structure the way in which we talk to and interview an elderly client and perpetrator, the situation is complex and will involve a number of more complex psychological determinants. The relationship which staff develop with the victim, and possibly with the perpetrator too, may increase the possibility that the worker is trusted and can be confided in, and this first step of talking about abuse is vital in moving on to develop further steps towards positive action and intervention. Contrary to the assumption that it is always difficult to detect abuse is the evidence that when staff do ask elderly clients and their carers about abuse, many carers and some elderly clients quite readily acknowledge abusive relationships. Homer and Gilleard (1990) found that a large proportion of carers, when asked about this in a respite care setting, and a smaller proportion of elderly victims *were* prepared to acknowledge abusive events in their relationship. However, taboos and prevailing social norms often make staff feel that it is difficult to address this issue directly with elders and their carers.

Staff working together

Relationships and interactions between staff working with victims and perpetrators of elder abuse are also vital to the process of managing cases appropriately. The American Medical Association's Council on Scientific Affairs recommended in their report on abuse and neglect (1987) that intervention and management of cases of abuse should be multidisciplinary (see further, Chapter 4, this volume).

Authorities on elder abuse, such as Wolf and Pillemer (1989), have also emphasized the importance of cooperation between agencies. However, staff working with older adults and who encounter instances of abuse and neglect are likely to hold a wide range of views about what constitutes abuse and whether and how action should be taken. A survey of staff attitudes within the team with which I work in Central Manchester indicated that even amongst staff who work closely together, there exists a wide range of views about risk factors, and about the type of liaison which it may be appropriate to engage in when encountering instances of abuse. In addition, staff were often unclear as to what their professional role should be and most indicated that they did not feel well informed about issues surrounding elder abuse and neglect (Marriott, 1996). In an editorial review, McDonald and Wigdor (1995) discuss the use of the Elder Abuse Attitude Test as a research-based measure of differing attitudes towards elder abuse, and note how different attitudes exist between staff as a consequence of factors such as the age of practitioners. Younger practitioners rated examples of elder abuse more severely than senior practitioners, and some strongly believed that society has a responsibility to act determinedly to end abuse. Beliefs such as these are likely to have an impact upon clinical practice.

It can be a strength of multidisciplinary teamwork that our different professional roles and backgrounds allow us to emphasize and detect aspects of casework which our colleagues fail to spot. With respect to elder abuse, these different professional emphases may allow, for example, the social worker in the team to detect the possibility of financial abuse more readily than other professionals not involved with the financial affairs of the client, or the nurse to detect physical changes in the client indicative of injuries more readily than staff who have less close physical contact with the client. However, the nature of the roles and the work which staff undertake with older people may also increase the chances of abuse occurring in some instances, and staff may become the perpetrators of abusive practices. Pillemer (1988) has suggested that abuse is more likely in staff who are less well qualified and less experienced, and this may be related to the psychological effects upon staff of undertaking low paid work, which is generally devalued and afforded little status by others. Gilleard (1994) has reviewed some of the evidence relating to staff burnout and elder abuse, and also discusses how 'extrapunitiveness', or the extent to which staff direct hostility outwards, has been found to be linked to negative responses towards patients on long-stay nursing wards (Firth et al., 1987). There are a number of circumstances which may be assumed to increase the risk of burnout in staff working with elderly people (for further discussion of this issue, see Chapter 11, this volume).

In work with frailer elderly people, the aims of care may be directed at maintaining the person's condition or slowing down deterioration, rather than 'cure', and this may be less personally reinforcing for staff. Low levels of general and staffing resources may also contribute to staff stress, and a feeling that one's own personal needs are not being met. One of the symptoms of burnout may be to be less concerned about the welfare of the client, and in these circumstances, abusive practices may be more likely to occur. There are other ways in which more general negative and ageist attitudes towards older people can adversely affect healthcare practices, and the practices which groups of staff and organizations adopt when working with older people. There is evidence that older people may be denied counselling more often than younger people or may be allocated less skilled staff to care for their needs (Borsay, 1989); and Solomon's work (1983a) has suggested that older people are less likely to be given life-saving care than are younger people. Clark-Daniels and Daniels (1995) undertook an empirical case study of service rationing and found that the context in which staff make decisions relating to cases of elder abuse had an influence on the types of decision taken and the degree of service rationing employed. Staff attitudes also affected other aspects of practice. Factors such as the age of the victim and the race of the victim had an effect upon the time scale within which staff took action and upon the type of action taken. These are examples of how staff attitudes may result in practices which are, in themselves, abusive and neglectful of some elderly people.

However, other forms of working practice, such as multidisciplinary teamwork, with elderly people have evolved in an attempt to improve the quality of care, and to emphasize the importance of having a range of contributions from staff to the process of assessment and to the package of care. One of the strengths of the multidisciplinary approach in the area of elder abuse is that it allows scope for a range of opinions and views to be addressed and discussed. A consensus may be reached after considering a wider range of viewpoints and options than a single worker could produce if working alone. This can be further strengthened by taking the viewpoints of the elderly client and other involved family members into account too, which is one of the strengths of the Care Programme Approach, when it operates effectively within mental health services: it involves clients and relatives, as well as staff, in a regular review of the situation and entails the production of clearly determined care plans, which are made available to all those involved.

However, although the multidisciplinary approach with its emphasis on shared discussion and decision-making has many advantages, it is not without its pitfalls. Evidence from the social psychological literature about the behaviour of individuals operating in groups suggests that in certain circumstances decision-making processes may be subject to various group effects, which do not necessarily have positive outcomes. One example of this derives from *social impact theory* and proposes that individuals operating in groups, particularly as group size increases, may make less effort than the sum total of the effect had each individual worked alone (Latane, 1973). One possible explanation for this effect was thought to be that individuals may reduce their output in group tasks in order to maintain an equitable distribution of labour. Hence each individual in the elder abuse case conference may adopt a position that allows them to feel that the burden and responsibility for risk is being shared between team members and that less individual effort and responsibility is essential. Unfortunately, this may result in a management strategy which is less stressful for team members, but potentially more risky for the elderly victim, as there may be no one individual in the group who makes the special effort, which is sometimes required, to ensure that 'things happen'.

Another finding from early social psychological research was that group working often has the effect of polarizing decisions. In some instances this can result in a 'shift to caution', where the group consensus is more cautious than any of the views of the individuals within it considered alone. In other groups there may be a 'risky shift', where the group's decision and consensus is more risky than the view of any individual member. Lamm and Myers (1978) reviewed this phenomenon with respect to a wide range of group situations, and it is clear that any tendency within groups towards polarized decision-making could have important implications for the decisions reached in elder abuse case conferences and team case discussions. In some instances, extreme forms of group polarization can affect decision-making to a point where the group ignore clear evidence which is contrary to their decision. Janis (1982) has described how a number of disastrous political decisions have been based upon a tendency in groups towards 'groupthink', where a cohesive group of individuals is overcome by a desire for consensus, which outweighs the evidence and available information. This is most likely to occur when groups are cohesive (a multidisciplinary team with good working relationships and a shared mission?); when the group is isolated from other sources of information (the team does not liaise with other agencies or involve the client and family?); and when its leader favours a particular position and expresses this strongly (a team where professional hierarchies and the power of individual members are unchallenged?).

Groups, then, may not always benefit from shared discussion in all circumstances, and it may be necessary to introduce a number of safeguards when the professional team debate important issues such as elder abuse. Promoting open inquiry and appointing a member of the team as 'devil's advocate' may be beneficial, as may the practice of individual team members separately recording their views and assessment findings prior to the team conference, and then re-referring to them after the group has arrived at a consensus. Involving other agencies, and including the views of the victim, perpetrator and other family members, may also help to preserve some diversity of viewpoint and perspective, and allow the benefits of staff working in teams to outweigh the potential disadvantages of group effects.

Psychological factors which are particular to individuals, such as attitudes, beliefs and perceptions, may have a significant impact upon how staff define and interpret abuse, upon how they report abuse and implement guidelines, and upon how they develop management strategies and interventions. Wider psychological issues may also have significant effects upon relationships and team-working. The impact of psychological factors should be considered with respect to the three key areas in which relationships develop when working in this area – the relationship between the victim and perpetrator, the relationship which staff establish with the victim and perpetrator, and the relationships within and between groups and teams of staff working with abused and neglected elderly people.

10
Insidious abuse? Who is Responsible for Societal Neglect?

Maggie Pearson and Sarah Richardson

Throughout the 1970s and 1980s, concerns were consistently expressed in Britain about the quality of life and care for older people living in large, long-stay institutions provided by local health authorities and social service authorities. As the development of the private sector in long-stay care was actively encouraged by government policy, similar concerns were expressed about standards in smaller scale residential and nursing homes, some of which could be described as 'mini-institutions' in the community. Besides specific publicized isolated cases of overt abuse of older people living in a range of long-stay facilities, statutory health and social care services were criticized for being inflexible and unresponsive to the individual needs of their disabled and older users (Audit Commission, 1986; Griffiths, 1988). These concerns about service quality combined with the government's over-riding concern about the spiralling costs of care funded in the private sector from public sources through social security payments, a matter which is referred to again in Chapter 11 of this volume.

The official policy documents and management guidance which underpinned the British community care reforms, implemented in 1993, stressed as key values clients' personal dignity, individuality, choice, and realization of their personal aspirations (Department of Health, 1989b, 1991a). These 'shared values' were seen as 'a solid foundation on which to build collaboration between agencies' involved in commissioning and providing care to people in their own homes or 'homely' settings in the community (Department of Health, 1991a: 26).

These are fine sentiments with which no one concerned with the rights, dignity and quality of life of our elders could disagree. From the outset, however, the scale of resources required for the reality of community care to live up to its noble promise was the subject of considerable debate. Prophetically, the policy's architect, Sir Roy Griffiths, who was a highly successful businessman asked by the government to review and redesign community care arrangements, warned that it was not acceptable 'to allow ambitious policies to be embarked upon without the appropriate funds' (Griffiths, 1988, para. 38: ix). Within two years of the policy's implementation, however, almost a quarter of local authorities were experiencing severe problems in meeting identified local needs from within their strictly limited community care budgets (Pearson and Wistow, 1995; Waterhouse,

1994; Wistow, 1995). Whereas most authorities had a scale of eligibility criteria and prioritized categories of need for community care, from an early stage some were able to respond only to those in most dire need, and deemed to be at most severe personal risk (Sequira, 1994). The net result has been that, in many areas, as local authorities have struggled to balance the two conflicting aspects of the community care reforms – containing expenditure and meeting local needs – few service users or their carers have experienced a positive change in the availability and nature of health and social care services in the community, particularly at home (Warner, 1994). Indeed, some authorities have reduced or withdrawn services to clients, resulting in at least one legal challenge in the High Court. Whilst data are not available of the numbers of people employed by private agencies or older people themselves to provide care in people's own homes, it is striking that the number of district nurses and domiciliary social services staff have respectively remained constant and fallen since 1988 (Department of Health, 1989c, 1995a).

Whilst all areas of publicly funded services in the UK have experienced strict financial limits in the last 15 years, the tight controls on community care spending at a time when other services have also been reduced, have a particular significance for elders who are ill or frail, and whose numbers are increasing. The number of hospital beds in England fell by a third from 343,000 to 220,000 between 1983 and 1993/94, with the number of cases per bed each year almost doubling from 19.5 in 1983 to 36.4 in 1993/94 (Department of Health, 1995a). Over the same period, the number of cases treated per 'geriatric' bed almost trebled from 5.7 to 14.8 (ibid.), but the overall trends in reductions in hospital beds and lengths of hospital stay are felt most by older people, since 48 per cent of all occupied beds were occupied by people aged 65 and over in 1994 (Chew, 1995).

This trend, of reduction in hospital resources which are provided without direct charge, without compensating rises in nursing and social care services at home (the latter of which incur direct charges) have a specific resonance for older people. Forty per cent of elders aged between 65 and 74 and 50 per cent of those aged 75 and over reported a longstanding illness, disability or infirmity in 1993 (Central Statistical Office [CSO], 1995). Whilst this self-reported illness may not necessarily limit daily activities, the figures nevertheless indicate the scale of potential need for services and support among elders living at home. In 1985, a quarter of elders aged 65 and over living at home had a 'moderate' or 'severe' disability (Arber and Ginn, 1991b), and many are likely to live alone. Among elders aged 75 and over who live alone, 28 per cent reported a moderate or severe disability in the 1985 General Household Survey (GHS), compared with 23 per cent living with others. The remainder are likely to live with another older person who may be their principal carer (Green, 1988; Arber and Ginn, 1991b). The frailty of the older population should not be overstated, but it is likely that some of these older spouse and sibling carers may themselves be becoming frail.

Suffering in silence: elders' accounts of community care

It is within this context that an in-depth study was undertaken of the health
and social care needs of disabled older people living at home in an impoverished inner city area in 1994 (Richardson and Pearson, 1994). The
research was commissioned jointly by a local health authority and social services department. The two agencies were concerned that, in the context of
increasing need for continuing care at home, there may be unmet needs
among disabled and frail elders living at home, which could be met by real-
locating resources duplicated where the two services provided similar care
to specific individuals. The findings which are summarized here have been
corroborated in another study recently completed in the same district
(Westlake and Pearson, 1995), and have been validated by colleagues and
practitioners in other areas at presentations given to a range of statutory
and voluntary sector providers.

Methods

An in-depth, semi-structured interview was conducted with 37 respondents
aged between 52 and 90 years, who were living at home; 22 of them lived
alone. Twenty-six were women and 11 were men. The 37 respondents represented a response rate of 70 per cent from a stratified sample of 53 people
who were users and potential users of domiciliary health and social care services. Participants were selected from four sub-groups: (1) 13 receiving
home help services only; (2) seven receiving services from district nurses
only; (3) 12 receiving care from both home helps and district nurses; and (4)
five people with continuing care needs who were receiving neither health
nor social care. Four of these had refused services which they had been
offered. The respondents from sub-groups (1) and (3) were randomly
sampled from home help service records. The names of those from group
(2) were provided by district nurses from their lists, but so few names were
provided that it was not necessary to generate a random sample. Respondents in group (4) were identified by general practitioners (GPs) and social
service information systems. Attempts proved impossible to contact by
other means people who were receiving no services.

The interview involved open-ended questions to draw out the individual
respondent's concerns, priorities and most pressing limitations in their daily
lives, and what they saw as the ideal care solutions; and a structured section
concerned with health and social care needs, including physical and mental
health, self-care, social/emotional needs, domestic tasks, finances and living
accommodation. Respondents were also asked for their views on any domiciliary care services they were receiving.

Respondents themselves identified three principal concerns, which have
been discussed more fully elsewhere (Richardson and Pearson, 1995): loneliness, bereavement and isolation; bathing and personal hygiene; the suffi-
ciency of domiciliary services.

Loneliness and isolation

The most significant and widespread problem to emerge was the poor social
and emotional well-being of many of the respondents, particularly among
those who lived alone. Over half of the participants interviewed (20)
reported that they were lonely, feeling very low, or anxious. As we were
concerned with the participants' own perceptions, we did not use clinical
measures of depression or anxiety. Respondents generally took some time
before revealing the extent of their loneliness, referring gradually to not
being able to get out as much as they would like to, and to finding that the
days dragged, being 'stuck at home' alone. For over half the 22 respondents
who lived alone, loneliness was a serious problem. One 88-year-old woman,
who was partially sighted and diabetic, admitted:

> 'No, I get depressed sometimes. I've got no near relatives, I might as well be alone
> in the world . . . Monday, I sat in that chair over there and I sobbed my heart out
> . . . it's just feeling sorry for yourself, it's all wrong I know . . . I think it's just being
> alone here.'

A man living alone rarely saw even his neighbours:

> 'No one, I never see no one, just one downstairs who's been in two, three or four
> times for half an hour. If I want to buy something I don't see anybody and I don't
> like to ask anybody . . . Where I was before, I helped anyone, now here no one
> even says hello, I never see anyone.'

Health problems were a major source of anxiety and were often a key factor
in the person's loneliness and isolation. Many felt very low about the unre-
lenting nature of their ill-health and about the limitations it imposed. One
67-year-old man, who was partially sighted and diabetic, worried a lot about
his health and got 'depressed' that he was so dependent on others. He felt
that his failing eyesight was the chief cause of his anxiety, but he had not
told his doctor or social worker about his worries, because he was becoming resigned to his situation and felt that there was little they could do.

   An 87-year-old woman who suffered from blackouts and nausea was very
depressed and anxious about her health and about living on her own.
Although she stayed in her own home during the day she spent the nights
at her son's:

> 'I'm not very well and it worries me of a night if I take ill . . . I couldn't cope stop-
> ping here, I can't stop in on my own, it's my nerves. I hate being on my own, I
> hate being on my own, I don't mind the day times, it's night times. How I'll stick
> another winter I don't know.'

Several participants appeared to be suffering from severe or prolonged
grief. Because each of these elders had relied heavily upon the person they
had lost, they were finding their health and practical problems particularly
difficult to bear alone, but none had received any counselling for their grief,
or heard of bereavement services. One man was still very depressed about
the loss of his mother five years previously, a loss which was especially difficult for him to bear because he had lived with her all his life. He still got

very upset when he came home to an empty house with no one there to greet him, and often cried about it:

> 'I'd like to have someone to talk to because I'm frightened that I'll have a nervous breakdown, 'cos I had a couple when I was younger and I'm not afraid to admit it.'

Another 87-year-old woman described how, since the loss of her best friend the previous year, her social life had come to an abrupt end because she did not want to go out on her own. She missed her friend coming to stay with her when she was unwell and missed having someone close to talk to.

The majority of participants seemed to feel that their loneliness, anxiety and despair were not legitimate problems to raise with health and social services, and that there was no solution. This is a poignant perception, since 19 of the 22 respondents living alone were receiving home help services, but the impression gained was of attempts to hide the extent of their distress from the home help, who may have been the only contact they had with formal services on a regular basis. A simultaneous observational study of primary health care nurses' practice with older people corroborated these elders' perceptions, for practice nurses undertaking annual health checks on people aged 75 and over rarely recorded the loneliness and isolation revealed to them, and did not refer the person to other professionals, often stating that there was 'nothing which could be done' (Quinney and Pearson, 1996: 39).

Many respondents who were lonely felt that 'to go out more' would improve their quality of life most. However, several were deterred by the effort, and some by the pain involved in getting ready. Others were afraid of being ill when they were out and others could not afford taxis or cope on public transport. Some had become completely resigned to being housebound, and several revealed that what they wanted more than anything else was close, personal contact with someone to whom they could turn whenever the need arose. Whilst some widows/widowers were clearly missing the support and company of their partners, others yearned for the support of a good friend, neighbour or son or daughter.

Dignity and personal hygiene

The question of personal hygiene has great potential for embarrassment and distress to elders becoming increasingly frail, who wish principally to do things as they always have done (Westlake and Pearson, 1995). However, our findings illustrate how constraints on care services are reducing people's choices in how, where, when and by whom they are bathed or washed, thereby threatening their personal dignity, which was a key value underpinning the *Caring for People* reforms (Department of Health, 1989b).

Most respondents had problems with bathing and washing, which tended to be exacerbated by the insufficiency of services to meet their specific wishes. The introduction of regulations on the lifting of patients and clients, to comply with EC health and safety regulations (Commission of the European Communities [CEC], 1990) prevented care staff from helping people into the bath alone, but resource constraints prevented two staff being available for domiciliary care either in social services or community nursing, and hoists were not readily available. Four of the seven receiving only district nursing services commented that they had problems with bathing, and two of the seven participants receiving strip-washes from district nurses would have liked them more often. Those receiving services from home helps only were less likely to have such problems, reflecting the recent extension of home help services into personal care, and the common practice reported by home helps themselves of contravening health and safety guidelines in order to ensure that their client could have a bath or shower to their satisfaction (Richardson and Pearson, 1994). Some clients receiving home help services had also had the requisite adaptations to their bathrooms, but others were on a waiting list of up to two years (see also Westlake and Pearson, 1995; Quinney and Pearson, 1996).

A severely disabled 78-year-old woman and her husband wanted the district nurse to come more than once a week to give the husband some respite from the physical strain of tending to his wife. Another woman found one wash per week inadequate, particularly in the hot weather:

'I was wondering whether she [district nurse] could come two days a week instead of one so that I could have two baths a week, 'cos honest to God I was wringing, streaming, sopping wet this morning.'

Other participants had requested help from domiciliary care services but had been refused. The home help of a 68-year-old man who was recovering from a stroke told him that although she could keep an eye on him while he was in the bath she was not allowed to physically assist him in any way. As he commented: 'I can't get in and out of the bath properly and I would like someone to come at least once a week to help me get out of the bath.'

Resource constraints had also led to reduced availability of baths at a local bathing centre, where there were long waiting lists and insufficient transport to enable people to attend. One woman had not applied to the centre because she had heard that there was a six-month waiting list and a 57-year-old man, who suffered with multiple sclerosis, had recently had his visits reduced from once a week to once a fortnight. He did not want to be strip-washed by a district nurse or a home help, and had been waiting for over a year for an occupational therapy assessment to have a special shower put into his bathroom: 'I've got to be honest, I miss a bath every week . . . I go to the bath centre, I used to go every week but it's every fortnight now.'

Insufficiency of services

Respondents' accounts of services were principally concerned with their insufficiency, rather than with their quality. Indeed, most participants were enormously grateful for the services they were receiving and were reluctant to pass comment on them. This echoes Wilson's observation (1993) that the combination of gratitude and low expectations may discourage older people from openly commenting upon (i.e. criticizing) services.

Local services were clearly unable to respond flexibly and sufficiently to people's wishes. Many respondents were dissatisfied with the frequency and length of visits by all care services and felt that their aspirations for social participation were thwarted by service limitations which prevented them from maintaining the personal standards and social roles which they had enjoyed before becoming disabled or frail.

A quarter of those receiving home help services would have liked more time to be spent on cleaning. In the two to four hours per week usually allotted to domestic work, there was not enough time for more than the minimum of dusting and vacuuming after the home help had done the bare minimum of shopping. Cupboards could not be turned out and cleaned very often and spare bedrooms could not be cleaned as much as respondents would have liked.

A 68-year-old man who had a paralysed hand and mobility problems after suffering two strokes was rated by the home help service as 'potentially highly dependent'. He received 10 hours of care per week from the home helps on weekdays and he was hoping that his allocation might be extended to include weekends:

> 'I asked [the home care organizer] whether there was any chance of having a home help at the weekend and she said "We're short-staffed and everything" and I said "Well, I could do with one" and only last week they tried to take the home help off me at breakfast time and I said "You can't do that!".'

Some respondents felt it was unfortunate that the home helps did not have enough time in their schedule to go to a main shopping centre to buy things like household items and clothing. It was evident that unless other sources of help were available to them, or home helps contravened management guidance and did extra shopping for them in their own time (Warren, 1990) it was impossible to participate in the consumption of anything other than basic groceries. This was particularly frustrating for participants who wanted to buy presents for their grandchildren, as they had always done, or to buy themselves something new to wear: basic and essential components of maintaining their established social role and dignity, and some modicum of independence amidst increasing dependency.

In addition to the insufficiency of some services, health and social care staff were clearly unable to tailor their visit times to suit the daily routines of some respondents, constraining or disrupting their social lives. For example, one insulin-dependent woman described how difficult it was for her to go out in the afternoons because she always had to be in at four o'clock for the district nurse's teatime injection call. Another couple complained that they missed out on the weekly coffee morning in their sheltered housing complex because it clashed with the district nurse's visit. Problems of service inflexibility such as this were seen to be less problematic for housebound participants, not only because they were less likely to be inconvenienced but also because they were usually extremely grateful for any visits they did receive. Respondents were often reluctant to ask for a change in visit times, however, lest they should seem ungrateful or lose the service altogether.

Dignity and personal aspirations: whose responsibility?

The findings from this study suggest that, in the study district as in many others, domiciliary health and social care services were not able to address people's needs in the ways which they would prefer, or to meet needs which people themselves felt were a priority. Despite their prominence in the government's strategy to improve the health of the nation (Department of Health, 1993a), mental health needs were not seen as a legitimate priority by respondents or, as our research in other studies suggests, by staff (Pearson et al., 1994; Quinney and Pearson, 1996). Furthermore, far from reflecting the 'shared values' underpinning community care policy (Department of Health, 1991a), our respondents' accounts indicated the same problems of little choice and dignity, and feelings of powerlessness, which have always characterized older people's lives in industrial societies (Shanas et al., 1968; Laslett, 1989a).

Denial of basic dignities

In this study, lack of staff time and other resources, rather than unsympathetic attitudes or behaviour, were apparently the problem. The intense pressures to increase cost-efficiency and accountability have prompted several responses including a skill-mix review in district nursing (Department of Health, 1992), which led to reductions in the numbers of highly qualified nurses and increases in the numbers of unqualified staff, who could perform the work more cheaply. In addition, personal care has almost silently become redefined as the responsibility of social rather than nursing care as community nursing services have withdrawn from providing baths which are not deemed to have a strictly 'health' purpose (Pearson and Wistow, 1995). However, in the home help service, savings have been made by steadily increasing charges to clients, reducing the service time allocated to individual clients and the 'targeting' of scarce resources on those in greatest need (Bebbington and Davies, 1993). The result has been that clients who are vulnerable and distressed, but of insufficiently high priority to receive complex care packages or residential and nursing home care, are experiencing service reductions and minimal physical maintenance which cannot attend to basic emotional and social needs and quality of life (Townsend, 1987; Doyal and Gough, 1991; Richardson and Pearson, 1995).

In some districts, these reductions have been subject to recent legal challenges. Our data confirm Caldock's observation that

> The universalistic and morally worthy image engendered by the use of the word 'care' is clearly inappropriate in situations where those entering the home of elderly people do so for a specific length of time, often to quarter-hour timings, to do a specific range of tasks and then move on to the next person. (1994: 135)

Besides reducing the quantity of services provided, both health and social services providers are also seeking to reduce costs by withdrawing from work which may be defined as outside their spheres of responsibility. This question, of the boundary between health and social care, has been sharpened in the last year by the introduction of Department of Health guidance on NHS responsibilities for continuing care (Department of Health, 1995b) which, within current resource constraints, will force further 'clarification' of personal care as outside the sphere of nursing (Pearson and Wistow, 1995). In the research area, clarification of responsibilities between home helps and district nursing was apparently almost absolute with virtually no overlaps between their responsibilities. So separately were their roles defined that the problems which did emerge were mainly those of gaps within and between services, but it is arguably *precisely* those gaps, in a task-oriented and financially constrained service, to which the key community care policy 'shared values' of personal dignity and personal aspirations fall victim.

Arguably the most disturbing finding from the research was the extent of searing loneliness, anxiety and unhappiness witnessed amongst our respondents, especially those who lived alone. Mental health promotion and protection have, it seems, also become invisible casualties of the emphasis on cost reductions and task definition, yet this intangible issue is crucially important for older people, who are known to be at particular risk. In this and other studies with disabled and frail older people (Pearson et al., 1994), the question of social support and participation was not seen by local health services to be their responsibility, despite their known contribution to a health priority for the nation of improving mental health (Department of Health, 1993a). Despite the stated aims of social service home help or home care services, which include social and emotional support amongst their main functions (Department of Health, 1993b), the limited domiciliary service resources available were clearly insufficient to provide care and support for those who were housebound, sick and lacking social support networks, yet not of the highest priority because they were not at risk of life and limb. If our respondents were children, they would be deemed to be 'at risk' and their interests would be protected by the Children Act 1989, which sees healthy development as paramount (Smith and Lyon, 1994). A range of services could be put in place to ensure that the risks to their health and well-being were minimized if not removed, and the family would be subject to regular surveillance to assess the risk of likely significant harm (Parton, 1991).

There is, however, no such protection for elders in our society. Their rights to care are difficult to define, and are relative rather than absolute. Furthermore, emotional needs such as loneliness and isolation are not accepted as any statutory authority's responsibility, despite the policy commitment to community care promoting 'the realization of an individual's aspirations and abilities' (Department of Health, 1991a: 25).

As the question of continuing care is .intensified by disputes between health and social service authorities about responsibility for its provision (Pearson and Wistow, 1995), the need to address the mental health and emotional needs of frail and disabled people living at home will become ever sharper. Unless the statutory services discover ways of meeting such needs, these ideals of community care will become a reality only for those who can mobilize their own social support, whether from within their social networks, connections with the voluntary sector, or by purchasing quality care from private agencies (Wilson, 1994). However, it is precisely those who are at greatest risk of spending their old age in undignified distress and isolation who are likely to be living in poverty, and in impoverished communities in which the social fabric is disintegrating in the face of systematic and continuous exclusion from social and economic participation. Whilst these elders may not be subject to overt physical abuse from individuals (though if they were, we might not know), their distressing accounts raise the crucial but all too silent question of their neglect by national and local society which protects them neither by adequate funding for services nor by statute from spending their old age with a poor quality of life which we would rightly never accept for a child.

11

The Mistreatment and Neglect of Elderly People in Residential Centres: Research Outcomes

Frank Glendenning

The dominant approach to elder mistreatment in the research literature has been to apply the family violence model. This has tended to underplay concern in residential centres (hospitals, nursing homes and residential care homes). So whilst the extent of abuse in informal or family settings is very unclear, its existence within institutions in Britain has been widely documented (Phillipson and Biggs, 1995: 189). Townsend published *The Last Refuge* in 1962 (in which he described the gradual process of depersonalization which overtook elderly people in residential care) and since then there have been reports by Robb on hospitals in 1967, Willcocks, Peace and Kellaher on residential homes in the public sector in 1986, Clough's hitherto unpublished overview of official inquiry reports, *Scandals in Residential Centres*, which was prepared at the request of the Wagner Committee (Clough, 1988a), Holmes and Johnson on private homes (1988), Horrock's analysis of Health Advisory Service reports on long-stay wards in hospitals (cited in Tomlin, 1989: 11), the Harman sisters' report on the first 96 cases considered under the 1984 Registered Homes Act in 1989 (Harman and Harman, 1989), Counsel and Care's reports on privacy and restraint in 1991 and 1992 together with their discussion paper on abuse in care homes (Bright, 1995) and Peace, Kellaher and Willcocks in 1997.

When discussing this subject it has been customary to draw a distinction between individual acts of abuse in institutions and actual institutional or institutionalized abuse. As Decalmer (1993: 59) has suggested, abuse of the person is common, but the commonest abuse of all is institutional abuse, where the environment, practices and rules of the institution become abusive in themselves. Bennett and Kingston have argued that there is a deficiency in research that could be used to explain and remedy the socialization processes that lead to abusing behaviour in institutions (Bennett and Kingston, 1993: 116). Higgs and Victor have also reminded us that there are few longitudinal studies that would enable us to examine the influence of age, or indeed other variables, like health status and availability of family care, on the probability of moving into institutional care (Higgs and Victor, 1993: 193). These comments are all important.

One commentator wrote in the *Nursing Times* at the time of the Nye Bevan Lodge scandal in 1987:

It is self-evident that when elderly, often confused residents are made to eat their own faeces, are left unattended, are physically manhandled or are forced to pay money to care staff and even helped to die, there is something seriously wrong. (Vousden, 1987: 19)

Phillipson has suggested that it is invidious to select any one setting for particular emphasis and that we should look for an approach that sees abuse as an issue which is not tied to any one context or relationship (Phillipson, 1993: 84). Nevertheless the evidence of abusive behaviour in residential settings is well documented in this country. The issue is how, with our existing knowledge, should we proceed in relation to our understanding of elder abuse and our search for strategies to prevent it?

It is necessary to place the discussion into some kind of context, without going back to demographic issues. Higgs and Victor have shown that between 1970 and 1990 the number of residential places in UK institutions nearly doubled, reaching nearly half a million places, over 200,000 being in the independent sector (for figures updated to 1994, see Peace et al., 1997). They trace the increase to the rapid growth of private residential and nursing home places during the 1980s resulting from a change in the supplementary benefit (SB) regulations. The regulations now enabled older people with low incomes to enter care at no cost to themselves. In 1980, SB offices were given discretion under regulation nine to pay board and lodging allowances to older people in private homes at rates which were 'reasonable'. This doubled the number of claimants between 1980 and 1983 and raised annual expenditure from £18 million to £102 million. By 1990, this had reached £5.5 billion (Higgs and Victor, 1993: 190). This unexpected growth in expenditure is the total antithesis of the policy objective of community care and led the Audit Commission's report in 1986 to argue that this was a 'perverse' incentive favouring institutionalization rather than community care (see Parker, 1990; Higgs and Victor, 1993). This provided the stimulus for the Griffiths Report and the 1990 NHS and Community Care Act. But with growth there had also been problems in standards of care. The Harmans in 1989 found 'evidence of abuse, binding residents with cord, misuse of drugs, fraud, fire hazard, lack of hygiene and a sorry tale of bruised and miserable residents'. They also found that the Registered Homes Act 1984 was not as detailed and as clearly drafted as it might have been and had not given the registration authorities or the tribunal wide enough powers to protect residents in homes (Harman and Harman, 1989: 4; see also Brammer, 1994: 436).

I intend first to summarize briefly the findings of various small-scale American studies and then to deal with Pillemer and Moore's study on maltreatment in nursing homes in 1987 in more detail, because their significant report has not been widely available in Britain (Pillemer and Moore, 1989).

As long ago as 1973, Stannard published a paper in the American journal *Social Problems* entitled 'Old folks and dirty work' based on his participant observation study of a nursing home where he identified slapping, hitting, shaking a patient, pulling hair, tightening restraining belts and terrorizing by gesture or word (Stannard, 1973).

Kimsey, Tarbox and Bragg in 1981 examined 1,000 nursing homes in Texas and wrote:

> Deliberate physical abuse by formal caretakers was less common. Physical neglect was far more common, for example the development of bedsores, inadequate nutrition, improper medication and vermin infestation. Psychological abuse was most frequent in the area of passive neglect with patients regarded as 'going to die anyway'. (Kimsey et al., 1981: 465)

Kimsey built up a profile of the total nursing home population in Texas of 77,000 as being: average age 82; 95 per cent over 65 and 70 per cent over 79; the ratio of women was 2:1; most patients were poor and isolated; more than 50 per cent had some mental impairment; half had no close relatives; and fewer than 50 per cent could walk alone.

Tarbox followed this report with a paper in 1983 on the psychological aspects of neglect in nursing homes, in which he emphasized the lack of cleanliness and attractiveness in the physical environment, inadequate diet, infantilization and passive neglect (Tarbox, 1983: 42–6).

Doty and Sullivan in 1983 reported on their study of statistics from the Federal Certification Agency. Out of a sample of 550 skilled nursing facilities nation-wide, with 54,000 beds, as of September 1980, 7 per cent were cited by the Agency

> as deficient on the requirement that patients' rights, policies and procedures ensure that each patient admitted to the facility is free from mental and physical abuse and free from chemical and (except in an emergency) physical restraints except as authorized by the physician. (Doty and Sullivan, 1983: 224)

Their study showed that a significant proportion were assessed as 'deficient on the requirement that each patient is treated with consideration, respect and full dignity', 15 per cent fitting this category in eight specific states and 7 per cent nation-wide (Pillemer and Moore, 1990: 11).

Doty and Sullivan also reported from their study of New York City nursing homes that there was evidence of over-medication and unsanitary conditions and that patients who were unable to feed themselves were not being fed. Further, they contended:

> it is not uncommon for problems of patient abuse, neglect and mistreatment in nursing homes to be dismissed on the grounds that the evidence is anecdotal. The implication is that a journalist or politician 'on the make' can always go out and uncover a horror story or two. (Doty and Sullivan, 1983: 223)

In 1980, over 3,000 cases of potential Medicaid fraud were being investigated in different states and Halamandaris, who was a senior lawyer at the time, published a paper in 1983 which listed a cavalcade of abuse in American nursing homes: theft from patients' funds, false claims by carers to Medicare and Medicaid, trading in real estate, fraudulent therapy and pharmaceutical charges, even involvement in organized crime (Halamandaris, 1983: 104–14).

Stathopoulos also reported in 1983 on the fact that a consumer advocacy organization (Consumer Advocates for Better Care) had to develop strategies in nursing homes in North Central Massachusetts to deal with financial abuse, denial of civil rights, removal from private or semi-private rooms to three- or four-bedroom wards, neglect, psychological abuse and various kinds of maltreatment (Stathopoulos, 1983: 336–54).

The organization developed strategies in the following way. The foremost goal was to improve the quality of care in nursing homes and to alter the power equilibrium in favour of the consumers. The Advocates focused on local, rather than on state, nursing homes. The organization sought funding on the understanding that it would have programme independence. It emphasized the importance of providing training for volunteer advocates and the importance of networking. At the end of the exercise, Stathopoulos reflected that 'elder abuse in institutions is one part of the continuum of abuse in our society. Public policy which supports institutionalization of the elderly to the exclusion of other forms of care in the community is in many instances the root of elder abuse in institutions' (Stathopoulos, 1983: 353).

Then Solomon investigated the pharmacological and non-pharmacological abuse of elderly patients by health care professionals and concluded that

> poorly trained caretakers can command lesser pay but have an extremely high turnover rate ... The frustrations of the job and the debility of the patients promote infantilization, derogation and actual physical abuse. (Solomon, 1983b: 159)

Cowell (l989: 249) cites Nusberg's 1985 study of the consumer's perspective of the quality of care in nursing homes, which was conducted under the auspices of the National Citizens' Coalition for Nursing Home Reform. She also described the progress made in California during the 1980s, which instituted its own studies of the quality of care in nursing homes (Blum, 1987). This led to legislation to deal with alleged abuse and neglect in health care facilities that received state medical insurance payments. Cowell suggested however that legislation on its own would not bring about change.

Finally in 1990, Fader et al. published a paper in the *Clinical Gerontologist* on a study of health care workers in long-term care settings in New York and the way in which they perceived elder abuse in relation to active and passive neglect. By using the student T-test, nurse aides were found to have significantly lower scores than licensed practical nurses and other groups when taken together. Questions relating to passive neglect were frequently answered incorrectly by all groups. The researchers' conclusion was that 'there must be ongoing education and training about abuse and neglect' (Fader et al., 1990; see also Foner, 1994).

There was no lack of awareness among North American investigators about the existence of the general problem of maltreatment in the 1980s. But apart from the Texas study, not until 1989 did we have a thorough review of abuse in nursing homes by Pillemer and Moore (1989, 1990), which Pillemer revisited with Lachs in 1995 (Lachs and Pillemer, 1995).

Although mentioned briefly by McCreadie in her study of abuse in domestic settings in 1991, their findings were not widely accessible in Britain until Bennett and Kingston obtained permission to publish them in 1993. Their conclusion was that when Pillemer and Moore's evidence is set alongside the evidence of the British official inquiry reports, it may be that, as Pillemer has indicated, abuse in institutions is relatively widespread (Bennett and Kingston, 1993: 126).

Pillemer and Moore, in attempting to establish the prevalence of elder abuse in nursing homes, came to the conclusion that the figures provided so far were likely to be underestimates of the actual incidence of maltreatment and that official statistics merely scratched the surface of the problem. They refer to the survey by Monk et al. in 1984 which found that over half the nursing home residents in the sample had refrained from making a complaint at one time or another, because they were fearful of reprisals if they complained to a nursing home ombudsman or other state official. In drawing a distinction between 'proprietary' and 'nonprofit' homes, Monk also found that there was less fear of reprisals in the latter (Pillemer, 1988: 232).

So Pillemer and Moore conducted a random sample survey of nursing home staff in one state. Fifty-seven nursing homes were invited to participate and the final sample was drawn from 32 homes, which ranged in size from 19 to 300 beds. This yielded a sample of 577 nurses and nursing aides and telephone interviews were conducted in spring 1987.

They recognized that it was critical to examine the issue of the extent of abuse and the causes of maltreatment within the general context of nursing home care. In order to achieve this, they built up a profile of staff and, recognizing the wide range of settings that exists, confined their investigation to skilled nursing facilities (which provided 24-hour care), and intermediate care nursing homes (where intensive care was not required but where the patients had functional impairments). 'Staff' were defined as registered nurses, licensed practical nurses and nursing aides. The profile showed that the average length of employment was under five years and the average length of total employment was 7.5 years. Ages ranged from 16 to 64, with an average age of 40.

The data which Pillemer and Moore obtained presented a picture of staff who were motivated by a desire to help others and to have meaningful employment. Staff believed that they were in an occupation that was recognized and accepted. Seventy-nine per cent felt that they had at least some authority in determining what tasks to perform and 91 per cent felt that they had some authority in setting the pace of their work. Thirty-two per cent found the job very stressful; 44 per cent moderately so; 15 per cent a little stressful; 10 per cent not at all. Although comparable data for other occupations were not available, these seemed to Pillemer and Moore to be high levels of job stress.

Lack of time was given as one reason for stress. The more personalized tasks like walking, talking and helping residents with personal care activities were identified as the ones not done (see also Baillon et al., 1996: 223).

Forty-three per cent reported that fewer staff turned up than were scheduled on their shift on three or more days a week. Many reported high levels of burnout, based on results gained from responses to a burnout inventory developed for human service workers (Maslach, 1982). Similarly, 57 per cent agreed that they sometimes treated patients more impersonally than they would like and 37 per cent said that the job hardened them emotionally. When all these data were collated, 32 per cent were classified as being in the 'high burnout' category. The study went on to show that burnout was strongly related to stress and therefore finding ways of reducing stress was a major priority for administrators. Training needs were seen to be critical for the management of patient behaviour and aggression.

Pillemer and Moore reported that 36 per cent of the sample had seen at least one incident of physical abuse during the preceding year. Seventy per cent had seen staff yelling at patients. Fifty per cent had seen staff insult or swear at patients during the preceding year. The majority said that such actions had occurred more than once. Ten per cent admitted that they themselves had committed such actions. Six per cent had used excessive restraint. Forty per cent had committed at least one act of psychological abuse during the preceding year. Denying food or privileges was reported by 13 per cent. Pillemer and Moore suggest that as the survey was based on staff self-reporting, some under-reporting of negative actions had probably occurred. These estimates, they admit, cannot be compared with other estimates, which do not exist in a compatible form. But there is sufficiently extensive evidence of abuse to merit concern (Pillemer and Moore, 1989: 314–20).

Separate statistical analyses were made to identify predictors of negative actions, paying attention to staff–patient conflict and level of burnout.

Pillemer developed his work on predictors in a paper with Bachman-Prehn in 1991. That study concludes that well-qualified staff do not choose to work in nursing homes. Work in nursing homes is physically taxing, the wages are poor and the job prestige is low (Pillemer, 1988: 232). Working in situations of very high conflict, staff also run serious risk of verbal and physical assault by patients. (This point is reiterated in the findings of a study in Bristol and published in the *British Medical Journal* in 1993: Eastley et al., 1993.) Pillemer also drew attention to the quality of care in nursing homes which had been shown to be better in homes which could afford to hire staff with better training and where staff–patient ratios were relatively high. High staff turnover rates could be correlated with poor quality care. Nurses and nursing aides with lower levels of education and younger staff members were likely to have more negative attitudes towards elderly people (Pillemer, 1988: 232).

The outcome of this survey was an endeavour to improve staff training. Together with Hudson and others, Pillemer developed a model abuse prevention programme for nursing assistants called *Ensuring an Abuse-Free Environment* (Coalition of Advocates for the Rights of Infirm Elders [CARIE], 1991; Pillemer and Hudson, 1993). In so doing they underscored the necessity of upgrading the quality of nursing home care. In brief, the model programme is made up of eight modules written in non-technical language and includes a module on the abuse of staff by residents. Pillemer's conviction that it was essential to improve staff training has recently been confirmed by British research (Baillon et al., 1996: 225).

Finally, Pillemer and Moore emphasized that inappropriate management practices and staff–patient interaction require further study. Staff shortages may be a factor in inadequate care. Staff screening and development are needed to protect patients and steps must be taken to reduce the stress experienced by staff.

In the following year, Wiener and Kayser-Jones published a paper about the interaction of nursing home staff with patients and their relatives. They showed that both staff and patients/relatives had complaints of the other: the staff complained largely of being short-staffed and the sense that they were not working as a team, with restrictions placed on them by a lack of resources and actual materials to do the job, such as sheets, towels and simple ointments (Wiener and Kayser-Jones, 1990: 95; cf. Kayser-Jones, 1981; see also Tellis-Nayak and Tellis-Nayak, 1979).

Goffman said 30 years ago:

> Many institutions, most of the time, seem to function merely as storage dumps for inmates, but they usually present themselves to the public as rational organizations designed consciously as effective machines for producing a few officially avowed and officially approved ends. (Goffman, 1968: 73)

Although the existence of elder mistreatment in domestic situations had been recognized by some investigators in Britain since the 1970s, little attention had been paid to it specifically in residential settings. In 1981, however, Clough published *Old Age Homes* and emphasized the rights and choices to which residents were entitled. Urging that they should achieve some degree of 'mastery' or self-determination, he said: 'The more services the staff provide, or the more they do for residents, the more power they have over their lives' (Clough, 1981: 162), thus drawing attention to the danger that is implicit in inhibiting personal growth by restricting freedom and movement. Since then, Clough has continually drawn attention to the quality of care in residential homes. In 1988, the Wagner Committee received his report *Scandals in Residential Centres*. This was an analysis of some 20 public inquiry reports about abuse and neglect in residential homes. It raised fundamental questions about the nature of residential institutions, but was never published. (Extracts are published here with the author's permission.) Clough reflected on what we had *not* learnt from the past and noted the published statement of a former Secretary for Social Services, in 1979:

> We have had a succession of public enquiries pointing up grave inadequacies in public hospitals . . . [but] little has changed for the better in some of them . . . I am determined that this gap between the good and the bad shall not remain as wide as it is today. (cited in Clough, 1988a)

Clough then set the scene by going back to this report written by a journalist in 1955:

John had been lying in a urine soaked bed.

Then the nurse came. He pulled back the three blankets which covered John and said 'You filthy bastard'. He took hold of the nightshirt. John took hold of the nightshirt. They tugged. John held on as if the split shirt was life. The nurse swore. John swore. The nurse lifted a closed fist and crashed it into John's stomach. John let go. The nurse changed John's nightshirt. John's nightshirt was changed several times before he died the next day.

He was sixty-three.
It was a chronics' ward.
It was a mental hospital.
It was a progressive hospital.
It was the twentieth century.
It was 1955.

Clough went on to comment on this example of abuse and the others that were to follow in his report, saying: 'Even [these examples] cannot convey what it must have been like for dependent, powerless people to live in fear of those who had the responsibility to look after them, *day after day after day*'.

In spite of the strength of the Minister's words in 1979, by 1987 there were to be at least two more public inquiries. One was a report illustrating the poor management of care homes for older people in Camden and there was the appalling report about pervasive abuse at Nye Bevan Lodge, Southwark. Even more reports were to follow. Wardhaugh and Wilding in their recent paper on the corruption of care, said of one scandal:

What is remarkable is that every level of management appears to have been guilty. Middle and senior management were equally contemptuous of complaints and dilatory in pursuing them. So were Hospital Management Committees, Regional Hospital Boards and the Department of Health and Social Security. As [Dick] Crossman's memoirs reveal (*Political Diaries*, Vol. 3. 411), the Department knew about the unsatisfactory conditions at Ely Hospital [Cardiff] long before the Howe Report. (Wardhaugh and Wilding, 1993: 18–19)

The Camden Report followed complaints about the standard of care in homes for older people in the borough. It revealed that the standard of care was poor in the majority of homes and concluded that 'effective management of residential care in Camden has broken down' (cited in Clough, 1988a). This was only nine years ago.

The same year, there was the Nye Bevan Lodge inquiry. The report stated that there was:

an atmosphere of deep mistrust and suspicion which [had] permeated every aspect of life in the home for many years resulting in a serious deterioration in the level of care provided [and] was such that a proper level of caring could never be restored given the same staff and officers. (cited in Clough, 1988a)

The actions of staff included: neglecting to wash or bath residents and charging them for bathing, probably as a means of reducing the number of people to be bathed; punishing those who complained by leaving one person's feet in excessively hot water for a long time; opening windows and removing blankets at night so that in consequence some residents caught pneumonia and died; some residents were involved in falls following altercations with staff; the bar in the home was used by a few staff and by outsiders who were rowdy and sometimes molested staff or residents (Clough, 1988a).

About the same time as Clough prepared his report, he suggested in the journal *Care Weekly* that the abuse of residents is more likely when:

> there have been a series of complaints over a long period and [these] relate to more than one member of staff; the establishment is run down and basic arrangements for laundry and hygiene are poor, for example a pervasive smell of urine; there are staff shortages and staff sickness; senior staff are on holiday; interaction between resident and worker takes place in private; there is little supervision of staff and they are able to develop their own patterns of work (we know little of what happens at night time); staff have been in charge of the unit with considerable authority for a long time; there is a high turnover of staff; staff drink alcohol regularly during breaks or when on duty; there is uncertainty about the future of the establishment; there are few visitors; residents are highly dependent upon staff for personal care; residents go out little or have few contacts; a particular resident has no-one taking an active interest in him or her; there is discord among the staff team or between staff and managers; the task or the people being cared for are ascribed little worth; the residents are troublesome, when their care makes heavy demands or when the task to be carried out is unpleasant. (Clough, 1988b: 7)

Why does abuse occur on such a scale? Wardhaugh and Wilding proposed an extension of Martin's reflective analysis of *Hospitals in Trouble* in 1984. Martin analysed the sequence of inquiries into scandals in long-stay hospitals in the late 1960s and 1970s, just as Clough was to do later in relation to residential centres, as were Holmes and Johnson on private homes in 1988 and the Harmans on the reports of the Registered Homes Tribunal in 1989. It is an astonishingly painful story. Such an analysis might enable us to see if it is possible to construct a general theory of the reasons for corruption in institutional care. Clough put forward a number of explanations in his 1988 report of what was to be learnt from the scandals that he reviewed:

> There was a failure within the managing agency to agree about purpose and tasks.
> There was a failure to manage life in the centre in an appropriate way.
> There was a shortage of resources and staff.
> There was confusion and lack of knowledge and frequent absence of guidelines.
> There was the attitude and behaviour of staff, inadequate staffing levels and training and low staff morale.
> Low status was ascribed to the work.
> There was a failure to perceive a pattern in events, individual events being treated in isolation. (Clough, 1988a)

Commenting on Clough's findings, Phillipson and Biggs (1995: 191) have suggested that they imply a model in which abuse and neglect may be related to three key factors: (a) *the home environment*; (b) *the staff* and (c) *the residents*. In this, they follow Pillemer, who first broached this as a provisional model (Figure 11.1) and found it validated by his subsequent research (Pillemer, 1996).

Figure 11.1 *Theoretical model of patient maltreatment (Pillemer, 1988: 230; published with permission)*

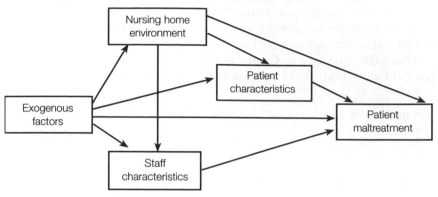

Phillipson and Biggs went on to suggest further that under these separate headings might be included the following factors:

(a) *the home environment* – the extent of custodial orientation (that is, the areas where residents can exercise control over their situation);

(b) *the staff* – low staff–patient ratios and staff turnover rate, which themselves may lead to maltreatment if they reach certain levels. They suggest also that the extent to which homes in the statutory sector are integrated into (rather than isolated from) the social services department may be important both in preventing and identifying abuse. Staff attitudes, they consider, will be conditioned by wider social attitudes to older people.

(c) *the residents* – they identify the fact that healthier patients receive more humane treatment from staff and regard socially isolated residents and patients as being at greatest risk of abuse (Phillipson and Biggs, 1992: 115–16; 1995: 192; see also Pillemer, 1988: 233). Bennett and Kingston also note Pillemer's suggestion in his model that there may be exogenous (or external) factors: namely, the supply and demand of hospital beds and the unemployment rate, which may need to be taken into account. (Pillemer, 1988: 234; Bennett and Kingston, 1993: 118)

Clearly both Pillemer and Clough, each working independently from the other, in countries on either side of the Atlantic Ocean, come to remarkably similar conclusions.

Bennett and Kingston have reminded us (1993) that abuse in residential settings can be traced back to practices under the nineteenth century Poor Laws (but see also Thomson, 1983; Norton, 1990). In fact, institutional malpractice was not discussed overtly and taken seriously in Britain until Townsend's *The Last Refuge* in 1962 and Robb's *Sans Everything: a Case to Answer* in 1967. Bennett and Kingston have listed the varied spectrum of abusive and neglectful behaviours encountered in elderly care which have been the subject of American and European studies: privacy, physical care and quality of life, erosion of individuality, resistance to change in geriatric care, physical working conditions, burnout, organizational factors, fraud and the taking of life (Bennett and Kingston, 1993: 117; see also Gilleard, 1994).

The Wagner Report on residential care (1988) said that living in a residential establishment should be a positive experience ensuring a better quality of life than the resident could enjoy in any other setting and that the contribution of staff should be recognized and enhanced. While this is indisputable, it is strange that Clough's findings were not included or referred to in the report. Indeed, Wagner studiously avoided raising the implications of the notorious public inquiry reports of the 1970s and 1980s. The literature surveys (Sinclair, 1988) which were attached as Volume 2 of the Wagner Report contain no reference to them. We are left with the distinct impression that Clough's findings were deliberately suppressed (Glendenning, 1996: 47).

The 1994 report on *Standards of Nursing in Nursing Homes* by the UK Central Council for Nursing, Midwifery and Health Visiting (UKCC) revealed that reported cases of misconduct in the nursing home sector had risen from 8 per cent to 26 per cent since 1990. The report said:

> Whilst the complaints reveal serious professional misconduct such as physical and verbal abuse, they also identify wholly inadequate systems of drug administration, ineffective management systems, lack of systematic care planning or effective record keeping and almost non-existent induction or in-service training. (UKCC, 1994: 7)

This is a penetrating comment from a professional organization. How much more difficult is it therefore in the case of professionally unqualified staff and care staff in the independent sector?

Willcocks, Peace and Kellaher in their 1986 study of 100 public sector homes concluded that the reality of the care home was that the needs of the institution had to be met. The physical environment was not designed to take into account residents' lifestyles and this was 'a substantial indictment of residential care' (Willcocks et al., 1986: 151; Peace et al., 1997), a view that was reinforced by Counsel and Care's report on privacy in 1991 and Bright's report on residential care in 1995. As Hughes has pointed out:

> Institutions, because of their semi-closed environment and the intimate nature of care required, appear to be environments in which abuse can occur unreported for significant periods of time. (Hughes, 1995: 136)

Conclusion

The messages that come from Pillemer and Clough are very clear and the American studies demonstrate that length of service and the effectiveness of staff training have a clear relation to stress and burnout. It is also neces-sary to admit that we have an insufficient understanding of staff–patient conflict, together with a lack of theoretical understanding of why abuse, mis-treatment, maltreatment and neglect in residential centres occurs. In addition, the implications of gender in elder abuse have been side-stepped for too long (see Kenny, 1990: 571–5; Peace, 1993: 140; Lee-Treweek, 1994; and also Chapter 8, this volume).

Additionally, we saw in Chapter 4 (above) that the taboo subject of sexual abuse is as relevant to an understanding of what is occurring in residential settings as it is in domestic situations. Unquestionably this category of abuse is a major area for research (Ramsey-Klawsnik, 1991: 73–90; 1996: 67–87; Bennett and Kingston, 1993: 103–6; Holt, 1993a: 16; 1993b: 63–71; Ker, 1996: 166–71).

It is astonishing that after all this time and countless reports from public inquiries, no government has understood that there is a public responsibility to fund research to enable us to understand the questions that this chapter has attempted to raise.

Note

This chapter is based on a paper originally given at an Action on Elder Abuse conference at Lancaster University in July 1995 (Glendenning, 1996).

12
Developing Social Work Practice in Protection and Assistance

Jill Manthorpe

In this chapter we shall explore the development of social work practice in the 1990s in the areas of detecting elder abuse, assisting those who have been mistreated or neglected and in contributing to systems of prevention, protection and public education. The focus is on social work in the British context but this professional activity is rarely carried out without reference to other disciplines or agencies. It is therefore important to note that social work practice may well describe a range of roles and activities that encompass the work of others from a variety of professional or organizational backgrounds.

The changing context of care

The National Health Service (NHS) and Community Care Act 1990 marked a major shift in British social and health care delivery, though there are considerable points of continuity. In terms of policy, five main themes arising from the White Paper *Caring for People* (Department of Health, 1989b) are highly relevant to elder abuse. These are:

- the award of lead responsibility for community care to local authorities
- the requirement for local authorities to establish inspection and registration units
- the exhortation to make maximum use of the independent (commercial and voluntary) sectors
- the emphasis on strategic development of services
- the encouragement of systems of care management to deliver a coordinated range of services and informal assistance. (sections 1.11 and 1.12)

Local authorities have implemented the community care reforms swiftly, though there persists a degree of variation between authorities for reasons associated with political preferences, local circumstances and managerial priorities. For example, the purchaser/provider split in social care has itself taken a great deal of work, with little immediate beneficial outcomes in some areas (Lewis et al., 1996). Similarly, concerning the transition to new processes such as care management, a recent commentary notes: 'Case management arrangements and performance differs greatly' (Davies et al.,

1996: 87). The implementation process is still continuing and although the policy context is clear in some respects, Community Care Plans for example are produced annually and inspection and complaints procedures are highly developed, much work remains to establish robust systems which can cope with the fundamental challenges raised when care is sub-optimal or abusive.

The five themes identified above merit some comment individually. First the onus of having lead responsibility raises questions about whether individual local authority officers (social workers) are *de facto* the lead professional in a hierarchical system of care planning. In some senses the social worker or care manager has assumed this role, being the person responsible for coordinating care services, for agreeing to budget expenditure and carrying out the duties of local authorities in terms of assessment now applicable to both eligible users and carers (under the Carers (Recognition and Services) Act 1995). However, social workers rightly query whether or not they have the powerful position implied. They are required to liaise with other agencies. They are compelled to place the majority of their extra budget in the independent sector and much of their work can feel reactive to decisions made by others, most notably in the area of discharge from hospital.

In relation to elder abuse, local authorities have taken the lead in terms of producing strategic documents about elder abuse. A survey conducted by Action on Elder Abuse in 1994 (AEA, 1995) discovered that three-quarters of responding social services departments had a policy on elder abuse and all responding recognized the need for such a policy. In contrast less than a quarter of health authorities/trusts had such a policy. Whilst this survey was confined to England and Wales and drew attention to 'remarkable variation' in what were presented as policies, it also noted that 80 per cent of local authorities with policies had responsible lead officers in this area.

Encouraged by the Social Services Inspectorate (1992), social services departments have therefore been the major agents of change in developing policies and procedures, simultaneously taking on lead responsibilities under the NHS and Community Care Act 1990. There are some interesting parallels in implementation, notably the interface with general practitioners. Means and Smith (1994: 159) draw attention to the complications surrounding the lead role of social services with the reluctance of GPs to become involved in the detail of care management while Action on Elder Abuse point to the total exclusion of GPs from all the policy documents identified in their survey.

The second theme arising from the strategy conceptionalized by *Caring for People* is the establishment of inspection units, which in 1991 was one of the earlier legislative changes in the area of community care reforms, predating the transfer of social security monies and assessment procedures by two full years. Until recently and with some rare exceptions theories of domestic and institutional abuse or mistreatment have been strangely separated in Britain. Reasons for this might be a 'tolerance factor'; the idea that institutional care is, by its very nature, abusive since its organization is the antithesis of so-called natural family care freely provided, ideally with love and respect. Alternatively it could lie in the origins of ideas about elder abuse as part of social concern about family, gendered and domestic violence (Kingston and Penhale, 1995) which initially formed part of critiques about family life and relationships and have been developed through work on informal, not formal care.

In terms of social work reorganization and practice the establishment of inspection units confirmed responsibilities under the Registered Homes Act 1984 and its Code of Practice, *Home Life* (Centre for Policy on Ageing, 1984). Such units, with their prescribed 'arm's length' and thus organizationally separate status have confirmed the distinction between residential and home-based care. For local authorities, issues of quality have often developed as part of the contracting process of review and monitoring for both in-house services and those provided by the independent sector. New working relationships have also had to evolve with complaints departments, their establishment again part of the duties of the NHS and Community Care Act 1990 under clause 50 and set up in April 1991.

Procedures and policies about elder abuse have to engage with a complex web of existing functional processes. Yet further complexities arise in relation to nursing home care, where the inspectorate is located in the health authority, the purchaser/commissioner, or where complaints involve health service personnel and thus become entwined with the NHS complaints procedure (revised as *Acting on Complaints*, Department of Health, 1995c). Both the community care changes and the NHS reforms, albeit enacted together, are somewhat discrete: a new area of professional concern such as elder abuse can quite rapidly point to the rough edges or areas of uncertainty that exist while major organizational changes take time to bed down.

Our third theme of relevant contextual debate lies in the rapid development of the independent sector as the major provider of residential services, a position only confirmed by the policy guidance since the independent sector had become virtually the exclusive provider of nursing home care and the majority provider of residential care before the NHS and Community Care Act 1990, particularly in relation to provision for older people (Darton and Wright, 1993).

Such a development and the confirmation that it would not be reversed raises important questions about the protection of older people. The independent sector has to become involved in self-regulation and internal monitoring to guard against abusive care practices, but as Gilleard (1994) points out, in the area of physical abuse in residential care and in hospitals there appears to be an intriguing lack of relationship between those characteristics associated with the quality of care, or the lack of it, and physical abuse in institutions, or its absence. For those involved in the interests of individual older residents, such as care managers or relatives, the many facets of residential care make for problems in assessing what is happening or in testing the strength of defences against abusive or neglectful practice.

To a large extent, negative perceptions of the independent sector have dominated the debate about elder abuse, although public sector care has never been immune from criticism; it has simply been rather muted. What has been missing is an acknowledgement that the independent sector has, *de facto*, become a significant provider of respite from domestic abuse or neglect and has the potential to be a key location for assistance to those who have been abused, from whatever quarter. It is within its walls that older people may be helped therapeutically and helped to rebuild their self-esteem, or to cope with feelings of self-blame and guilt.

Concentration on definition and discovery of elder abuse among professional circles needs to move on to focus on what is helpful for survivors of abuse. Individual care managers who contract with a provider of residential care, from whatever organizational setting, need to devote considerable energy and imagination to devising useful programmes for individuals, with the provider, beyond the important aspects of physical security and the satisfaction of basic needs. The onus on the care manager is part of that role. However, great help may be available from local psychology services, community nurses or medical practitioners within the health service, while voluntary organizations may also be key sources of counselling, victim support or self-help groups. Further links may be established at local level among the survivors of domestic violence or mental health problems, while religious or culturally specific groupings or individuals may have significant meaning to the individuals concerned. Such networks move the care manager beyond simplistic notions of 'care packaging' for domestic services or personal care to a much broader interpretation of the role – particularly developing and seeing a residential placement as being part of the complex raft of assistance for the older person in the provision of immediate safety, crucially, but also in the provision of healing and social relationships.

At the level of policy our fourth theme notes the responsibility of social services departments to move to an enabling role, establishing through the production of annual Community Care Plans (clause 46 of the Act) a strategy for local services development. This has resulted in consultation rounds, with a degree of variety among plans, but these symbolize an advance in thinking strategically about developments in line with other organizations and in consultation with users and with carers. The next step in development may be increased coherence with other departmental policies so that, for example, particular issues such as elder abuse can form the subject of agreed action. A community care plan is not a policy on elder abuse, but the two need to be cognizant of each other. In drawing together such material, individual workers may benefit from the ironing out of procedural problems such as how issues of protection are to be discussed in a community care assessment. Otherwise there is a danger of elder abuse issues being at a remove from community care assessments which can be under pressure to progress swiftly with minimal levels of participation. As Futter and Penhale (1996: 55) note: 'Care management and assessment processes appear to be developing predominantly as managerial systems concerned with the cost-effective administration of resources.' This pessimistic picture of care management from the field should alert those interested in issues of elder abuse that as yet 'unmentionable' subjects such as resources, rationing and priorities are seen to affect good practice generally. The optimism of Community Care Plans may be at variance with the experiences of staff delivering assessment of care services. We have little information about the implementation of elder abuse procedures at the level of practitioners; this is not simply a gap in knowledge of underlying theories but a lack of detail about how staff juggle the competing demands of individuals who all have social care needs.

We finish this section with a comment on the theme of care management, the system nationally adopted but with local variations (Davis et al., 1995). Care management is ideally placed to assist in the discovery of possible abusive or neglected care practices with its focus on the individual's needs, its ability to coordinate information, its potential for engaging in a trusting and empathetic relationship with the user. As Smale and Tuson note, assessors need to be experts in:

- facilitating people to articulate their own needs and clarify what they want
- being sensitive to differences
- helping people through major transitions
- negotiating and conciliating (Smale and Tuson, 1993: 13–15)

They advocate an exchange model of assessment to assist in the complex processes of 'reorganizing, understanding and intervening in the patterns of relationships between individuals and between groups and organizations that precipitate and perpetuate social problems'.

As we have noted, early work on elder abuse was concentrated on definition and detection (see Hugman, 1995) in much the same way as early emphasis on care management has been on assessment and targeting. The two come closer together as the helping processes move to determine what is to be done and how the situation is to be reviewed or monitored. In social work, the separation of domiciliary-based care from residential care has perpetuated the idea that a residential solution removes or ameliorates problems. Trained staff and imaginative ways of working, for example, have been more concentrated in services outside the residential sector for many user groups, as the Wagner Report (1988) implied.

Care management systems and the way in which they incorporate or ignore issues of abuse and neglect appear to converge around the notion of risk. Narrowly interpreted, risk can be perceived as simply danger and for older people this may be construed paternalistically or infantilizingly. For example, people can be seen as literally being 'at risk' in a general sense with no real evaluation of the likelihood of the danger occurring or the seriousness of the danger (Carson, 1995). Further work in this area will have to incorporate ideas about 'risk factors' which seem to pervade professional literature but again occupy an uncertain realm. Debate continues, for example, about the róle of dementia as a significant risk factor – is it a trigger that increases carer stress or a characteristic that increases an individual's vulnerability by removing barriers around privacy and autonomy (Manthorpe, 1995)? As the literature on child abuse confirms, there are unlikely to be simple patterns of relationships.

The monitoring and review functions of care management should assist us to listen to the experiences of the survivors of abuse since the process is designed to be continuous and wide-ranging. Much will depend though on the priority given to these tasks in the context of pressure to achieve good quality initial assessments, particularly those which enable rapid hospital discharge. There also needs to be some continuity and agreement on the sharing of information when assessment and review are carried out by different personnel.

In the short term the intersection of the two areas of care management and elder abuse may be the most fruitful area of the conundrum which has begun to dominate discussion in protecting older people – what can be done to protect that does not further abuse or oppress the individual?

Social work dilemmas

This section focuses on some current questions which are distilled from social work commentary and the wider research and practitioner community; now noticeably distinguished by multidisciplinary work. It raises a series of interrelated points which are relevant at both philosophical and practical levels.

Adults or elders?

The concept of elder abuse signifies that age is a fundamentally important characteristic of the victim or abused person. It raises questions about whether being old makes for increased vulnerability or whether specific duties or obligations are owed to older people. Currently the social division between child and adult reflects legal notions of when capacity, in terms of making contracts or decisions, is presumed and also when the notion of citizenship is acquired. For older people both capacity and citizenship may be problematic since, although their adult status is accepted, it may be undermined by processes of infantilization and social discrimination. Biggs et al. draw attention to citizenship as the 'unifying force' in the debate about elder abuse, claiming that 'An exclusive focus on the most deprived, and the prejudices that thereby receive support, have resulted in the paradoxical situation whereby abuse can be recognized whilst very little is done to prevent it' (Biggs et al., 1995: 122).

Such arguments are familiar to social work practitioners since their work in the area of acute need for social care has similarly meant that their focus is on a small percentage of older people; in a sense they have always had their attention directed to the extremes of vulnerability.

Drawing attention to older people as citizens moves us to assess whether it might be more beneficial to consider elder abuse as adult abuse. In Britain, some social services departments have moved in this direction by developing policies and procedures for adults at risk of abuse. There may be an organizational justification for this in that the services are organized around children and adults. Equally it may reflect a shift in priorities away from the notion that 'elderly services' could be separated functionally from services for other adults. The survival and ageing of people with physical disabilities and people with learning disabilities may also have blurred previous distinctions.

The designation of adulthood imputes autonomy and control, yet some adults are not the focus of social work attention and have their self-determination limited by a lay or professional judgement that they need protection or it is in their best interests to receive assistance with aspects of personal care or daily living. The term 'adult abuse' is therefore too broad a notion to take on as an anti-ageist alternative to elder abuse. Indeed as work on domestic violence confirms (N. Johnson, 1995; Lloyd, 1995), some forms of violence in the domestic setting receive far more professional and political attention than others.

Elder abuse therefore is located in the general span of social care services for those older people already assessed as requiring or deserving community care provision but also as a factor which can alter the classification of the individual. At one level a home care worker (from whatever agency) may develop suspicions about the mistreatment of his or her 'client'; at another, evidence or suspicion of mistreatment may start the process of assessment and may justify the provision of resources to an individual whose social care needs appear minimal. Currently there are few tailored services available to victims or survivors of elder abuse, so a similar service may be provided to those with such experience and those whose circumstances have no relevance to abusive practices. We have little idea of the meaning and experiences of residential care when it is used as a sanctuary for an abused older person rather than for someone who has made a positive choice to enter residential care and is well supported by the wider environment of family or previous carers.

Social work with older people has had a chequered history, and the care management system described earlier is one move towards bridging the traditional gap between services for older people and other social work clients or users. In terms of practice there are advantages in being more precise about the reasons for social care, particularly when resources are in such short supply. Such precision however can be problematic since privacy and confidential relationships can be breached if need has to be argued, defended and defined. Multidisciplinary working, with all its benefits, is sometimes rather silent on the extent to which certain information can be kept confidential. For social workers, their ambiguous professional status

(Shardlow, 1995) may also lead to dilemmas about whether to pass on information about mistreatment to other agencies.

A feminist approach, seeing the construct of elder abuse as an attempt to disguise the fact that the majority of abusers are male (Whittaker, 1996a; see also Chapter 8, this volume), is also relevant to the issue of adulthood versus elder status. Drawing attention to gender raises a wide and controversial range of philosophical and research questions but in practice it confirms the position that social work services are generally delivered to women by women, a prime example being residential or day care, which can operate in a female environment almost exclusively. Whittaker argues that the general decriminalization of elder abuse needs to be challenged and that interventions, in terms of providing a safe refuge or excluding the perpetrator, must be developed.

This approach moves us from seeing elder abuse as part of the care system for adults or elder people to locating it within family systems in particular. In doing so it returns the debate to the domestic sphere and to conceptualizations of abuse as largely manifested by physical violence. Social workers have access to domestic environments and those places which are home yet not home; many also now will have experience in working with a range of adults who have social care needs. What are missing still are models of work with those adults who do not fall neatly into organizational or policy priority areas.

The spectre of child protection?

Procedures and policies about elder abuse or the abuse of vulnerable adults are often based on the child protection model since this model is familiar and relevant and, despite criticisms, has stood the test of time. Yet professional discourse makes much of reminding practitioners that the areas are distinct and raises the spectre of child protection to warn practitioners and policy-makers that there are dangers in following the models too closely, lest the area of elder abuse become associated with the mistakes and image of child protection.

There are two threads to this debate. First, the view that the child protection system has not fulfilled its aims of protection, indeed that it has resulted in further abuse or labelled families as abusive erroneously, with untold damage to the children and parents concerned. Equally, the system of child abuse is blamed for not saving certain children from the dangerous or inadequate care of certain parents or caregivers. As Parton notes, the role of the social worker in assessment and management is to avoid 'both harm to children and unwarrantable interventions in the family' (Parton, 1996: 11), a dualism which is pertinent to elder abuse, particularly in the domestic setting. One thread in differentiating elder abuse from child protection is to avoid being associated with the latter's perceived failings.

This polarization does have its drawbacks. It means that elder abuse theory and practice develops largely without the benefits of learning from the lessons of child protection. The 20 individual studies arising from the Department of Health's research (summarized in Department of Health, 1995d and known as the Blue Book), raise important questions about response to referrals of allegations of abuse and the effectiveness of interventions. It is unlikely that individual practitioners working with older people will be able to benefit from this research unless trainers and commentators draw out the relevance of its findings and can convince practitioners that the area of child protection is not so discredited that elder abuse services should distance themselves from it; a position that will not necessarily convince the wider world.

The second thread has more substance and concerns the validity of child protection systems to the world of adults. Much of the initial work on elder abuse was not about adults or elders in general but about those who are intellectually impaired, either through learning disabilities or a degree of mental confusion such as that related to dementia. Most case studies in training materials refer to examples where there is doubt about the individual's ability to make informed choices, to recall, to communicate, or the extent of their ability to distinguish reality from fantasy. Such problems may already have brought individuals to the attention of care services. Wilson (1994), for example, reports very high rates of abuse and neglect among mentally ill older people, even though she considered staff abuse had been under-reported.

Conceptualizing the 'victim' of elder abuse as an adult places great onus on staff to find out the meaning of abuse to the older person. Does he or she see the pilfering of his or her pension by a caregiving relative as important or not? It also means accepting the person's choice to allow a situation to continue in the light of the acceptability or availability of other courses of action. It can mean defending the right of the individual against the views of other staff or relatives that 'something must be done' or that it is in the person's best interests (but contrary to his or her wishes) to take action. Part of the multi-faceted role of the social worker may lie in this advocacy function rather than as an investigator.

For individuals, where the extent of mental impairment appears to cloud the ability to make choices or to be self-protective, the social work task, as is common for other professionals, lies in making judgements about the extent of intervention. Here again, the child protection system has something to offer in protecting vulnerable adults. For example, liaison with the police in domestic and child care cases may be well developed and a useful link for social work agencies. The police are also the key resource in giving advice about the collection of evidence or whether a crime has been committed. Their expertise in helping older people who have been the victims of crimes (such as burglary and deception) has been remarkably under-researched and under-used by welfare professionals.

The dilemmas explored here concern whether social work can distance itself from the image and reality of child protection by developing new and better systems of protecting adults. Alternatively, should social workers in adult services liaise closely with their colleagues who have great experience in this area? The wider policy community is still cautious about professional expansion in this area. We may have to accept that social workers will not find work in elder abuse any easier or more 'legitimate' than child protection. The fundamental difficulty for both is identical: there is no certainty that intervention will be totally or universally beneficial. It is nonetheless better than the alternative of inertia and inaction.

Developing a value base

This section explores some of the values espoused by social work practitioners in the 1990s and relates them to work in protecting individuals from elder abuse or neglect. The dilemma lies in assessing the extent to which the profession has a coherent set of values and whether in practice certain values conflict with the declared aim of protection. Whilst any discussion of values could be extensive, the discussion here revolves around the concepts of empowerment, protection and anti-oppressive practice.

Phillips (1996: 135) argues that social work has to embrace more positive images and models of ageing in order to respond to the changing role of older people, particularly as their consumption of goods and services extends to the care arena. The theory of empowerment lends itself to this pluralistic world, as the social worker or care manager enables the consumer to become an active participant in the process. However, empowerment is relatively undeveloped in the area of elder mistreatment and the relationship of consumer/provider is especially ambiguous in domestic settings where caregiving is not generally driven by commercial relationships. Both caregiver and recipient may have little power and their histories may be entwined by many years of inter-generational or spousal abuse. As a theory, empowerment seeks to redress imbalances of power and has been particularly effective in countering stereotypes that people are adequately served by well-meaning professionals or family members.

In this sense empowerment acts as a useful concept to explain the principle of handing over power or challenging authority. However, for professionals this individualistic focus is made somewhat difficult by their attempts to rightly empower a range of individuals, particularly those who have become known, almost inseparably, as 'users and carers'. Although the interests of users and carers do coincide to a large extent, this can be overestimated, and of course if one party is abusive to the other, there can be significant areas of conflict (see Manthorpe and Twigg, 1995). To empower both the older person and the carer can seem contradictory, especially if both allege that there is no cause for concern. It may be that the social worker, in consultation with colleagues from other services, accepts that self-determination for an adult who is mentally capable means precisely that. The multidisciplinary team or network is not there just to protect the worker from blame if things go wrong: it may also suggest different strategies (see Penhale, 1993a). Similarly, the social worker will need the backing and support of his or her agency to 'let go' of situations, or move them to a monitoring or review process, if the adult concerned has indicated that intervention is unwelcome at this stage. While Payne (1995: 181) rightly observes that self-determination can be criticized, in linking it to advocacy and participation he reminds us that provision for older people in terms of self-help groups and specialist services is lacking. An individual worker may genuinely wish to empower the older person in theory, but he or she needs to reflect on issues of power at an individual level.

This wider service context is relevant to dilemmas about protection, since removal of the vulnerable person or the abuser is no guarantee that the need for protection will end. As Clough (1996) illustrates, institutional care can be abusive despite the safeguards of inspection and self-regulation. Some older people, at times, are exceptionally vulnerable and may attract those committed to abusive behaviours. To offer guarantees of safety may itself be so intrusive as to be abusive or simply optimistic.

As yet, little work exists on involving older people in measures for self-protection. By far the most developed area is that of money; a subject which the social work profession has largely ignored apart from some individuals' or departments' interests in welfare rights, or more latterly, charging for social care (see Bradley and Manthorpe, 1995). As a distinct category, financial abuse has been greatly informed by Langan and Means's research (1996) which found inconsistency in policies relating to elder abuse and to the management of individuals' finances where decisions had been taken that they could no longer administer their own money. Social workers are being placed in the unenviable position of protecting the same money that they may later authorize to be spent in order to purchase care; a position which can be justified, but one which begs the question about the purpose of protection by, say, a cynical relative. It is clear that protection needs to be more clearly formulated and its motives made more transparent, particularly when other people may stand accused of being over-protective. A spouse, for example, who protects his or her partner from the dangers of the outside world may do so from a variety of motives. The word 'protect' is rarely used objectively in such circumstances and professionals may find their own motives more closely questioned.

The last dilemma concerns the question of what constitutes anti-oppressive practice and how it may be operationalized. In the area of elder abuse, oppression as a concept fits in well with the social position of many older people both economically and in terms of gender. However, since the publication of the first edition of this book, little has changed in terms of engaging older people themselves in the debate concerning what is to be done about elder abuse. Unlike work in domestic violence and more like child protection, their voices have been quiet. As an agenda for research and for service development, we need to make opportunities to listen to the experiences of survivors and to the experiences of those who are labelled as perpetrators. We also need to assess whether increased media attention has begun to impact upon older people in general. Do they now fear being abused in old age and does this affect their relationships with family members or care professionals? To see older people as active in the construction of solutions to the problem of elder abuse may take us further in practice.

13

Key Issues for Nursing: the Need to Challenge Practice

Michael Davies

This chapter is intended principally for nurses practising in any setting and it will explore the implications associated with elder abuse from this perspective.

There is little doubt that nurses, whether in hospitals, institutions, community, nursing or residential homes, are essentially placed to identify areas of possible or actual abuse of clients and their carers, although these same practitioners often feel disinclined to report it, or to act upon their observations. The reason for this 'inaction' could be due to the fact that protocols are not available or are inaccessible, or there is fear of being exposed to aggressive management systems. The fear of scapegoating may be another important reason for inaction. Furthermore, questions will be raised as to whether these practitioners are aware of their own professional standards. These issues will be explored in some detail, and I will outline possible areas where professionals and others could be accused of actual or potential abuse, while carrying out their nursing care role, particularly with their frail elderly patients. Areas of possible staff abuse will also be addressed, and the apparent lack of guidelines available for staff to follow will also be questioned.

Central to this chapter will be the firm belief that if we are to bring about change in the total field of elder abuse, more still needs to be done by those involved in nurse education to expose present and future practitioners to all aspects of the abuse of elderly people. This can only be achieved by introducing the topic into nurse education programmes, at pre- and post-basic level, and the value of a multidisciplinary approach to training will be emphasized. An update regarding the progress made on the introduction of the assessment tools described in the 1993 edition of this book and a brief review of some recent training manuals will also be given.

A cause for concern?

The majority of professionals and their assistants who work with elderly people are becoming more aware that elder abuse and neglect exist and can present in a variety of ways.

In recent times there have been significant changes in the way in which elderly people are cared for. With many long-stay wards closing, and the consequent contraction in the number of hospital beds for elderly patients, the emphasis on caring has moved from the hospital to a more community-orientated service. This does not, of course, preclude the need to question the probability of abuse in these areas, or in other health settings, specifically in the so-called acute care and rehabilitation wards, or within medicine, surgery, orthopaedics and so on where the majority of patients admitted to acute hospitals today are over 65 years old.

This change in emphasis has reduced the period of time that the elderly person remains in hospital. The reduced length of stay for patients often leads to inappropriate discharge to residential homes. This may lead to care assistants undertaking delegated tasks for which they are inadequately supervised and for which they are not clinically competent or trained (O'Kell, 1995). Community nursing staff are called upon to provide nursing care for these residents, delegating complex nursing tasks, thus increasing the risk and workload for both parties. The RCN (1992) found that half the nurses working in residential and nursing homes thought older people were being placed in the wrong kind of home. Indeed it could be argued that we have now 'shifted' the incidence of abuse to other environments within the community. These changes are not perceived as better care provision by the profession.

Writing recently in the *Nursing Times* Waters (1996: 29–31) suggested that there is evidence that nurses are concerned by the perceived lack of specialist care being afforded to patients in residential homes, and that these patients are frequently moved to other homes if their care needs change. This view is supported by Nazarko, who catalogues tasks carried out by unqualified staff on patients who are clearly in need of professional care (Nazarko, 1996: 31–3). This early discharge of elderly people into the community – into their own homes or other institutions such as residential/nursing homes – has resulted in an increased demand for more acute nursing care in these situations and as Castledine makes clear: 'Nurses must concern themselves with the care that is to be provided for elderly people in the future – at present, many elderly people are cared for by unqualified staff under poor direction and supervision. Although quality is expensive in terms of both nurses' time and money, this trend must be reversed' (Castledine, 1996: 191).

A more rigorous inspection procedure and a single inspectorate with single care homes are needed. One must also question whether the present fragmented system of monitoring standards and activities within hospitals and institutions – by bodies such as the King's Fund, the Royal Colleges, the United Kingdom Central Council for Nursing, Midwifery and Health Visiting (UKCC), the English National Board and the Mental Health Commission – provides the necessary 'holistic' powers needed to safeguard the interests of the more vulnerable elderly population.

There is a case here for increasing the power of community health councils, which are the only statutory bodies directly representative of the public; all their members are volunteers. Their power could effectively be expanded to cover all facilities which care for older people.

Professional practice issues

Elder abuse is an emotive subject, and action by staff to do something about it is often met by opposition, resistance and criticism, largely because what may be seen as abusive to one person may not seem so to another. The way that older people are perceived can also be an important factor (as we have seen in Chapter 2 of this volume). The vast majority of patients admitted into elderly care units are in a poor state of health, either physically, psychologically or socially, but very often due to all three factors. Demographic trends indicate that the number of these patients will increase. However, the quality of life that these people can expect is not guaranteed, and the provision of their care is uncertain.

In hospitals and other elderly care settings the speciality of geriatrics is under threat. Many hospital trusts are looking to replace geriatric with acute and rehabilitation medicine. The implication of this could be that the specialist care of the chronically ill and frail elderly will disappear. Continuing care will be left in untrained hands. With such a negative attitude towards elderly people, nursing staff are much less likely to be attracted to elderly care settings.

Gilleard has suggested that this would lead to understaffing, lack of training, poor management and poor practice, predisposing towards institutional abuse (Gilleard, 1994: 104). Evidence of this is now beginning to be documented. Cohen has noted that the UKCC Professional Conduct Committee recently dealt with 86 complaints, of which 36 per cent involved nursing homes and 15 per cent mental illness (Cohen, 1995: 18). Over a third of the practice-related allegations that were examined concerned cases of physical or verbal abuse of clients. 'Few would argue that abuse cannot be tolerated, whatever form it takes: basic humanity dictates that, not just our Code of Professional Conduct. We must make every effort to understand such abuse, before looking closely at our own practice, and asking whether we are aiding and abetting it' (Booth, 1995: 26).

Professionals may attempt to 'explain away' abusive behaviour, but we need to question such an attitude when we know anecdotally that certain practices occur. The following examples of abusive behaviour are categorized into restraint, disempowerment, management and neglect.

Categories of abusive behaviour

Restraint

(a) Inappropriate use of medication for challenging behaviour.
(b) Inappropriate use of chemical and mechanical restraints.

Disempowerment

(a) Placing patients arbitrarily in side rooms.
(b) Professional autonomy, which denies elderly persons the information necessary to ensure informed consent before treatment.
(c) The exclusion of patients from the decision-making process.
(d) Violation of the Patient's Charter.
(e) Labelling of patients.
(f) Lack of privacy for personal hygiene, e.g. eliminating, vomiting.
(g) Over-familiarity with the patient, without permission.

Management

(a) Delays and waiting times.
(b) Failure to carry out continuing care because of inadequate resources, including staff who are uncommitted to elderly people.

Neglect

(a) Inadequate supervision of toiletting.
(b) Denial of fluids/food for whatever reason and in whatever way, e.g. making it difficult for patients to reach food or drink.
(c) Condoning incontinence.

It should be remembered that some types of behaviour or action may be perfectly acceptable to one professional, but not to another. For example, a patient who is the victim of a stroke requires a rehabilitation programme to mobilize and dress him/herself. This may be seen by some staff as cruel when the patient appears to be totally incapable of performing either task. But others may perceive it as forceful therapeutic intervention, for which the patient is likely to be grateful later.

Staff working in elderly care settings are themselves likely to be abused. Patients who are highly dependent and vulnerable, and are also confused and aggressive, are liable to scratch, pinch, swear and threaten on occasions. Outbursts of physical or verbal aggression are not uncommon from both patients and relatives. Although there may be good explanations for their behaviour, it can still be difficult to deal with. Elderly care units are often under-resourced, lacking appropriately qualified staff with the skills necessary to assess the patient's total needs, and recent reports suggest that staff are being expected to take on tasks previously undertaken by junior doctors. There have also been reports that nurses are being requested by health and social services to undertake financial assessment as part of their role; a task usually undertaken by social workers (ACE, 1996: 41). In addition, Langan and Means (1994) found that many community staff were also anxious about handling the finances of people with dementia, because they feared the accusation of abuse. If staff are to handle finances, appropriate systems to protect them should be in place. The issues that all this raises are (1) the need to train staff how to deal with unacceptable behaviour; (2) resource and skills implications; and (3) the changing role of the nurse (ACE, 1996).

Working with dependent elderly patients is both physically and emotionally tiring, and yet in some areas the 12-hour shift concept has either been introduced or is being contemplated. But a six-hour or maximum eight-hour shift is more than sufficient to work within these environments. Each case should be individually assessed in relation to the work and pressure involved in managing each group of patients.

Every effort should be made to ensure that elderly care units are well resourced in terms of appropriately qualified, trained and highly motivated staff, with adequate equipment and informed management support. If we fail to achieve this, we will continue the legacy of elderly care nursing being perceived as a poor quality service with nurses struggling to maintain only minimum standards where abuse can and will occur, unreported; and, more importantly, where it will remain unnoticed.

Reporting cases of mistreatment

Identifying elder abuse and knowing how to respond to it still presents problems for nursing staff, carers and vulnerable older people. Responsible registered nurses are expected to report bad practice. But factors such as professional loyalty, fear of recrimination, or the misinterpretation of events and the absence of adequate protocols for training and support interfere with this process. Without these protocols in place, how can unqualified staff who witness a registered nurse abusing an elderly person report this? The older person concerned may not be able to raise the alarm and the situation may continue to deteriorate if those who witness the incident do not pass on what they know. Some patients are reluctant to complain, feeling that they are fortunate to receive any kind of service and fearful that complaints might lead to reprisals (Cang, 1989; Allen et al., 1992).

There seems little doubt that the abuse of elderly people in any setting is likely to continue, until nurses and care workers feel able to 'blow the whistle' on fellow members of staff. Bright has found that abusers are sometimes allowed to move from one home to another, even after being detected (Bright, 1995: 23). Senior staff, particularly managers it would appear, are often willing to conceal abuse for fear that adverse publicity would lead to a loss of contract, especially in the new purchaser/provider culture. Heath has recently reported that she has been contacted by nurses who are afraid of losing their jobs if they complain about the care (Heath, 1996: 5). But unless people are protected when raising concerns, there will be no real accountability and the well-being of patients could be jeopardized. Brown has suggested that health-care settings tend to be hierarchical and bureaucratic. Such large organizations are usually anonymous and require obedience from their employees, not discussion and consensus (Brown, 1995: 60). Tschudin argues that 'the individual's needs count less than the corporate ones, and ideally, the relationship between employer and employee should be based on the same principles as those between practitioner and patient, that is, care based on receptivity, reciprocity and responsivity' (Tschudin, 1992: 112).

Everyone involved in the care of older people has a responsibility to prevent mistreatment. Staff education could go some way to assist the process, as could adequate systems for monitoring care and supervising new and non-qualified staff. No matter where staff carry out their caring role, they must be encouraged to question care practices continually and raise concerns in the knowledge that they will be supported when they speak out.

To enable this, all health care settings should develop policies and operational guidelines for handling situations of mistreatment of older people. A recent report by Action on Elder Abuse (AEA) found that although social services departments had made considerable progress in the development of policies, developments within health authorities and National Health Service trusts were much slower (AEA, 1995: 8).

The way forward

The importance of raising the profile of the care of elderly people cannot be over-emphasized, but professional education alone does not provide a panacea: changes in social attitudes are also required. Patients' quality of life is closely associated with that of the nursing staff, who share with them the human need for recognition of worth and self-esteem. All staff working with elderly people must be skilled and confident and should be given the opportunity to initiate better methods of care and ways of working. Supporting patients with their family and friends to come to terms with irreversible disability, or to accept death, can be rewarding. Staff need to understand and believe in what they are doing and above all to know that their contribution is valued. Staff also have the right to effective management and leadership, an efficient communication system and continuing professional education opportunities.

Podnieks (1985) identified key areas which contributed to possible neglect and abuse of elderly people by staff as: negative attitudes towards ageing, a lack of understanding of the ageing process, inadequate staff preparation and opportunity for professional growth. In the main, basic education/training programmes for nurses are delivered at diploma/degree level, students following a common foundation programme (CFP) and electing to train for a specific branch: adults, children, mental health, etc. Elderly care nursing preparation falls within the generic adult branch. This could be seen as disadvantaging the elderly patient/client, as it is argued that not enough emphasis is given to this speciality. This view is compounded by a recent survey which the author carried out among 40 institutions of further/higher education who deliver both pre- and post-registration training. Thirty replies were received. Specific details were requested relating to the number of hours spent on teaching 'Gerontological Aspects of Care' during the CFP. This averaged out at approximately five to six hours, similar to the findings of Kingston et al. (1995: 358). Only two institutions taught aspects relating to elder abuse throughout the three-year programme, but the number of hours was not specified. With regard to the experience/qualification of the teaching staff, none stated the length of experience other than expressing an interest during their initial training and beyond, and only four staff responsible for teaching held a diploma/degree in gerontology. This must be seen as a significant reflection on the priority given to the initial preparation of future practitioners in this speciality. Responses to the post-registration surveys were similar. Again specific details were requested relating to the number of post-basic courses offered for qualified staff, and how many hours were devoted to aspects of elder abuse. Eleven institutions responded that they delivered the English National Board (ENB) course 941 (Nursing Elderly People) but only four stated that they included specific sessions on elder abuse. Three indicated that they were aware of policies/guidelines for staff dealing with abuse within trusts. With regard to qualifications of tutors and lecturers, 11 post-basic lecturers held a Master's degree in gerontology, yet only one indicated that it did cross-teaching between pre-/post-registration programmes. Two lecturers supplied assessment tools which they used in their abuse teaching sessions. Opportunities for qualified staff to enrol on ENB post-basic courses on the care of elderly people must be made available, and some key personnel should be afforded the opportunity to study for a diploma or degree in gerontology. These courses are equally relevant for both specialist and generalist nurses. Study days and short courses are also important, particularly if specifically focused training is required.

Gradually, training material is becoming available, for example, Phillipson and Biggs (1992) and Pritchard (1992, 1995). Pillemer and Hudson have reported that an elder abuse prevention training programme (Coalition of Advocates for the Rights of Infirm Elderly [CARIE], 1991), used with nursing assistants working in long-term care, reduced the incidence of reported abusive episodes between staff and patients (Pillemer and Hudson, 1993: 130). A report by the Royal College of Nursing (RCN, 1987) suggested that we need to ask:

- Are all the multidisciplinary team involved, including night staff?

- Are opportunities available for staff to share knowledge and skills and express feelings and attitudes in their day-to-day work?
- Are there adequate learning resources available? (adapted from Royal College of Nursing, 1987)

Educational and training materials are urgently needed for use by all staff who have any dealings with elderly patients in any setting. Only then will we begin to raise the profile of the nursing of elderly people. Ideally, such training should be multidisciplinary, involving social work, psychology, medical and nursing staff, both hospital and community based. The involvement of members of other professions, such as occupational therapy and physiotherapy, could also be included. Together they should form supporting teams to collaborate in producing the training materials that are required. Phillipson and Biggs and Pritchard, taken together, would make a good starting point.

Assessment

The assessment tool introduced in the first edition of this book (Davies, 1993: 112–16) was designed to help staff to identify the potential abuse of patients when they were admitted from their home to hospital or other residential setting. Since that time, several pilot studies have been carried out using hospital and community staff and the feedback from these pilots has been embodied in the revised protocols which may be found in Appendices D and E (p. 233–8).

Implications for practice

The need to improve the detection and prevention of the abuse of elderly people has direct implications for nursing practice. Nurses must be aware of the importance of a comprehensive nursing history. Meticulous attention, using the individualized patient care documentation, in identifying the elderly person's specific needs and problems should be employed to help nurses identify the elderly at risk. There is clearly also a need for a reliable tool which will assist practitioners to detect neglect and abuse.

Perhaps the biggest problem in assessing the extent of abuse, is that the abused person is reluctant to report the incident for fear of retaliation (Ross et al., 1985: 36–9). This may be because of pride, shame, fear, bewilderment or confusion, or because of heavy dependence on the abuser, with the elderly person blaming him/herself for the situation. However, the UKCC's Code of Professional Conduct leaves us in no doubt of our responsibility to our clients. The Code states that nurses should 'act always in such a way as to promote and safeguard the well being and interests of patients/clients' (UKCC, 1992: 2). If nurses are to maintain their role as the patient's advocate, they must be willing to act to prevent abuse to one of the most vulnerable groups in our society.

Detection

Detection is often problematic because of the victim's reluctance to admit that abuse is taking place. The nurse's assessment role in cases of physical abuse begins at the initial contact with the elderly person and continues with each subsequent interaction. During routine physical assessment, the nurse must be alert for clinical symptoms that are inconsistent with the information collected from the patient's history. This becomes difficult when the elderly individual has cognitive defects and exhibits confusion and disorientation. In such cases it is advisable to locate the primary carer or, where appropriate, other workers who have been involved in the care of the patient, to confirm details. Often neighbours and relatives have additional information that may clarify the nature of the injury and its cause. The nurse's observational skills are paramount in all cases, whether or not the patient's mental state is functional or organic. Indicators of abuse should be considered in clusters of categories because although these do not prove the existence of abuse, they certainly indicate a risk (see also Chapter 4, this volume and Decalmer and Davies, 1993).

Nurses also need to be trained in the recognition of indicators of possible psychological and financial abuse.

In the psychological context, possible indicators would include:

Humiliation
(a) shame
(b) blame
(c) ridicule and aggression of and by the elderly person
(d) rejection
(e) cowering, helplessness, hopelessness and infantilization
(f) tearfulness
(g) expression of ambivalence towards family/carers

Harassment
(a) insults
(b) intimidation
(c) fearfulness
(d) agitation

Mental health problems
(a) confusion
(b) depression
(c) anxiety
(d) paranoid reactions.

In the financial context:

(a) theft, often presenting as an unusual interest in the elderly person's financial affairs;
(b) deprivation, insufficient assets being provided for personal needs, for example soap, sweets, newspapers;
(c) coercion: being forced to sign documents without explanation;
(d) manipulation of information, especially financial, with blocked access to property and contracts;
(e) misuse of professional authority, that is, by people who have responsibility for financial affairs; denying access to money required for care or personal needs.

In cases where these indicators are present, it would be advisable to involve other professionals, for example district nurse, health visitor, social worker, solicitor, bank manager, accountant and police, who would be able to advise if there were suspicions, because they might have access to additional information.

Carers

When nurses are carrying out patient assessment, they need to be aware of the vital part that carers play. In any case where there may be reason to believe that abuse has taken place, the assessment must involve the primary carer(s). This must be conducted with great sensitivity. In cases that 'appear' to indicate neglect, it is important to assess the carer's level of understanding, the resources they have available, and the elderly person's willingness to accept care. Older people have the right to self-determination and may knowingly refuse the care necessary to sustain health. Many carers find themselves overburdened, with other family and employment commitments making considerable demands on their time, energy and loyalties.

It should also be remembered that it is not only carers who do the abusing. Carers can also be physically abused by the persons they are caring for; this is quite a common occurrence when a dependent person has behaviour problems associated with dementia. Carers can also experience a great deal of emotional abuse, for example verbal insults, threats, humiliation, etc. Carers can suffer financially if they are unaware that they are entitled to state benefits (ACE, 1996).

Observing carers for signs of abuse is not easy, as they too may be reluctant to volunteer information, but nevertheless an assessment is important if we are to be able to build up a complete picture, which could lead to a resolution of the situation.

Perhaps the best indicator that all is not well with the carer will be signs of stress, and the role of the nurse is to attempt to measure the intensity of feeling associated with some of the common signals that might be expected. These could include:

• frequent requests for help (self or patient), which includes admission to

care;
- aggression: frustration or despair often towards staff;
- signs of physical or mental illness, exhaustion;
- non-visiting or telephone enquiry;
- non-participation in discharge planning;
- anxiety and worry, feeling isolated, lonely, low self-esteem;
- indifferent relationship with patient;
- signs of alcohol/drug dependence;
- being 'over-critical' regarding aspects of care for the patient.

A carer will often express a lack of time for self, or say that they cannot see an end to the situation, that there is no future – that all has gone beyond their control. These signals indicate carer stress and are not necessarily indications that abuse is taking/has taken place. But assessment and recording of these indicators are important pointers in collating the most appropriate package of care for both the patient and the carer and may well help to prevent an abuse situation.

Precise, informed detection skills on the part of nurses, and the completion of the necessary assessment protocols, though perceived as lengthy and time-consuming, will provide definitive information regarding suspected cases of abuse. This in itself may be sufficient to instigate action or at least to alert relevant professionals to the need for further investigation.

The assessment protocols (Appendices D and E), one for use with patients and the other for use with carers, are designed to complement the existing, history-taking process that exists within the individualized patient care documentation, thus allowing for a universal screening mechanism, including identification of possible abuse as a matter of routine.

14

The General Practitioner and Elder Abuse

John F. Noone and Peter Decalmer

How is a family doctor to know if one of his elderly patients is being abused, physically or otherwise? If such abuse is brought to his attention, perhaps by a neighbour or by a health professional who has stumbled onto this knowledge in the course of routine visiting, what is the general practitioner (GP) to do with this information?

The context of general practice

Doctors, generally, have not been trained to recognize elder abuse. They have not been in the habit of screening for it and they may not be aware of high risk factors for elder abuse.

Since 1 April 1990, general practitioners have been required to offer all patients over the age of 75 years an annual consultation and/or a home visit, to assess whether any personal medical services or social services are required (Department of Health, 1989a). Assessment should cover:

- general health
- coping
- sensory functions
- mobility
- mental condition
- physical state, including social environment

In 1990–91 in one Manchester practice, 50 of 268 patients refused the offer of a home visit for assessment, although 16 of these were subsequently assessed at home fortuitously, after they had requested a home visit for an acute illness. Seventeen patients did not respond to the invitation and an attempt was made to visit them to carry out the assessment. After failing to gain access to the first six addresses in the computer-generated register, time constraints forced a halt to the exercise. In five of the six cases, neighbours reported that the patients appeared well and regularly went out without assistance, or drove their own motor car. In the sixth case, no neighbour information was forthcoming.

The morbidity register was inaccurate, in that 11 of the 268 patients listed on 1 April 1990 were deceased, leaving a target population of 257 (10 per cent of the total practice list compared with the regional average of about 6 per cent). Of these, 240 (93.4 per cent) were assessed. Thirty-four assessments were carried out at the surgery only and 206 at home only, or both at home and at the surgery. The assessments were almost all done by the GP, with less than 10 per cent carried out by the practice nurse (Noone, 1993: 137). They added significantly to the workload of the GP and the secretarial staff, which has been overburdened by this and other aspects of the new GP contract, such as child health surveillance, the setting up of health promotion clinics and the annual check-ups for over-75s.

The question of the follow-up of elderly people who ignore or refuse the GP's invitation for a regular check-up is a difficult one. In many cases, an assessment can be made fortuitously when a home visit has been requested for some other coincidental medical problem. In other cases, liaison with a home care worker, community nurse or relative may bring suspected abuse to the GP's attention. In cases where there is no evidence or even suspicion of abuse, it is very difficult not to respect the rights of elderly people to their privacy.

GPs' morale

Many GPs feel under pressure and undervalued. The perception among GPs is that they and their staff are required to work harder. Bureaucracy is frequently cited as a cause of disaffection. The recent report on general practice (National Health Service Executive, 1995) records that the Department has identified a number of factors contributing to the lowered morale of GPs. The examples quoted were: out-of-hours arrangements, violence against GPs , bureaucracy, and patient expectations. GPs and their staff face increased demands arising from: demography – the increasing elderly population; changing trends in clinical practice – which allows earlier hospital discharges and more patients to be in primary and community care settings; consumerism – the growing expectations of a better informed public that is less reticent about expressing choice. It is within this context, then, that one needs to consider the two questions posed in the opening paragraph:

- How does a family doctor discover elder abuse?
- What should he/she do with the knowledge?

Screening in primary care

A number of investigators have described conditions that may be manifestations of abuse or neglect or may be associated with a high risk of abuse. O'Malley et al. (1983), for example, produced a lengthy checklist of conditions that may be associated with abuse and neglect, and this was described in Chapter 3 above. The Social Services Inspectorate (SSI) practice guidelines *No Longer Afraid* (1993) contained a list of indications of abuse which is clear and concise. Either of these would made a useful appendix to the screening cards or sheets used by many British GPs when carrying out their statutory annual assessment of their patients aged 75 and over. Many of the conditions referred to would be recognized as pointers to high risk without such a checklist, but the fact of assessing and recording each one on paper helps to ensure that the chances of overlooking or not following up such instances are reduced.

Ogg and Bennett (1992a) have recommended a six-point elder abuse screening checklist of good practice for the GP and practice nurse. The list includes knowledge of high risk factors (present and future); the involving of family and carers (but interviewing them separately from the elderly person); being prepared to see the elderly person on more than one occasion, using procedural guidelines where they are available; working closely with other agencies; and introducing recording mechanisms to detect significant changes in the elderly person.

More recently, a screening instrument for primary care physicians has been devised by O'Brien (1996). Questions which address the problems of abuse should be incorporated into the physician's approach, especially when assessing quality of life and independence issues. We know that abuse can escalate over time and early recognition can alleviate symptoms and improve outcome. Early recognition of carer stress and the provision of support may prevent serious abuse. It is, however, important to point out that the fewer false negatives there are, the better the screening instrument. (A false negative is a case not identified by the screening.)

Screening in primary care involves collecting vital information on, for example, personal health, functional ability, mental capacity, social and economic resources and living arrangements (Ferguson and Beck, 1983). This information needs to be collected over a period of time to form a database. The screening instrument helps to identify high risk factors, or those factors which were previously unrecognized. It could easily be added to the over-75's physical assessment to be administered by the general practitioner or practice nurse. O'Brien suggests the following questions:

1   Are you sad or lonely?
2   Do you know anyone who is reliable and can help you in a crisis?
3   Are your finances adequate?
4   Do you support someone?
5   Do you need any assistance with taking care of yourself?
6   Do you take your own medicines and balance your own checkbook?
7   Describe a typical day.
8   Do you have enough privacy in your own home?
9   Are you uncomfortable with anyone in your family?
10 Who makes decisions about your life, such as how or where you will live?
11 Does anyone in your family drink too much or have problems with drugs or medicine?
12 Have you had any injuries, hospitalizations, or emergency room visits recently? Describe them. (O'Brien, 1996: 54)

The primary care physician should then turn to issues relating to the victim's health and functional status and clinically address the following:

- What medical problems exist?
- Is a condition present that may have resulted from abuse?
- Has a medical problem worsened as a result of withheld treatment?
- Is a condition present that may reflect an overuse of a medication?
- Is a medical problem, such as insulin-dependent diabetes, present that requires close monitoring and supervision?

Additionally, if the perpetrator is a patient of the GP, issues relating to the perpetrator's health and functional status need to be assessed:

- What medical problems exist?
- Is a condition present that may result in abuse?
- Is a medical/psychiatric problem such as schizophrenia or learning disability in a sibling present that requires close monitoring and supervision, which without treatment may lead to abuse? (adapted from O'Brien, 1996: 56)

The answers that are obtained will often determine what action the GP should take, such as requesting specialist medical or psychiatric advice/intervention. It will be necessary to interview victims of abuse and neglect. If primary care staff are trained they can use the techniques that were suggested in Chapter 4 above. If they are not trained, referral should be made to a specialist social worker or team who deal with elder mistreatment. In Bury and Rochdale, for example, north of Manchester, most nurses, social workers and primary care physicians have basic training in the recognition of and initial intervention in abuse cases, but liaise closely with specialists who assist with assessment. It is essential for the primary care team to be vigilant, because abuses may present in a variety of situations. Ramsey-Klawsnik (1996) summarized these situations as follows:

1 *Elderly patient discloses abuse to provider:*
- During routine health care the patient discloses abuse but physical evidence of abuse may or may not be present.
- The patient requests treatment for condition reportedly inflicted by abusive action.

2 *Physical evidence of abuse observed, but no disclosure of abuse:*
- During routine care, injury or infection symptomatic of abuse is observed but the patient does not report abuse.
- The patient presents for treatment of injury or infection symptomatic of abuse but does not report abuse as the cause.

3 *Others seek assistance:*
- Family members or paid caregivers suspect abuse and seek advice from the elderly person's health care provider.
- Health care providers are asked to provide the patient's medical and social histories during abuse investigation.

- The physician is asked to conduct forensically oriented medical examination for possible abuse.
- Health care professional is a member of an interdisciplinary team assessing elder abuse allegations and may provide diagnostic examination and/or consultation. (Ramsey-Klawsnik, 1996: 74)

Thus health care providers may be called upon to assess possible abuse, even when only routine care such as dressings or bathing are being provided. This is most common when a trusting relationship has developed between the provider and the elder. Often these disclosures are in private, or are historical. We know that they are likely to recur.

When a disclosure is made in a trusting relationship, it is strongly recommended to follow the guidelines proposed recently by Ramsey-Klawsnik:

Do not display alarm, personal reactions, or disbelief.
Express concern and invite the patient to provide more information.
Do not conduct investigative interview unless trained to do so and in a role in which this is appropriate.
Validate the patient's expressed feelings about the abuse.
Explain the limits of confidentiality.
Assess whether the patient has any injuries, infection, or bruises.
Conduct or arrange for medical examination as appropriate.
Document and preserve medical evidence of abuse.
Document the disclosure and observations of the patient.
File all necessary reports.
Assess the patient's needs.
Make referrals for required services.
Use discretion and judgement in sharing disclosures with others. (Ramsey-Klawsnik, 1996: 78)

It is important that the providers should not conduct the investigative interview, as only those who have been trained clinically and legally should be involved at this stage.

Need for guidelines for action

In May 1992, the Law Commission supported by Age Concern and the Royal College of Psychiatrists called for local authorities to be given a statutory duty to investigate suspicions of elder abuse, with officers having powers to enter premises and take away suspected victims under place of safety orders.

But it is precisely because of the lack of national and local guidelines that GPs are reluctant to act when they find evidence of elder abuse. The Department of Health recommended such practice guidelines in *No Longer Afraid* in 1993 (SSI, 1993). But the response has been by no means universal. However, if guidelines are available to the family doctor any referrals of suspected abuse can be reported to the local social services department. The case would then be investigated by a social worker or duty officer, a case conference should be called and proper follow-up and recording would be ensured. There would be continuing negotiations with the elder and carer on the delivery of mutually acceptable levels of support and care, and these would be agreed, thus removing much of the uncertainty and anxiety that has been generated by all parties. Traditionally, social services departments have experienced difficulty in involving GPs in assessment procedures and care management meetings. Relationships on the ground between social and health care staff, especially GPs, need to be improved, if we are to meet the challenge of detecting and managing and where possible preventing elder abuse.

The role of the family doctor

It is essential that the cooperation of the GP is sought at the earliest possible stage, and that his/her particular role in detecting and managing elder abuse is carefully considered. The involvement of the GP, with his or her unique position as physician, counsellor and sometimes arbiter in family health and related matters, is likely to be crucial in cases of elder abuse or neglect.

On the one hand, it might be thought that a conflict of interest would arise where both victim and perpetrator are patients of the same GP. On the other hand, experienced GPs are well used to managing situations where their professionalism is rigorously tested. Family doctors in Britain still enjoy a degree of influence and a status which enables them to mediate successfully in domestic crises, where others would not be in a position to do so. A negative effect of the family doctor's status may, however, manifest itself in that because of his/her professional detachment, he/she is less likely to be approached in the first place by the abused elder or a third party who suspects abuse.

The GP is also well placed to assess carer stress, and its impact on the elderly person, due to his/her long-term professional involvement with the family. The Cost of Care Index by Kosberg and Cairl, which is cited in Ogg and Bennett (1992a), is a possible screening instrument for avoiding future distress. This may not transfer well from the American situation. Robinson's Caregiver Strain Questionnaire (see p. 232) is much simpler to understand and can be used easily by primary care staff.

Case conferences

The case conference system should ensure that abused or neglected elderly people enjoy the same access to a caring professional team approach as do abused children. The difficulties of the situation and the potential conflicts involved are, if anything, greater in elder abuse. The abused child can be taken from the parents to a place of safety; the abused elder may choose to stay with the carer in spite of the abuse or inadequate care. The carer may decline help and support when it appears obvious to the professional that such help is essential.

It may well be that the continuing responsibility for the following up and monitoring of elder abuse or neglect is too much for a single key worker. Perhaps a better way forward would be the formation of a sub-group from the case conference to follow up and monitor the progress of cases. One possible sub-group might be elder, carer, key social worker, community nurse and GP. Brief meetings, held once a month between case conferences or at a defined interval determined by the members of the group, would enable the group to compare notes and to modify strategy. It would be necessary for this group to call (or bring forward) a case conference should changing circumstances warrant it. One member of the group, probably the key social worker, would be responsible for the recording of information at these meetings. It is essential to record the conference in writing and to get each participant – including, if possible, the elder and the carer – to agree that the decisions are binding. The overall responsibility for this is the care manager's.

An important practical point for the GP is the timing of case conferences and the amount of notice given. In the year ending 31 March 1994 in one health district, the GPs attended 41 out of 210 case conferences held for suspected child abuse (i.e. 19.5 per cent) (Bury Social Services, 1994). This is a disappointing statistic, as it relates to case conferences in an area where national guidelines are well established and a strong legal framework exists. However, these case conferences are often called at short notice and held at a time which clashes with a previously booked surgery. GPs in the United Kingdom have a contractual obligation to be available at their surgeries at fixed hours which are published in local directories. Many are single-handed and are not able to absent themselves from their patients without adequate notice and many do not make the effort because, rightly or wrongly, they believe inter-disciplinary case conferences to be a waste of time. Unlike the situation with child abuse, the lack of payment for attending these meetings is a contributory factor.

Case examples

Four cases of physical elder abuse encountered in one practice are now described. They represent the most obvious manifestations of elder abuse. Hidden cases of psychological, sexual, financial and other types of abuse present even more complex and difficult management implications.

Case example 1

A 73-year-old woman presented to the GP with early dementia characterized by a deterioration from her personal skills as an excellent home-maker and provider to a person who neglected herself and her household tasks. Her short-term memory deteriorated. She started to hide items in the house and failed to make decisions. Her husband, who was 74, was a professional man with marked obsessional traits who found his role changing as he was losing his wife's support, having to make decisions for her and take over household duties which previously he had not performed. The diagnosis was confirmed by a consultant psychiatrist with the help of a CT scan. The husband found it difficult to accept help but was supported by a community psychiatric nurse and day care. In less than a year the family were reporting to the GP physical (slapping) and psychological (shouting) abuse by the husband. A further psychiatric opinion revealed the patient's further deterioration in behaviour; her mood was labile, her behaviour unpredictable and she was not able or allowed to carry out the simplest of tasks. Her husband's obsessional coping mechanisms meant that he had to be in control and he was the only one who could provide the best care. Further assessment by a psychiatrist and a social worker provided him with more support and more successful coping mechanisms such as 'time out' for him to be away from the stress. Holiday relief and day care are still refused, but they are coping together with only occasional episodes of shouting. Slowly more services are being accepted and the situation is stabilizing.

General comments

This case illustrates the following risk factors for and pointers to abuse:

- a degree of imposed isolation, elder and carer;
- moderately severe cognitive impairment in the elder;
- moderate degree of dependency on the carer;
- carer's obsessional personality (the appearance of a resultant paranoid reaction would lead to a failure of coping mechanisms and a sudden withdrawal of the caring role);
- mention of physical violence by the carer;
- refusal of outside services by both victim and perpetrator.

Case review 1

This case demonstrates many of the difficulties in balancing caregiving with the risk of abuse. The predisposing factors of the abused person are that she is over 73, demented, physically frail, dependent on her husband, has lost her skills as a housewife and is no longer able to be independent. Her husband (the abuser) is obsessionally rigid, has difficulty in coping with change or interference and needs to feel that he is in control. When confronted by unreasonable or threatening behaviour he will decompensate, developing a paranoid reaction, often resulting in abuse.

The GP is in an ideal position to help. He or she may have a longstanding relationship with them both and because he/she is trusted may be able to be more directive, giving practical instructions on how to help the abused and abuser: for example arranging specialist help, putting them in touch with supportive organizations such as the Alzheimer's Society, and allowing the husband to ventilate his frustrations. Social services can offer help with social support, day care, home care and financial advice, but always ensuring that he feels that he is in control and people are merely advising rather than controlling him. His wife needs medical and social work support to cope with her own emotional needs and frustration. Thus the GP is pivotal in making sure that this couple can stay together and be supported. A case conference is essential to ensure that each worker and the patient's family know their role and what they should do.

Case example 2

An 88-year-old woman suffered a long history of manic depressive illness and self-poisonings. She suffered from heart failure as well as looking after her husband who was diagnosed as having a dementing illness, chronic bronchitis and partial blindness. As a result of this, he had become physically and verbally abusive. The problems were identified by the community psychiatric nurse who noticed personal deterioration, a dressing apraxia, and increased confusion. The GP found the wife depressed, suicidal and not complying with her medication, as a result of carer stress. A further assessment by the consultant psychiatrist and social services identified the need for day care for the couple, home care and meals-on-wheels. The GP ensured compliance with antidepressant medication by supportive visits. Her mental state improved with resultant coping. The abuse ceased. A stepdaughter started to support her. Unfortunately, her husband became physically so frail that he was admitted to continuing care. His wife remains unhappy and lonely, but is slowly adapting to her new role.

General comments

This case illustrates the following risk factors for and pointers to abuse:

- elder's depression and fearfulness;
- reversal of roles due to deterioration in the carer's mental state with cognitive impairment;
- inadequate treatment of medical problems;
- elder's financial dependency;
- risk of suicide/homicide.

Case review 2

This case illustrates how abuse can occur in someone who is dementing and losing their coping skills. The abused person may be the elderly carer who, because of a depressive illness, loses her coping skills. The community nurse was the alerting agent. The GP was able to identify clearly various key people to perform specific tasks. The consultant psychiatrist was able to assess both parties' mental states, suggest treatment, arrange day care and eventual continuing care; the social services provided practical help with home care and meals-on-wheels; a stepdaughter gave emotional support with weekly visits. Once again, the GP is pivotal here, providing monitoring of any change, a regular review of antidepressant medication, and support, all of which resulted in the abuse ceasing and the reduction of suicidal risk which is not uncommon in cases like this. The GP was able to help the wife to be positive in her outlook, to start to look after her husband and to cope with the trauma of her husband going into continuing care. Suicidal and homicidal acts, often combined, are not uncommon cases with this profile.

Case example 3

Mrs C is an 81-year-old who has been a widow for six years and lives with her 41-year-old unmarried son. She suffers from longstanding hypertension and severe deafness, requiring a hearing aid, and regularly attends the GP. Her son, who suffers from severe migraine, was known to have personality difficulties, being diagnosed as inadequate and immature by a consultant psychiatrist. He did not abuse alcohol or smoke. Her married daughter identified to the GP physical and emotional abuse from the son. She noted that her father had exhibited similar abuse to her mother before his death. The son was seen by the GP about his migraine, and sensitive questioning about his mother revealed the son's feelings of depression, failure and frustration. He admitted to losing his temper and abusing his mother. His worsening migraine and unemployment were significant precipitants. The GP achieved success by reviewing and successfully treating his migraine, and by referral to a stress management group and positive support of the son. The abuse ceased.

General comments

This case illustrates the following risk factors for and pointers to abuse:

• the elder's depression, fearfulness and deafness;
• dependency, physical and social;
• the carer's personality disorder and social and medical problems;
• family history of violence.

Case review 3

This case illustrates the problem of a competent elderly person who has chronic physical problems and sensory deficits. She has been subject to two abusers (husband and son), suggesting that the son's behaviour is a learned response. Her son, the main carer, has personality problems, is depressed and has migraine. He has a very negative cognitive set, reinforced by unemployment. He is not a substance abuser and cares deeply about his mother, which is very positive as he is quite prepared to discuss his problems with the GP. The daughter who identified the abuse remains peripheral and is quite accusatory and judgmental, but not prepared to get practically involved. This is not unusual and increases the carer's stress. The GP is the first and only contact. He is trusted by all parties. He identifies the stress factors of migraine which he treats, deals with the son's poor coping skills, using a stress management group, and supports the son. By helping him as a carer, the GP removes the guilt of unemployment. Thus a happy outcome.

Case example 4

Mrs D, a 78-year-old widow, presented to the GP with depression and fearfulness. She suffered a traumatic perforated eardrum in 1984, needing specialist treatment. In 1991 she developed breast cancer and also had a heart attack. She lives with her 41-year-old daughter who was diagnosed as an immature histrionic psychopath by many consultant psychiatrists. Her daughter was very unstable and the police requested the mother to press charges for assault when neighbours identified incidents. The mother was very protective towards her daughter, insisting that she was ill. With community support and psychiatric treatment for the daughter, the abuse was lessened and the daughter's personality has matured. The relationship between mother and daughter has grown and they have stayed together.

General comments

This case illustrates the following risk factors for and pointers to abuse:

- the elder's recurring injuries;
- the elder's depressive fearfulness;
- the carer's psychiatric condition.

Case review 4

This case illustrates that sometimes it is necessary to work with potentially very dangerous situations and identify and accept the risks. The positive aspects of this case are (a) the strong mother/daughter relationship; (b) the daughter's continued cooperation with psychiatric and psychological treatment which led to her eventual mental health improvement and maturing relationship with her mother; (c) the refusal of the mother to report episodes of violence, because of her loyalty to the daughter; the mother also would have felt she had failed as a parent. The emotional stress of this abuse may well have played a part in the mother's psychical problems. The community and psychiatric services organized by the GP led to the eventual improvement of this chronic case, but careful monitoring by the GP was essential as non-compliance might well have been fatal.

Conclusion

In the four cases described, two became obvious to the GP in the course of consultations; one was brought to his notice by a concerned relative and one by a community psychiatric nurse. Important knowledge about patients of all ages is often received by the GP at second or third hand, passed on by other health professionals, by concerned relatives or from other sources.

It may be that the traditional aura of respect and authority that surrounds the GP precludes the direct disclosure of sensitive information in many cases. Women may report incontinence to a practice nurse when they are too embarrassed to mention it to the doctor. An elderly woman who has seen her GP a month before about her arthritis may disclose to a sympathetic home carer over a cup of tea that her husband has been shouting at her because she was too slow in reaching the toilet. The carer may not pass on the information for fear of the consequences. The clear implication is that there is a need for better communication. Informal carers need to know how they can get the help and support that they frequently require. Professional carers, social workers, community nurses, health visitors and voluntary workers need guidance and direction as well.

In addition, it must be recognized that GPs find themselves faced with distinct conflicts of interest and, in the absence of nationally accepted guidelines, definite uncertainty about their legal position. As the law stands at the moment, the burden of responsibility for action and intervention is unclear and, while the management of both victim and perpetrator may be medically, psychologically and socially positive, the GP is by no means confident of his or her ground legally and ethically in relation to what further action may be advisable. This is a major reason why so many GPs do not wish to become involved.

One further issue may well be a result of the changing image of the GP and family doctor. Very many GPs need assistance to understand that in the contemporary world of care in the community, they may head the primary health care team, but they are still only representing one of a number of disciplines which contribute to the well-being of the patient. A refusal to admit to the possible existence of elder abuse, when recorded information is presented, amounts to a rejection of the findings of another professional from a para-medical or social work discipline, or risks ignoring information presented by an informal carer or relative. GPs must learn to share their knowledge and decision-making. Their traditional élitism can become a cloak for ignoring what they do not wish to hear.

GPs need additional undergraduate and postgraduate training in the management of elderly people and their carers, and in the early recognition of abuse and neglect. Failure to gain this will lead clinicians to continue to harbour ageist attitudes and have a low index of suspicion. They only see what they are trained to see and they also need a strong reassurance from the National Health Service that if they do become involved in such cases, their input will contribute to an improvement in the quality of life of their elderly patients and their carers.

In his book *Old Age Abuse*, Eastman regarded the role of the general practitioner as being of the utmost importance (Eastman, 1984: 75). This judgement has not changed. Wolf in the United States of America went further, maintaining that 'Physicians can make a major contribution to the advancement of knowledge, practice and policy, with regard to elder abuse and neglect' (Wolf, 1988: 761). The teaching of general practice in medical schools and in departments of postgraduate medicine must now, in the face of the growing evidence, ensure that the primary health care physician is enabled to take a lead role in the detection of the mistreatment, abuse and neglect of elderly people, with adequate training in multidisciplinary case management and the legal aspects of elder mistreatment. Otherwise the general practitioner is left in a very vulnerable position.

'It is important that physicians recognize and respond to the stresses of families under their care,' wrote Taler and Ansello (1985: 113) and more recently, Lachs and Pillemer wrote: 'Recent guidelines (1992) from the American Medical Association suggest that older adults may be asked by their physicians about family violence, even in the absence of symptoms potentially attributable to abuse or neglect. This recommendation is reasonable, given the prevalence of the problem and the tendency for "asymptomatic" family violence to go unrecognized' (Lachs and Pillemer, 1995: 438; see also Wolf, 1994: 18). Similar observations have already been mentioned during the discussion of the role of physician in Chapter 3 of this volume. The current task is to develop this sensitivity at the heart of general practice. This will be best achieved by the establishment of multidisciplinary guidelines at a national level, which are reinforced by locally agreed policies based upon close liaison, discussion and agreement.

15

Sustaining Meaning: a Key Concept in Understanding Elder Abuse

Michael Nolan

The manner in which we define a given concept is not only central to our recognition of it (would we know it if we saw it?) but also largely determines the success or otherwise of interventions designed to predict, prevent or ameliorate instances of that concept. Many of the challenges we currently face with respect to elder abuse arise from the lack of consensus on the meaning of this term and the various dimensions that are subsumed within it. A similar lack of conceptual clarity is apparent with respect to the meaning of care or caregiving. The chapter is based on the premise that elder abuse can most fruitfully be considered in the context of a caregiving relationship and that an adequate understanding of abuse will not emerge until there is a greater appreciation of the nuances and complexity of care. In particular it is suggested the meanings attributed to caring have to be explored and the various dimensions of this construct have to be plumbed in more depth. This is a significant undertaking both conceptually and empirically and is beyond the scope of a single chapter. Therefore in order to confine debate to reasonable parameters, the primary emphasis here is placed on the satisfactions of caring and their potential relationship to elder abuse. Whilst the major focus is on family (informal) carers, reference is also made to professional carers, particularly those providing care within institutional settings.

As Biegel et al. (1991) noted some time ago, use of the term 'caregiving' is now so ubiquitous that its meaning is taken for granted, yet what the word actually denotes is not always clear. Certainly within the caregiving literature there has been an undue emphasis on the physical aspects of care and a marked tendency to view it in 'pathologizing' terms (Twigg and Atkin, 1994), which has provided the 'predominant focus' for much of the research in this field (Kahana and Young, 1990). Consequently it is suggested that caregiving burden represents one of the most studied topics in the gerontological literature (Kane and Penrod, 1995). This has resulted in the emergence of a somewhat partial and incomplete picture of caring, which fails adequately to account for its dynamic and temporal nature. More recently there have been calls to return to basic questions such as 'what is this thing some call caregiving'? (Gubrium, 1995: 268) in order that a better understanding can be achieved. In attempting to answer this question and building on the work of Bowers (1987, 1988), it has been suggested that there are nine conceptually distinct but empirically overlapping *types* of care (Nolan et al., 1995, 1996) which are differentiated by purpose or meaning rather than the act of caring itself. Such a view provides a counterpoint to those who focus on the objective circumstances of caring. On the other hand, alternative frameworks are also emerging which whilst still motivated by a desire to develop more 'sophisticated' typologies of care, continue to root their models within a primarily physical or instrumental paradigm (Parker and Lawton, 1994). It is tensions such as these that need to be resolved before services and interventions can adequately respond to carers' needs in both non-abusive and abusive relationships.

As Wenger et al. (1997) argue, caring most often represents a continuation of long-term, usually familial, relationship and must be understood in this context. The same is true of most abusive situations. Therefore in order better to understand abuse it is helpful to consider the manner in which 'ordinary' families negotiate responsibilities. Finch and Mason (1993) assert 'with some certainty' that such negotiations are not circumscribed by normative rules but emerge out of a dynamic process, reflecting family history and biography. The main purpose of such negotiations is to maintain a sense of reciprocity and balance within family relationships. To achieve this, negotiations, particularly those concerning help and assistance, are usually tacit and implicit, with the potential recipient of help often being deliberately excluded (Finch and Mason, 1993). However, such exclusions are intended to protect rather than disempower individuals, thereby providing a positive contextual meaning. In other circumstances such an act of deliberate exclusion might be perceived in a far more negative light. This illustrates the importance of understanding an act in terms of its intentions, rather than its more objective parameters.

Although Finch and Mason (1993) argue that there are no fixed rules determining the manner in which negotiations in families unfold they nevertheless believe that there are guidelines for action which are underpinned by implicit and subtle reciprocities. For example, most people consider it wrong to expect to receive help as a right, but having to ask for help is also seen as something to be avoided if possible. In situations where the need for help is apparent, offering to provide it before someone has to ask is the most psychologically satisfactory outcome for all parties (Finch and Mason, 1993).

This approach to understanding family negotiations provides us with a picture of the complex dynamics of family life. Similar models have been postulated with respect to abusive family relationships, with one of the most useful being that suggested by Phillips and Rempusheski (1986).

While adopting a broad theoretical stance, their model is located primarily within a symbolic interactionist perspective. The approach is essentially cognitive and is centred around a number of key variables which are used to give meaning to the caring situation. Such meanings then largely determine subsequent behaviour. The model highlights the dynamic and interactive nature of caring and stresses the importance of individual carers' evaluation of their behaviour. It is suggested that carers hold an image of caring which determines both their relationship with the cared-for person and the quality of the care given. Factors considered influential in creating this image are the carer's perception of their past relationship with the cared-for person and the reconciliation of the present situation with this past image. Where carers have a normalized view of their past relationship (in which both positive and negative factors are acknowledged but which remains positive overall) and when present interactions are consistent with this, then carers are more likely to be accepting of certain behaviours and less likely to adopt caring styles that revolve around the cared-for person conforming. Alternatively, if carers have a 'stigmatized' (only negative perceptions) or 'deified' (only very positive perceptions) past relationship and if the stigmatized view remains or the deified relationship has been spoilt, then carers are less tolerant and have a greater expectation of conformity from the cared-for person. The carer's general beliefs as to what constitutes healthy living, a good quality of life and the nature of family relationships and responsibilities are also influential. Where there is congruence or fit between the carer's beliefs and the behaviour of the cared-for person then carers are said to adopt a style of caring which is more open and protective and in which they have fewer expectations that the cared-for person will conform. Where behaviours and beliefs are incongruent or do not fit, then carers are more likely to adopt a punitive style and expect the cared-for person to be more suppliant. In the latter circumstances the authors suggest that abuse is far more likely to occur.

Steinmetz (1988) has reached a similar conclusion with respect to abusive situations and her results add further support to the type of model suggested by Phillips and Rempusheski (1986). She notes that abuse is not so much the result of instrumental dependency (that is, the need for physical care) but often arises when there is a conflict of values between carer and cared-for person. Situations are particularly fraught when the cared-for person is demanding and resorts to manipulative behaviour as a means of establishing control. She suggests that interpretation of interactions between carer and cared-for must be considered when attempting to predict abuse and that there are higher levels of abuse amongst stressed carers: 'In as much as a person's perception of a situation is a better predictor of behaviour than objective criteria, caregivers who report a sense of burden may have a greater potential for using abusive or neglectful behaviours' (Steinmetz, 1988: 70).

Approaches such as these are consistent with transactional models of stress and coping. A transactional model is based upon the belief that each individual has a differing response to potentially stressful events (stressors) and that the degree to which any event is actually stressful is determined by the way in which each person views that event. What is stressful for one person is therefore not automatically stressful for another. Indeed, the same event can also be stressful to a person one day and not stressful the next. Central to the production of stress within the transactional model are the subjective perceptions of the carer as opposed to the objective circumstances of care.

Transactional models are also concerned with all the factors that might influence behaviour and recognize the possibility that potentially stressful situations can also be interpreted as a challenge and thereby have a positive effect. Encouragingly, there is now growing recognition that satisfying aspects of caring are also possible. Indeed it is suggested that it is the balance between the burdens and satisfactions, or hassles and uplifts, of caring (Kinney and Stephens, 1989) that provides a better overall understanding than does either alone (Nolan et al., 1996). A fuller appreciation of the positive aspects of caring is therefore likely to assist us in the identification of potentially abusive relationships.

The satisfactions of caring: a brief literature review

Compared to the literature on the stresses and burdens of care, that on the rewards and gratifications is still sparse. Nevertheless, the possibility that caring may provide positive outcomes is not new (Davies, 1980), with a number of studies providing descriptive accounts of the frequency of certain sources or types of satisfaction. Others have attempted to go further by seeking to build a more adequate theoretical understanding using concepts such as *mutuality* (Hirschfield, 1981, 1983) and *enrichment* (Archbold et al., 1992, 1995; Cartwright et al., 1994).

The early literature on the satisfactions of care clearly signalled the importance of relationships to achieving or construing rewards (Fengler and Goodrich, 1979; Davies, 1980). Davies (1980) for example argued that satisfactions are only possible when the recipient of care is seen as a valued person rather than as a problem. Similarly, in dementia Hirschfield (1981, 1983) contended that the development of mutuality (the ability to find gratification and meaning in caregiving) was dependent largely on the extent to which the cared-for person was perceived to reciprocate 'by virtue of their existence'.

A closely related notion is that of the meaning ascribed to caring, with the suggestion being that if caring is to be construed as positive there has to be at least some element of meaning or worth attached to it (Given and Given, 1991; Farran et al., 1991; Archbold et al., 1992; Jivanjee, 1993). The most detailed arguments appear to be those suggested by Farran et al. (1991) who contend that caring can be seen as meaningful in terms of provisional and ultimate meanings. Provisional meanings are constructed within the day to day elements of care whereas ultimate meanings are more intimately tied to the philosophical or spiritual beliefs that an individual holds. Caring, Farran et al. (1991) suggest, provides a number of avenues to finding meaning including: *creative* routes (as a means of developing new skills, for example); *experiential* routes (through relationships and feelings) and *attitudinal* routes (through the exploration of personal beliefs and values).

A not dissimilar concept is that of *caregiving enrichment* (Cartwright et al., 1994) which is also dependent upon the meanings ascribed to care. These authors define enrichment as 'the process of endowing caregiving with meaning or pleasure for both caregiver and care-recipient'. The linking of meaning and pleasure with a satisfying relationship highlights the iterative nature of these concepts, consistent with the conclusions of a number of authors (Davies, 1980; Hirschfield, 1981, 1983). Satisfaction within caring relationships is often linked to apparently trivial or mundane events, for example Jivanjee (1993: 9) in a study of dementia caregiving recounts being surprised at the creativity carers bring to bear in finding rewards in seemingly insignificant events or activities. Such findings mirror those of other studies which suggest that simply seeing the cared-for person happy and contented is a source of considerable satisfaction for carers (Lawton et al., 1989; Clifford, 1990; Grant and Nolan, 1993; Cartwright et al., 1994; Kane and Penrod, 1995).

At a much more abstract level it has been suggested that maintaining the dignity and self-esteem of the cared-for person is also a major source of satisfaction (Nolan and Grant, 1992a; Grant and Nolan, 1993). In order to achieve this, carers often draw on their intimate knowledge of the cared-for person, particularly in terms of sustaining or rebuilding meaningful roles. There is also evidence that the interpersonal relationships between carer and cared-for person provide satisfactions which are more obviously of mutual benefit to both parties. For example Clifford's (1990) study indicated that 62 per cent of carers of older people and 50 per cent of carers of people with learning difficulties felt closer to the cared-for person than they did at the beginning of the caring experience. Other authors have reached similar conclusions (Motenko, 1988; Walker et al., 1990; Nolan and Grant, 1992a; Grant and Nolan, 1993; Coleman et al., 1994). Such improved relationships are not confined solely to the caregiving dyad, with studies also reporting that caring has resulted in an improved relationship within families (Stoller and Pugliesi, 1989; Farran et al., 1991; Nolan and Grant, 1992a; Grant and Nolan, 1993; Patterson, 1993; Burr et al., 1994; Kane and Penrod, 1995).

An extensive range of other potential rewards from caring have also been identified in the literature. These include: expressions of appreciation (Lewis and Meredith, 1988a, 1988b; Grant and Nolan, 1993; Beresford, 1994); providing life with a purpose or meaning (Davies, 1980; Farran et al., 1991; Harris, 1993); developing a sense of competency and mastery (Motenko, 1988; Jivanjee, 1993; Langer, 1993); enhancing personal qualities such as greater tolerance and patience (Clifford, 1990). Such rewards are often seen to provide carers with a sense of self-esteem (Motenko, 1988; Given and Given, 1991; Cartwright et al., 1994). These types of satisfaction are conceptually different from those relating directly to the interpersonal dynamic between carer and cared-for person as they derive more from the intrapsychic orientation of the carer (Grant and Nolan, 1993).

Many carers believe that their intimate knowledge of the cared-for person means that they can provide better care than anyone else. Twigg and

Atkin (1994) suggest that carers often become the 'arbiter of standards', monitoring the quality of care given by individuals other than themselves. Related sources of satisfaction are concerned with seeing the cared-for person grow and develop or overcome difficulties and obstacles. Such satisfactions are generally motivated by a desire to promote positive outcomes for the cared-for person (Grant and Nolan, 1993).

As will be appreciated from this brief review, the potential sources of reward and gratification in caring are diverse, complex and often subtle. However, most of the empirical data on satisfactions collected to date have emanated from small, non-random samples or have been collected as a small part of a larger study, the main purpose of which was to explore other dimensions of caring.

Consequently we still know very little about the prevalence of satisfactions within caring. Recently, however more substantial empirical evidence has emerged.

The satisfactions of caring: an empirical exploration

Although the satisfactions of caring are of considerable interest theoretically it is the suggestion that an absence of satisfactions can serve as an indicator of potentially poor caring relationships (Clifford, 1990; Walker et al., 1990; Archbold et al., 1992, 1995) that is of most relevance in the present context. If satisfactions are to serve as a risk indicator, however, they must be reasonably prevalent. If the majority of carers experience little or no satisfaction from their role then this represents a normative pattern and is of limited predictive value. On the other hand if satisfactions are reasonably commonplace and are also associated with more positive caring circumstances, their absence might serve as a useful marker of possibly abusive situations.

What is required is an approach that will allow a clearer picture of the satisfactions of caring to emerge. The Carers' Assessment of Satisfactions Index (CASI, Nolan and Grant, 1992a) was developed with the express purpose of exploring the nature and frequency of satisfactions that carers experience. This index consists of 30 items which were derived from an extensive postal survey of carers and a number of in-depth semi-structured interviews (see Nolan and Grant, 1992a). Items are therefore empirically generated from sources of satisfaction identified by carers themselves. In completing the scale, carers are asked to indicate if each item: doesn't apply to them; applies but does not provide a source of satisfaction; applies and provides quite a lot of satisfaction; or applies providing a great deal of satisfaction. The index can be either interviewer administered or form part of a postal survey. The results reported here are based on two main sources of data. The first data were generated from in-depth interviews with 38 carers of people with dementia (Keady and Nolan, 1993a, 1993b), whilst the remaining data were collected using a postal questionnaire survey. The questionnaire, which was comprised of CASI, and a range of other variables such as age, gender, caregiving relationship, self-perceived emotional and physical well-being, levels of physical and mental frailty and so on, was distributed by the Alzheimer's Disease Society newsletter in Wales and Scotland and the Cross-roads Care network in Wales. This represents a non-random sample and the limitations of generalizing from such data are well recognized. However, the majority of caregiving research is based on non-random, usually clinical samples (Kane and Penrod, 1995) and the results reported here are therefore just as robust as those within the general caring literature.

In total, data were collected from 206 individuals and the results outlined below relate to the 200 who were caring for either a partner or a parent. A fuller account of these analyses can be found elsewhere (Nolan et al., 1996), and reporting here is restricted to a broad overview which is used to demonstrate both the pervasiveness and breadth of satisfaction that carers experienced.

Of the 30 items of which CASI comprises, 12 were identified as providing a source of satisfaction for 75 per cent of the sample or over, a further six were identified as a source of satisfaction by 50 per cent or more of the sample and no single item applied to less than 25 per cent of the sample. Those aspects of caring identified as satisfying by 75 per cent or more of the sample are summarized in Table 15.1.

Even a cursory glance at this table provides a clear indication of the pervasive nature of satisfactions experienced by the present sample of carers. Notwithstanding the methodological limitations of the survey noted above, these results reaffirm many previous studies based on smaller samples or less well developed data collection instruments. Taken together these add validity to the suggestion that more attention must be paid to the nature of caring rewards and the role they play in ameliorating burden or stress (Levesque et al., 1995).

Table 15.1   *Aspects of caring identified as satisfying by 75 per cent or more of the sample* (n = 200)

	%
Maintaining the dignity of the cared-for person	96
Seeing the cared-for person well turned out	91
Knowing I'll have done my best	90
Expressing my love for the cared-for person	89
Seeing the cared-for person happy	88
Giving pleasure to the cared-for person	87
Seeing their needs tended to	79
Knowing they'd do the same for me	79
Keeping the cared-for person out of an institution	78
Providing the best possible care	78
Just enjoying helping people	78
Helping the cared-for person overcome difficulties	75

Nolan et al. (1996) suggest that caregiver satisfactions have a number of implications for the design and delivery of services to carers and they consider these under three main headings:

- Satisfactions as a coping resource/therapeutic intervention
- Satisfactions as a quality control measure
- Satisfactions as a 'risk' indicator

It is the latter area that is particularly relevant in the present context. In highlighting the use of caregiving satisfaction as an indicator of risk Nolan et al. (1996) argue that this can be conceived of as operating in two areas: risk of poor emotional health; and risk of fragile and potentially abusive relationships. Such an idea is not new but the recent data provide more convincing evidence of the utility of such an approach. Hirschfield (1981, 1983) suggested some time ago that mutuality was the key to understanding caregiving relationships and she contended that in situations where there was high mutuality then carers could cope even in objectively adverse circumstances. Alternatively, low mutuality was seen as an indicator of a poor caring relationship, even if objectively the situation appeared unproblematic.

Lewis and Meredith (1989) believe that the potentially most fraught caring circumstances are those in which there is no positive feedback and it seems that those carers who can identify no positive aspects to their role are likely to be near breaking point (Clifford, 1990). On this basis it has been suggested that there is a need to target carers who get no satisfaction (Walker et al., 1990; Archbold et al., 1992) and either provide additional support or seek alternative caregiving arrangements. Accordingly, low mutuality should be 'taken very seriously' (Archbold et al., 1992).

Accepting this suggestion raises a number of issues about the assessment of caregiver satisfaction at various stages in the caring history or trajectory and the nature of past and present relationships. This is particularly important at the start of caring as carers frequently adopt their role during a health crisis, at the point of hospital discharge. They often do so without a full consideration of the impact this may have on their lives (Nolan and Grant, 1992a; Opie, 1994) and with little or no preparation, either emotionally or physically, for their roles (Nolan and Grant, 1992b; Stewart et al., 1993). Limited thought is given to a potential carer's willingness or ability to care, or to the nature and quality of past or present relationships. Similarly, caring competencies are rarely assessed. As Nolan et al. (1996) argue, this represents something of a paradox for in circumstances where there were doubts about a mother's ability to care for a child or the quality of their relationship was in question then every effort would be made to assess the situation fully. Yet the concept of this happening in any systematic way prior to a daughter assuming caring responsibilities for her mother would be alien to most practitioners.

A key notion which might aid our thinking here is that of preparedness (Archbold et al., 1992), or the extent to which carers feel competent to take on their role. This relates to the acquisition of the knowledge, skills and emotional support necessary to care effectively. Feeling confident and prepared is associated with lower levels of depression and burden, and vice versa (Braithwaite, 1990; Archbold et al., 1992; Harvarth et al., 1994). However, most carers do not initially have such a sense of competence and usually acquire their skills by a process of trial and error (Stewart et al., 1993; Lea, 1994; Harvarth et al., 1994); this has been described as 'flailing about' (Stewart et al., 1993). Taraborrelli (1993) argues that carers generally 'take it on' in a state of 'initial innocence' in which they have very little information and advice and are usually ignorant of both the extent and the nature of the care they will be expected to deliver. This is by no means uncommon (Lewis and Meredith, 1988a, 1988b; Bell and Gibbons, 1989; Nolan and Grant, 1992a). Moreover, there appears to be little professional input at this time, and the limited support that is offered is confined to the physical aspects of care (Stewart et al., 1993). A simple but persuasive argument is offered by Braithwaite (1990) who contends that there is probably more to be learnt about becoming a carer than there is about becoming a parent, yet we do not have the equivalent of ante-natal classes for carers.

The start of a caregiving relationship therefore represents a key period during which poor existing relationships can be identified and efforts can be made to ensure that carers are fully prepared for their role.

For those individuals who have been caring for some time, satisfactions should play a more overt role in the assessment process. Here the absence of satisfactions, which often go hand in hand with a poor caring relationship (Nolan and Grant, 1992a) can and should be viewed as a risk factor, as a sign that a fragile caring situation exists. In a recent survey of the coping strategies carers adopt (Nolan et al., 1996) the most frequently used and most useful strategy was realizing that the cared-for person was not to blame for their present situation. On this basis, the absence of satisfactions and the presence of a 'blaming' culture may well represent a particularly potent set of risk factors.

The satisfactions of caring: extending the logic

Although this chapter has focused primarily on family caring relationships a similar logic can be applied to professional or paid caring, particularly in institutional settings. Kyle (1995) suggests that caring is probably one of the most widely used but least understood concepts in the human services literature and consequently, as Scott (1995) points out, we cannot assume a shared meaning. Moreover even when definitions are agreed considerable work remains to be undertaken before good care can be assured (Scott, 1995). Scott argues that good care is constructive care, which is technically proficient yet also recognizes the 'humanness' of the care receiver. This requires that staff see themselves as the instrument of care and have a personal investment in the people they are caring for. In other words the recipient of care has in some way to 'matter'. Yet it is the failure to accord elderly people in residential and nursing home care the full status of a human being that underlies much of the abuse in such environments.

For example Kayser-Jones (1981) suggested that four major forms of abuse in institutional care could be identified: these have been already discussed in Chapter 7 of this volume.

Jacelon (1995) argues that older individuals are often construed as 'non-people' and, as Dimond (1986) suggests, the objectification of care in institutions in America creates a predominant perception that older people are 'out of it'. This for example then makes it legitimate for older people to be viewed as 'feeders' rather than individuals who require help with their nutritional needs (Dimond, 1986). Eight years later, Lee-Treweek (1994) portrays a depressingly similar picture of life in a nursing home in Britain. She suggests that the motivation underpinning the activity of unqualified care staff, who give the majority of 'hands-on care', is to present the 'lounge standard patient'. This is an individual who is smartly attired and looks neat and tidy while on public display in the lounge. Within the working world of care staff the presentation of a 'well-ordered body' symbolizes a job well done. In order to achieve this, it is both necessary and legitimate to be ruthless in the delivery of care. Individuals who do not reach the required 'lounge standard' are confined to their own rooms, but in order to ensure that as many individuals as possible are presentable, 'mistreatment and being hard towards patients' is seen as an essential attribute of the good worker (Lee-Treweek, 1994).

In part such a situation exists because work in these environments is accorded little recognition and status and staff derive limited satisfaction from what they do. A failure to gain any satisfaction or reward from caring activity may be the key to understanding abuse in both paid and family caring relationships. (There is further discussion of abuse and neglect in residential institutions in Chapter 11, this volume.)

Conclusion

In a recent conspectus on the nature of coping theory Lazarus (1993), one of the most influential writers in this field, reflected on several decades of research. He reached the conclusion that a central determinant of coping is the 'personal meaning' that each individual brings to a potentially stressful encounter. He summarizes this in the following way:

> To truly understand coping requires that we zero in on the main threat meanings of a particular stress situation and how they change across time and across situational contexts. (Lazarus, 1993: 24)

He goes on to state that the ability to 'sustain serviceable meanings' represents the single most important key to understanding coping. I would suggest here that the same is probably true of abusive situations, whether these occur in family or institutional settings. Individuals need to be able to create a meaning or purpose for what they do and derive at least some form of satisfaction from it. In circumstances where this is not possible most of us desist from that activity. In caregiving, this is not usually a viable option and so people carry on, possibly with a mixture of conflicting and increasingly negative emotions. If we are to grasp the nettle that abuse presents us with, there must be a fundamental recognition that if people or actions no longer matter then abuse is the likely corollary. We need to develop more subtle and dynamic indications that may provide us with an 'early warning system'. Caregiving satisfaction is one such indicator.

16

Vulnerability and Public Responses

Jeremy Ambache

Since we were alerted a decade ago to the existence of abuse of elderly people the reaction to it has been slow and faltering; the reasons for this are worth examining. This chapter describes the limited national policy in relation to this problem. Comparisons, from which lessons can be drawn, are made with the fields of child abuse in this country and of elder abuse in the United States. Local policy and service responses to elder abuse are examined. Although the obstacles to a coherent national policy are acknowledged some suggestions are made to possible ways forward.

National policy

Elder abuse was 'discovered' here in the 1970s, as it was in America where it came very much to prominence towards the end of the decade, leading to legislation and policy development in most states during the 1980s. In Britain the problem was raised by letters in medical journals in the mid-1970s (Baker, 1975; Burston, 1975, 1977) and more recently by Eastman, then a social worker, and by Age Concern England in the early 1980s. Age Concern published Eastman's *Old Age Abuse* in 1984. This led to an influential conference organized by the British Geriatrics Society in 1988 attended by over 400 people, including geriatricians, other health care professionals and social workers. The prevalence study by Ogg and Bennett in 1992 (1992b: referred to in Chapter 3, this volume) established that 'abuse is already taking place' in the words of the Social Services Inspectorate (SSI) of the Department of Health. The SSI issued *No Longer Afraid* in 1993 as guidance to local authority social service departments who were advised to work together with other local agencies. No specific guidance was given to health authorities or to the police. The guidance provided the following overall definition of abuse: 'It [abuse] may be intentional or unintentional, or the result of neglect. It causes harm to older people, either temporarily or over a long period of time.' More specifically, abuse is divided into four categories: physical, emotional, sexual and neglect (SSI, 1993: 3).

The guidance describes areas that need to be addressed but does not suggest the contents of each local policy. The guidance advises that policy statements should cover values, equal opportunities and reflect inter-agency working arrangements. It also advises that local implementation strategies should include guidelines, setting and maintaining standards, and integration with care management; arrangements should include staff training and supervision, monitoring and review (SSI, 1993: 9–20).

Social Service Departments (SSDs) received *No Longer Afraid* in July 1993, just three months after the implementation of the long-planned-for and much heralded community care changes. Directors and managers were focusing their energies on these major additional responsibilities, such as managing the new special transitional grants, community care planning and care management. These changes came under close scrutiny from the Social Services Inspectorate. In contrast, central government was providing only guidance in relation to elder abuse and there was apparently no sanction should it remained unheeded. Dealing with elder abuse was perceived as a matter of much less importance than the community care changes. Furthermore, although *No Longer Afraid* recommended a strong inter-agency approach, central government addressed the guidance to SSDs and not to other key statutory bodies.

There is a number of reasons why central government did not give a high priority to elder abuse. The community care agenda for vulnerable adults was to some extent moving in a different direction. Community care encouraged elderly people to remain in their own homes, thereby putting more stress on carers. Underlying the community care reforms was the government's concern to contain the escalating costs of residential and nursing care. SSDs were taking on the new responsibilities for assessing, rationing and allocating provision, including residential care services which had previously been provided on request through Social Security. This change coincided with the political ideology of 'the family' and family care as opposed to an all-providing state. Government was also able to introduce a means test for nursing home care and shift the provision away from a free service of long-term care provided by the NHS. An additional aim was to promote the private and voluntary care sectors to enable a greater 'mixed economy of care'. Central government's economic policy has been influenced recently by the desire to restrict local government finance. It was not eager to embrace new responsibilities requiring further funding. The problem of elder abuse has not as yet caused major public debate or influenced public opinion, although politicians have responded in a limited way.

Local policy and response

The national policy in relation to elder abuse has encouraged a variety of differing local approaches. Some SSDs working with the health service and the police have taken a vigorous policy initiative on elder abuse, whilst others have done little. About half of the local policies deal with the abuse of vulnerable adults, e.g. those with disabilities and older people, and the other half focus exclusively on the mistreatment of elders. The minority (some 20 per cent) of local policies have established the maintenance of 'at risk registers' (Penhale, 1993c: 13). These hold the names of people who have been abused *and* are considered to be at risk of further abuse. The purpose of these registers (as in child protection registers) is to facilitate effective communication between agencies about 'at risk' individuals. However, it is generally considered that this communication can be effected by a single agency (usually social services) playing a leading role in coordinating abuse information without the need for a register. Some SSDs have developed their own policy whilst others developed an inter-agency policy from the outset.

Elder abuse is currently an area for evolving policy. The author was involved in 1995 in organizing a conference for the 17 North-West SSDs in conjunction with health authorities, the police and the voluntary sector. The policy documents from all these authorities showed some variations in the definition of abuse categories, though all included physical, psychological/emotional, neglect, financial and sexual abuse. However, there was consistency in the procedural stages to be followed in responding to abuse: investigation, assessment, case conference, care plan and review, and all specified that action to ensure safety would be taken in urgent situations.

There were similarities in the areas in which the various authorities were working to develop their services:

1 the formation of inter-agency policies (where they did not exist);
2 training in awareness and specialist intervention;
3 procedures for institutional abuse.

The most recent survey on the state of policy formation was conducted by Action on Elder Abuse (AEA) in 1995. It found that a significant number of SSDs and the majority of health authorities do not have policies. It was reported that three-quarters of social services departments had policies whilst a quarter did not. Amongst health authorities and health care trusts less than a quarter had policies. A number of health authorities indicated that they did see a need for such policies. The majority of authorities (both health and social services) which had policies, did not have plans to monitor and review them.

In summary, it is a matter for concern that a significant number of SSDs and the majority of health authorities do not have policies on elder abuse. The existing policies vary widely as to their contents, and few agencies actively review how services are delivered in practice (AEA, 1995: 8).

The experience from the United States of America

Elder abuse and the response to this problem has received more attention in the United States than in any other country. It achieved national prominence when a joint hearing of the Senate and House of Representatives Select Committee on Aging met in 1980 (Filinson and Ingman, 1989: 130). The committee produced the report *Elder Abuse: The Hidden Problem*

(United States Congress House Select Committee on Aging, 1981). This heralded the start of a 10-year campaign to achieve recognition of the problem and legislation. The media played an important part in highlighting the problem, but the abuse situation was oversimplified and inaccurately stereotyped as that of elders dependent on family carers being abused by their carers. Widespread public recognition of the problem was achieved, which galvanized the state and federal governments into action. However, there was not enough political support for national legislation, and so Congress amended the Older Americans Act in 1990 and 1992 in order to provide funding to state governments. The states were able to define their approach to these issues, and this has been done in a wide variety of ways, through 50 different state laws. To obtain funding each state had to provide preventive and treatment services. A National Centre on Elder Abuse was created to provide a focus for conducting and disseminating research. It has played a key role in providing guidance to states on reporting, investigation, assessment and treatment of abuse and neglect. Elder abuse has assumed a more prominent position since the Older Americans Act in 1992, under a new title – 'vulnerable elder rights protection' (Wolf, 1994: 12).

Following the pattern of the child abuse laws in America, most of the states have enacted legislation in relation to elder abuse and neglect. By 1988, 43 states had mandatory reporting laws (Bennett and Kingston, 1993: 8). These require health care workers to inform the official state agency of any suspected abuse. Those reporting suspected abuse are protected against litigation.

The states require those who suspect abuse, care professionals and others, to report their concerns to the Adult Protection Services (APS), which are part of (or closely associated with) the state's legal prosecution office. They have three main functions: to investigate the suspected abuse, to assess the elderly person's needs, and to provide services that reduce the risks of further abuse. The APSs control few support services and therefore need to work closely with the other social services, health and voluntary agencies.

There is much controversy as to whether an emphasis on law enforcement and mandatory reporting are appropriate responses. Campaigners wanted recognition and assistance for a hidden problem. There was a strongly held view that many of those subject to elder abuse were helpless and unable to protect themselves. Legislators argued that the state had to take firm action to uncover the problem and assist these dependent individuals. It was considered that the strident approach taken by APSs, including mandatory reporting, would identify the extent of the problem. Additionally, the use of the criminal justice system was seen as a particularly appropriate response to financial and material abuse.

Some commentators have argued that mandatory reporting is 'an inappropriate, ineffective and ageist response' to abuse (Faulkner, 1982: 69; see also Crystal, 1986: 338). Crystal regarded the mandatory reporting statutes as an 'invasion of traditional privileged relationships with physicians, clergy, other professionals, and even spouses' treating all older people as less than competent, leading to infantilization and infringement of civil rights. He went on to say that the statutes were popular because legislators and governors are anxious to find a way to 'do something' about a highly visible problem without the need to spend substantial sums on new services.

Other American studies have also cast doubt on the effectiveness of mandatory reporting legislation. O'Brien, for example, found that in Michigan and North Carolina, 70 per cent of physicians in both states were unaware of the reporting laws (O'Brien, 1986: 621). Writing two years before this, Salend et al. (1984a), had noted that by January 1981, 16 states had legislation for mandatory reporting in place and when the practice in those states was reviewed three years later, the amount and quality of the information generated by the reporting system was 'disappointing'. South Carolina had the earliest reporting statute, in 1974, but ten years later Salend et al. found that all their respondents suspected under-reporting and that on average, only 45 per cent of suspected cases of abuse were subsequently substantiated. They also pointed out that more than half the state statutes failed to mandate a central state-wide registry for establishing a database of information about cases of abuse and neglect. Taken together, the statutes failed to provide a definitional basis for classifying types of abuse (Salend et al., 1984: 62–4). In the 1990s, such a situation was still being confirmed (Wolf, 1994: 12; Lachs and Pillemer, 1995: 437).

The examination of risk factors associated with the likelihood of abuse is relevant for those who are planning services. Those elders who are frail are particularly vulnerable because they are not able to defend themselves. But Lachs and Pillemer's research review (1995: 438) suggests that age and impairment are not primary risk predisposing factors. It is considered that the main predeterminants of abuse are characteristics associated with the abuser. He or she is likely to:

1   suffer from mental illness;
2   misuse drugs;
3   be financially or materially dependent on the elderly person;
4   have a history of violence or anti-social behaviour;
5   live with the abused elder.

Wolf and Pillemer concluded that: 'abusers are less likely to be stressed care givers than they are to be troubled and impaired individuals' (1989b: 155).

These findings run counter to the popular belief that abuse is brought on by the burden of caring. It appears to be caused by the pathology of the abuser. Therefore services need to address the needs of the abuser as well as of the abused.

The American research examines 'outcomes' of intervention. In one study (Foelker et al., 1990: 561) a third of abused elders refused help and clearly this presented difficulties. The same study found that neglect involving carers was particularly difficult to resolve. An early study of APSs in Cleveland (cited in Crystal, 1986: 337) reported that intervention by the

APS was associated with removal from home (both short- and long-term) and Faulkner (1982) stated that this was linked to a higher morbidity than for those remaining at home. An interesting outcome was that there was little use of court action and that APSs considered legal action a strategy of last resort.

There was a broad agreement that the provision of comprehensive services and strong inter-agency working are a precondition for an effective service. Wolf (1994: 14–16), describes a number of innovative model projects which achieved positive results, namely:

1   the development of a senior advocacy programme using volunteers who were highly trained and supported;
2   victim support groups to build confidence and provide a supportive network;
3   specialist casework training to Master's level for those working in APSs;
4   inter-agency awareness training, particularly including the police.

The continuing high profile of elder abuse is illustrated by the estimate of two million abused elders by the 1991 Senate Select Committee on Aging (Lachs and Pillemer, 1995: 437). The recognition of this problem is much higher than in Britain. The legislative response involving mandatory reporting has provoked formidable criticism, although in practice the APSs operate to resolve social problems rather than use the law. American research findings and innovations in service delivery give strong pointers for the development of services in Britain, and Biggs et al. have concluded that Britain needs to be aware that difficulties will be encountered if policy initiatives are not grounded in adequate research (Biggs et al., 1995: 52).

Comparisons with child protection

Both similarities and differences are found when comparing elder abuse with child abuse. Child abuse has attracted the attention of government, research and training institutions and so there are lessons from there. An obvious common theme is that of effective inter-agency working. One would hope that the breakdown of communications between agencies that has been highlighted in numerous child abuse inquiries, and the strategies proposed in *Working Together under the Children Act 1989* (Department of Health, 1991b) would be helpful in the field of elder abuse.

There are many differences between childhood and old age. Childhood is a period of rapid growth from total dependency to increasing autonomy, but with parental and adult limitations on autonomy. On the other hand, personality has matured by the time of old age. When elderly persons need caring help, they are entitled to full choice, autonomy and civil rights. The laws concerning children are based on concepts of normal development and dependency on adult carers. But the law for adults and older people assumes full independence except in particular circumstances where there is 'mental incapacity' (see further, Chapter 6, this volume). Children are provided with universal services, including health care and schools. But for older people there is no similar state provision to nurture and monitor vulnerable individuals. Perhaps most importantly, children benefit from positive attitudes towards them, whilst elders are undervalued and held in low regard. These values are epitomized by the way that children are described as 'the hope of the future', whilst elders are frequently described as 'retired', 'unproductive' and 'non-contributing'. Typically, the response by society to older people does not enhance their position.

There are a number of areas where there is much to learn from the comparison of dealing with child protection. These are:

1   public recognition and the response from politicians through government policy;
2   policy formation and development;
3   how the various agencies work together as a system to prevent and respond to abuse.

Child abuse, like elder abuse, was highlighted in Britain in the decade after it was discovered in America (the 1970s). Henry Kempe, the paediatrician, used the term 'battered baby syndrome' to gain credibility from paediatricians, and he proposed the therapeutic treatment of parents and families through a process of 're-parenting'. The National Society for the Prevention of Cruelty to Children (NSPCC) founded their Battered Child Research Unit in 1968 to bring the American experience to this country. In the early 1970s, the NSPCC and others were using the term 'non-accidental injury' which marked a shift in emphasis from a medical to a wider social problem. The terminology changed again in the 1980s to child abuse (including neglect and sexual abuse), an even wider social and legal definition. Latterly, the term 'child protection' has been used to emphasize the response to the problem. This change illustrates how the problem was redefined. Similarly, elder abuse has evolved from the 1970s term 'granny bashing' (see further Chapter 3, this volume). There is no agreed definition of elder abuse and much debate about categories of abuse, particularly whether neglect is a form of abuse or a different type of social problem.

The publicity attracted by the numerous child abuse inquiries, from Maria Colwell in 1973, following deaths of children at the hands of their carers provoked widespread public concern. A number of authors, notably Parton (1985), have described the 'moral panic' which was fuelled by politicians and the media. The family, which is typically seen as a positive and nurturing institution, and 'family values' emphasized by all political parties, was under attack. Further, the welfare state was seen as failing in its role to protect children. Unfortunately these tragedies were examined in the full glare of the media and were inappropriately judged with the 'wisdom of hindsight'. The care professionals were frequently made scapegoats. A positive outcome was that the government was encouraged to take an active approach to this problem. Guidance was issued to health and social services authorities in 1976 that led to the setting up of inter-agency area review committees. In the 1980s, these became the area child protection committees with their responsibility for management coordination and cooperation in relation to child abuse. The government then defined and subsequently revised categories of abuse, the current categories being physical, sexual, emotional and neglect. The category of 'grave concern' was removed in 1994. This meant that local statistics became comparable from one area to another, and that national statistics could be collected from the late 1980s. The government issued guidance on agency and inter-agency practice in the 1985 version of *Working Together*, which was reissued as *Working Together under the Children Act 1989*. Detailed guidance followed the Cleveland, Orkneys, Rochdale, Staffordshire and Leicestershire inquiries. These later reports led to the extension of national guidance to cover 'organized' and 'institutional abuse'.

A main theme for practitioners in this field has been to get the balance right between being too intrusive into the privacy of the family and intervening to protect children. Major 'errors' have been identified in the child protection system intervening inappropriately (Cleveland) and on the other hand not intervening to protect children (for example, the Tyra Henry and Jasmine Beckford inquiries). Government guidance on good practice has emphasized the need to work with families, encouraging attendance and participation at key decision-making meetings such as case conferences. In the early 1990s, the government funded major research which examined the effectiveness of child protection intervention. This work has directly influenced policy guidance. The recent publication of this work, in *Child Protection: Messages from Research* (Department of Health, 1995d), has led to greater emphasis on supporting children and families rather than the child protection focus that is often seen by families as punitive.

There is much to learn from the mistakes and achievements during the last quarter of a century of child protection work in this country, much of which is applicable to the field of elder abuse. The national policy response to elder abuse is at an early stage, similar to that of child abuse in the 1970s when the major preoccupation was with identifying and redefining the problem. In child protection work, the delicate balance between state intervention and the privacy of the family has been re-examined and refined as a result of experience and public debate. The very nature of human risk and risk management makes it impossible to assess and get it right all the time. However, a body of knowledge which covers good practice policy and procedure has evolved. Child protection work has had the advantage of gaining wide interest with the public and the government, and this has ensured a nation-wide approach.

The field of elder abuse would benefit from greater recognition. Without this, much elder abuse will continue to remain unrecognized. A strong lead is required by government to ensure that agencies develop policies *and* work together. This might take the form of an abuse protection committee for disabled and vulnerable adults. The Department of Health should standardize the categories of abuse so that comparable national data become available. This would help research, which is currently extremely limited. Research on 'outcomes of intervention' should inform practice, as it has done with child abuse. Government should sponsor such research and then promote good practice guidance. Without a lead by government, the services will remain patchy, fragmented and not informed by a researched knowledge-base.

The way forward

The hesitant lead from the British government has contributed to the slow development of a response to elder abuse. The lack of guidance both to health authorities and to the police, and the rather general nature of the guidance to Social Services Departments (SSDs), has led to a wide range of differing policies emerging 'from the grass roots'. Hence, there is an uneven response to elder abuse across the country. The government could do much to provide a national strategy. The Department of Health should issue common criteria for the categories of abuse and start to collect national data. The government should determine which agency (presumably health or social services) should take the lead in coordinating this work, both for care management and for the development of local policies. Stronger and more authoritative national guidance should be issued to all the statutory agencies. The government should commission research into the nature of elder abuse (similar to *Messages from Research* on child protection) with emphasis on the efficacy of various approaches that are being taken to tackle it. If the government took this lead there would be a more consistent response by all the main agencies, in particular from those who at present have failed to address this issue.

There is much to learn about the development of effective services (as well as policy) from the American experience. An important theme is the need for a broad range of 'mainstream' services to support elders. Specialist services that respond to elder abuse should dovetail with mainstream services. From America, there is some interesting research evaluation of service interventions to help both abused and abusers. In this country, there is very limited experience of this work and no research. Since the main feature of abuse situations is the characteristics of the abusers it is important to help and 'deal with' their behaviour. Therefore services for abused elders should interrelate effectively with the services dealing with psychiatry, drug misuse, and the law. Special programmes to help those who have abused should be developed, such as counselling, group work, volunteer support and advocacy. Of current concern is the issue of institutional abuse and it will be necessary to identify and share best practice in tackling this. Perhaps it is most important at this early stage in the understanding of

17
Looking to the Future

Frank Glendenning and Peter Decalmer

During the course of this book, we have drawn attention to a considerable number of issues, the principal one being that of the definition of elder abuse. *Action on Elder Abuse* has essayed a definition to which we referred in Chapters 3 and 4. This definition was agreed by a majority of experts who attended a meeting for that purpose at Bristol University in 1995. The debate which preceded the acceptance of the definition demonstrated that differing views continued to exist, and it is well to recognize this. Kingston drew attention to this dilemma several years ago, when he warned against a replication of the American debate about *definitions* in the 1980s (Kingston, 1990). We also subscribe to that view, although since 1993 we have seen little reason to change the *categories* of abuse proposed by Wolf and Pillemer in 1989, and which, again, have already been discussed in Chapters 3 and 4.

Development of guidelines for action

What is noticeable about the British situation is that there has been a growing recognition since the mid-1970s that elder abuse exists and in 1991 a consortium composed of the British Geriatrics Society (BGS), Age Concern England (ACE), the British Association of Social Workers, the Carers' National Association and the Police Federation of England and Wales published guidelines for action and for carers (ACE, 1991). These were published with permission in the 1993 edition of this book and have recently been revised (AEA, 1996). In 1991 also, the Royal College of Nursing produced its own guidelines, but although Kent Social Services had produced guidelines in 1987 (revised in 1989), other departments and health districts and National Health Service trusts were slow to follow this lead.

Assessing the situation in 1991, Hildrew pointed out that while some social services departments had begun to follow the British Geriatrics Society et al. guidelines (ACE, 1991), others based their early drafts on the Kent guidelines which were influenced by child protection procedures, while others followed Gloucestershire Social Services' guidelines, *Adults at Risk* (Gloucestershire Social Services Department, 1991), which is detailed and procedural, involving an 'at risk' register and has been regarded by some as being too rigid.

elder abuse that front-line staff receive training and supervision to ensure that this problem is recognized and not 'brushed under the carpet'.

The experience from child protection and elder abuse in America points to the importance of strong family support services and effective inter-agency collaboration, a point that Stevenson has recently underlined (Stevenson, 1996).

What had already emerged by 1993, in general terms, was that it was not at all clear that decision-making about the abuse and neglect of old people was reliably research based and the result of informed discussion. Phillipson (1992b), referring to the Department of Health Social Services Inspectorate report, *Confronting Elder Abuse* (SSI, 1992), suggested that the area of abuse and neglect was so muddled and ill-defined that departments should proceed with utmost caution when trying to develop appropriate policies (Phillipson, 1992b: 2). This observation came after a number of social services departments and health districts had already implemented or drafted guidelines, often without reference to one another. It would have been helpful to have established a compatible model first, which would then have enabled a national database to have been more easily compiled, and to have assisted in the setting up of incidence and prevalence studies on a planned basis.

In 1993, the SSI developed its own practice guidelines, *No Longer Afraid: the Safeguard of Elderly People in Domestic Settings*, and copies were distributed to all social services departments with the requirement that local authorities apply principles of care management and assessment to the cases referred to them (SSI, 1993: 9–10). It further said clearly that policies should be developed on an inter-departmental and an inter-agency basis, and in particular (p. 9) that policies should be formulated in consultation with the social services, legal and housing departments, the police, the health authorities and the new National Health Service (NHS) trusts, together with the private and voluntary sectors, and formally adopted.

The results of this recommendation have not proved to be entirely successful, as indicated several times above and was manifestly evidenced by the Action on Elder Abuse survey (AEA, 1995). Brief reference has been made to this survey in Chapter 3 and elsewhere in this volume.

Questionnaires were sent by AEA to 515 social services departments, and the Association of Directors of Social Services (ADSS) (1995: 16) noted that the AEA survey had reported that of the 58 policy documents received from social services departments in response to the questionnaire, 43 per cent 'were concerned with abuse of vulnerable adults, which included older people'. AEA (1995), however, made the point that the SSI in 1993 had recommended that the abuse of older people should be considered *separately* from other forms of abuse. The survey demonstrated that only 3 per cent of social services policy documents referred to adults over 65.

The chief elements in all local guidelines should involve ensuring that staff at every level are trained to recognize abuse and high risk situations and to know what action to take. Since the Gloucestershire guidelines, there has been discussion about the establishment of 'at risk' registers. There is little research available on the effectiveness of such registers.

Eastman first broached the issue in *Old Age Abuse* in 1984. In 1990, the ADSS mentioned registers in a guarded way in their guidance document *Adults at Risk* (ADSS, 1991), but the matter was not raised in their subsequent discussion document on the mistreatment of older people (ADSS,

1995). Since 1990, there has also been a good deal of reflection on the issues of adults at risk and elders at risk, and whether it is appropriate to subsume both within the same generic register, with the possibility of failure to address the special needs of elderly people who are at risk. The AEA survey found that the number of registers was small and the SSI guidelines of 1993 stated firmly that *adequate monitoring systems* should reduce the need for a register (SSI, 1993: 20). The AEA also suggested that registers raised ethical implications for elderly people, which agencies needed to consider carefully (AEA, 1995: 19). However, for those who are mentally ill, the Care Programme Approach Supervision Register and Supervised Discharge (Mental Health Act, 1995), protection is offered, but *not* to those who are competent and do not suffer from mental health problems.

Questionnaires were also sent to 399 health authorities and National Health Service (NHS) trusts. Thirty-nine of these sent copies of their policy documents, which showed that only 4 per cent referred specifically to adults over 65 (AEA, 1995: 17). Thus in spite of the leadership provided by the government through the SSI and its further reports (SSI, 1993, 1994), by 1995 the situation had not changed a great deal. With neither the SSI nor the NHS Executive apparently wishing to be prescriptive, and with policies being left to departments, authorities and trusts, for some years it has remained difficult to see how the situation can be progressed in the overall national interest.

Recently however, some advancement has become evident. Among the more recent guidelines and training developments have been those in Bury and Rochdale. These guidelines are exceptionally well written, thorough and concise in our view.

The main categories of abuse which have been included in the Bury and Rochdale guidelines are physical abuse (including sexual abuse), negligence, self-neglect, financial exploitation, psychological and verbal abuse and violation of rights. A summary of the guidelines is to be found in Appendix F, this volume and the full text will be found in *Working Together: Elder Abuse Guidelines* (Bury and Rochdale Partnership Group for Older People, 1993). The primary health care teams, many of whom have been trained in care management, use the guidelines alongside this system. Care managers in Bury and Rochdale include nurses and social workers who have been formally trained in the recognition and management of elder mistreatment. The training (which was mentioned in Chapters 4 and 14, above) has included:

1   identification and recognition.
2   care management of cases
3   assessment
4   case conferences
5   documentation
6   legal aspects

Elder abuse and child abuse

The SSI noted in the 1993 guidelines that care should be taken not to link elder abuse with child abuse. We believe that it is inadvisable to make this linkage. Finkelhor and Pillemer (1988: 248) drew attention to the fact that elder abuse within the context of family violence was compared to child abuse more frequently than spouse abuse 'because of certain apparent similarities . . . The relationship between caretaker and elder in such cases is often thought to have a parent–child character in the extreme dependency of the elder.' As was suggested in Chapter 3, the carer may well be the 'dependant' and Breckman and Adelman (1988) have pointed out that even when it is the elderly person who is dependent, the conditions of dependency are quite different from those of young children. Lessons that can be learnt from child protection procedures are a quite different matter from actually following child abuse guidelines, in response to elder abuse, as was the case in some areas seven or eight years ago (Kingston, 1990). In this respect a recent paper on elder protection and child protection (Stevenson, 1996) is of great interest and importance, drawing a distinction between policies and procedures and laying stress on inter-agency cooperation.

Inter-agency cooperation

'Cooperation between agencies is perhaps the most critical contribution to the success or failure of a project' (Wolf and Pillemer, 1989: 149). Such cooperation is an important part of working within the context of elder mistreatment. Health authorities and trusts are usually involved, as are social services, housing departments or housing associations, the police, voluntary agencies, and of course the general practitioner who should, with the primary health care team, be central not only at case conferences but also in the establishing of joint guidelines so that there is as little misunderstanding as possible concerning local procedures. Cooperation of this kind is the bedrock of everything that we mean by 'community care' and 'caring for people'. This will not be achieved unless each agency attempts to understand the role and ethos of the others and unless all are adequately resourced; furthermore, it is essential that the infrastructure required to make this possible is adequately resourced as well. Inter-agency cooperation implies in addition that a complete rethinking is needed of the context of existing professional, post-qualifying and in-service training.

Nevertheless, it has to be admitted that working together in a real sense is fraught with difficulty. The difficulty occurs not only because of attempting to meld the aspirations of different agencies who were previously autonomous and independent and, in the case of social services, accountable to local government, but also because of practical problems encountered through terms of service and professional attitudes. Far too little attention has been paid by the makers of social policy in Britain to such factors and far too little attention has been paid to the concept of joint responsibility and what working together really means, in relation both to training and to good practice.

Guidelines for institutions

It has long been evident that investigators and practitioners have been seeking to understand elder mistreatment, and advising about good practice, by applying the family violence model, dealing with the mistreatment of elderly people almost exclusively within domestic settings (Glendenning, 1993: 33; Phillipson and Biggs, 1995: 189). Decalmer (1993: 59) drew attention also to institutional abuse, where the environment, practices and rules found in residential settings become abusive in themselves.

There is well-documented evidence from the numerous official inquiries in Britain of both active and passive abuse in homes and hospitals (see also Chapters 3 and 11, this volume). Apart from the need for increased resources, rigorous staff training and clear aims and objectives, it continues to be necessary to reinforce the resolve of those who before and after the Wagner Report on residential care in 1988, have been deeply committed to the provision of more than adequate care in residential settings and to the wiping out of abuse in all its forms (see especially, Clough, 1996).

At the very least, we need to have in place quality assurance programmes, adequate levels of staffing, a charter for service users, with independent advocacy services, clear procedures for hearing complaints and investigating alleged abuse in institutional care, a clear contract governing the provision of services to users, and their cost, together with services which meet the needs of multi-ethnic society (McCreadie, 1991, 1996a).

We also need to bear in mind that similar principles apply to hospitals as much as to residential homes for elderly people, for as Horrocks (formerly of the government's Health Advisory Service) speaking of institutional passive abuse 'on a massive scale' remarked in 1988: 'We seem to be running institutions, not care programmes' (Tomlin, 1989: 12).

Home Life: A Code of Practice for Residential Care was a landmark text when it was published by the Centre for Policy on Ageing in 1984, as was *Community Life: A Code of Practice for Community Care* (Centre for Policy on Ageing, 1990). Neither has been emulated by government departments, who devolve accountability and standards for good practice to local responsibility. More recently, and of relevance to residential care, is *Creating a Home from Home: A Guide to Standards* (1996) published by the National Institute of Social Work.

The increase in the number of residential care homes in the private sector, as indicated in Chapter 11, makes legislative regulation a crucial issue, and from April 1991 all local authorities were obliged to establish arm's length inspection units, under the National Health Service and Community Care Act 1990. Under the present regulations, social services departments register care homes and health authorities register nursing homes and homes for the elderly mentally infirm. There is therefore the inherent problem of two registering authorities. When abuse is identified in a residential setting, the evidence has to be strong enough to be examined in a court of law, as withdrawal of registration may lead to challenge in the courts, with all its inherent costs. This will often have the effect that minor forms of abuse are not reported, or there may be a reluctance by some authorities to meet the potential escalating costs of litigation. Brammer, in a paper on the 1984 Registered Homes Act, has pointed up a number of deficiencies in the legislation itself and has commented that 'governmental attitudes demonstrate a preference for the non-interventionist approach and cast doubts on the existing system of regulation as imposing an excessive burden on business'. She comments that 'the impetus behind such measures must be to secure greater protection for the elderly and not to lessen the regulatory burden on businesses' (Brammer, 1994: 436). There is on this evidence a strong argument for the appointment of an ombudsman or commissioner who can deal with complaints or issues of serious contention, as we proposed in the 1993 edition. The fact that we are still without such a commissioner underlines the inability to set national standards and to take action against cases of abuse.

A significant contribution to any discussion about an ombudsman has been made recently by the long-term care 'ombudsman' for Ohio. Her reflections have led her to express her conviction that there must be a strong focus for the long-term care ombudsman as a client advocate and that 'ombudsmen must work with and depend upon professionals in many disciplines ... [this] is extremely important to the ombudsman's ability to achieve the client's desired outcomes' (Skelley-Walley, 1996: 111).

Matters of law

Attention needs to be paid to legislative needs, and Griffiths et al. have demonstrated very clearly in Chapter 6 of this volume the areas in which action should be taken. It is also advisable for social services departments to have available lists of lawyers who have a special expertise in this area, whose advice they can draw on when it is more appropriate to seek such advice, rather than routinely inform the police. As this book was being prepared for the press the Family Law Act 1996 received Royal Assent. For the first time, there is legislation on the statute book covering abusive situations in the elder's home.

Pointers from other countries

Crystal (1986) declared his misgivings about mandatory reporting in the USA when he drew attention to the stereotypical language used to describe older people in state mandatory reporting legislation. Moreover he suggested that there was a marked tendency for politicians to support mandatory reporting on the grounds that reporting an increased number of cases was proving that elder abuse was being controlled and that there was no need for substantial financial resources to develop new services. This illusory sense of progress, he concluded, was a real problem! For a useful overview of public responses to the American legislation, see Filinson and Ingman (1989). More recently, Mixson has reviewed adult protective services in America in the context of existing protocols and their ethical values. Her conclusions emphasize the value of multidisciplinary teamwork (Mixson, 1996: 64–86).

Kingston, in 1990, suggested that because the American literature on assessment tools far exceeded the entire British literature on elder abuse, British policy-makers needed to learn from this. It is not clear that many have so learnt but a number of tables of indicators and protocols for identification, assessment and screening have been mentioned or included in this volume.

Considering the topic of elder mistreatment from a world-wide perspective, Kosberg and Garcia suggest that the extent of elder abuse is 'speculative and believed to be an underestimation' (Kosberg and Garcia, 1995: 185) and they identify a number of explanations for the phenomenon: dependency, economic conditions, cultural changes, continuing marital abuse, substance abuse, personal problems, isolation, gender, homogeneity and prejudice, housing and societal violence. These are all matters that we recognize.

Training

As McCreadie has recently suggested, 'awareness of the possibility of abuse depends very largely on the training and education of a wide range of professionals and others in contact with older people' (McCreadie, 1996a: 101). Replication is required everywhere, for as Action on Elder Abuse claims, this is 'Everybody's business' (AEA, 1995).

Continuing research

In the first edition, we ended by including a list of matters which in our view required further research. They were similar to many of the issues raised by McCreadie in her exploratory study of elder abuse in 1991. We have updated them to include:

- studies of incidence and prevalence;
- studies of victims and perpetrators;
- studies of caregiver stress;

- the consequences of abuse on the perpetrator as well as the victim;
- the nature of family violence;
- the relationship between child abuse, spouse abuse, adult abuse and elder abuse;
- different types and perceptions of abuse;
- abuse from a stranger;
- issues of neglect and self-neglect;
- a study of abuse in residential institutions (for which we have waited a long time in view of the British record in public inquiries);
- the development of screening instruments;
- a study of standardization in recording.

McCreadie was one of the first investigators in this country to draw attention to the important work of Rosalie Wolf and Karl Pillemer in America (McCreadie, 1991). In the second and enlarged edition of her study (1996a), she emphasizes the necessity for rigorous methodology and quality research in this difficult area. From the early 1980s, the studies of Wolf and Pillemer led them to the conclusion that 'the importance of using control groups cannot be over-emphasized' (Wolf and Pillemer, 1989). Those who are familiar with their work will appreciate exactly what McCreadie means. When Pillemer lectured in England in 1993, he underscored this theme, affirming that their most useful studies had been those which had used case-control groups. These, for example, had enabled them to recognize that abuser characteristics were more powerful indicators of elder mistreatment than victim characteristics. After his Boston study, referred to in Chapter 3 above, Pillemer applied the same methodological instruments in Canada with Podnieks; this led him to believe that in general, the extent of elder abuse was lower than had been previously reported (Pillemer, 1994: 5). This evidence should encourage British social science researchers to assess whether the methodology of Wolf and Pillemer could be adapted for use in Britain.

There is an urgent need to develop quality research studies in Britain. Apart from the topics that have just been listed, there are also studies on victims' mental health problems as well as those of caregivers, outcome measures and risk analysis. We also need to standardize recording and achieve compatibility in policy guidelines so that a national database can be established. This would enable us both to utilize the empirical data and to develop the consequent theory which together would help us to obtain legitimation for public recognition of this distressing social phenomenon. It is also our hope that more elderly victims of abuse and neglect will find it possible to make their voices heard and that we may, as a result of what we learn from them, find ways to increase the quality of life of all elderly people.

However, as Holstein reminds us:

> Practitioners rarely have the luxury of working in ideal circumstances. For those who work with abused and neglected older adults, the likelihood of achieving an ideal solution is slim. While the public may be appalled at newspaper descriptions of elder mistreatment, that dismay rarely translates into political action. Despite

outrage, few understand the roots of problems that lead to elder abuse and neglect, and therefore, few assume responsibility for activities designed to address these deeper causes . . . It is unlikely that this picture will change in the immediate future. (Holstein, 1996: 180)

That is the challenge with which we are all faced.

Appendix A
Indicators of Possible Elder Mistreatment

I PHYSICAL	II PSYCHOLOGICAL	III SOCIOLOGICAL	IV LEGAL
A. Medication misuse	A. Humiliation	A. Isolation	A. Material misuse
1. Absence	1. Shame	1. Involuntary withdrawal	1. Property mismanagement
2. Improper use	2. Blame	2. Voluntary withdrawal	2. Contract mismanagement
3. Adverse interaction	3. Ridicule	3. Inadequate supervision	3. Blocked access to property
4. Unnecessary use	4. Rejection	4. Improper supervision	4. Blocked access to contract
B. Bodily impairment	B. Harassment	B. Role confusion	B. Theft
1. Unmet medical needs	1. Insult	1. Competition	1. Stealing property
2. Poor hygiene	2. Intimidation	2. Overload	2. Stealing contracts
3. Ingestion problems	3. Fearfulness	3. Inversion	3. Extorting property
4. Rest disturbance	4. Agitation	4. Dissolution	4. Extorting contracts
C. Bodily assaults	C. Manipulation	C. Misuse of living arrangements	C. Misuse of rights
1. External injuries	1. Information withheld	1. Household disorganized	1. Denied contracting
2. Internal injuries	2. Information falsified	2. Lack of privacy	2. Involuntary servitude
3. Sexual assault	3. Unreasonable emotional deprivation	3. Unfit environment	3. Unnecessary guardianship
4. Suicide/homicidal act	4. Interference with decisions	4. Abandonment	4. Misuse of professional authority

Source: Johnson, 1991: 392. Copyright © T.F. Johnson. Published with the author's permission.

See also Johnson (1991) for Health Status Risk Assessment Evaluation Form, Glossary of Indicators of Elder Mistreatment and Evaluation Categories for the Health Status Risk Assessment.

Appendix B
High Risk Placement Worksheet

Name of client/patient: _____

A.	Characteristics of older person	Existence of risks
1.	Female	_____
2.	Advanced age	_____
3.	Dependent	_____
4.	Problem drinker	_____
5.	Inter-generational conflict	_____
6.	Internalizer	_____
7.	Excessive loyalty	_____
8.	Past abuse	_____
9.	Stoicism	_____
10.	Isolation	_____
11.	Impairment	_____
12.	Provocative behaviour	_____

B.	Characteristics of caregiver	Existence of risks
1.	Problem drinker	_____
2.	Medication/drug abuser	_____
3.	Senile dementia/confusion	_____
4.	Mental/emotional illness	_____
5.	Caregiving inexperience	_____
6.	Economically troubled	_____
7.	Abused as child	_____
8.	Stressed	_____
9.	Unengaged outside the home	_____
10.	Blamer	_____
11.	Unsympathetic	_____
12.	Lacks understanding	_____
13.	Unrealistic expectations	_____
14.	Economically dependent	_____
15.	Hypercritical	_____

C. Characteristics of family system — Existence of risks

   1. Lack of family support   ———————

   2. Caregiving reluctance   ———————

   3. Overcrowding   ———————

   4. Isolation   ———————

   5. Marital conflict   ———————

   6. Economic pressures   ———————

   7. Intra-family problems   ———————

   8. Desire for institutionalization   ———————

   9. Disharmony in shared responsibility   ———————

D. Congruity of perceptions between older person and (potential) caregiver — Existence of risks

   1. Quality of past relationship   ——— ———

      a. Perception of older person

      _____

      b. Perception of caregiver

      _____

   2. Quality of present relationship   ———————

      a. Perception of older person

      _____

      b. Perception of caregiver

      _____

   3. Preferred placement location   ———————

      a. Perception of older person

      _____

      b. Perception of caregiver

      _____

   4. Ideal placement location   ———————

      a. Perception of older person

      _____

      b. Perception of caregiver

      _____

Source: Kosberg, 1988: 48. Copyright © The Gerontological Society of America. Published with permission.

Appendix C
Caregiver Strain Questionnaire

I am going to read a list of things other people have found to be difficult in helping out after somebody comes home from the hospital. Would you tell me whether any of these apply to you? (GIVE EXAMPLES)

	(Yes = 1)	(No = 0)
Sleep is disturbed (e.g. because _____ is in and out of bed or wanders around at night)	_____	_____
It is inconvenient (e.g. because helping takes so much time or it's a long drive over to help)	_____	_____
It is a physical strain (e.g. because of lifting in and out of a chair, effort or concentration is required)	_____	_____
It is confining (e.g. helping restricts free time or cannot go visiting)	_____	_____
There have been family adjustments (e.g. because helping has disrupted routine; there has been no privacy)	_____	_____
There have been changes in personal plans (e.g. had to turn down a job; could not go on vacation)	_____	_____
There have been other demands on my time (e.g. from other family members)	_____	_____
There have been emotional adjustments (e.g. because of severe arguments)	_____	_____
Some behaviour is upsetting (e.g. because of incontinence; _____ has trouble remembering things; or _____ accuses people of taking things)	_____	_____
It is upsetting to find _____ has changed so much from his/her former self (e.g. he/she is a different person than he/she used to be)	_____	_____
There have been work adjustments (e.g. because of having to take time off)	_____	_____
It is a financial strain	_____	_____
Feeling completely overwhelmed (e.g. because of worry about ———; concerns about how you will manage)	_____	_____
Total score (count yes responses)*	_____	

*Scores range from 0 to 13

Appendix D
Elder Abuse Assessment Protocol for Nurses

(adapted from Fulmer, 1984; Ross et al., 1985)

Before attempting to carry out the assessment, reference should be made to the section on 'detection' in Chapter 13 (p. 183) and the checklist of indicators of physical abuse in Chapter 4 of this volume (p. 47). The assessment is meant to serve as a screening procedure and to document cases of suspicion of abuse or neglect.

You are not asked to 'rate' any particular section but rather to use your powers of observation, instinct and 'gut feeling'. Remember, seldom will you find isolated symptoms but a 'cluster' of symptoms which may give rise to suspicion, and should not be ignored.

Any suspicion will need to be fully explained in the 'Assessor's summary and general opinion' section [in Appendix E].

A tick (✔) should be placed against the applicable description and, where appropriate, expanded upon in the summary section.

For example, if you tick Physical Assessment 1. Bruising: Shoulders ✔ left; colour: purple/yellow 2", in the summary section, you will need to expand, for example: bruise left shoulder, approximately 2" in diameter, purple in centre with yellow ringed edge.

In cases where the patient is not able to communicate or cooperate, this fact should be indicated in the summary, and if an advocate/representative was present during the assessment process, this should be clearly documented.

Note

It is acknowledged that the protocol does not specifically indicate the following: medication being taken, any medical or psychiatric condition, general practitioner involvement, respite care and housing status. If it is felt by the assessor that these issues are relevant, they should be included in your 'summary and general opinion' section.

A continuation sheet may be used if there is insufficient room for your remarks. These sheets should be securely fixed to the other documents.

General assessment

Clothing:
Torn
Soiled
Disarrayed

Hygiene:
Body odour
Unclean

Grooming:
Unkempt hair
Uncut nails;
Finger
Feet

Nutrition:
Pallor
Lips
Mouth
Hydration

Skin:
PAs:
sites

Ulcers:
sites

Urine burns:
sites

Excoriation:
sites

Physical assessment: evidence of:

1. Bruising:

Site: Colour of bruise/size
Shoulders
Buttocks
Thighs
Forearm
Lips
Mouth
Face
Eyes
Other

Colour of bruise – Please indicate black/purple/yellow
(this may give some indication of age of bruise)

2. Abrasion/laceration:

Site: Colour/state
Mouth
Lips
Gums
Genitalia
Buttocks
Others

Please state colour/state: e.g. red/pink/open/closed/
scarred/scabbed/tenderness etc.

Please indicate site of bruising/abrasion/
laceration on torso.
Colour code: Bruise (black Biro)
Abrasion/laceration (red Biro)

3. *Alopecia/haemorrhaging*
   Comment:

4. *Obvious deformities*
   Comment/site: _____

   Contractions _____
   Comment/site:

	Site
Pain	____
Tenderness	____
Swelling	____

5. *Sexual abuse*   (By observation not examination)

   Genitalia – vaginal and anal area

   Bruising _____
   Bleeding _____
   Pain _____
   Redness _____
   Itching _____
   Scratch marks _____
   Discharge _____
   Marked embarrassment evident _____
   Comment:

6. *Cognitive/emotional assessment:*
   a. Worried/anxious _____
   b. Aggressive _____
   c. Depression:
      Sad _____
      Loss of interest _____
      Feeling hopeless _____
      Withdrawn _____
      Tearful _____
   d. Slurred speech _____
   e. Drowsiness _____
   f. Reduced responsiveness _____
   g. Cowering _____
   h. Irritable, easily upset _____
   i. Defensive _____
   j. Evasive _____
   k. Guarded _____
   l. Suspicious _____
   m. Confused _____
   n. Disorientated _____
   o. Sleep disturbances _____
   p. Evidence of infantilization _____

   Comment:

7. *Relationship with carer:*
   a. Defensive _____
   b. Guarded _____
   c. Hostile _____
   d. Passive _____
   e. Afraid _____

   Any change after carer has left?

   Comment:

8. *Personal possessions:*

   Petty cash _____
   Toiletries _____
   Tissues _____
   Newspaper _____
   Writing material _____
   Stamps _____
   Confectionery _____
   Cordials _____
   Personal clothing _____

Signed: ....
Date(s): ....

Appendix E
Carer Abuse Assessment Protocol for Nurses

(adapted from Fulmer, 1984; Ross et al., 1985)

Before attempting to carry out the assessment, reference should be made to the section in Chapter 13, this volume, referring to 'Carers' (p. 184).

The assessment is designed to identify indications of possible stress and its intensity.

Again you are not being asked to 'rate' particular sections, but to use your powers of observation and the 'Assessor's summary and general opinion' section should be used to explain your observations.

For example in Section 7, if you tick 'exhaustion', you will need to explain how this was displayed ('appears continually drained, tired, listless, etc.').

Note

It is acknowledged that the protocol does not specifically indicate the following: general practitioner involvement, respite care and housing status. If it is felt by the assessor that these issues may be relevant they should be referred to in the 'Assessor's summary and general opinion' section.

A continuation sheet may be used if there is insufficient room for your remarks and this sheet should be securely fixed to the other documents.

The carer abuse assessment protocol for nurses

1. *Relationship to patient:*
   Relative
   Other

2. *Age range:*
   Under 21
   21–39
   40–59
   60–75
   75+

3. *Gender:*
   Male/Female

4. *Marital status:*
   Married
   Single
   Separated
   Divorced
   Widowed
   Other

5. *Domestic arrangements:*
   Alone
   With patient
   With spouse
   With children
   With others

6. Evidence of:
   Alcohol dependence
   Drug dependence
   Physical illness
   Mental illness
   Mental retardation
   Financial dependence
   History of family
      violence
   Other

7. *Evidence of stress:*
   Frustration
   Exhaustion
   Anxiety
   Low self-esteem
   Lack of leisure time
   Problems with
      children/marriage

8. *Knowledge of patient's situation:*

	Good	Poor
a. *Physical/ emotional health*		
b. *Assistance with ADLs:* Bathing Dressing Eating Mobility Toiletting		
c. *Any treatment regime:* Medication Nutrition Exercise Treatments Others		

9. *Attitude towards patient:*
   a. Angry
   b. Blaming
   c. Critical
   d. Over-concerned
   e. Resentful
   f. Non-concerned

10. *Attitudes towards staff:*
    a. Defensive
    b. Aggressive
    c. Irritable
    d. Suspicious

11. *Behaviour with patient during visiting:*
    Demonstrates lack of:
       Physical contact
       Facial contact
       Eye contact
       Verbal contact

Signed: ....

Date(s): ....

Assessor's Summary and General Opinion

Signed ....

Date(s) ....

Appendix F
Bury and Rochdale Partnership Group for Older People – Guidelines for Staff

GUIDELINES FOR STAFF TO FOLLOW WHEN THE ABUSE OF OLDER PEOPLE IS SUSPECTED OR CONFIRMED

Introduction

How Common is the Abuse of Older People?

Currently little hard statistical information is locally available which indicates the extent to which older people are abused. However, many staff and practitioners feel able to give instances of situations where abuse, as defined in these guidelines has occurred. These guidelines have therefore been prepared in an attempt to provide support for staff and practitioners who are concerned about the abuse of older people both generally and specifically with regard to an individual service user, patient and carer.

Fundamental Principles

These guidelines are based upon the following fundamental principles:

a. The recognition that abuse occurs in many different places, for example an older person's own home, a day care centre or hospital ward or a residential or nursing home.
b. When a situation of abuse is suspected, alleged or confirmed, then it is the responsibility of all those involved with the older person, irrespective of their agency or professional status, to ensure that appropriate action is taken and that a referral to a Care Manager, so that an assessment can be carried out and appropriate services provided, is made as soon as possible.
c. Unpaid carers should receive the practical and emotional support which their needs require before a situation enters a crisis.
d. All paid carers should receive good quality support, supervision and training appropriate to their duties.
e. That all situations of alleged, suspected or confirmed abuse should be investigated by a Care Manager as soon as possible but certainly within 24 hours of the referral having been made.

The Aim in Producing These Guidelines

There has for some time been increasing concern within the Borough about the abuse of dependent older people. This concern has been raised by the Partnership Group for Older People, Carers Groups, Staff of Rochdale Social Services Department, Rochdale Health Care NHS Trust, Rochdale FHSA and Rochdale Health Authority.

In order to increase understanding and provide good guidance about the recognition and management of abuse of older people, these guidelines have been produced by a multi-disciplinary working group.

There are two main aims behind these guidelines. Firstly to bring forward procedures based on good practice for dealing with abuse and secondly to foster awareness of the difficulties faced by paid and unpaid carers. Over a period of time these difficulties can become stressful and wearing, whether people are cared for at home or in a residential establishment. With the increasing numbers of elderly people needing care these pressures will increase.

The starting point for these guidelines is that older people and their carers have a right to have their anxieties, fears, anger and distress, heard and acknowledged by professionals. It is also important that within the limits of resources available, personal support and practical help should be offered to carers, and that our efforts should be geared to prevention as well as the management of abuse.

It is intended therefore that these guidelines will clarify the issues, help staff to recognize situations where risks may be present and enable them to take effective action to maintain the safety and well-being of older people and their carers.

At the back of these guidelines you will find:

- a checklist which will help you to decide whether abuse is taking place and what action you should take.
- a list of social services offices and telephone numbers; the Social Services Department will be responsible for ensuring that your concerns are properly listened to and that where necessary an assessment takes place. The duty officer in each office is the first point of contact.

The list of phone numbers also includes arrangements for contacting the Social Services Emergency Duty Team, who provide cover out of office hours.

Assessment and Care Management

These guidelines are the result of work which has been based around the implementation of the 1990 NHS and Community Care Act, and have been prepared by a multi-disciplinary working group.

The approach described in these guidelines provides basic guidance for everyone to follow. The approach outlined has been designed to be integrated into local Assessment and Care Management arrangements which together with these guidelines have received the formal approval of local agencies and should now be implemented.

1.0 What is Meant by the Abuse of Older People?

1.1 Abuse is the term used to describe those situations where the power of carers (either paid or unpaid) over dependent older people is used in such a way as to deny them their rights – to dignity, to respect, and to self determination or to basic needs such as security, warmth and food. Sometimes this abuse may be suspected, alleged, or confirmed. In all situations however it would be non-accidental. For the purpose of these guidelines abuse can be divided into seven main areas.

1.2 Physical Abuse

This is probably the most easily identified form of abuse. It is violence resulting in bodily harm or mental distress. It includes assault, unjustified denial or violation of another's rights, restrictions of the freedom of movement and in its most extreme form murder. This category also includes hypothermia and malnutrition where the older person is living with others who do not appear to be similarly affected.

1.3 Sexual Abuse

This involves an older person being subjected to any sexual activity which is not of his/her own choosing.

1.4 Negligence

Negligence is the breach of duty or carelessness that results in injury or the violation of rights. This area includes the deprivation of help in performing activities of daily living. Sometimes abuse in this area may be passive, and may include a failure to understand or respond to the implications of a medical situation. It needs to be recognized however that sometimes this lack of understanding may result from inadequate counselling, supervision and training, or publicity.

1.5 Self-Neglect

This includes self-inflicted physical harm and the failure to take care of personal needs. It may stem from the individual's diminished physical or mental abilities and can be brought on by the attitude and behaviour of carers both paid and unpaid who may treat the individual in an over-protective way.

1.6 Financial Exploitation

This involves a theft or conversion of money or objects belonging to an individual by a relative or carer. It is accomplished by force or through misrepresentation.

1.7 Psychological and Emotional Abuse

This is the provoking of the fear of violence or isolation including name calling and other forms of verbal assault. It also includes threats of placement outside the family home into institutional care, or the change in the placement between institutions or units. It can be sudden, or can take place over a long period of time and can be accompanied by other types of abuse.

1.8 Violation of Rights

This is the breaching of rights of individuals as citizens of the country in which they reside or within a particular community or residential establishment.

2.0 Where Does Abuse Take Place?

2.1 It is vital to accept that abuse takes place in every conceivable setting. Whilst it may be thought to be most common where an older person lives in close proximity to a relative, it is equally likely to happen within a hospital, residential or day care establishment. In short it is likely to occur in any situation where one individual is dependent (for whatever reason) on another. In this situation a power structure exists and the carer, whether paid or unpaid, is usually the one with power and is therefore in a position to dictate the terms of the care or abuse administered, although there are occasions when the situation may be reversed and the dependent older person holds the dominant position.

3.0 How Does Abuse Come About?

3.1 While some abuse arises from relationships that have never been positive, it is often the case that abuse will take place within apparently close loving relationships. Partial explanation for this can be said to arise from the way in which caring, i.e. dependency relationships, differ from other relationships. Lack of training, support, supervision, and procedures may also be key factors in allowing abuse to develop.

3.2 For a relationship to remain viable in the long term a balance has to be maintained between giving and taking, between the rights and needs of one particular individual and the rights and needs of others in that relationship.

3.3 The difficulty in maintaining this balance lies at the heart of many problems described by carers and those who depend upon them. People can find it hard to estimate what is fair or reasonable to expect from each other and as the expectations begin to differ they may slide towards the problems we would define as abuse. Once again the lack of good support and supervision, and the failure of managers to lay down what is expected of staff can contribute towards this process.

4.0 What is my Role as a Practitioner or Member of Staff?

4.1 Carers need considerable encouragement to recognize and attend to their own needs and it is the duty of all professionals who come into contact with carers, and their dependants, to ensure that they are both made aware of and given access to the appropriate services.

4.2 The carer and the older person both have needs and rights. These must be addressed by careful and considerate assessment, appropriate counselling and regular planned staff supervision. Above all whether the carer is paid or unpaid, **the role of the professional must**

be to identify situations where abuse could occur and offer counselling, support and appropriate services to prevent a crisis arising. When a deterioration has taken place and abuse is suspected, alleged or confirmed, a professional must take sensitive but honest action to prevent further occurrence.

4.3 Professionals also need to understand that unpaid carers cope with intensely demanding and stressful situations, often without having the opportunity to exercise the right not to care. In some situations where an unpaid carer constantly copes with an elderly relative whose behaviour is highly challenging, and eventually breaks down under this pressure, there may be real doubts about who is abusing whom.

4.4 General Guidance for Professionals

4.5 It needs to be recognized that in a small minority of situations the danger of further abuse can only be prevented by the older person and the carer agreeing to separate. This may be a painful decision and the person and carer involved will need considerable support. It also needs to be remembered however that carers and their dependants are often fearful of professionals.

They may not be very clear about the role of the professional or the resources available through them. Professionals may sometimes have the attitude that relatives ought to care for their dependants and they may appear critical when they are unable to do this. This can only add to the carer's guilt, their anxiety, and levels of stress.

5.0 What are the Danger Signals?

5.1 The following list indicates some of the common stress factors which may signal that a caring situation is moving towards breakdown and intervention is required to correct the balance.

5.2 Social Isolation

This is characterized by inadequate support coupled with the continuity of care of another adult. There is a feeling of total responsibility for another human being and negative feelings resulting from this situation can build up over a long period of time.

5.3 Physical Dependence

Situations where a high degree of care is required, including activities such as giving medication and assistance with personal tasks. Misuse of medication may be a feature of abuse associated with this danger signal.

5.4 Multi-Generational Family Structure

Situations where there may be a conflict of interests and personal loyalties. It may also be demonstrated in the role reversal which has taken place between the dependant person and their carer.

5.5 Poor Communication

This may vary from hostile exchanges to minimal communication or both, between the carer and the dependant person.

5.6 Challenging Behaviour

Poor eating habits, inappropriate behaviour, faecal smearing, incontinence, and changes in personality are all examples of challenging behaviour which carers may find very stressful and difficult to cope with.

5.7 Stigma

It may be that relatives and other carers become embarrassed and/or fearful of the older person's condition.

5.8 Carer's Own Health

The carer's physical and mental health is crucial in the support they are able to offer to their dependant relative. Carers risk a high level of depression, fatigue, frustration, and loss of sleep. Some effects of menopause may also be significant.

5.9 Resentment of Caring Role

The carer may experience feelings of being trapped. Equally the carer's own contribution to the dependent older person's well-being may be minimized and misunderstood by relatives, neighbours or professionals. There may also be times when the carer will resent a role which in some circumstances they have little choice in taking on.

What to Do if Abuse is Suspected, Alleged or Confirmed

6.0 Who is Likely to be Concerned About Abuse?

6.1 Potentially, a wide range of staff may identify an incident of abuse. These staff could range from a homecare worker to a general practitioner, a practice nurse or a doctor based in an accident and emergency department, ward staff or a residential or day care worker. Unpaid carers may also come across this. It is important therefore that they refer their concerns as soon as possible to a worker who has been especially trained to intervene in situations where abuse is taking place.

IDENTIFICATION OF ABUSE IS THE RESPONSIBILITY OF ALL STAFF WHO WORK WITH OLDER PEOPLE AND THEIR CARERS

7.0 All Practitioners and Staff Who are Concerned About Possible Abuse Should Take the Following Action, No Matter What Agency or Setting They Work in.

7.1 Obtain emergency medical treatment if appropriate.

7.2 Record their reasons for concern together with any observations regarding the health and social circumstances of the older person and their carer.

7.3 Throughout any action which they may take, staff and practitioners should keep in close contact with their line manager. At the minimum they should report their observations and concerns to the line manager as soon as possible.

7.4 All staff practitioners should take action as soon as possible to refer the older person into the assessment and care management system.

7.5 This is done by:

checking records within health and social services to find out whether a care manager or practitioner is currently involved. The practitioners who will take responsibility for investigating the concern will be:

Social Workers
Health Visitors
District Nurses
Community based Occupational Therapists
Community Psychiatric Nurses

7.6 Where a member of staff as outlined above is currently involved, the situation should be referred to them as soon as possible.

7.7 Where no worker is currently involved, the situation should be referred to the social services duty officer at the relevant office, who will liaise with their line manager. The line manager will be responsible for discussion with other agencies to determine which agency and member of staff will be responsible for the assessment. A list of phone numbers and contact points can be found at the back of these guidelines.

7.8 Where concern arises out of office hours, then the situation should be referred to the Social Services Emergency Duty Team as soon as possible. The phone number can be found at the back of these guidelines.

8.0 Abuse Suspected in a Residential or Nursing Home Placement

8.1 Where the situation concerns the placement of an older person in a residential or day care establishment the above action should still be taken, alongside any action the agency responsible for an establishment may take themselves. **It is vital that a care manager is able to assess the situation from the user and unpaid carer's point of view**.

8.2 The organizations responsible for the establishment concerned will also wish to investigate any incident and the care manager will work closely with them in order to avoid any distress to the user and carer.

8.3 If a situation of abuse is suspected by a worker, and the person suspected to be carrying out the abuse is the worker's line manager, then the worker concerned is responsible for following the complaints procedure of the relevant agency for whom they work, if necessary with the support of their professional association.

8.4 If the establishment concerned is a private, voluntary or not for profit organization then the member of staff should contact the Inspection and Registration unit responsible for the establishment. Namely:

* Rochdale Social Services Department; for Rest Homes
* Rochdale Health Authority; for Nursing Homes

8.5 Staff from these Inspection and Registration units will then, in addition to their own responsibilities, ensure that the process outlined in 7.1–7.8 is followed.

In addition to the process outlined in section 7.0 (above) the following guidance is also available for nursing staff.

9.0 The Role of Nursing Staff in Situations of Suspected, Alleged or Confirmed Incidents of Abuse of Older People

9.1 Nursing staff must be familiar with the relevant Guidance laid down in the UKCC Code of Professional Conduct. This Guidance includes advice on exercising accountability and confidentiality.

9.2 This Guidance advises nursing staff to clearly record their observations paying particular attention to the health of the dependent person, their carer, and other parties involved.

9.3 Within the bounds of confidentiality staff are advised to check if any records are held by NHS staff and practitioners or the Social Services Department. All relevant details should be checked.

9.4 As part of this process nursing staff will need to discover if a care manager is involved and report their information to them.

9.5 It will then be necessary for nursing staff to report their concerns, the information they have obtained and action they have taken to their line manager. It is important to remind staff at this point that any person with a recordable qualification on the UKCC's register is governed by the UKCC's Code of Professional Conduct. This is binding wherever the person is working, be it in hospital, in a nursing home or in the community.

The Code of Conduct will require the professional to ensure that they are 'acting always in the interest of the client'. It needs to be remembered however that the older person may not only be the abused person; it may also be their carer. Staff are clearly advised to follow the professional guidance contained in the UKCC Code of Conduct.

Checklist for all practitioners and staff

1.   IS THERE A CARER?   YES/NO

1.1 Does the carer have other dependants whose needs they have to meet?
     YES/NO   specify _____

2.   WHAT RELATIONSHIP EXISTS BETWEEN CARER AND DEPENDANT?

     i.   Family member   _____
     ii. Friend   _____
     iii. Paid carer   _____
     iv. Volunteer   _____

3.   WHO IS REFERRING THIS CARE?

     _____

4.   WHAT FORM DID ANY SUSPECTED ABUSE TAKE?

i.   Physical injury
     Inadequately explained bruising   _____
     Inadequately explained burns   _____
     Inadequately explained lacerations   _____
     Rough handling   _____
     Threats   _____
     Other   _____

ii. Negligence
     Malnourishment   _____
     Hypothermia   _____
     Harassment   _____
     Withdrawal of communication   _____
     Lack of cleanliness of body   _____
     ('elder is inappropriately or improperly dressed')
     Lack of cleanliness of house   _____

iii. Self-neglect
iv. Financial exploitation
v.   Psychological and emotional abuse
vi. Violation of rights

5.   WHERE DID THE ABUSE TAKE PLACE?

     i.   Dependant's own home   _____
     ii. Other premises   _____
     Please specify _____

6.   WAS MEDICAL HELP REQUIRED? YES/NO

     Please specify _____

7.   ACTION TAKEN

     Referred to:

Date:
Time:
          CHECKLIST COMPLETED BY:

Source: Bury and Rochdale Partnership Group for Older People: *Working Together*
(1996). Published with permission.

References

Action on Elder Abuse (AEA) (1995) *Everybody's Business: Taking Action on Elder Abuse.* London: AEA.

Action on Elder Abuse (AEA) (1996) *The Abuse of Older People at Home: Information for Workers.* London: AEA.

Age Concern England (ACE) (1991) *Abuse of Elderly People: Guidelines for Action.* Mitcham: Age Concern England.

Age Concern England (ACE) (1996) 'Annus freneticus', *Elderly Care*, 8(1): 41.

Allen, I. and Perkins, E. (1995) *The Future of Families for Older People.* London: HMSO.

Allen, I., Hogg, D. and Peace, S. (1992) *Elderly People: Choice, Participation and Satisfaction.* London: Policy Studies Institute.

American Medical Association (AMA) Council on Scientific Affairs (1987) 'Elder abuse and neglect', *Journal of the American Medical Association*, 257(7): 966–71.

Anderson, M. (1974) *Family Structure in Nineteenth Century Lancashire.* Cambridge: Cambridge University Press.

Arber, S. and Evandrou, M. (1993) *Ageing, Independence and the Life Course.* London: Jessica Kingsley Publishers.

Arber, S. and Ginn, J. (1991a) 'Gender class and income inequalities in later life', *British Journal of Sociology*, 42(3): 369–96.

Arber, S. and Ginn, J. (1991b) *Gender and Later Life: A Sociological Analysis of Resources and Constraints.* London: Sage Publications.

Arber, S. and Ginn, J. (eds) (1995) *Connecting Gender and Ageing: A Sociological Approach.* Buckingham: Open University Press.

Archbold, P.G., Stewart, B.J., Greenlick, M.R. and Harvath, T.A. (1992) 'The clinical assessment of mutuality and preparedness in family caregivers of frail older people', in S.G. Funk, E.M.T. Tornquist, S.T. Champagne and R.A.Wiese (eds), *Key Aspects of Elder Care: Managing Falls, Incontinence and Cognitive Impairment.* New York: Springer.

Archbold, P.G., Stewart, B.J., Miller, L.L., Harvath, T.A., Greenlick, M.R., Van Buren, L., Kirschling, J.M., Valanis, B.G., Brody, K.K., Schook, J.E. and Hagan, J.M. (1995) 'The PREP system of nursing interventions: a pilot test with families caring for older members', *Research in Nursing Health*, 18: 1–16.

Ashton, G. (1994) 'Action on elder abuse', *Eagle*, April–May: 7–9.

Ashton, G. (1995) *Elderly People and the Law.* London: Butterworths and Age Concern, England.

Association of Directors of Social Services (ADSS) (1991) *Adults at Risk: Guidance for Directors of Social Services.* Stockport: ADSS.

Association of Directors of Social Services (ADSS) (1995) *Mistreatment of Older People: a Discussion Document.* Wolverhampton: ADSS.

Audit Commission (1986) *Making a Reality of Community Care.* London: HMSO.

Bailey, S.H., Harris, D.J. and Jones, B.L. (1991) *Civil Liberties Cases and Materials.* London: Butterworths.

Baillon, S., Boyle, A., Neville, P.G. and Scothern, G. (1996) 'Factors that contribute to stress in care staff in nursing homes for the elderly', *International Journal of Geriatric Psychiatry*, 11: 219–26.

Baker, A.A. (1975) 'Granny battering', *Modern Geriatrics*, 5(8): 20–4.

Ball, C., Harris, R., Roberts, G. and Vernon, S. (1988) *The Law Report: Teaching and Assessment of Law in Social Work Education*. London: Central Council for Education and Training in Social Work (CCETSW).

Ball, C., Preston-Shoot, M., Roberts, G. and Vernon, S. (1995) *Law for Social Workers in England and Wales: Guidance for Meeting the DipSW Requirements*. London: CCETSW.

Bardwell, F. (1926) *The Adventure of Old Age*. Boston: Houghton Mifflin.

Baumhover, L.A. and Beall, S.C. (eds) (1996) *Abuse, Neglect and Exploitation of Older Persons: Strategies for Assessment and Intervention*. London: Jessica Kingsley Publishers.

Bebbington, A. and Davies, B. (1993) 'Efficient targeting of community care: The case of the homehelp service', *Journal of Social Policy*, 22(3): 373–92.

Bebbington, P.F. and Hill, P.D. (1985) *A Manual of Practical Psychiatry*. Oxford: Blackwell Scientific.

Bell, R. and Gibbons, S. (1989) *Working with Carers: Information and Training for Work with Informal Carers of Elderly People*. London: Health Education Authority.

Benbow, S.M., Egan, D. and Marriott, A. (1990) 'Life cycle issues and the later life family', *Journal of Family Therapy*, 12: 321–40.

Bennett, D. and Freeman, M.R. (1991) *Community Psychiatry*. Melbourne and London: Churchill Livingstone.

Bennett, G.C.J. (1990a) 'Action on elder abuse in the '90s: new definitions will help', *Geriatric Medicine*, April: 53–4.

Bennett, G.C.J. (1990b) 'Shifting emphasis from abused to abuser', *Geriatric Medicine*, May: 45–7.

Bennett, G.C.J. (1990c) 'Abuse of the elderly: prevention and legislation', *Geriatric Medicine*, October: 55–60.

Bennett, G.C.J. (1992) 'Elder abuse', in J. George and S. Ebrahim (eds), *Health Care for Older Women*. Oxford: Oxford Medical Publications.

Bennett, G.C.J. and Kingston, P. (1993) *Elder Abuse: Concepts, Theories and Interventions*. London: Chapman and Hall.

Beresford, B. (1994) *Positively Parents: Caring for a Severely Disabled Child*. London: HMSO.

Berger, P. and Luckman, T. (1972) *The Social Construction of Reality*. London: Allen Lane.

Bernard, M. (ed.) (1988) *Positive approaches to ageing: Leisure and Lifestyle in Later Life*. Stoke-on-Trent: Beth Johnson Foundation and Centre for Social Gerontology, University of Keele.

Bernard, M., Itzin, C., Phillipson, C. and Skucha, J. (1995) 'Gendered work, gendered retirement', in S. Arber and J. Ginn (eds), *Connecting Gender and Ageing: A Sociological Approach*. Buckingham: Open University Press. pp. 56–68.

Beveridge, W. (1942) *Social Insurance and Allied Services*. Report of the Committee on the Coordination of Social Insurance. London: HMSO.

Bexley Social Services Department (1988) *Report of a Working Party and Seminar on Abuse of Elderly People*. Bexley: London Borough of Bexley.

Biegel, D.E., Soles, E. and Schulz, K. (1991) *Family Caregiving in Chronic Illness*. Newbury Park, CA: Sage Publications.

Biggs, S. (1993) *Understanding Ageing: Images, Attitudes and Professional Practice*. Buckingham: Open University Press.

Biggs, S. (1994a) 'Up to all the angles', *Community Care*, 24 March: 24–5.

Biggs, S. (1994b) 'Failed individualism in community care: the case of elder abuse', *Journal of Social Work Practice*, 8(2): 137–50.

Biggs, S. (1995) 'The development of an elder abuse policy in Britain', *Social Work in Europe*, 2(3): 30–4.

Biggs, S. (1996) 'A family concern: elder abuse in British social policy', *Critical Social Policy*, 16(2): 63–88.

Biggs, S. and Kingston, P. (1995) 'Elder abuse in Europe', *Social Work in Europe*, 2(3): 1–2.

Biggs, S. and Phillipson, C. (1994) 'Elder abuse and neglect: developing training programmes', in M. Eastman (ed.), *Old Age Abuse: A New Perspective*. London: Chapman and Hall.

Biggs, S., Phillipson, C. and Kingston, P. (1995) *Elder Abuse in Perspective*. Buckingham: Open University Press.

Binstock, R.H., Post, B. and Whitehouse, P.J. (eds) (1992) *Dementia and Ageing: Ethics, Values and Policy Choices*. Baltimore, MD: Johns Hopkins University Press.

Block, M.R. and Sinnott, J.D. (1979) 'The battered elderly syndrome: an exploratory "study" '. Unpublished manuscript cited in M.F. Hudson and T.F. Johnson (1987), 'Elder neglect and abuse: a review of the literature', in C. Eisdorfer (ed.), *Annual Review of Gerontology and Geriatrics*, Vol. 6. New York: Springer. pp. 84–5.

Bloom, J.S., Ansell, P. and Bloom, M.N. (1989) 'Detecting elder abuse: a guide for physicians', *Geriatrics*, 44(6): 40–56.

Blum, S. (1987) *New and Continuing Impediments to Improving the Quality of Care in California's Nursing Homes*. Sacramento, CA: Little Hoover Commission.

Blumer, H. (1969) *Symbolic Interactionism*. Englewood Cliffs, NJ: Prentice-Hall.

Bond, J. (1992) 'The politics of caregiving: the professionalization of informal care', *Ageing and Society*, 12(1): 5–21.

Booth, B. (1995) 'Clinical reports. Editor's notes', *Nursing Times*, 91(42): 26.

Bornat, J., Phillipson, C. and Ward, S. (1985) *A Manifesto for Old Age*. London: Pluto Press.

Borsay, A. (1989) 'First child care, second mental health, third the elderly', *Research, Policy and Practice*, 7: 27–30.

Bowers, B.J. (1987) 'Inter-generational caregiving: adult caregivers and their ageing parents', *Advances in Nursing Science*, 9(2): 20–31.

Bowers, B.J. (1988) 'Family perceptions of care in a nursing home', *The Gerontologist*, 28(3): 361–7.

Bowlby, J. (1982) 'Attachment and loss: retrospect and prospect', *American Journal of Orthopsychiatry*, 52(4): 664–78.

Bradley, G. and Manthorpe, J. (1995) 'The dilemmas of financial assessment: professional and ethical difficulties', *Practice*, 7(4): 21–30.

Braithwaite, V.A. (1990) *Bound to Care*. Sydney: Allen and Unwin.

Brammer, A. (1994) 'The Registered Homes Act 1984: safeguarding the elderly', *Journal of Social Welfare and Family Law*, 4: 423–36.

Brammer, A. and Biggs, S. (in preparation) 'Competing definitions of elder abuse and their social construction', *Journal of Socio-Legal Studies*.

Brazier, M. (1988) *Street on Torts*. London: Butterworths.

Brearley, P. (1982) 'Old people in care', in V. Carver and P.Liddard (eds), *An Ageing Population*. London: Hodder and Stoughton/Open University Press.

Breckman, R. and Adelman, R. (1988) *Strategies for Helping Victims of Elder Mistreatment*. London: Sage Publications.

Bright, L. (1995) *Care Betrayed*. London: Counsel and Care.

Brillon, Y. (1987) *Victimization and Fear of Crime among the Elderly*. Toronto: Butterworths.

British Broadcasting Corporation (BBC) (1995) *Home Truths: Radio 2's Guide on How to Overcome Elder Abuse*. London: BBC Books.

British Medical Association (BMA)/Law Society (1995) *Assessment of Mental Capacity: Guidance for Doctors and Lawyers*. London: BMA/Law Society.

Bromley, D.B. (1988) *Human Ageing: An Introduction to Gerontology*. London and Harmondsworth: Penguin Books.

Brown, A. (1995) 'In their own best interests', *Nursing Times*, January, 91(4): 60.

Brubaker, T.H. (1990) 'An overview of family relationships in later life', in T.D. Brubaker (ed.), *Family Relationships in Later Life*. Newbury Park, CA: Sage Publications. pp. 13–26.

Bruce, N. (1980) *Team Work for Preventative Care: Research Study Presentation*. New York: Wiley.

Burr, W.R., Klein, S.R. and Associates (1994) *Re-examining Family Stress: New Theory and Research*. Thousand Oaks, CA: Sage Publications.

Burston, G.R. (1975) 'Granny battering', *British Medical Journal*, 6 September: 592.

Burston, G.R. (1977) 'Do your elderly patients live in fear of being battered?', *Modern Geriatrics*, 7(5): 54–5.

Bury, M. (1995) 'Ageing, gender and sociological theory', in S. Arber and J. Ginn (eds),

Connecting Gender and Ageing: A Sociological Approach. Buckingham: Open University Press. pp. 15–29.

Bury and Rochdale Partnership Group for Older People (1993) *Working Together: Elder Abuse Guidelines.* Bury: Author.

Bury Social Services Department (1994) *Annual Report 1993–94.* Bury: Social Services Department.

Butler, R.N. (1975) *Why Survive? Growing Old in America.* New York: Harper and Row.

Butler, R.N. (1996) 'Global ageing: challenges and opportunities of the next century', *Ageing International*, 23(1): 12–32.

Butler, R.N. and Lewis, M.L. (1982) *Ageing and Mental Health*, 3rd edition. St Louis: C.V. Morsby.

Bytheway, B. (1995) *Ageism.* Buckingham: Open University Press.

Caldock, K. (1994) 'Policy and practice: fundamental contradictions in the conceptualization of community care for elderly people?', *Health and Social Care in the Community*, 3(2): 133–41.

Callahan, D. (1987) *Setting Limits: Medical Goals in an Aging Society.* New York: Simon and Schuster.

Callahan, J.J. (1982) 'Elder abuse programming: will it help the elderly?', *Urban Social Change Review*, 15(Summer): 15–16.

Callahan, J.J. (1986) 'Guest editor's perspective', *Pride Institute Journal of Long Term Home Health Care*, 5: 3.

Callahan, J.J. (1988) 'Elder abuse: some questions for policymakers', *The Gerontologist*, 28(4): 453–8.

Cang, S. (1989) 'Open to criticism', *Health Service Journal*, 99(5159): 886.

Carnegie (1992) *The Carnegie Inquiry into the Third Age: Reports 1–9.* Dunfermline: The Carnegie UK Trust.

Carson, D. (1985) 'Registered homes: another fine mess', *Journal of Social Welfare Law*, March: 67–85.

Carson, D. (1995) 'Calculated risk', *Community Care*, 26 October: 26–7.

Cartwright, J.C., Archbold, P.G., Stewart, B.J. and Limandri, B. (1994) 'Enrichment processes in family caregiving to frail elders', *Advances in Nursing Science*, 17(1): 31–43.

Cassell, E.J. (1989) 'Abuse of the elderly: misuses of power', *New York State Journal of Medicine*, March: 159–62.

Castledine, G. (1996) 'Nursing elderly people with dignity and respect', *British Journal of Nursing*, 5(3): 191.

Central Statistical Office (CSO) (1995) *Social Trends 25*, 9th edition. London: HMSO.

Centre for Policy on Ageing (CPA) (1984) *Home Life: A Code of Practice for Residential Care.* London: CPA.

Centre for Policy on Ageing (CPA) (1990) *Community Life: A Code of Practice for Community Care.* London: CPA.

Chapman, H. and Chapman, R. (1993) 'Reflections on a movement: the US battle against women', in M. Schuler, *Women's Strategies from around the World.* New York: Wyld Books.

Chen, P.N., Bell, S., Dolinsky, D., Doyle, J. and Dunn, M. (1981) 'Elderly abuse in domestic settings: a pilot study', *Journal of Gerontological Social Work*, 4(Fall): 3–17.

Chew, R. (1995) *Compendium of Health Statistics*, 9th edition. London: Office of Health Economics.

Clark, P. (1993) 'Public policy in the US and Canada: individualism, familial obligations and collective responsibility in the care of the elderly', in J. Hendricks and C.J. Rosenthal (eds), *The Remainder of their Days: Domestic Policy and Older Families in the United States and Canada.* New York: Garland Publishing.

Clark-Daniels, C.L. and Daniels, R.S. (1995) 'Street-level decision-making in elder mistreatment policy: an empirical case study of service rationing', *Social Science Quarterly*, 76: 461–73.

Clements, L. (1994) 'European convention: human rights and family cases', *Family Law*, 24: 452–4.

Clifford, D. (1990) *The Social Costs and Rewards of Care.* Aldershot: Avebury.

Cloke, C. (1983) *Old Age Abuse in the Domestic Setting: A Review.* Mitcham: Age Concern England.

Clough, R. (1981) *Old Age Homes*. London: Allen and Unwin.
Clough, R. (1988a) *Scandals in Residential Centres: a Report to the Wagner Committee.* Unpublished report.
Clough, R. (1988b) 'Danger: look out for abuse', *Care Weekly*, 7 January.
Clough, R. (ed.) (1995) *Elder Abuse and the Law*. London: Action on Elder Abuse.
Clough, R. (ed.) (1996) *The Abuse of Care in Residential Institutions*. London: Whiting and Birch.
Coalition of Advocates for the Rights of the Infirm Elderly (CARIE) (1991) *Ensuring an Abuse-free Environment: A Learning Program for Nursing Home Staff.* Philadelphia: CARIE.
Cochran, C. and Petrone, S. (1987) 'Elder abuse: the physician's role in identification and prevention', *Illinois Medical Journal*, 171(4): 241–6.
Cohen, P. (1995) 'Men behaving badly', *Nursing Times*, 91(45): 18.
Cole, T. (1992) *The Journey of Life*. Cambridge: Cambridge University Press.
Cole, T.R. and Winkler, M.G. (eds) (1994) *The Oxford History of Aging*. New York: Oxford University Press.
Coleman, C.K., Piles, L.L. and Poggenpoel, M. (1994) 'Influence of caregiving on families of older adults', *Journal of Gerontological Nursing*, November: 40–9.
Commission of the European Communities (CEC) (1990) *Council Directive on the Minimum Health and Safety Requirements for the Manual Handling of Loads where there is a Risk particularly of Back Injury to Workers*. Directive 89/391/EEC. Brussels: Commission of the European Communities.
Community Care (1993) Elder abuse campaign, 1. July.
Costa, J. (1984) *Abuse of the Elderly: A Guide to Resources and Sources*. Lexington: D.C. Heath.
Counsel and Care (1991) *Not Such Private Places*. London: Counsel and Care.
Counsel and Care (1992) *What If They Hurt Themselves*. London: Counsel and Care.
Cowell, A. (1989) 'Abuse of the institutionalized aged: recent policy in California', in R. Filinson and S.R. Ingman (eds), *Elder Abuse: Practice and Policy*. New York: Human Sciences Press. pp. 242–54.
Craig, Y. (1992) 'Elder mediation', *Generations Review*, 2(3): 4–5.
Craig, Y. (1994) 'Elder mediation: can it contribute to the prevention of elder abuse and the protection of the rights of elders and their carers?', *Journal of Elder Abuse and Neglect*, 6(1): 83–96.
Cretney, S. (1993) 'Comment', *Family Law*, 23: 679–80.
Crystal, S. (1986) 'Social policy and elder abuse', in K.A. Pillemer and R.S.Wolf (eds), *Elder Abuse: Conflict in the Family*. Dover, MA: Auburn House. pp. 331–40.
Cummings, E. and Henry, W.E. (1966) *Growing Old: The Process of Disengagement*. New York: Basic Books.
Daniels, R.S., Baumhover, L.A. and Clark-Daniels, C.L. (1989) 'Physicians' mandatory reporting of elder abuse', *The Gerontologist*, 29(3): 321–7.
Darton, R.A. and Wright, K.G. (1993) 'Changes in the provision of long-stay care, 1970–1990', *Health and Social Care in the Community*, 1(1): 11–25.
Davies, A.J. (1980) 'Disability, home-care and the care-taking role in family life', *Journal of Advanced Nursing*, 5: 475–84.
Davies, B., Baines, B. and Chesterman, J. (1996) 'The effects of care management on efficiency in long-term care: a new evaluation model applied to British and American data', in J. Phillips and B. Penhale (eds), *Reviewing Care Management for Older People*. London: Jessica Kingsley Publishers.
Davies, B., Warburton, W. and Fernandez, J. (1995) 'Do different case management approaches affect who gets what? Preliminary results from a comparative British study', *Care Plan*, December: 26–30.
Davies, M. (1993) 'Recognizing abuse: an assessment tool for nurses', in P. Decalmer and F. Glendenning (eds), *The Mistreatment of Elderly People*. London: Sage Publications. pp. 102–16.
Decalmer, P. (1993) 'Clinical presentation', in P. Decalmer and F. Glendenning (eds), *The Mistreatment of Elderly People*. London: Sage Publications. pp. 35– 61.

Decalmer, P. and Davies, M. (1993) 'Checklist of possible physical indicators', in P. Decalmer and F. Glendenning (eds), *The Mistreatment of Elderly People*. London: Sage Publications. pp. 39–41.

Decalmer, P. and Glendenning, F. (eds) (1993) *The Mistreatment of Elderly People*. London: Sage Publications.

Decalmer, P. and Marriott, A. (1993) 'The multidisciplinary assessment of clients and patients', in P. Decalmer and F. Glendenning (eds), *The Mistreatment of Elderly People*. London: Sage Publications, pp. 117–35.

Denton, F.T., Feaver, C.H. and Spencer, B.G. (1987) 'The Canadian population and labour force: retrospect and prospect', in V.W. Marshall (ed.), *Aging in Canada*. Markham, Ontario: Fitzhenry and Whiteside. pp. 11–38.

Department of Health (DOH) (1989a) *Terms of Service for Doctors in General Practice*. London: DOH.

Department of Health (1989b) *Caring for People: Community Care in the Next Decade and Beyond*.Cmd. 849. London: HMSO.

Department of Health (1989c) *Health and Personal Social Services Statistics for England*, 1989 edition. London: HMSO.

Department of Health (1991a) *Care Management and Assessment: Manager's Guide*. London: HMSO.

Department of Health (1991b) *Working Together under the Children Act 1989*. London: HMSO.

Department of Health (1992) *The Nursing Skill Mix in the District Nursing Services*. EL(92)69. London: DOH.

Department of Health (1993a) *Health of the Nation. A Health Strategy for England*. London: HMSO.

Department of Health (1993b) *Developing Quality Standards for Home Support Services*. London: HMSO.

Department of Health (1995a) *Health and Personal Social Services Statistics for England*, 1995 edition. London: HMSO.

Department of Health (1995b) *NHS Responsibilities for Meeting Continuing Health Care Needs*. HSG(95)8. London: DOH.

Department of Health (1995c) *Acting on Complaints*. London: HMSO.

Department of Health (1995d) *Child Protection: Messages from Research*. London: HMSO.

Derbyshire County Council (1979) *Report of the Social Services Sub-Committee on its Investigation into the Alleged Ill-Treatment of Residents and Other Complaints Relating to Stonelow Court Aged Persons Home, Dronfield*. Matlock: Derbyshire County Council.

Dimond, T. (1986) 'Social policy and everyday life in nursing homes: a critical ethnography', *Social Science and Medicine*, 23(12): 1287–95.

Dobash, R. and Dobash, R. (1992) *Women, Violence and Social Change*. London: Routledge.

Dollard, J. (1939) *Frustration and Aggression*. New Haven, CT:Yale University Press.

Donovan, T. and Wynne-Harley, D. (1986) *Not a Nine to Five Job*. London: Centre for Policy on Ageing.

Doty, P. and Sullivan, E. W. (1983) 'Community involvement in combating abuse, neglect and mistreatment in nursing homes', *Milbank Fund Quarterly/Health and Society*, 32: 222–51.

Douglass, R.L. (1983) 'Domestic neglect and abuse of the elderly: implications for research and service', *Family Relations*, 32: 395–402.

Downey, R. (1991) 'Waiting for parity', *Social Work Today*, 13 June: 9.

Doyal, L. and Gough, I. (1991) *A Theory of Human Need*. Basingstoke: Macmillan.

Dunn, P.F. (1995) 'Elder abuse as an innovation to Australia: a critical overview', in J.I. Kosberg and J.L. Garcia, *Elder Abuse: International and Cross-Cultural Perspectives*. New York: The Hawarth Press. pp. 13–30.

Durkheim, E. (1952) *Suicide: A Study in Sociology*. London: Routledge and Kegan Paul.

Dyer, C. (1996) 'Doctors and lawyers unite on incapacity laws', *British Medical Journal*, 312: 203.

Eagle (1994) 'Editorial', *Eagle*, 6: 3.

Eastley, R. J., MacPherson, R., Richards, H. and Mia, I. H. (1993) 'Assaults on professional carers of elderly people', *British Medical Journal*, 307: 845.

Eastman, M. (1983) `Granny battering: a hidden problem', *Community Care*, 27 May : 11–15.

Eastman, M. (1984) *Old Age Abuse*. Mitcham: Age Concern England.

Eastman, M. (ed.) (1994) *Old Age Abuse: a New Perspective*. London: Chapman and Hall (2nd edition).

Eastman, M. and Sutton, M. (1982) `Granny battering', *Geriatric Medicine*, 12(11): 11–15.

Estes, C.L. (1979) *The Aging Enterprise*. San Francisco: Jossey Bass.

Estes, C.L. (1986) 'Politics of ageing in America', *Ageing in Society*, 6 (2): 121–34.

Estes, C.L. (1991) 'The new political economy of aging: introduction and critique', in M. Minkler and C.L. Estes (eds), *Critical Perspectives on Aging: The Moral and Political Economy of Growing Old*. New York: Baywood Publishing.

Estes, C. (1993) 'The aging enterprise revisited', *The Gerontologist*, 33(3): 292–8.

Fader, A., Koge, N., Gupta, K. L. and Gambert, S. R. (1990) 'Perceptions of elder abuse by health care workers in a long-term care setting', *Clinical Gerontologist*, 10(2): 87–9.

Farran, C.J., Keane-Hogarely, E., Salloway, S., Kupferer, S. and Wilkin, C.S. (1991) 'Finding meaning: an alternative paradigm for Alzheimer's Disease family caregivers', *The Gerontologist*, 31(4): 483–9.

Faulkner, L.R. (1982) 'Mandating the reporting of suspected cases of elder abuse: an inappropriate, ineffective, and ageist response to the abuse of older adults', *Family Law Quarterly*, 16: 69–91.

Featherstone, M. and Hepworth, M. (1989) 'Ageing and old age: reflections on the postmodern life course', in B. Bytheway, T. Kell, P. Allatt and A. Bryman (eds), *Becoming and Being Old*. London: Sage Publications.

Featherstone, M. and Hepworth, M. (1991) *The Body: Social Process and Cultural Theory*. London: Sage Publications.

Fengler, A.P. and Goodrich, N. (1979) 'Wives of disabled men: the hidden patients', *The Gerontologist*, 26(3): 248–52.

Fennell, G., Phillipson, C. and Evers, H. (1989) *The Sociology of Old Age*. London: Open University Press.

Ferguson, D. and Beck, C. (1983) 'Health, attitudes, living arrangements and finances (H.A.L.F) protocol, a tool to assess elder abuse within the family', *Geriatric Nursing*, 4 (5): 301–4.

Festinger, L. (1957) *A Theory of Cognitive Dissonance*. Stanford, CA: Stanford University Press.

Filinson, R. (1989) 'Introduction', in R. Filinson and S.R. Ingman (eds), *Elder Abuse: Practice and Policy*. New York: Human Resources Press.

Filinson, R. and Ingman, S.R. (1989) *Elder Abuse: Practice and Policy*. New York: Human Resources Press.

Finch, J. (1989) *Kinship Obligations and Social Change*. Cambridge: Polity Press.

Finch, J. (1995) 'Responsibilities, obligations and commitments', in I. Allen and E. Perkins (eds), *The Future of Family Care for Older People*. London: HMSO.

Finch, J. and Mason, J. (1990) 'Filial obligations and kin support for the elderly', *Ageing and Society*, 10(2): 151–78.

Finch, J. and Mason, J. (1993) *Negotiating Family Responsibilities*. London: Routledge.

Finkelhor, D. and Pillemer, K.A. (1988) 'Elder abuse: its relationship to other forms of domestic violence', in G.T. Hotaling, D. Finkelhor, J.T. Kirkpatrick and M.A. Straus (eds), *Family Abuse and its Consequences: New Directions in Research*. Newbury Park, CA: Sage Publications. pp. 244–54.

Firth, H., McKeown, P., McIntee, J. and Britton, P. (1987) 'Professional depression, "burnout" and personality in long stay nursing', *International Journal of Nursing Studies*, 24: 227–37.

Fisk, J. (1991) 'Abuse of the elderly', in R. Jacoby and C. Oppenheimer (eds), *Psychiatry in the Elderly*. Oxford: Oxford University Press. pp. 901–14.

Foelker, G.A., Holland, J., Marsh, M. and Simmons, B.A. (1990) 'A community response to elder abuse', *The Gerontologist*, 30 (4): 560–2.

Foner, N. (1994) 'Nursing home aides: saints or monsters?', *The Gerontologist*, 34(2): 245–50.

Forbes, W.F., Jackson, J.A. and Kraus, A.S. (1987) *Institutionalization of the Elderly in Canada*. Toronto: Butterworths.

Formby, W. (1992) 'Should elder abuse be decriminalized?', *Journal of Elder Abuse and Neglect*, 4(4): 121–30.

Foucault, M. (1977) *Discipline and Punish: The Birth of the Prison*. London: Penguin.

Foucault, M. (1979) *The History of Sexuality*. London: Penguin.

Fox, N. (1995) 'Postmodern perspectives on care', *Critical Social Policy*, 44/45: 107–25.

Fricker, N. (1992) 'Personal molestation and harassment: injunctions in actions based on the law of tort', *Family Law*, 22: 158–63.

Fulmer, T. (1984) 'Elder abuse assessment tool', *Dimensions of Critical Care Nursing*, 3(4): 216–20.

Fulmer, T. and O'Malley, T.A. (1987) *Inadequate Care of the Elderly*. New York: Springer.

Futter, C. and Penhale, B. (1996) 'Needs led assessment: the practitioner's perspective', in J. Phillips and B. Penhale (eds), *Reviewing Care Management for Older People*. London: Jessica Kingsley Publishers.

Garrod, G. (1993) 'The mistreatment of older people', *Generations Review*, 3(4): 9–12.

Gelles, R. (1987) *Family Violence*. London: Sage Publications.

Gelles, R. and Straus, M. (1987) 'Is violence towards children increasing?', *Journal of Interpersonal Violence*, 2(2): 212–22.

General Medical Council (1995) *Good Medical Practice*. London: General Medical Council.

George, L. (1989) *Heroes of Their Own Lives: The Politics and History of Family Violence*. London: Virago.

Gesino, J.P., Smith, H.H. and Keckich, W.A. (1982) 'The battered woman grows old', *Clinical Gerontologist*, 1(Fall): 59–67.

Gibbs, J., Evans, M. and Rodway, S. (1987) *Report of the Inquiry into Nye Bevan Lodge*. London: London Borough of Southwark Social Services Department.

Giddens, A. (1991) *Modernity and Self-Identity*. Cambridge: Polity Press.

Gilleard, C. (1994) 'Physical abuse in homes and hospitals', in M. Eastman (ed.), *Old Age Abuse: a New Perspective*. London: Chapman and Hall.

Gioglio, G.R. and Blakemore, P. (1983) 'Elder abuse in New Jersey: the knowledge and experience of abuse among older New Jerseyians'. Unpublished manuscript, Department of Human Services, Trenton, NJ quoted in M.F. Hudson and T.F. Johnson, 'Elder neglect and abuse: a review of the literature', in C. Eisdorfer et al. (eds), *Annual Review of Gerontology and Geriatrics*, Vol. 6. New York: Springer. pp. 81–133.

Given, B.A. and Given, C.W. (1991) 'Family caregivers for the elderly', in J. Fitzpatrick, R. Tauton and A. Jacox (eds), *Annual Review of Nursing Research*, Vol. 9. New York: Springer.

Glendenning, F. (1993) 'What is elder abuse and neglect?', in P. Decalmer and F. Glendenning (eds), *The Mistreatment of Elderly People*. London: Sage Publications. pp. 1–34.

Glendenning, F. (1995) 'Changing perceptions of ageing and intelligence', in F. Glendenning and I. Stuart-Hamilton (eds), *Learning and Cognition in Later Life*. Ashgate: Aldershot. pp. 3–21.

Glendenning, F. (1996) 'The mistreatment of elderly people in residential institutions', in R. Clough (ed.), *The Abuse of Care in Residential Institutions*. London: Whiting and Birch. pp. 35–49.

Gloucestershire Social Services Department (1991) *Adults at Risk: Procedural Guidelines for Professionals*. Gloucester: Gloucestershire County Council.

Gnaedinger, D. (1989) *Elder Abuse: A Discussion Paper*. Ottawa: National Clearing House on Family Violence, Health and Welfare, Canada.

Godkin, M.A., Pillemer, K.A. and Wolf, R.S. (1986) 'Maltreatment of the elderly: a comparative analysis', *Pride Institute Journal of Long Term Home Health Care*, 5: 10–14.

Godkin, M.A., Wolf, R.S. and Pillemer, K.A. (1989) 'A case-comparison analysis of elder abuse and neglect', *International Journal of Aging and Human Development*, 28(3): 207–25.

Goffman, E. (1968) *Asylums*. Harmondsworth: Penguin.

Goldberg, D.R. and Huxley, P. (1980) *Mental Illness in the Community: A Pathway to Care*. London: Tavistock.

Goldberg, D.R. and Huxley, P. (1992) *Common Mental Disorders: A Biosocial Model*. London and New York: Tavistock/Routledge.

Graebner, W. (1980) *A History of Retirement: The Meaning and Function of an American Institution (1885–1978)*. New Haven: Yale University Press.

Grant, G. and Griffiths, A. (1993) 'Shouting for a Samaritan', *Baseline*, 52: 43–5.

Grant, G. and Nolan, M. (1993) 'Informal carers: sources and concomitants of satisfaction', *Health and Social Care*, 1(3): 147–59.

Green, H. (1988) *Informal Carers*. OPCS Series GHS, no. 15, Supplement A. London: HMSO.

Green, R.F. (1969) 'Age-intelligence relationship between ages 16 and 64: a rising trend', *Developmental Psychology*, 1: 618–27.

Griffiths, A. (1980) 'The legacy and present administration of English law: some problems of battered women in context', *Cambrian Law Review*, 11: 29–39.

Griffiths, A. and Roberts, G.(eds) (1995) *The Law and Elderly People*, 2nd edition. London: Routledge.

Griffiths, A., Grimes, R. and Roberts, G. (1990) *The Law and Elderly People*. London: Routledge.

Griffiths, R. (1988) *Community Care: Agenda for Action*. London: HMSO.

Groves, D. (1993) 'Work, poverty and older women', in M. Bernard and K. Meade (eds), *Women Come of Age*. London: Edward Arnold. pp. 43–62.

Gubrium, J. (1995) 'Taking stock', *Qualitative Health Research*, 5(3): 267–9.

Haber, D. and Gratton, B. (1994) *Old Age and the Search for Security*. Indiana: Indiana University Press.

Halamandaris, V.J. (1983) 'Fraud and abuse in nursing homes', in J.I. Kosberg (ed.), *Abuse and Maltreatment of the Elderly: Causes and Interventions*. Boston: John Wright. pp. 104–14.

Hall, P.A. (1989) 'Elder maltreatment patterns: items, sub-groups and types, policy and practical implications', *International Journal of Aging and Human Development*, 28(3): 196–205.

Hansard (1995) *Proceedings of the House of Commons*. London: HMSO.

Harman, H. and Harman, S. (1989) *No Place Like Home: A Report of the First Ninety-six Cases of the Registered Homes Tribunal*. London: NALGO.

Harris, L. (1981) 'Americans believe government should take major responsibility in coping with the abuse problem' (news release). New York: Harris Polls.

Harris, P.B. (1993) 'The misunderstood caregiver? A qualitative study of the male caregiver of Alzheimer's disease victims', *The Gerontologist*, 33(4): 551–6.

Harvath, T.A., Archbold, P.G., Stewart, B.J., Godow, S., Kirschling, J.M., Miller, L.L., Hogan, J., Brody, K. and Schook, J. (1994) 'Establishing partnerships with family caregivers: local and cosmopolitan knowledge', *Journal of Gerontological Nursing*, 20(2): 29–35.

Havighurst, R. (1954) 'Flexibility and the social roles of the retired', *American Journal of Sociology*, 59: 309–11.

Heath, H. (1996) 'Reluctance to report bad practice', *Elderly Care*, 8(1): 5.

Hibbs, P.J. (1991) 'Freedom or restraint'. Paper presented at Counsel and Care Conference, autumn 1991, London.

Hickey, T. and Douglass, R.L. (1981a) 'Mistreatment of the elderly in the domestic setting: an exploratory study', *American Journal of Public Health*, 71: 500–7.

Hickey, T. and Douglass, R.L. (1981b) 'Neglect and abuse of older family members: professionals' perspectives and case experiences', *The Gerontologist*, 21(1): 171–6.

Higgs, P. and Victor, C. (1993) 'Institutional care and the life course', in S. Arber and M. Evandrou (eds), *Ageing, Independence and the Life Course*. London: Jessica Kingsley Publishers. pp. 186–200.

Hildrew, M.A. (1991) *Guidelines on Elder Abuse: Which Social Services Departments have them?* London: British Association of Social Workers.

Hirschfield, M.J. (1981) 'Families living and coping with the cognitively impaired', in L.A. Copp (ed.), *Care of the Ageing*. Edinburgh: Churchill Livingstone.

Hirschfield, M.J. (1983) 'Home care versus institutionalization: family caregiving and senile brain disease', *International Journal of Nursing Studies*, 20(1): 23–32.

Hirst, S.P. and Miller, J. (1986) 'The abused elderly', *Journal of Psycho-Social Nursing*, 24(10): 28–34.

Hocking, E.D. (1988) 'Miscare – a form of abuse in the elderly', *Update*, 15 May: 2411–19.

Hocking, E.D. (1994) 'Caring for carers: understanding the process that leads to abuse', in M. Eastman (ed.), *Old Age Abuse: A New Perspective*. London: Chapman and Hall. pp. 51–63.

Hoggett, B. (1990) *Mental Health Law*. London: Sweet and Maxwell.

Holmes, B. and Johnson, A. (1988) *Cold Comfort: the Scandal of Private Rest Homes*. London: Souvenir Press.

Holstein, M. (1996) 'Multidisciplinary ethical decision-making: uniting differing professional perspectives', in T.F. Johnson (ed.), *Elder Mistreatment: Ethical Issues, Dilemmas and Decisions*. New York: Haworth Press. pp. 169–82.

Holt, M. G. (1993a) 'Elder sexual abuse in Britain', in C. McCreadie (ed.), *Elder Abuse: New Findings and Policy Guidelines*. London: Age Concern Institute of Gerontology, King's College London. pp. 16–18.

Holt, M. G. (1993b) 'Elder sexual abuse in Britain: preliminary findings', *Journal of Elder Abuse and Neglect*, 5(2): 63–71.

Holt, M. G. (1993c) 'Sexual abuse – whose problem is it anyway?', *Action on Elder Abuse Bulletin*, September/October.

Homer, A.C. and Gilleard, C. (1990) 'Abuse of elderly people by their carers', *British Medical Journal*, 301: 1359–62.

Hooyman, N.R. (1983) 'Elderly abuse and neglect: community interventions', in J.I. Kosberg (ed.), *Abuse and Maltreatment of the Elderly: Causes and Interventions*. Boston: John Wright. pp. 376–90.

Horrocks, P. (1988) 'Elderly people: abused and forgotten', *Health Service Journal*, 22 September: 1085.

Hudson, B., Soffer, B. and Menio, D. (1991) *Ensuring An Abuse-Free Environment: A Learning Programme for Nursing Home Staff*. Philadelphia: Coalition of Advocates for the Rights of Infirm Elderly (CARIE).

Hudson, J.E. (1988) 'Elder abuse: an overview', in B. Schlesinger and R. Schlesinger (eds), *Abuse of the Elderly: Issues and Annotated Bibliography*. Toronto: University of Toronto Press. pp. 12–31.

Hudson, M.F. (1986) 'Elder mistreatment: current research', in K.A. Pillemer and R.S. Wolf (eds), *Elder Abuse: Conflict in the Family*. Dover, MA: Auburn House. pp. 125–66.

Hudson, M.F. and Johnson, T.F. (1986) 'Elder neglect and abuse: a review of the literature', in C. Eisdorfer et al. (eds), *Annual Review of Gerontology and Geriatrics*, Vol.6. New York: Springer. pp. 81–133.

Hughes, B. (1995) *Older People and Community Care: Critical Theory and Practice*. Buckingham: Open University Press.

Hugman, R. (1995) 'The implication of the term "elder abuse" for problem definition and response in health and social welfare', *Journal of Social Policy*, 24(4): 493–507.

Hwalek, M. and Sengstock, M. (1986) 'Assessing the probability of elder abuse: toward the development of a clinical screening instrument', *Journal of Applied Gerontology*, 5(2): 153–73.

Hytner, B.A. (1977) *Report into Allegations concerning Moorfield Observation and Assessment Centre*. Salford: City of Salford.

Isaacs, B. (1971) 'Geriatric families: do their families care?', *British Medical Journal*, 30 October: 282–6.

Jacelon, C.S. (1995) 'The effects of living in a nursing home on socialization in elderly people', *Journal of Advanced Nursing*, 22(3): 539–46.

Jack, R. (1994) 'Dependence, power and violation: gender issues in abuse of elderly people by formal carers', in M. Eastman (ed.), *Old Age Abuse: A New Perspective*. London: Chapman and Hall. pp. 72–92.

Janis, I.L. (1982) *Groupthink: Psychological Studies of Policy Decisions and Fiascoes*, 2nd edition. Boston: Houghton Mifflin.

Jensen, B. (1995) 'Abuse of the elderly in the Netherlands', *Social Work in Europe*, 2(3): 18–23.

Jivanjee, P. (1993) 'Enhancing the well-being of family caregivers to patients with dementia'.

Paper given at International Mental Health Conference, Institute of Human Ageing, Liverpool.

Johns, S. and Juklestad, O. (1995) 'Norway: developing elder protective services', *Social Work in Europe*, 2(3): 2–7.

Johnson, N. (1995) 'Domestic violence: an overview', in P. Kingston and B. Penhale (eds), *Family Violence and the Caring Professions*. London: Macmillan.

Johnson, T.F. (1986) 'Critical issues in the definition of elder mistreatment', in K.A. Pillemer and R.S. Wolf (eds), *Elder Abuse: Conflict in the Family*. Dover, MA: Auburn House.

Johnson, T.F. (1991) *Elder Mistreatment: Deciding Who is At Risk*. Westport, CT: Greenwood Press.

Johnson, T.F. (ed.) (1995) *Elder Mistreatment: Ethical Issues, Dilemmas and Decisions*. New York: Haworth Press.

Johnson, T.F., O'Brien, J.G. and Hudson, M.F. (1985) *Elder Neglect and Abuse: An Annotated Bibliography*. Westport, CT: Greenwood Press.

Johnson, P., Conrad, C. and Thomson, D. (eds) (1989) *Workers versus Pensioners: Intergenerational Justice in an Ageing World*. Manchester: Manchester University Press.

Jones, S. (1976) 'Education for the elderly', in F. Glendenning and S. Jones (eds), *Education and the Over-60s*. Stoke-on-Trent: Beth Johnson Foundation and Keele University Adult Education Department. pp. 9–20.

Kahana, E. and Young, R. (1990) 'Clarifying the caregiving paradigm: challenges for the future', in D.E. Biegel and A. Blum (eds), *Ageing and Caregiving: Theory, Research and Policy*. Newbury Park, CA: Sage Publications.

Kane, R.A. and Penrod, J.D. (1995) *Family Caregiving in an Aging Society: Policy Perspectives*. Thousand Oaks, CA: Sage Publications.

Kappeler, S. (1992) *The Will to Violence:The Politics of Personal Behaviour*. Cambridge: Polity Press.

Kastenbaum, R. (1992) 'The creative process: a lifespan approach', in T. Cole, D. Van Tassel, R. Kastenbaum (eds), *Handbook of the Humanities and Aging*. New York: Springer.

Kayser-Jones, J.S. (1981) *Old and Alone, Care of the Aged in the UK and Scotland*. Berkeley: University of California Press.

Kayser-Jones, J. and Wiener, C.L. (1990) 'The uneasy fate of nursing home residents: an organisational interaction perspective', *Sociology of Health and Illness*, 12(1): 84–104.

Keady, J. and Nolan, M.R. (1993a) 'Coping with dementia: understanding and responding to the needs of informal carers'. Paper given at the Royal College of Nursing Research Conference, University of Glasgow, April.

Keady, J. and Nolan, M.R. (1993b) 'Coping with dementia: towards a comprehensive assessment of the needs of informal carers'. Paper given at International Conference on Mental Illness in Old Age, Institute of Human Ageing, Liverpool.

Keller, B.H. (1996) 'A model abuse prevention training program for long-term care staff', in L.A. Baumhover and S.C. Beall (eds), *Abuse, Neglect and Exploitation of Older Persons: Strategies for Assessment and Intervention*. London: Jessica Kingsley Publishers. pp. 221–40.

Kenny, T. (1990) 'Erosion of individuality in care of elderly people in hospital: an alternative approach', *Journal of Advanced Nursing*, 15: 571–6.

Ker, H. J. (1996) 'Training residential staff to be aware of sexual abuse in old age', in R. Clough (ed.), *The Abuse of Care in Residential Institutions*. London: Whiting and Birch. pp. 166–71.

Kertzer, D.I. and Laslett, P. (eds) (1995) *Aging in the Past: Demography, Society and Old Age*. Berkeley: University of California Press.

Kimsey, L. R., Tarbox, A. R. and Bragg, D. F. (1981) 'Abuse of the elderly: the hidden agenda 1. The caretakers and the categories of abuse', *American Geriatrics Society Journal*, 29: 465–72.

Kingston, P. (1990) 'Elder abuse'. Unpublished MA dissertation, University of Keele.

Kingston, P. (ed.) (1994) *Proceedings of the First International Symposium on Elder Abuse*. London: Action on Elder Abuse.

Kingston, P. and Penhale, B. (eds) (1995) *Family Violence and the Caring Professions*. London: Macmillan.

Kingston, P., Penhale, B. and Bennett, G.C.J. (1995) 'Is elder abuse on the curriculum? The relative contribution of child abuse, domestic violence and elder abuse in social work, nursing and medicine qualifying curricula', *Health and Social Care in the Community*, 3(6): 353–62.

Kinney, J.M. and Stephens, M.A.P. (1989) 'Hassles and uplifts of giving care to a family member with dementia', *Psychology and Ageing*, 4: 402–8.

Kitwood, T. (1997) *Dementia Reconsidered: the Person Comes First*. Buckingham: Open University Press.

Kosberg, J.I. (1988) 'Preventing elder abuse: identification of high risk factors prior to placement decisions', *The Gerontologist*, 28(1): 43–50.

Kosberg, J.I. and Garcia, J.L. (1995) *Elder Abuse: International and Cross-cultural Perspectives*. New York: The Hawarth Press.

Kurrle, S. (1995) *The Hidden Problem of Abuse of Older People*. Sydney: New South Wales Office of Ageing.

Kurrle, S.R. and Sadler, P.M. (1993) 'Australian service providers: responses to elder abuse', *Journal of Elder Abuse and Neglect*, 5(1): 57–76.

Kurrle, S. and Sadler, P. (1994) *Assessing and Managing Abuse of Older People*. Sydney: New South Wales Office on Ageing.

Kyle, T.U. (1995) 'The concept of caring: a literature review', *Journal of Advanced Nursing*, 21(3): 506–14.

Lachs, M.S. and Pillemer, K.A. (1995) 'Abuse and neglect of elderly persons', *New England Journal of Medicine*, 332(7): 437–43.

Lamm, H. and Myers, D.G. (1978) 'Group induced polarization of attitudes and behaviour', in L. Berkowitz (ed.), *Advances in Experimental Social Psychology*, Vol. 11. New York: Academic Press.

Langan, J. and Means, R. (1994) *Money Matters in Later Life: Financial Management and Elderly People in Kirklees. Anchor Studies 1*. Oxford: Anchor Housing Association.

Langan, J. and Means, R. (1996) 'Financial management and elderly people with dementia in the U.K.', *Ageing and Society*, 16(3): 287–315.

Langer, S.R. (1993) 'Ways of managing the experience of caregiving for elderly relatives', *Western Journal of Nursing Research*, 15(5): 582–94.

Laslett, P. (1989a) *A Fresh Map of Life: The Emergence of the Third Age*. London: Weidenfeld and Nicolson.

Laslett, P. (1989b) 'The demographic scene – an overview', in J. Eekelaar and D. Pearl (eds), *An Ageing World: Dilemmas and Challenges for Law and Social Policy*. Oxford: Clarendon Press.

Latane, B. (1973) *A Theory of Social Impact*. St Louis: Psychonomic Society.

Lau, E. and Kosberg, J.I. (1979) 'Abuse of the elderly by informal care providers', *Aging*, 299–301: 11–15.

Law Commission (1995) *Mental Incapacity*. Law Com 231. London: HMSO.

Law Society (1994) *Improving and Developing Legal Services for Elderly People*. London: Law Society.

Lawton, M.P., Kleban, M.H., Moss, M., Rovine, M. and Glicksman, A.(1989) 'Measuring caregiver appraisal', *Journal of Gerontology*, 44: 61–71.

Lazarus, R.S. (1993) 'Coping theory and research: past, recent and future', *Psychosomatic Medicine*, 55: 234–47.

Lea, A. (1994) 'Defining the roles of lay and nursing caring', *Nursing Standard*, 9(5): 32–5.

Lee, G. (1985) 'Kinship and social support: the case of the United States', *Ageing and Society*, 5: 19–38.

Lee-Treweek, G. (1994) 'Bedroom abuse: the hidden work in a nursing home', *Generations Review*, 4(2): 2–4.

Lehman, H.C. (1953) *Age and Achievement*. Princeton, NJ: Princeton University Press.

Levesque, L., Cossette, J. and Laurin, L. (1995) 'A multidimensional examination of the psychological and social well-being of caregivers of a demented relative', *Research on Aging*, 17(3): 322–60.

Lewis, J. and Meredith, B. (1988a) *Daughters Who Care: Daughters Caring for Mothers at Home*. London: Routledge and Kegan Paul.

Lewis, J. and Meredith, B. (1988b) 'Daughters caring for mothers', *Ageing and Society*, 8(1): 1–21.

Lewis, J. and Meredith, B. (1989) 'Contested territory in informal care', in M. Jeffreys (ed.), *Growing Old in the Twentieth Century*. London: Routledge.

Lewis, J. with Bernstock, P., Bovell, V. and Wookey, F. (1996) 'The purchaser/provider split in social care: is it working?', *Social Policy and Administration*, 30(1): 1–19.

Lloyd, S. (1995) 'Social work and domestic violence', in P. Kingston and B. Penhale (eds), *Family Violence and the Caring Professions*. London: Macmillan. pp. 149–77.

Lomas, G. (1991) 'Middleton Elderly Resource Intervention Team (MERIT)', Private communication.

Lowther, C.P. and Williamson, J. (1966) 'Old people and their relations', *The Lancet*, 31 December: 1459–60.

McCall, G.J. and Simmons, J.L. (1966) *Identities and Interactions*. New York: Free Press.

McCallum, J., Matiasz, S. and Graycar, A. (1990) *Abuse of the Elderly at Home: the Range of the Problem*. Adelaide: Office of the Commissioner for the Ageing.

McCreadie, C. (1991) *Elder Abuse: An Exploratory Study*. London: Age Concern Institute of Gerontology, King's College, London.

McCreadie, C. (ed.) (1993) *Elder Abuse: New Findings and Policy Guidelines*. London: Age Concern Institute of Gerontology, King's College, London.

McCreadie, C. (1994) 'Introduction: the issues, practice and policy', in M.Eastman (ed.), *Old Age Abuse: A New Perspective*. London: Chapman and Hall.

McCreadie, C. (1996a) *Elder Abuse: Update on Research*. London: Age Concern Institute of Gerontology, King's College, London.

McCreadie, C. (ed.) (1996b) *Elder Abuse: New Perspectives and Ways Forward: Report of Two Conferences*. London: Age Concern Institute of Gerontology, King's College, London.

McDonald, L. and Wigdor, B. (1995) 'Taking stock: elder abuse research in Canada', *Canadian Journal on Ageing*, 14: 1–6.

McEwan, E. (ed.) (1989) *Age: The Unrecognised Discrimination*. London: Age Concern.

McEwan, J. (1989) 'Documentary hearsay evidence: refuge for the vulnerable witness', *Criminal Law Review*, 692–742.

McMullin, J. (1995) 'Theorizing age and gender relations', in S. Arber and J. Ginn (eds), *Connecting Gender and Ageing: A Sociological Approach*. Buckingham: Open University Press. pp. 30–41.

McPherson, B. (1990) *Ageing as a Social Process*. Toronto: Butterworths.

Manthorpe, J.(1993) 'Elder abuse and key areas in social work', in P. Decalmer and F. Glendenning (eds), *The Mistreatment of Elderly People*. London: Sage Publications. pp. 88–101.

Manthorpe, J. (1995) 'Elder abuse and dementia', *Journal of Dementia Care*, November/December.

Manthorpe, J. and Twigg, J. (1995) 'Carers and care management', *Baseline*, 59(October): 4–18.

Marriott, A. (1996) 'Elder abuse: staff attitudes and beliefs', *Psychology Special Interest Group for the Elderly*, 55: 14–17.

Marshall, M. (1993) 'New trends and dilemmas in working with people with dementia and their carers', in A. Chapman and M. Marshall (eds), *Dementia: New Skills for Social Workers*: London: Jessica Kingsley Publishers.

Martin, J. P. (1984) *Hospitals in Trouble*. Oxford: Blackwell.

Martin Matthews, A. and Campbell, L.D. (1995) 'Gender roles, employment and informal care', in S. Arber and J. Ginn (eds), *Connecting Gender and Ageing*. Buckingham: Open University Press. pp. 129–43.

Maslach, C. (1982) *Burnout: the Cost of Caring*. Englewood Cliffs, NJ: Prentice-Hall.

Mason, J. and McCall Smith, A. (1994) *Law and Medical Ethics*. London: Butterworths.

Means, R. and Smith, R. (1994) *Confronting Elder Abuse*. London: HMSO.

Mechanic, D. (1989) *Mental Health and Social Policy*, 3rd edition. Englewood Cliffs, NJ: Prentice-Hall.

Medd, P. (1976) *Committee of Inquiry into Incidents at Besford House Community House.* Shrewsbury: Shropshire County Council.

Mildenberger, C. and Wessman, H.C. (1986) 'Abuse and neglect of elderly persons by family members', *Physical Therapy*, 66(4): 537–9.

Millard, P. (1984) 'Views of a geriatrician', in M. Eastman (ed.), *Old Age Abuse*. Mitcham: Age Concern England. pp. 94–5.

Minkler, M. and Estes, C. (eds) (1991) *Critical Perspectives on Aging*. New York: Baywood Publishing.

Minkler, M. and Robertson, A. (1991) 'The ideology of age/race wars', *Ageing and Society*, 11: 1–22.

Minois, G. (1989) *History of Old Age*. Cambridge: Polity Press.

Mitchell, D. (1991) 'The long and the short of it', *Community Care*, 7 November: 8.

Mixson, P.M. (1996) 'An adult protective services perspective', in T.F. Johnson (ed.), *Elder Mistreatment: Ethical Issues, Dilemmas and Decisions*. New York: Haworth Press. pp. 69–87.

Monk, A. (1990) 'Gerontological social services: theory and practice', in A. Monk (ed.), *Handbook of Gerontological Services*. New York: Columbia University Press. pp. 3–26.

Monk, A., Kaye, L. W. and Litwin, H. (1984) *Resolving Grievances in the Nursing Home: A Study of the Ombudsman's Program*. New York: Columbia University Press.

Moody, H. R. (1992) 'Bioethics and aging', in T. Cole, D.Van Tassel and R. Kastenbaum (eds), *Handbook of the Humanities and Aging*. New York: Springer.

Moon, A. and Williams, O. (1993) 'Perceptions of elder abuse and help seeking patterns among African-American, Caucasian-American, and Korean-American elderly women', *The Gerontologist*, 33: 386–95.

Motenko, A.K. (1988) 'Respite care and pride in caregiving: the experience of six older men caring for their disabled wives', in S. Reinharz and G. Rowles (eds), *Qualitative Gerontology*. New York: Springer.

Murphy, E. and Bean, P. (1992) 'Sweet freedom', *Social Work Today*, 29 October: 15.

Murphy, J. (1931) 'Dependency in old age', *Annals of the American Academy of Political and Social Science*, 154: 38–41.

Nathanson, P. (1983) 'An overview of legal issues, services and resources', in J.I. Kosberg (ed.), *Abuse and Maltreatment of the Elderly: Causes and Interventions*. Boston: John Wright. pp. 303–15.

National Health Service (1969) *Report into Allegations of Ill-Treatment at Ely Hospital, Cardiff*. London: HMSO.

National Health Service Executive (NHSE) (1995) *Patients not Paper: Report of the Efficiency Scrutiny into Bureaucracy in General Practice*. London: NHSE.

National Institute of Social Work (NISW) (1988) *Residential Care: A Positive Choice*. London: HMSO.

National Institute of Social Work (1996) *Creating a Home from Home: A Guide to Standards*. London: NISW.

Nazarko, L. (1996) 'The single care home', *Nursing Times*, 92(4): 31–3.

New South Wales Office on Ageing (1995) *Behind Closed Doors: a Training Kit with Video*. Sydney: NSW Office of Ageing.

Nolan, M. R. and Grant, G. (1992a) *Regular Respite: An Evaluation of a Hospital Rota Bed Scheme for Elderly People*. London: Age Concern England.

Nolan, M.R. and Grant, G (1992b) 'Helping new carers of the frail elderly patient: the challenge for nursing in acute care settings', *Journal of Clinical Nursing*, 1: 303–7.

Nolan, M., Grant, G. and Ellis, N. (1990) 'Stress is in the eye of the beholder: reconceptualizing the nature of carer burdens', *Journal of Advanced Nursing*, 15: 554–5.

Nolan, M.R., Grant, G. and Keady, J. (1996) *Understanding Family Care: A Multidimensional Model of Caring and Coping*. Buckingham: Open University Press.

Nolan, M.R., Keady, J. and Grant, G. (1995) 'Developing a typology of family care:

implications for nurses and other service providers', *Journal of Advanced Nursing*, 21: 256–65.

Noone, J.F. (1993) 'The general practitioner and elder abuse', in P. Decalmer and F. Glendenning (eds), *The Mistreatment of Elderly People*. London: Sage Publications. pp. 136–47.

Norman, A. (1987) *Aspects of Ageism: Discussion Paper*. London: Centre for Policy on Ageing.

Norton, D. (1990) *The Age of Old Age*. London: Scutari Press.

O'Brien, J.G. (1986) 'Elder abuse and the physician', *Michigan Medicine*, 85: 618–20.

O'Brien, J.G. (1996) 'Screening: a primary care clinician's perspective', in L.A. Baumhover and S.C. Beall (eds), *Abuse, Neglect and Exploitation of Older Persons: Strategies for Assessment and Intervention*. London: Jessica Kingsley Publishers. pp. 51–64.

O'Donnell, J. (1995) 'Protection of family life: positive approaches and the ECHR', *Journal of Social Welfare and Family Law*, 17(3): 261–80.

Ogg, J. (1993a) 'International perspectives on elder abuse', in C. McCreadie (ed.), *Elder Abuse: New Findings and Policy Guidelines*. London: Age Concern Institute of Gerontology, King's College, London. pp. 19–24.

Ogg, J. (1993b) 'Elder abuse: the European context', *Geriatric Medicine*, September: 15.

Ogg, J. and Bennett, G.C.J. (1992a) 'Screening for elder abuse in the community', *Geriatric Medicine*, February: 63–7.

Ogg, J. and Bennett, G.C.J. (1992b) 'Elder abuse in Britain', *British Medical Journal*, 305: 998–9.

O'Kell, S. (1995) *Care Standards in the Residential Care Sector*. York: York Publishing Services.

O'Malley, H.C., Segal, H.D. and Perez, R. (1979) *Elder Abuse in Massachusetts: Survey of Professionals and Paraprofessionals*. Boston: Legal Research and Services to the Elderly.

O'Malley, T.A., Everitt, D.E., O'Malley, H.C. and Campion, E.W. (1983) 'Identifying and preventing family-mediated abuse and neglect of elderly persons', *Annals of Internal Medicine*, 98: 998–1005.

O'Malley, T.A., O'Malley, H.C., Everitt, D.E. and Sarson, D. (1984) 'Categories of family-mediated abuse and neglect of elderly persons', *Journal of the American Geriatrics Society*, 32(5): 362–9.

Opie, A. (1994) 'The instability of the caring body: gender and caregivers of confused older people', *Qualitative Health Research*, 4(1): 31–50.

Oppenheim, C. (1993) *Poverty: The Facts*. London: Child Poverty Action Group.

Pahl, J. (ed.) (1985) *Private Life and Public Policy. The Needs of Battered Women and the Response of the Public Services*. London: Routledge and Kegan Paul.

Parker, G. and Lawton, D. (1994) *Different Types of Care, Different Types of Carer: Evidence from the General Household Survey*. London: HMSO.

Parker, R. (1990) 'Private residential homes and nursing homes', in I. Sinclair, R. Parker, D. Leat and J. Williams (eds), *The Kaleidoscope of Care: A Review of Research on Welfare Provision for Elderly People*. London: HMSO.

Parkin, A. (1995) 'The care and control of elderly or incapacitated adults', *Journal of Social Welfare and Family Law*, 17(4): 431–44.

Parton, N. (1985) *The Politics of Child Abuse*. London: Macmillan.

Parton, N. (1991) *Governing the Family: Child Care, Child Protection and the State*. London: Macmillan.

Parton, N. (1996) 'Introduction', in N. Parton (ed.), *Social Theory, Social Change and Social Work*. London: Routledge.

Patel, N. (1990) *A Race against Time?* London: Runnymede Trust.

Patterson, J.M. (1993) 'The role of family meanings in adaptation to chronic illness and disability', in A.P. Turnbull, J.M. Patterson, S.K. Behr, D.L. Murphy, J.G. Marquis and M.J. Blue-Banning (eds), *Cognitive Coping: Families and Disability*. Baltimore, MD: Paul H. Brookes.

Paveza, G.J., Cohen, D. and Eisdorfer, C. (1992) 'Severe family violence and Alzheimer's disease: prevalence and risk factors', *The Gerontologist*, 32: 493–7.

Payne, M. (1995) *Social Work and Community Care*. London: Macmillan.

Peace, S. (1986) 'The forgotten female: social policy and older women', in C. Phillipson and A. Walker (eds), *Ageing and Social Policy*. Aldershot: Gower.

Peace, S. (1993) 'The living environments of older women', in M. Bernard and K. Meade (eds), *Women Come of Age*. London: Edward Arnold.

Peace, S., Kellaher, L. and Willcocks, D. (1997) *Re-evaluating Residential Care*. Buckingham: Open University Press.

Pearson, M. and Wistow, G. (1995) 'The boundaries of health and social care', *British Medical Journal*, 311: 208–9.

Pearson, M., Bogg, J., Pursey, A. and Quinney, D. (1994) *Users' and Carers' Views of NHS Day Hospitals for Older People*. London: National Audit Office.

Penhale, B. (1993a) 'The abuse of elderly people: considerations for practice', *British Journal of Social Work*, 23(2): 95–112.

Penhale, B. (1993b) 'Abuse on the map', *Community Care*, 10 June.

Penhale, B. (1993c) 'Local authority guidance and procedures', in C. McCreadie (ed.), *Elder Abuse: New Findings and Policy Guidance*. London: Age Concern Institute of Gerontology. pp. 8–15.

Penhale, B. and Kingston, P. (1995a) 'Recognizing and dealing with the abuse of older people', *Nursing Times*, 91(42): 27–8.

Penhale, B. and Kingston, P. (1995b) *Family Violence and the Caring Professions*. London: Macmillan.

Phillips, J. (1996) 'The future of social work with older people in a changing world', in N. Parton (ed.), *Social Theory, Social Change and Social Work*. London: Routledge.

Phillips, L.R. (1986) 'Theoretical explanations of elder abuse', in K.A. Pillemer and R.S. Wolf (eds), *Elder Abuse: Conflict in the Family*. Dover, MA: Auburn House. pp. 86–93.

Phillips, L.R. (1989) 'Issues involved in identifying and intervening in elder abuse', in R. Finlinson and S. Ingman (eds), *Elder Abuse: Practice and Policy*. New York: Human Sciences Press. pp. 197–217.

Phillips, L.R. and Rempusheski, V.E. (1986) 'Caring for the frail elderly at home: towards a theoretical explanation of the dynamics of poor quality family care', *Advances in Nursing Science*, 8(4): 62–84.

Phillipson, C. (1977) *The Emergence of Retirement*, Working Papers on Sociology No. 14. Durham: Department of Sociology, University of Durham.

Phillipson, C. (1982) *Capitalism and the Construction of Old Age*. London: Macmillan.

Phillipson, C. (1991) 'Intergenerational relations: conflict or consensus in the 21st century', *Policy and Politics*, 19: 27–36.

Phillipson, C. (1992a) 'Challenging the "spectre of old age": community care for older people in the 1990s', in N. Manning and R. Page (eds), *Social Policy Review No. 4*. London: Social Policy Association.

Phillipson, C. (1992b) 'Confronting elder abuse: fact or fiction?', *Generations Review*, 2(3): 2–3.

Phillipson, C. (1993) 'Abuse of older people: sociological perspectives', in P. Decalmer and F. Glendenning (eds), *The Mistreatment of Elderly People*. London: Sage Publications. pp. 76–87.

Phillipson, C. (1996a) *Family Networks and Social Support for Older People*. Keele: Keele University, Centre for Social Gerontology.

Phillipson, C. (1996b) 'Interpretations of ageing: perspectives from humanistic gerontology', *Ageing and Society*, 16(3): 359–69.

Phillipson, C. and Biggs, S. (1992) *Understanding Elder Abuse: A Training Manual for Helping Professionals*. London: Longman.

Phillipson, C. and Biggs, S. (1995) 'Elder abuse: a critical overview', in P. Kingston and B. Penhale (eds), *Family Violence and the Caring Professions*. London: Macmillan. pp. 181–203.

Phillipson, C. and Walker, A. (eds) (1986) *Ageing and Social Policy: A Critical Assessment*. Aldershot: Gower.

Pillemer, K.A. (1986) 'Risk factors in elder abuse: results from a case-control study', in K.A. Pillemer and R.S. Wolf (eds), *Elder Abuse: Conflict in the Family*. Dover, MA: Auburn House. pp. 239–64.

Pillemer, K.A. (1988) 'Maltreatment of patients in nursing homes', *Journal of Health and Social Behavior*, 29(3): 227–38.

Pillemer, K.A. (1993) 'Abused offspring are dependent', in R. Gelles and D. Loseke (eds), *Current Controversies in Family Violence*. Newbury Park, CA: Sage Publications. pp. 237–50.

Pillemer, K.A. (1994) 'Methodological issues in the study of elder abuse', in P. Kingston (ed.), *A Report on the Proceedings of the First International Symposium on Elder Abuse*. London: Action on Elder Abuse. pp. 1–10.

Pillemer, K.A. (1996) Private Communication.

Pillemer, K.A. and Bachman-Prehn (1991) 'Helping and hurting: predictors of maltreatment of patients in nursing homes', *Research on Aging*, 13(1): 74–95.

Pillemer, K.A. and Finkelhor, D. (1988) 'The prevalence of elder abuse: a random sample survey', *The Gerontologist*, 28(1): 51–7.

Pillemer, K.A. and Finkelhor, D. (1989) 'Causes of elder abuse: caregiver stress versus problem relatives', *American Journal of Orthopsychiatry*, 59: 179–87.

Pillemer, K.A. and Hudson, B. (1993) 'A model abuse prevention programme for nursing assistants', *The Gerontologist*, 33(1): 128–31.

Pillemer, K.A. and Moore, D. W. (1989) 'Abuse of patients in nursing homes: findings from a survey of staff', *The Gerontologist*, 29(3): 314–20.

Pillemer, K.A. and Moore, D. W. (1990) 'Highlights from a study of abuse in nursing homes', *Journal of Elder Abuse and Neglect*, 2(1/2): 5–29.

Pillemer, K.A. and Wolf, R.S. (eds) (1986) *Elder Abuse: Conflict in the Family*. Dover, MA: Auburn House.

Pitsiou-Darrough, E.N. and Spinellis, C.D. (1995) 'Mistreatment of the elderly in Greece', in J.I. Kosberg and J.L. Garcia (eds), *Elder Abuse: International and Cross-Cultural Perspectives*. New York: Haworth Press. pp. 45–64.

Podnieks, E. (1985) 'Elder abuse', *The Canadian Nurse*, 81(11): 36–9.

Podnieks, E. (1988) 'Elder abuse: it's time we did something about it', in B. Schlesinger and R. Schlesinger (eds), *Abuse of the Elderly: Issues and Annotated Bibliography*. Toronto: University of Toronto Press. pp. 32–42.

Podnieks, E. (1990) *National Survey on Abuse of the Elderly in Canada: The Ryerson Study*. Toronto: Ryerson Polytechnical Institute.

Podnieks, E. and Pillemer, K.A. (1989) *Survey on Abuse of the Elderly in Canada*. Toronto: Ryerson Polytechnical Institute.

Pollard, J. (1995) 'Elder abuse – the public law failure to protect', *Family Law*, 25: 257–9.

Powell, S. and Berg, R.C. (1987) 'When the elderly are abused', *Educational Gerontology*, 13(1): 71–83.

Poxton, R. (1996) *Joint Approaches to a Better Old Age: Developing Services through Joint Commissioning*. London: King's Fund Publishing.

Pratt, M. and Norris, J. (1994) *The Social Psychology of Ageing*. Oxford: Blackwell.

Pritchard, J. (1989) 'Confronting the taboo of the abuse of elderly people', *Social Work Today*, 5 October: 12–13.

Pritchard, J. (1990a) 'Old and abused', *Social Work Today*, 15 February: 22–3.

Pritchard, J. (1990b) 'Charting the hits', *Care Weekly*, 19 October: 10–11.

Pritchard, J. (1992) *The Abuse of Elderly People: A Handbook for Professionals*. London: Jessica Kingsley Publishers.

Pritchard, J. (1993) 'Gang warfare', *Community Care*, 8 July: 22–3.

Pritchard, J. (1995) *The Abuse of Older People: A Training Manual for Detection and Prevention*, 2nd edition. London: Jessica Kingsley Publishers.

Quinn, M.J. and Tomita, S.T. (1986) 'Elder abuse and neglect: written protocol for identification and assessment', in M.J. Quinn and S.T. Tomita (eds), *Elder Abuse and Neglect*. New York: Springer. pp. 267–74.

Quinney, D. and Pearson, M. (1996) *Different Worlds, Missed Opportunities? Primary Health Care Nursing in a North Western Health District*. Liverpool: Health and Community Care Research Unit, University of Liverpool.

Ramsey-Klawsnik, H. (1991) 'Elder sexual abuse: preliminary findings', *Journal of Elder Abuse and Neglect*, 3(3): 73–90.

Ramsey-Klawsnik, H. (1996) 'Assessing physical and sexual abuse in health care settings', in

L.A. Baumhover and S.C. Beall (eds), *Abuse, Neglect and Exploitation of Older Persons: Strategies for Assessment and Intervention*. London: Jessica Kingsley Publishers. pp. 67–97.

Rathbone-McCuan, E. (1980) 'Elderly victims of family violence and neglect', *Social Casework: The Journal of Contemporary Social Work*, May: 296–304.

Rathbone-McCuan, E. and Voyles, B. (1982) 'Case detection of abused elderly parents', *American Journal of Psychiatry*, 139(2): 189–92.

Richardson, S. and Pearson, M. (1994) *Suffering in Silence? Hidden Health and Social Care Needs in Tranmere*. Liverpool: Health and Community Care Research Unit, University of Liverpool.

Richardson, S. and Pearson, M. (1995) 'Dignity and aspirations denied? Unmet health and social care needs in an inner city area', *Health and Social Care in the Community*, 3(5): 279–87.

Ripamonte, E. (1995) 'The abuse of the elderly in Italy', *Social Work in Europe*, 2(3): 15–17.

Robb, B. (1967) *Sans Everything: a Case to Answer*. Edinburgh: Nelson.

Roberts, R. (1978) *The Classic Slum: Salford Life in the First Quarter of the Century*. Harmondsworth: Penguin.

Robinson, B. (1983) 'Caregiver strain questionnaire', *Journal of Gerontology*, 38(3): 344–8.

Rogers, W.V.H. (1989) *The Law of Tort*. London: Sweet and Maxwell.

Rosenmayer, L. and Kockeis, E. (1963) 'Propositions for a sociological theory of aging and the family', *International Science Journal*, XV: 410–46.

Ross, M., Ross, P.A. and Ross, C. (1985) 'Abuse of the elderly', *The Canadian Nurse*, 81(2): 36–9.

Royal College of Nursing (RCN) (1987) *Improving Care of Elderly People in Hospital*. London: RCN.

Royal College of Nursing (1992) 'A scandal waiting to happen?', *Elderly People and Nursing Care in Residential and Nursing Homes*. London: RCN. pp. 18–20.

Royal Commission on Criminal Justice (1993) *Report*. Cmd. 2263. London: HMSO.

Sadler, P., Kurrle, S. and Cameron, I. (1995) 'Dementia and elder abuse', *Australian Journal on Ageing*, 14: 36–40.

Salend, E., Kane, R.A., Satz, M. and Pynoos, J. (1984a) 'Elder abuse reporting: limitation of statutes', *The Gerontologist*, 24: 61–9.

Saunders, E. (1995) 'Private prosecution by the victims of violent crimes', *New Law Journal*, 29 September: 1423–4.

Saveman, B.-I. (1994) *Formal Carers in Healthcare and the Social Services Witnessing Abuse of the Elderly in Their Homes*. Umea, Sweden: Umea University.

Schaie, K.W. (1990) 'Intellectual development in adulthood', in J.E. Birren and K.W. Schaie (eds), *Handbook of the Psychology of Aging*, 3rd edition. San Diego: Academic Press. pp. 291– 309.

Schlesinger, B. and Schlesinger, R. (eds) (1988) *Abuse of the Elderly: Issues and Annotated Bibliography*. Toronto: University of Toronto Press.

Scott, P.A. (1995) 'Care, attention and imaginative identification in nursing practice', *Journal of Advanced Nursing*, 21(6): 1196–200.

Seccombe, W. (1991) *Millennium of the Family: Feudalism to Capitalism in Northwest Europe*. London: Verso.

Sengstock, M.C. and Barrett, S. (1986) 'Elderly victims of family abuse, neglect and maltreatment: can legal assistance help?', *Journal of Gerontological Social Work*, 9: 43–60.

Sengstock, M. C. and Liang, J. (1982) 'Identifying and characterizing elder abuse'. Unpublished manuscript, Wayne State University Institute of Gerontology, quoted in B. Hudson and T.F.Johnson (1986) 'Elder neglect and abuse: a review of the literature', in C. Eisdorfer et al. (eds), *Annual Review of Gerontology and Geriatrics*, Vol. 6. New York: Springer. pp. 81–133.

Sequira, R. (1994) Presidential address to Association of Directors of Social Services Conference, 1 November, Harrogate, Yorkshire.

Shanas, E., Townsend, P., Wedderburn, D., Friis, H., Milhoj, P. and Stehouwer, J. (1968) *Old People in Three Industrial Societies*. London: Routledge and Kegan Paul.

Shardlow, S. (1995) 'Confidentiality, accountability and the boundaries of client-work relationships', in R. Hugman and D. Smith (eds), *Ethical Issues in Social Work*. London: Routledge.

Sharpe, G. (1988) 'The protection of elderly mentally incompetent individuals who are victims of abuse', in B. Schlesinger and R.Schlesinger (eds), *Abuse of the Elderly: Issues and Annotated Bibliography*. Toronto: University of Toronto Press. pp. 64–74.

Sheldon, J.H. (1948) *The Social Medicine of Old Age*. London: Nuffield Foundation in association with Oxford University Press.

Shell, D.J. (1988) 'Elder abuse: summary of results – Manitoba', in B. Schlesinger and R. Schlesinger (eds), *Abuse of the Elderly: Issues and Annotated Bibliography*. Toronto: University of Toronto Press. pp. 75–85.

Sinclair, I. (ed.) (1988) *Residential Care: the Research Reviewed*, Vol. 2 of the Wagner Committee Report. London: HMSO.

Skelley-Walley, J.E. (1996) 'An Ombudsman perspective', in T.F. Johnson (ed.), *Elder Mistreatment: Ethical Issues, Dilemmas and Decisions*. New York: Haworth Press. pp. 89–113.

Skidmore, D. and Friend, W. (1984) 'Community Psychiatric Nursing', *Nursing Times Community Outlook*, 80(1): 179–81, 203–5, 257–61, 299–301, 310–12, 369–71.

Sladden, S. (1979) *Psychiatric Nursing in the Community*. Edinburgh: Churchill Livingstone.

Smale, G. and Tuson, G. (1993) *Empowerment, Assessment, Care Management and the Skilled Worker*. London: National Institute for Social Work.

Smeaton, D. and Hancock, R. (1995) *Pensioners' Expenditure*. London: Age Concern Institute of Gerontology, King's College, London.

Smith, F. and Lyon, C. (1994) *Personal Guide to The Children Act 1989 & Consent/Refusal of Medical Assessment/Treatment of Children for Health Professionals in England and Wales*. Surrey: Children Act Enterprises.

Social Trends 18 (1988) London: HMSO.

Solomon, K. (1983a) 'Victimization by health professionals and the psychologic response of the elderly', in J.I. Kosberg (ed.), *Abuse and Maltreatment of the Elderly: Causes and Interventions*. Boston: John Wright. pp. 150–71.

Solomon, K. (1983b) 'Intervention for victimized elderly and sensitization of health professionals', in J.I. Kosberg (ed.), *Abuse and Maltreatment of the Elderly: Causes and Interventions*. Boston: John Wright. pp. 404–21.

Sonntag, J. (1996) 'A case manager's perspective', in T.F. Johnson (ed.), *Elder Mistreatment: Ethical Issues, Dilemmas and Decisions*. New York: Haworth Press. pp. 115–30.

Sontag, S. (1978) 'The double standard of aging', in V. Carver and P. Liddiard (eds), *An Ageing Population*. London: Hodder and Stoughton. pp. 72–80.

Soule, D.J. and Bennett, J.M. (1987) 'Elder abuse in South Dakota', *South Dakota Journal of Medicine*, 40(10): 7–19 and (11): 5–8.

Sprey, J. and Matthews, S. (1989) 'The perils of drawing policy implications from research: the case of elder mistreatment', in R. Filinson and S. Ingman (eds), *Elder Abuse: Practice and Policy*. New York: Human Sciences Press. pp. 51–64.

SSI: Department of Health Social Services Inspectorate (1989) *Homes Are For Living In*. London: HMSO.

SSI: Department of Health Social Services Inspectorate (1992) *Confronting Elder Abuse: An SSI London Region Survey*. London: HMSO.

SSI: Department of Health Social Services Inspectorate (1993) *No Longer Afraid: the Safeguard of Elderly People in Domestic Settings: Practice Guidelines*. London: HMSO.

SSI: Department of Health Social Services Inspectorate (1994) *Abuse of Older People in Domestic Settings: a Report of two SSI Seminars*. London: HMSO.

Stannard, C. (1973) 'Old folks and dirty work: the social conditions for patient abuse in a nursing home', *Social Problems*, 20: 329–42.

Stathopoulos, P. A. (1983) 'Consumer advocacy and abuse of elders in nursing homes', in J.I. Kosberg (ed.), *Abuse and Maltreatment of the Elderly: Causes and Interventions*. Boston: John Wright. pp. 336–54.

Stearns, P. (1986) 'Old age family conflict: the perspective of the past', in K.A. Pillemer and R.S. Wolf (eds), *Elder Abuse: Conflict in the Family*. Dover: Auburn House. pp. 3–24.

Steinmetz, S.K. (1977) *The Cycle of Violence: Assertive, Aggressive and Abusive Family Interaction*. New York: Praeger.

Steinmetz, S.K. (1978) 'Battered parents', *Society*, 15: 54–5.

Steinmetz, S.K. (1983) 'Dependency, stress and violence between middle-aged caregivers and their elderly parents', in J.I. Kosberg (ed.), *Maltreatment of the Elderly: Causes and Interventions*. Boston: John Wright. pp. 134–49.

Steinmetz, S.K. (1988) *Duty Bound: Elder Abuse and Family Care*. Beverly Hills, CA: Sage Publications.

Steinmetz, S.K. (1990) 'Elder abuse: myth or reality', in T.D. Brubaker (ed.), *Family Relationships in Later Life*. Newbury Park, CA: Sage Publications. pp. 193–211.

Steuer, J. and Austin, E. (1980) 'Family abuse of the elderly', *Journal of the American Geriatrics Society*, 28(8): 372–6.

Stevenson, O. (1989) *Age and Vulnerability*. London: Edward Arnold.

Stevenson, O. (1996) *Elder Protection in the Community: What Can We Learn From Child Protection?* London: Department of Health Social Services Inspectorate.

Stewart, B. J., Archbold, P.G., Harvath, T.A. and Nkongho, N.O. (1993) 'Role acquisition in family caregivers of older people who have been discharged from hospital', in S.G.Funk, E.H. Tornquist, M.T. Champagne and R.A. Weise (eds), *Key Aspects of Caring for the Chronically Ill: Hospital and Home*. New York: Springer.

Stoller, E.P. and Pugliesi, K.L. (1989) 'Other roles of caregivers: competing responsibilities or supportive resources?', *Journal of Gerontology* (Social Sciences), 44.6(5): 231–8.

Straus, M. (1980) 'A sociological perspective on the causes of family violence', in M. Green (ed.), *Violence and the Family*. Boulder, CO: Westview. pp. 7–31.

Taler, G. and Ansello, E. (1985) 'Elder abuse', *Association of Family Physicians*, 32(2): 107–14.

Taraborrelli, P. (1993) 'Exemplar A: becoming a carer', in N.Gilbert (ed.), *Researching Social Life*. London: Sage Publications.

Tarbox, A. R. (1983) 'The elderly in nursing homes: psychological aspects of neglect', *Clinical Gerontologist*, 1: 39–52.

Tellis-Nayak, V. and Tellis-Nayak, M. (1979) 'Quality of care and the burden of two cultures: when the world of the nurse's aide enters the world of the nursing home', *The Gerontologist*, 29: 307–13.

Thomas, K. (1978) *Religion and the Decline of Magic*. London: Penguin Books.

Thompson, D. (1989) 'The welfare state and generational conflict', in P. Johnson, *Workers vs Pensioners*. Manchester: Manchester University Press. pp. 23–35.

Thomson, D. (1983) 'Workhouse to nursing home: residential care of elderly people in England since 1840', *Ageing and Society*, 3(1): 43–69.

Tomlin, S. (1989) *Abuse of Elderly People: An Unnecessary and Preventable Problem*. London: British Geriatrics Society.

Townsend, P. (1957) *The Family Life of Old People*. London: Routledge and Kegan Paul.

Townsend, P. (1962) *The Last Refuge*. London: Routledge.

Townsend, P. (1963) *The Family Life of Old People*. London: Penguin Books.

Townsend, P. (1981) 'The structured dependency of the elderly: a creation of social policy in the twentieth century', *Ageing and Society*, 1(1): 5–28.

Townsend, P. (1986) 'Ageism and social policy', in C. Phillipson and A.Walker (eds), *Ageing and Social Policy*. London: Gower. pp. 15–44.

Townsend, P. (1987) 'Deprivation', *Journal of Social Policy*, 16(2): 125–46.

Traynor, J. and Hasnip, L. (1984) 'Sometimes she makes me want to hit her', *Community Care*, 2 August: 20–1.

Troyansky, D. (1996) 'The history of old age in the western world', *Ageing and Society*, 16(2): 233–43.

Tschudin, V. (1992) *Ethics in Nursing*. Oxford: Butterworths and Heinemann.

Twigg, J. and Atkin, K. (1994) *Carers Perceived: Policy and Practice in Informal Care*. Buckingham: Open University Press.

Ungerson, C. (1987) *Policy is Personal: Sex, Gender and Informal Care*. London: Routledge and Kegan Paul.

United Kingdom Central Council for Nursing Midwifery and Health Visiting (UKCC) (1992) *Code of Professional Conduct*, 3rd edition. London: UKCC.

United Kingdom Central Council for Nursing (UKCC) (1994) *Professional Conduct. Occasional Report on Standards of Nursing in Nursing Homes*. London: UKCC.

United States Congress House Select Committee on Aging (1981) *Elder Abuse: The Hidden Problem*. Washington DC: Government Printing Office.

United States Department of Commerce (1990) *Statistical Abstracts of the United States*. Washington DC: Bureau of Census.

United States Department of Health and Social Services (1980) USDHEW Publication 79–3021 OHDS. 47–8. Washington DC: USDHEW.

United States House of Representatives Select Committee on Aging, Sub-Committee on Health and Long-Term Care (1990) *Elder Abuse: A Decade of Shame and Inaction*. Washington DC: US Government Printing Office.

Vadasz, M. (1988) 'Family abuse of the elderly', in B. Schlesinger and R. Schlesinger (eds), *Abuse of the Elderly: Issues and Annotated Bibliography*. Toronto: University of Toronto Press. pp. 91–4.

Victor, C. (1991) *Health Care in Later Life*. Buckingham: Open University Press.

Vousden, M. (1987) 'Nye Bevan would turn in his grave', *Nursing Times*, 83(32): 18–19.

Wagner Committee (1988) *Residential Care: A Positive Choice*, Report of the Independent Review of Residential Care Vol.1. London: HMSO (for Vol. 2 see Sinclair, 1988).

Walker, A. (1980) 'The social creation of dependency in old age', *Journal of Social Policy*, 9: 45–75.

Walker, A. (1981) 'Towards a political economy of old age', *Ageing and Society*, 1(1): 73– 94.

Walker, A. (1983a) 'Dependency and old age', *Social Policy and Administration*, 16(2): 115–35.

Walker, A. (1983b) 'Social policy and elderly people in Great Britain: the construction of dependent social and economic status in old age', in A. Guillemard (ed.), *Old Age and the Welfare State*. Beverly Hills, CA: Sage Publications. pp. 143–67.

Walker, A. (1986) 'Pensions and the production of poverty in old age', in C. Phillipson and A. Walker (eds), *Ageing and Social Policy*. London: Gower. pp. 184–216.

Walker, A. (1996) *The New Generational Contract: Intergenerational Relations, Old Age and Welfare*. London: University College of London Press.

Walker, A. and Warren, L. (1996) *Changing Services for Older People: The Neighbourhood Support Units Innovation*. Buckingham: Open University Press.

Walker, A.S., Skin, H.Y. and Bird, N.D. (1990) 'Perceptions of relationship change and caregiver satisfaction', *Family Relations*, 39: 147–52.

Wall, A. (1992) 'Relationships between the generations in British families past and present', in C. Marsh and S. Arber, (eds), *Families and Households: Divisions and Change*. London: Macmillan.

Wardhaugh, J. and Wilding, P. (1993) 'Towards an explanation of the corruption of care', *Critical Social Policy*, 47: 4–31.

Warner, N. (1994) *Community Care: Just a Fairy Tale?* London: Carers National Association.

Warren, L. (1990) ' " We're home helps because we care": the experience of home helps caring for elderly people', in P. Abbott and G. Payne (eds), *New Directions in the Sociology of Health*. London: Falmer Press. pp. 70–86.

Waterhouse, R. (1994) 'Cash crisis hits twenty nine councils', *The Independent*, 24 November: 11.

Waters, J. (1996) 'How care in the community has affected older people', *Nursing Times*, 92(4): 29–31.

Wenger, C. (1984) *The Supportive Network: Coping with Old Age*. London: Allen and Unwin.

Wenger, G.C., Grant, G. and Nolan, M. (1997) 'Elderly people as providers and recipients of care', in V. Minichiello, N. Chappell, A. Walker and H. Kendig (eds), *Sociology of Ageing*. International Sociological Association.

Weschler, D. (1958) *The Measure and Appraisal of Adult Intelligence*. New York: The Commonwealth Fund.

Westlake, D. and Pearson, M. (1995) *Maximizing Independence, Minimizing Risk: Older People's Management of their Health*. Liverpool: Health and Community Care Research Unit, University of Liverpool.

Wetzels, P., Greve, W., Mecklenburg, E., Bilsky, W. and Pfeiffer, C. (1995) *Kriminalität im Leben alter Menschen*. Stuttgart: W. Kohlhammer.

Whitehead, T. (1983) 'Battered old people', *Nursing Times*, 79(46): 16–22.

Whittaker, T. (1995) 'Gender and elder abuse', in S. Arber and J. Ginn (eds), *Connecting Gender and Ageing: A Sociological Approach*. Buckingham: Open University Press. pp. 144–57.

Whittaker, T. (1996a) 'Violence, gender and elder abuse', in B. Fawcett, B. Featherstone, J. Hearn and C. Toft (eds), *Violence and Gender Relations: Theories and Interventions*. London: Sage Publications.

Whittaker, T. (1996b) 'Talking about abuse: some theoretical and methodological implications'. Paper presented at Action on Elder Abuse Conference, March.

Wiener, C. L. and Kayser-Jones, J. (1990) 'The uneasy fate of nursing home residents: an organizational-interaction perspective', *Sociology of Health and Illness*, 12(1): 84–104.

Wigdor, B.T. (1991) *Elder Abuse: Major Issues from a National Perspective*. Ottawa: National Advisory Council of Aging.

Willcocks, D., Peace, S. and Kellaher, L. (1986) *Private Lives in Public Places*. London: Tavistock.

Williams, G. (1983) *Textbook of Criminal Law*. London: Stevens.

Williams, G. and Hepple, B.A.(1984) *Foundations of the Law of Tort*. London: Butterworths.

Williams, J. (1994) 'Elder abuse: the legal framework', in R. Clough (ed.), *Elder Abuse and the Law*. London: Action on Elder Abuse.

Willmott, P. and Young, M. (1960) *Family and Class in a London Suburb*. London: Routledge.

Wilson, G. (1991) 'Models of ageing and their relation to policy formation and service provision', *Policy and Politics*, 19(1): 37–47.

Wilson, G. (1993) 'Users and providers: different perspectives on community care services', *Journal of Social Policy*, 22(4): 507–26.

Wilson, G. (1994) 'Abuse of elderly men and women among clients of a community psychogeriatric service', *British Journal of Social Work*, 24(6): 681–700.

Wistow, G. (1995) 'Aspirations and realities: community care at the crossroads', *Health and Social Care in the Community*. 3(4): 227–40.

Wolf, R.S. (1988) 'Elder abuse: ten years later', *Journal of the American Geriatrics Society*, 36(8): 758–62.

Wolf, R.S. (1992) 'Victimization of the elderly', *Clinical Gerontology*, 2: 269–76.

Wolf, R.S. (1994) 'Responding to elder abuse in the USA', in P. Kingston (ed.), *Proceedings of the First International Symposium on Elder Abuse*. London: Action on Elder Abuse. pp. 11–19.

Wolf, R.S. and Pillemer, K.A. (1989) *Helping Elderly Victims: The Reality of Elder Abuse*. New York: Columbia University Press.

Wolf, R.S. and Pillemer, K.A. (1994) 'What's new in elder abuse programming? Four bright ideas', *The Gerontologist*, 34: 126–9.

Woman's Own (1987) 'Interview with Prime Minister Thatcher', 31 October.

Worsam, B. (1991) 'Assessment', in M.W. Shaw (ed.), *The Challenge of Ageing*, 2nd edition. Melbourne and London: Churchill Livingstone. pp. 120–7.

Index

abuse,
  child, 33
  indicators of, 27, 29, 34, 183
  material/financial, 17, 21, 56, 57, 62, 65, 98,
    212, 241
  medical, 17
  physical, 17, 21, 47, 55, 56, 59, 65, 130, 131,
    135, 152, 165, 212, 240
  psychological, 17, 21, 56, 57, 62, 66, 98, 130,
    153, 212, 241
  of residents,
    key factors, 159–60
    reasons for, 159
  sexual, 27, 48, 64, 65, 100, 212, 240
  societal, 141–50
  socio-economic context of, 2
  spouse, 25, 26, 33, 39, 89
  stranger, 227
  survivors of, 166, 168, 172
    and families, 39
    and physican, 34, 35, 37
  and victims, 39
  see also definitions of elder abuse and
    neglect; elder abuse; maltreatment of
    old; mistreatment; neglect; theories of
    abuse
abuse of civil liberties, 43
abuse and instrumental dependency, 201
abusers, 33
abusing incidents, 129
abusive behaviour, 178
abusive family relationships, 200
abusive practices, 169
abusive situations, 82, 126, 128
  and carer, 82
  and carer support, 82
  relationships, 121, 126
abusive society, 124
accountability, 52–3, 180
Acting on Complaints, 165
  procedure, 165
Action on Elder Abuse, 1, 2, 12, 26, 30, 42, 77,
    164, 180, 212, 220, 221, 222, 226
  definition of elder abuse, 1
    weakness of, 43
  as a pressure group, 1, 76
  survey, 41, 164, 180
  telephone response line, 2
active neglect, 17, 21, 57, 59, 71, 100, 101

Acts of Parliament; see Carers (Recognition
  and Services) Act 1995; Family Law
  Act 1996; Health Services and Public
  Health Act 1968; Mental Health Act
  1983; National Assistance Act 1947;
  National Health Service and
  Community Care Act 1990; Old Age
  Pensions Act 1908; Registered Homes
  Act 1984
'add on' approach, 119, 120, 121, 124, 127–8
adult protection legislation, 76
adult protection services, 29, 36, 37, 131
  surveys of, 30
adults at risk, 167, 169
advocates and autonomy, 169
age and gender, 118
  and power, 118, 119, 126
  and power inequality, 119
age and vulnerability, 168
Age Concern England, 15, 179, 184, 190, 210,
  220
age discrimination, 104
ageing,
  as gendered process, 117
  and gender imbalance, 118
  positive images of, 172
'ageing enterprise', 76, 113
ageism, 5, 7, 8, 38, 40
  and old age inequality, 40
ageist attitudes, 5–12, 112, 173
alcohol, 25, 130
Allen, I., Hogg, D. and Peace, S., 179
Allen, I. and Perkins, E., 105
American Medical Association, 29, 30, 31, 35,
  137
antecedents, behaviour and consequences,
  136-7
apocalyptic demography, 117
approved social worker, 67, 69
Arber, S. and Evandrou, M., 125
Arber, S. and Ginn, J., 6, 117, 142
Archbold, P.G., Stewart, B.J., Greenlich,
  M.R. and Harvath, T.A., 202, 204, 206,
  207
arm's length, 165
Ashton, G., 38, 101
assault, 90, 91, 92, 93
Association of Directors of Social Services,
  221